D0887600

Actium and Augustus

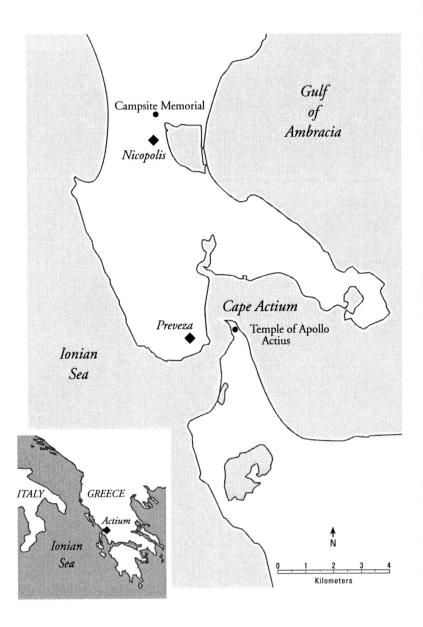

Gulf
of
Ambracia

Campsite Memorial

Nicopolis

Cape Actium

Preveza

Temple of Apollo
Actius

Ionian
Sea

ITALY   GREECE

Actium

Ionian
Sea

N

0   1   2   3   4
Kilometers

ACTIUM

Actium
and Augustus

The Politics and Emotions
of Civil War

Robert Alan Gurval

Ann Arbor

THE UNIVERSITY OF MICHIGAN PRESS

LONGWOOD COLLEGE LIBRARY
FARMVILLE, VIRGINIA 23901

PA
6019
.G87
1998

First paperback edition 1998
Copyright © by the University of Michigan 1995
All rights reserved
Published in the United States of America by
The University of Michigan Press
Manufactured in the United States of America
⊗ Printed on acid-free paper

2001 2000 1999 1998   4 3 2 1
A CIP catalogue record for this book is available
from the British Library.

Library of Congress Cataloging-in-Publication Data

Gurval, Robert Alan, 1958–
    Actium and Augustus : the politics and emotions of civil war /
Robert Alan Gurval.
        p.   cm.
    Revision of the author's doctoral thesis.
    Includes bibliographical references and index.
    ISBN 0-472-10590-6 (hardcover)
    1. Rome—History—Civil War, 43–31 B.C.—Literature and the war.
2. Augustus, Emperor of Rome, 63 B.C.–14 A.D.—In literature.
3. Rome—History—Civil War, 43–31 B.C.—Historiography.   4. Actium,
Battle of, 31 B.C.—Historiography.   5. Actium, Battle of, 31 B.C.,
in literature.   6. Politics and literature—Rome—History.   7. Latin
poetry—History and criticism.   8. Propertius, Sextus—Contemporary
Rome.   9. Horace—Contemporary Rome.   10. Virgil—Contemporary Rome.
11. War in literature.   I. Title.
PA6019.G87   1995
937'.05'072—dc20   95-1844
                                                                      CIP

ISBN 0-472-08489-5 (pbk : alk. paper)

No part of this publication may be reproduced, stored in a
retrieval system, or transmitted in any form or by any means,
electronic, mechanical, or otherwise, without the written
permission of the publisher.

LONGWOOD COLLEGE LIBRARY
FARMVILLE, VIRGINIA 23901

In memory of
Richard Lyle Welsh,
1958–1986

forsitan hoc etiam gaudeat ipsa cinis

LONGWOOD LIBRARY

1000327453

Acknowledgments

Many people have contributed to the original ideas, substantive revisions, and publication of this book. My first and greatest debt is to my teachers and the supervisors of my dissertation. William S. Anderson, Florence Verducci, and Erich S. Gruen formed an illustrious, but never imperious, triumvirate who guided my endeavors with generous assistance and kind benevolence. For their unfailing promptness, ever meticulous care, and penetrating criticism, I am forever grateful. Their influence on my scholarly attitudes and approaches is immense and deeply felt. In addition to my doctoral committee, various scholars, colleagues, and friends have supplied an unending source of knowledge, counsel, and inspiration. William E. Metcalf, chief curator of the American Numismatic Society, provided a helpful and informed introduction for the neophyte of coin types and legends. Professors Glen W. Bowersock, Elaine Fantham, Denis C. Feeney, John Nicols, Kurt A. Raaflaub, and Garth Tissol read earlier drafts of individual sections. To all these scholars I extend my gratitude. Two readers offered invaluable support and firm guidance, without whom this work would never have been completed. Michael C. J. Putnam—my former teacher who initiated me in the wondrous imagination and artifice of Latin poetry—and Sander M. Goldberg—my colleague and mentor, whose candor and honest criticism I have always respected—graciously read through the manuscript, rescued me from many flagrant and embarrassing errors, and tried to rescue me from more. Whatever improvements are found in this book I owe to them. All the shortcomings and errors remain my own. My trio of research assistants, Darel T. Engen, Michael Lovano, and Edward W. Powers, alleviated some of the burdens of checking footnotes and arranging a bibliography. My good friend, Michael Uhlenkott, assisted in the preparation of the plates and frontispiece. I also acknowledge my fond gratitude to my editor, Ellen Bauerle, who was forever patient, and who is chiefly responsible for this work's publication.

Finally, I wish to dedicate this book in memory of my fellow student and friend, Richard Lyle Welsh. His premature death preceded my initial research on this topic, but his keen intellect, subtle humor, and gentle spirit have never been far from my mind.

O qui complexus et gaudia quanta fuerunt!
Nil ego contulerim iucundo sanus amico.

Contents

Abbreviations

AA	*Archäologischer Anzeiger*
AArchAnth	*Annals of Archaeology and Anthropology*
ABSA	*Annual of the British School at Athens*
AClass	*Acta Classica*
AE	*Ἀρχαιολογικὴ Ἐφημερίς*
Age of Augustus	R. Winkes, ed. *The Age of Augustus: Interdisciplinary Conference Held at Brown University, April 30–May 2, 1982.* Archaeologica Transatlantica 5. Louvain-la-Neuve and Providence, 1985.
AJA	*American Journal of Archaeology*
AJN	*American Journal of Numismatics* (formerly *American Numismatic Society, Museum Notes)*
AJP	*American Journal of Philology*
ANRW	H. Temporini and W. Haase, eds. *Aufstieg und Niedergang der römischen Welt. Geschichte und Kultur Roms im Spiegel der neueren Forschung.* Berlin and New York, 1972–.
ANSMN	*American Numismatic Society, Museum Notes*
ANSNNM	*American Numismatic Society, Numismatic Notes and Monographs*
AUMLA	*Journal of the Australasian Universities Language and Literature Association*
BEFAR	*Bibliothèque des Écoles Françaises d'Athènes et de Rome*
Between Republic and Empire	K.A. Raaflaub and M. Toher, eds. *Between Republic and Empire: Interpretations of Augustus and His Principate.* Berkeley and Los Angeles, 1990.
BJ	*Bonner Jahrbücher des Rheinischen Landesmuseums in Bonn und des Vereins von Altertumsfreunden im Rheinlande*
BMCRE	H. Mattingly and R.A.G. Carson. *Coins of the Roman Empire in the British Museum.* 6 vols. London, 1923–.
BMCRR	H.A. Grueber. *Coins of the Roman Republic in the*

	British Museum. 3 vols. London, 1910. Reprinted 1970.
Caesar Augustus	F. Millar and E. Segal, eds. *Caesar Augustus: Seven Aspects.* Oxford, 1984.
CAH	*Cambridge Ancient History*
CB	*Classical Bulletin*
CIG	*Corpus Inscriptionum Graecarum*
CIL	*Corpus Inscriptionum Latinarum*
CJ	*Classical Journal*
Courtney, *FLP*	E. Courtney, ed. *The Fragmentary Latin Poets.* Oxford, 1993.
CP	*Classical Philology*
CQ	*Classical Quarterly*
CR	*Classical Review*
Crawford, *RRC*	M.H. Crawford. *Roman Republican Coinage.* 2 vols. Cambridge, 1974. Reprinted (with corrections) Cambridge, 1989. Cited by catalog numbers unless otherwise noted.
CSCA	*California Studies in Classical Antiquity*
CW	*Classical Weekly*
FD III	É Bourguet et al., eds. *Fouilles de Delphes.* Vol. 3, *Épigraphie.* Fasc. 1, *Inscriptions de l'entrée du sanctuaire au trésor des Athéniens.* Paris, 1929.
Giard, *BNC*	J-.B. Giard. *Bibliothèque Nationale. Catalogue des monnaies de l'empire romain.* Vol. 1, *Auguste.* Paris, 1976. Cited by catalog numbers.
HSCP	*Harvard Studies in Classical Philology*
ICos	W.R. Paton and E.L. Hicks. *The Inscriptions of Cos.* Oxford, 1891.
ICS	*Illinois Classical Studies*
IG	*Inscriptiones Graecae*
IGRR	*Inscriptiones Graecae ad res Romanas pertinentes.* 4 vols. Paris, 1906–27.
ILS	H. Dessau. *Inscriptiones Latinae Selectae.* 3 vols. Berlin, 1892–1916.
IvEphesos	R. Merkelbach et al. *Inschriften griechischer Städte aus Kleinasien.* Vol. 16.6, *Die Inschriften von Ephesos.* Bonn, 1980.
IvOlympia	W. Dittenberger and K. Purgold. *Olympia. Die Ergebnisse der von dem deutschen Reich veranstalteten Ausgrabung.* Vol. 5, *Die Inschriften.* Berlin, 1896.
IvPergamon	M. Fränkel. *Altertümer von Pergamon.* Vol. 8.1–2, *Die Inschriften.* Berlin, 1890–95.
JDAI	*Jahrbuch des Deutschen Archäologischen Instituts*
JEA	*Journal of Egyptian Archaeology*
JNG	*Jahrbuch für Numismatik und Geldgeschichte*

JÖAI	*Jahreshefte des Österreichischen Archäologischen Instituts*
JRA	*Journal of Roman Archaeology*
JRS	*Journal of Roman Studies*
Kaiser Augustus	M. Hofter, ed. *Kaiser Augustus und die verlorene Republik. Eine Ausstellung im Martin-Gropius-Bau, Berlin 7. Juni–14. August 1988.* Mainz, 1988.
LEC	*Les Études Classiques*
MAAR	*Memoirs of the American Academy in Rome*
MélRome	*Mélanges d'Archéologie et d'Histoire de l'École Française de Rome, Antiquité*
Milet	A. von Gerkan and F. Krischen. *Milet. Ergebnisse der Ausgrabungen und Untersuchungen seit dem Jahre 1899.* Vol. 1.9, *Die Thermen und Palaestren.* Berlin, 1928.
Moretti, IAG	L. Moretti. *Iscrizioni agonistiche greche.* Rome, 1953. Cited by catalog numbers unless otherwise noted.
MusHelv	*Museum Helveticum*
NAC	*Numismatica e Antichità Classiche. Quaderni Ticinesi*
Nicopolis I	E. Chrysos, ed. *Nicopolis I: Proceedings of the First International Symposium on Nicopolis (23–29 September 1984).* Preveza, 1987.
NouvClio	*La Nouvelle Clio*
NumChron	*Numismatic Chronicle*
NumCirc	*Numismatic Circular*
OpusArch	*Opuscula Archaeologica*
PAPS	*Proceedings of the American Philosophical Society*
PCPS	*Proceedings of the Cambridge Philological Society*
Poetry and Politics	T. Woodman and D. West, eds. *Poetry and Politics in the Age of Augustus.* Cambridge, 1984.
PP	*La Parola del Passato*
PQ	*Philological Quarterly*
PVS	*Proceedings of the Virgil Society*
QUCC	*Quaderni Urbinati di Cultura Classica*
RBN	*Revue Belge de Numismatique et de Sigillographie*
RE	A. Pauly and G. Wissowa et al., eds. *Real-Encyclopädie der Classischen Altertumswissenschaft.* Stuttgart, 1893–.
RecPhL	*Recherches de Philologie et de Linguistique, Louvain*
REG	*Revue des Études Grecques*
REL	*Revue des Études Latines*
RendPontAcc	*Atti della Pontificia Accademia Romana di Archeologia, Rendiconti*

RevArch	*Revue Archéologique*
RevNum	*Revue Numismatique*
RevPhil	*Revue de Philologie, de Littérature et d'Histoire Anciennes*
RhM	*Rheinisches Museum*
RIC²	C.H.V. Sutherland and R. Carson. *Roman Imperial Coinage.* Vol. 1. Rev. edition. London, 1984.
RIN	*Rivista Italiana di Numismatica e Scienze affini*
RivFil	*Rivista di Filologia e di Istruzione Classica*
RömMitt	*Mitteilungen des Deutschen Archäologischen Instituts, Römische Ableitung*
RPC	A. Burnett, M. Amandry, and P.P. Ripollès. *Roman Provincial Coinage.* Vol. 1, *From the Death of Caesar to the Death of Vitellius (44 BC–AD 69).* Part 1, introduction and catalog. Part 2, indexes and plates. London and Paris, 1992.
RSC	*Rivista di Studi Classici*
Sarikakis, ῎Ακτια	Th. Sarikakis. "῎Ακτια τὰ ἐν Νικοπόλει." *AE* 15 (1965): 145–62. Cited by catalog numbers listed in his appendix.
SEG	*Supplementum Epigraphicum Graecum*
SGDI	H. Collitz et al., eds. *Sammlung der griechischen Dialekt-Inschriften*, 4 vols. Göttingen, 1884–1915.
SIFC	*Studi Italiani di Filologia Classica*
Sydenham, *CRR*	E.A. Sydenham. *The Coinage of the Roman Republic.* Revised with indexes by G.C. Haines. Ed. L. Forrer and C.A. Hersh. London, 1952. Cited by catalog numbers.
SymbOslo	*Symbolae Osloenses*
TAPA	*Transactions and Proceedings of the American Philological Association*
Vahlen	J. Vahlen, ed. *Ennianae poesis reliquiae.* 2d ed. Leipzig, 1928.
VBW	*Vorträge der Bibliothek Warburg*
WJA	*Würzburger Jahrbücher für die Altertumswissenschaft*
WS	*Wiener Studien. Zeitschrift für klassische Philologie und Patristik*
Zanker, *Power of Images*	P. Zanker. *The Power of Images in the Age of Augustus.* Trans. A. Shapiro. Jerome Lectures Series 16. Ann Arbor, Mich., 1988. Originally published as *Augustus und die Macht der Bilder.* Munich, 1987.
ZN	*Zeitschrift für Numismatik*
ZPE	*Zeitschrift für Papyrologie und Epigraphik*

Introduction

On the second day of September in 31 B.C.E., the heir to the political legacy and name of Julius Caesar defeated the joint naval forces of Antony and Cleopatra off the coast of northwestern Greece. The outcome of the battle was not immediate, but the confrontation proved decisive and momentous. The vanquished pair fled to Egypt, and after seven tense days of protracted negotiations, the nineteen Roman legions that Antony had left behind at Actium surrendered to Octavian on equal terms with the victorious side. Foreign allies abandoned what was perceived as the losing cause and declared their allegiance to the victor. With the capture of Alexandria in the following year, Antony and the Egyptian queen were forced to commit suicide, and Octavian emerged as the sole and undisputed ruler of the Roman world. Peace was firmly established and officially proclaimed by the formal closure of the Temple of Janus. The Senate graciously rewarded the victor on his return to Italy with an accumulation of extraordinary honors, titles, and privileges. A political regime, which later generations would call the Augustan Principate, gradually evolved and, with it, a system of government that endured for more than four centuries. The Roman Empire had begun.

Actium constitutes a potent and enduring turning point in the course of Roman history and indeed of Western civilization. The significance of this victory hardly needs any long defense or complex explanation. Subsequent generations have not failed to recognize the serious consequences of the battle and to render their own verdict and individual bias. From the fawning Tiberian chronicler, who exclaimed that he could not record all the blessings that one day of fighting brought forth to the world,[1] to the more censorious author of the *Annales*, who viewed Octavian's victory at Actium as the lamentable sign of a failing Republic's demise,[2] to the later Greek historian

---

1. Vell. 2.86.1: *quid ille dies terrarum orbi praestiterit, ex quo in quem statum pervenerit fortuna publica, quis in hoc transcursu tam artati operis exprimere audeat?*

2. Tac. *Ann.* 1.3.7: *iuniores post Actiacam victoriam, etiam senes plerique inter bella civium nati: quotus quisque reliquus qui rem publicam vidisset?* And *Hist.* 1.1: *postquam bellatum apud Actium atque omnem potentiam ad unum conferri pacis interfuit, magna illa ingenia cessere.*

of the Severan Age, who marked the date of the military engagement as the beginning of a new political regime in Rome,[3] the judgment of posterity is firm and unequivocal: Actium signals the commencement of a new era.

The following study adopts a new approach to a familiar topic.[4] In the first half of this century, a host of historians attempted to sort out the particulars of the naval battle, the preliminary operations, opposing strategies, and varied maneuvers that ultimately secured the victory for Octavian. The solutions to the vexatious questions that once provoked discussions remain neither clear nor certain. Whether the battle at Actium was a "shabby affair, the worthy climax to the ignoble propaganda against Cleopatra," as Ronald Syme branded the famous naval engagement in an authoritative voice,[5] is a question of both import and consequence, but it is not the focus of this study. My interest lies instead in the political aftermath of Actium. This book examines the official celebration and public commemoration of the Actian victory in the contemporary period. What are the "Actian" monuments that the victorious Octavian erected at the site of the battle and later in Rome on his triumphal return in the summer of 29? What role did the Actian victory play in the formation of the Augustan Principate and its public ideology? And, finally, how did contemporary poetry respond to Actium?

The role of the Actian victory in the political ideology of the Augustan Principate has not been a topic of scholarly discussion or serious dispute.[6] It

---

3. Dio 51.1.1–2: τοιαύτη τις ἡ ναυμαχία αὐτῶν τῇ δευτέρᾳ τοῦ Σεπτεμβρίου ἐγένετο. τοῦτο δὲ οὐκ ἄλλως εἶπον (οὐδὲ γὰρ εἴωθα αὐτὸ ποιεῖν) ἀλλ᾽ ὅτι τότε πρῶτον ὁ Καῖσαρ τὸ κράτος πᾶν μόνος ἔσχεν, ὥστε καὶ τὴν ἀπαρίθμησιν τῶν τῆς μοναρχίας αὐτοῦ ἐτῶν ἀπ᾽ ἐκείνης τῆς ἡμέρας ἀκριβοῦσθαι.

4. The most recent and convincing discussions on the naval battle are found in J.M. Carter, *The Battle of Actium: The Rise and Triumph of Augustus Caesar* (London, 1970), 220–27, and J.R. Johnson, "Augustan Propaganda: The Battle of Actium, Marc Antony's Will, the Fasti Capitolini Consulares, and Early Imperial Historiography" (Ph.D. diss., University of California, Los Angeles, 1976), 22–69. The list of earlier discussions is long. Of the most important, cf. J. Kromayer, "Die Entwicklung der römischen Flotte vom Seeräuberkriege des Pompeius bis zur Schlacht von Actium," *Philologus* 56 (1897): 426–91; "Kleine Forschungen zur Geschichte des zweiten Triumvirats. VII. Der Feldzug von Actium und der sogenannte Verrath der Cleopatra," *Hermes* 34 (1899): 1–54; "Zur Schlacht von Actium," in *Antike Schlachtfelder. Bausteine zur einer antiken Kriegsgeschichte* (Berlin, 1931), 4.4:662–71; and "Actium. Ein Epilog," *Hermes* 68 (1933): 361–83; A. Ferrabino, "La battaglia d'Azio," *RivFil* 52 (1924): 433–72; W.W. Tarn, "The Battle of Actium," *JRS* 21 (1931): 173–99; "Antony's Legions," *CQ* 26 (1932): 75–81; and "Actium: A Note," *JRS* 28 (1938): 165–68; M.A. Levi, "La battaglia d'Azio," *Athenaeum* 20, n.s. 10 (1932): 3–21; G.W. Richardson, "Actium," *JRS* 27 (1937): 153–64; and J. Leroux, "Les problèmes stratégiques de la bataille d'Actium," *RecPhL* 2 (1968): 29–61.

5. R. Syme, *The Roman Revolution* (Oxford, 1939), 297.

6. Two important studies have sought to assemble a comprehensive inventory of what have been deemed the "Actian" monuments: J. Gagé, "*Actiaca*," *MélRome* 53 (1936): 37–100, and

is generally assumed that the victor would not have ignored the opportunity to exalt the battle to establish his newly secured position in Rome. The judgment of the esteemed author of *The Roman Revolution,* boldly articulated more than fifty years ago, has not been challenged.

> For some years, fervent and official language had celebrated the crusade of all Italy and the glorious victory of Actium—for Actium was the foundation-myth of the new order.

> In the official version of the victor, Actium took on august dimensions and an intense emotional colouring, being transformed into a great naval battle, with lavish wealth of convincing and artistic detail. More than that, Actium became the contest of East and West personified, the birth-legend in the mythology of the Principate.[7]

Historians view the public glorification of Actium as something spontaneous, clearly and forcefully defined by an official regime, fixed and invariable, as if the political outcome decided in the waters of the Ambracian Gulf held the same meaning to everyone in the Roman world throughout the forty-five years of Augustan rule. But we may rightly ask if the victor's activities in the Greek East—the foundation of a Nicopolis at the site of the battle, the celebration of quinquennial games, and the refurbishment of a neglected temple to Apollo—should be understood in the same political and ideological terms as the resolutions of the Roman Senate, which included the traditional honors of a triumphal ceremony, an arch, the formal closure of a temple's doors, and solemn prayers and vows on the anniversaries of the occasion of battle and the victor's birthday? Could Actium evoke the same emotions and carry the same message in the immediate and uncertain aftermath of victory, when an anxious Horace wrote his epode on the naval battle, and more than fifteen years later, when a defiant Propertius composed his hymn to Apollo? Modern critics fail to distinguish the passage of years and the evolving political climate. Actium, so it is claimed, was the military achievement that Augustus at once proclaimed his greatest success

---

T. Hölscher, "Denkmäler der Schlacht von Actium. Propaganda und Resonanz," *Klio* 67 (1985): 81–102. The discussions, however, do not critically assess what role Actium played in the political ideology of its age and how representations and perceptions of the victory changed during the Augustan Principate. The image of Actium, much like that of the victor himself, was never fixed or constant but must be seen in a process of political development, adaptation, and refinement. See later in this chapter my criticisms of modern presumptions of Actium's prominence or its political message in Augustan artwork and ideology.

7. Syme, *Roman Revolution,* 335 and 297, respectively.

and the start of a new world order, the victory that the proud ruler kept prodding his reluctant poets to celebrate in epic verse.

Scholars of the art and architecture of Augustan Rome follow the same presumptions. Paul Zanker's *The Power of Images in the Age of Augustus* is the art historian's essential companion piece to Syme's earlier investigation into the propaganda of the Principate, an impressive and masterful study of the complex interrelationship of art and public ideology in the Augustan political regime. Zanker rejects the once credible and popular notion that an officially directed propaganda machine operated in Augustan Rome. He is most persuasive when he explains that "what appears in retrospect as a subtle program resulted in fact from the interplay of the image that the emperor himself projected and the honors bestowed on him more or less spontaneously, a process that evolved naturally over long periods of time."[8] For Zanker, however, Actium is the exception or at least the "Great Turning Point," as he titles his third chapter. That the consequences of Actium effected changes in the Roman political world is without dispute, but it does not and should not follow that the image of Actium (or rather of the Actian victor) characterized this change and that this change, whatever its nature, was direct, immediate, and consciously transferred to the public art and architecture of the period. In his initial chapter, Zanker cogently argues that the influence of Hellenistic art and the borrowed images of Alexandrian monarchies had already pervaded the politics of Rome in the late Republic, contradicted and subverted Roman values (perhaps even contributed to their dissolution), and increasingly defined the nature and character of the fierce rivalry for power following the assassination of Julius Caesar in 44. Two major monuments of so-called Augustan Rome, the Temple of Apollo on the Palatine and the Mausoleum of Augustus, were both planned in the years before the battle at Actium and stood, as Zanker states, "purely as propaganda for an ambitious general, with no regard for the traditions of the Republic."[9] Nonetheless, Actium is viewed as the critical, if not singular, event in the formation and development of a "New Imperial style" in contemporary art and architecture.

Zanker's overall interpretation of an "official" glorification of Actium throughout the Augustan Principate is flawed by occasional inaccuracies and sometimes striking omissions in the examination of the ancient evidence. When Zanker misplaces Actium in the order of the Augustan triple triumph ("Illyrium, Egypt, and the Battle of Actium"),[10] indicating the celebration of

---

8. Zanker, *Power of Images*, 3.
9. Zanker, *Power of Images*, 24.
10. Zanker, *Power of Images*, 79.

the naval battle as the final and climactic triumph, he contributes to the popular (and inaccurate) belief that the whole affair was simply an official exaltation of Actium. The Egyptian triumph, in fact, concluded the three-day ceremonies and far surpassed the prior two in cost, extravagance, and public attention. Zanker virtually ignores the difficulties and considerable doubts surrounding the erection of an arch in commemoration of the naval battle (often called by modern scholars with the undocumented and mis-leading title "Actian") and, what is more serious, misquotes the assumed legend of the arch's architrave. The legend, which is actually an inscription now lost and perhaps attached to another monument, refers to the *res publica conservata* (not the *res publica restituta*). The former phrase belongs to the political vocabulary of Cicero and most often suggests the reestablishment of authority and order following a national crisis or the turmoil of civil conflict. The modern and popular notion that Augustus boasted of a "re-stored Republic" cannot be supported here and certainly cannot be part of a reconstructed political ideology.[11] More importantly, the arch displayed no dedicatory inscription or ornate artwork that celebrated the glory of the naval battle at Actium. The coinage of Octavian, an invaluable source of contemporary imagery and propaganda, also receives a rather arbitrary and inconsistent treatment throughout Zanker's work. His dating of the numis-matic evidence is selective and unexplained. He assigns some issues to the period after Octavian's victory at Naulochus over Sextus Pompey in 36 (like Actium, a naval battle) and yet others from the same denarii series, without any apparent or recognized distinction, but on which he prefers to find Actian motifs, to a later date after the decisive victory over Antony and Cleopatra.[12] This selective list of neglected particulars and slighted scholarly controversy does not in any serious way detract from the overall impact of Zanker's contribution to our understanding of the intricate relationship between politics and art. Nonetheless, it demonstrates that the public image of the Actian victory in the contemporary period has not been properly

---

11. On the phrase *res publica restituta* in Augustan political ideology, see the compelling discussion by E. Judge, "*Res Publica Restituta*: A Modern Illusion?" in *Polis and Imperium: Studies in Honour of Edward Togo Salmon*, ed. J.A.S. Evans (Toronto, 1974), 279–311, who argues that the phrase belongs more to Mommsen and modern conjecture than to ancient testimony and epigraphical evidence.

12. For example, Zanker claims, without explanation, that the issue that depicts a nude male figure standing on a globe (*RIC*² 256) belongs to a series minted after the decisive naval battle at Naulochus in 36 and thus alluded to a famous work that celebrated the victory over Sextus Pompey (*Power of Images*, 39), but later he dates select issues from the same series five years later, after Actium, because of the symbolic allusions to a naval victory on the coins (pp. 79–80).

evaluated and is poorly understood. The subject demands a comprehensive and circumspect investigation.

Literary critics are equally guilty when they bring the same presumptions—and the same mistakes—to the significance and meaning of Actium. The idea persists, and is almost unanimously endorsed, that Augustus ardently desired and indirectly requested through the agency of Maecenas that the poets compose verses to celebrate his martial glory and accomplishment at Actium. Though this poetic response to Actium has been interpreted to vary from reluctant compliance to stubborn defiance, the premise is much the same: the Augustan poets felt compelled by the political regime to incorporate recognition and praise of the victory at Actium. The testimony on this viewpoint is not difficult to assemble.

> The battle was not long over before there were signs that Augustus . . . was looking for a poet who could put his achievements in their proper light. He wanted, in short, an epic poem with himself as the hero.[13]

> He [Horace] did celebrate the victory in *Epode* 9, perhaps at official suggestion.[14]

> But Propertius and the other Augustan poets were called upon to write, not of any war, but of civil war.[15]

> Poets were driven to tackle Actium in symbolic or indirect ways.[16]

The subject of the Augustan poets' attitude toward the battle at Actium is not lacking in comprehensive and detailed treatments. Since no less than four individual studies have taken up this topic,[17] some explanation seems in order to defend yet another foray on this well-trodden ground. The presumptions underlying prior discussions on the theme of Actium among the

---

13. K. Quinn, *Virgil's Aeneid: A Critical Description* (London, 1968), 26.

14. E.T. Salmon, "The Political Views of Horace," *Phoenix* 1.2 (1946–47): 10.

15. F. Sweet, "Propertius and Political Panegyric," *Arethusa* 5 (1972): 173.

16. J. Griffin, "Augustus and the Poets: 'Caesar qui cogere posset,'" in *Caesar Augustus*, 198.

17. The list includes L. Hartmann, *De pugna Actiaca a poetis Augusteae aetatis celebrata* (Darmstadt, 1913); F. Wurzel, *Der Krieg gegen Antonius und Kleopatra in der Darstellung der augusteischen Dichter* (Ph.D. diss., Heidelberg, 1941); Frère Léon-Marcien, "L'interprétation de la bataille d'Actium par les poètes latins de l'époque augustéenne," *LEC* 24 (1956): 330–48; and M.L. Paladini, *A proposito della tradizione poetica sulla battaglia di Azio*, Collection Latomus 35 (Brussels, 1958).

Augustan poets are similar: the poets are the "witnesses . . . the echo of a political propaganda, intense and cleverly orchestrated."[18] Particular attention has been directed to the participants and details of the naval battle. How do the poets allude to the role of Antony in their accounts of the Actian battle? What is their attitude toward the Egyptian queen, her involvement in the battle and flight? These are serious and important questions that have stimulated prior studies on the attitude of the Augustan poets toward Actium, but answers to these questions, if there are indeed answers, do not really confront the central issue of this study, the public image and consciousness of the Actian victory in the emergent and evolving Augustan Principate. The rejection of prior assumptions on poetic intent invites new questions and queries. Are the poets merely (whether sometimes or always) the prompted transmission of or the defiant response to an official propaganda and public ideology, shaped by a victor's extravagant boasts and vainglorious aspirations? What if the victory at Actium failed to earn the immediate and direct attention that later generations expected and bestowed on the naval battle? What if the clever victor was never the dupe of his own rhetoric, distortions, and falsehoods—certainly essential in winning a war, but not in establishing a political regime, modeled on the institutions and values of the past? Furthermore, what if Actium was not, at least certainly not in the formative years of the Augustan Principate, the "foundation myth" and potent symbol of a new political order in Rome? How then do we assess the images of victory and defeat, the vivid memories of battle, and the mixed emotions of the poets?

Chapter 1 in this study begins with Octavian's triumphal return to Rome in the summer of 29. The victor chose to celebrate his triple triumph on three consecutive days. The significance and implications of this calculated decision by the grand showman in Rome have not been previously recognized. The ancient sources are certain on one point: the final day, which celebrated the conquest of Egypt and the victory over Cleopatra, was the most magnificent and striking, the dramatic climax to the three-day extravaganza. Actium merited its own triumph, an undisputed and important fact. But the carefully arranged staging of the Actian triumph, squeezed into the middle of the three-day affair, cannot be ignored or simply dismissed as an inadvertent oversight. The tradition of the Roman triumph and, in particular, the

---

18. Léon-Marcien, "L'interprétation de la bataille d'Actium," 330: "témoignages . . . l'écho d'une propaganda politique intense, fort habilement menée."

lavish celebrations of victory in civil war by the multiple triumphs of Julius Caesar offer an indication of Octavian's intentions in his triumphal ceremonies and of his audience's reaction.

From my discussion of the triumphal ceremonies, I turn to the so-called Actian arch, a complicated and controversial subject of inquiry. Excavations in the Roman Forum in the early 1950s have not removed earlier doubts over the construction and exact site of an arch honoring the Actian victory. The accumulation of evidence that had supported the claims of an "Actian" arch was meager and inconclusive, but an impressive consensus of scholars now finds agreement on the arch's actual erection and commemorative purpose. Current opinion maintains that an arch of a single span, voted by the Senate in the aftermath of the Actian victory, joined the Temples of Divus Julius and of Castor and Pollux, while archaeological discoveries suggest that this "Actian" arch either was later torn down and replaced by a triple arch that commemorated the victory acclaimed over the Parthians or was never erected. Removal of the single arch has now been linked with political motives and ideological exigencies; the exaltation of Actium and civil war later yielded to the glorification of a foreign campaign and victory in the East. But the actual erection of an "Actian" arch is still far from certain; the remains of the two foundation piers may belong to another commemorative structure (perhaps not even an arch). The problems that once cast serious doubt on the erection of an "Actian" arch have not been resolved.

The coinage of Octavian is the subject of examination in the third section of chapter 1. Two large groups of coins, distinguished by the simple, but potent, legends CAESAR DIVI F(ilius) and IMP(erator) CAESAR, feature a prominent motif of victory and the monuments of victory. The groups have recently been interpreted as the "triumphal series" that exalted the success at Actium. The period of mintage for both groups has been fixed to a brief span of years shortly before and immediately after Actium. The current confidence in this chronology, however, is unwarranted. Early editors of numismatic catalogs assigned the issues from either one or both groups to a more indefinite span of years extending from Octavian's victory at Naulochus in 36 to the formal adoption of the title Augustus in 27 B.C.E. The absence of any specific titulature on the coinage, the depictions of symbols and monuments of victory that may allude to the naval success at either Actium or Naulochus just five years earlier, and the disputed identification for the coin types suggest that there still remains substantial cause to question the rigid dating of these issues. The issues testify to a conspicuous and significant transformation in the public image of Octavian, but the victory at Actium may not have been the impetus for this grand transformation.

Discussion of the monuments of Actium in the East—the victory city and the quinquennial games—concludes chapter 1. The very name of the city and the celebration of Actian games, not only at Nicopolis, but in various cities throughout the Greek East, broadcast an official message of Octavian's victory at Actium. The substance of this message and its intended audience are important factors in any assessment of these "Actian" monuments. Celebration of victory in the Greek East had an old and well-established tradition of cults, rituals, and festivals that the Roman conquerors in this region readily adopted to exploit their own interests. Though he may have exceeded the actions and intentions of his predecessors, Octavian only inherited and continued this practiced tradition. Athletic games and victory cities established by the victor at Actium must be judged in the context of Octavian's efforts at reorganization and settlement of power in the Greek East and should not be confused with the formation of an imperial ideology shaped and articulated in Rome.

Chapter 2 inspects the ancient evidence and perceptions of the Augustan Temple of Apollo on the Palatine. The temple has often been seen by modern observers as the most visible and prominent monument in Rome of the victory at Actium. The public and direct association of this temple with Apollo Actius has not been questioned. It is generally assumed that the recognition that Octavian bestowed on Apollo at the site of his naval victory (a temple of the god stood on the promontory of Actium) was immediately carried over to Rome and his new temple, officially dedicated in 28. The subject demands a comprehensive and judicious review.

My inquiry is divided into two sections. The first inspects and seeks to reassess the claims of an early and close association between Apollo and Octavian. The association, so it has long been maintained, was political in nature and fundamentally shaped and influenced the public image of Caesar's heir in Rome. This popular view, however, has rested on implausible and unsupported assumptions. The scenario that has been widely imagined for the period of the Triumvirate, where rivals waged war through their surrogate divine patrons (Neptune and Sextus Pompey; Hercules, later Dionysus, and Antony; and Apollo and Octavian) has been exaggerated and distorted. The few and scattered reports that link Octavian and Apollo in the narratives of later historians must be placed beside the absence of corroborative testimony in the literary, epigraphical, and numismatic evidence of the contemporary period.

The second section moves to the circumstances that led to the vow of a new temple to Apollo in 36 and the formal dedication ceremonies eight years later. The efforts to associate either the initial vow to erect a temple with the victory at Naulochus or the later dedication with the victory at Actium cannot be supported by the evidence. The testimony on the "Actian" games at the dedication of Apollo's temple on the ninth day of October in 28 must be reviewed with circumspection and care. Finally, I seek to reconsider and question the merit of recent claims that the choice and arrangement of the temple's varied artwork indicate a glorification of Actium by overtly propagandistic or subtle allegorical images and motifs.

The final four chapters shift attention from imperial intentions to literary themes and poetic pursuits. Octavian's victory evoked mixed emotions from contemporary poets. Initial joy at the naval success at Actium may have later yielded to more profound reflection on the consequences of the victory. The response of Horace to Actium in *Epode 9*, most likely composed in the immediate aftermath of the battle, and in *Odes* 1.37, perhaps a reaction to the eager anticipation and public enthusiasm of Octavian's triple triumph ceremony in 29, cannot be judged against the same background as the central scene of battle and subsequent triumph on the shield of the hero in Vergil's *Aeneid* or the vivid image of the *Actiacum mare* in the elegies of Propertius. The slow passage of time, the political changes in Augustan Rome and the realizations of these changes, and, above all, the distinctive and dissimilar objectives of individual poets, far from any constant and uniform intention to applaud (or bemoan) the outcome at Actium, constitute proper and serious considerations in any assessment of the contemporary literature devoted to the theme of Actium.

Horace's *Epode 9* is the focus of attention in the examination of the lyric poet's attitude toward the victory at Actium. It could not be otherwise. Though Horace alludes to the new and exalted status of the Actian victor in his second book of *Satires* and in his collection of *Odes*, apart from the so-called Actian epode and Cleopatra ode, the poet avoids any direct reference to, much less any celebration of, the famed naval battle. To be sure, Horace is quick to praise Augustan victories and conquests in Spain, Gaul, and, above all, the East; subjugation of the Parthian enemy is proclaimed almost a decade before the Roman standards were returned and a triumph awarded (and graciously declined). The impressive military and civic accomplishments of the princeps earn the poet's sincere respect and his prophecy of the ruler's future deification. His record of Roman civil war (the battles at Mutina, Philippi, Perusia, Naulochus, and Actium), however, is conspicuously absent from the Horatian corpus. The ninth epode demands a close analysis of the text. The poem has become a source of fierce dispute and controversy among historians and literary critics alike. Modern appraisal of the epode has varied from a "running commentary" on the progress of the campaign and naval battle, to a "true war poem" of ugly propaganda and extreme Roman pride, to an enthused and spontaneous expression of uncomplicated joy, a "victory ode" in the Pindaric tradition. Close observation of the progress of the epode's narrative and of its sudden shifts in tone reveals a more complex and mixed response to the outcome at Actium.

My analysis of the early elegies of Propertius, composed in the formative years of the Augustan Principate, serves as a fitting transition between Horace's lyric compositions and Vergil's epic poem. Placed beside Horace's *Epode* 9, the Propertian elegies document a public discourse and poetic attitude before the reception of Vergil's *Aeneid* and evidence what I regard as the impetus of a national myth on Actium, the victory and its historic significance. My examination is divided into two sections. The first explores the nature and content of the Propertian response toward Actium in his second book. In the opening piece of this book, the elegist makes the Actian trophies of war the culmination of a triumphal parade of civil war, the final scene in the poet's *recusatio* to sing of Octavian's military glory. This introduction to Actium should not be forgotten when the elegist incorporates the scene of the battle in *Elegies* 2.15 and 2.16 and in the concluding elegy of the book, 2.34. The specific context of these passages in the individual poems must be carefully evaluated.

The second section examines the theme of Actium in *Elegy* 3.11. This long and troublesome poem employs Rome's past fear of Cleopatra as the defense of a lover's shameful submission to a woman. The predominant role of the queen in the elegy and the rather abrupt and surprising conclusion, where the nameless sailor is asked to remember Caesar throughout the Ionian Sea, a conspicuous allusion to Actium, have led modern commentators to view the Propertian elegy as sincere panegyric to Augustus and his Actian victory. One editor defines the elegy as an attempt at "patriotic poetry."[19] I reject this common view. The elegy offers more than an impressive display of Propertian rhetoric and artifice, something much different from a reluctant endeavor to praise Actium. The veiled allusions to past civil war, the recurrent accusations of shame against Rome for fearing a woman, and the nature of the elegy's final message argue against the notion that Propertius has begun to modify or abandon his attitude toward Actium.

Vergil's *Aeneid* exalts the battle at Actium in an epic setting. The consequences of this public gesture are profound and immediate. The central scene on the shield of Aeneas portrays Augustus leading the representatives of Roman authority into battle against Antony, his Egyptian *coniunx*, and

---

19. W.A. Camps, ed. *Propertius: Elegies, Book III* (Cambridge, 1966), 104.

the barbaric forces and divinities of the East. A mighty struggle ensues, fierce and cosmic in its dimensions. The appearance of Apollo Actius secures the victory. The scene shifts suddenly to Rome and concludes with a triumphal parade, where Augustus sits on the throne of Phoebus and receives the tribute of the conquered peoples. The remark by one scholar that "the poet discharges his obligation to commemorate the conclusion of the civil war" by the inclusion of Actium on the shield of Aeneas characterizes the modern approach toward the passage.[20] Vergilian critics, even those who once were inclined to discern the more dark and tragic aspects of the epic, regard the poet's depiction of the Actian conflict and the subsequent scene of the Augustan triple triumph as one of the few pure and untainted moments of proud Roman glory in the *Aeneid*. The presumptions of the poet's political voice or unwavering allegiance to the Augustan regime have biased interpretations of the passage, whether the scholar may be labeled positivist or pessimist. Vergil's Actium is not an isolated and obtrusive expression of a naive optimism or reluctant acceptance of Roman imperialism; the central scene on the Trojan hero's shield must be judged in the context of the Vergilian epic, as part of the fabric in the *Aeneid*'s rich patchwork of blurred images and potent symbols.

In chapter 6, I confront perhaps the most controversial of the "Actian" poems. Scholarly interpretations have run the gamut from reading Propertius' *Elegy* 4.6 as sincere eulogy to recognizing the poet's words as ironic parody. The elegy has most recently been seen by some critics as the final acknowledgment of, or the uneasy surrender to, the persistent demands of the political regime to honor Actium. Others have even asserted that the elegy honored the official ceremonies of the "Actian" games that are widely assumed to have been celebrated before the Temple of Apollo on the Palatine in 16 B.C.E. I approach the elegy from a different perspective. The Propertian scene of the battle at Actium profoundly differs from the depictions in Horace and Vergil. The enemies of Rome in this confrontation are neither formidable nor impressive; the battle is won without any real fighting; and Apollo Actius, not Augustus, is hailed as the victor at the end of the hymn. In the distance of at least fifteen years from the date of battle to the poet's composition, the reality of civil war has given way to the myth of a great battle. The influence of Vergil's *Aeneid* must be assumed and assessed. Perhaps more than any action of Augustus, the epic poet's vision of Actium on the shield of Aeneas articulated a new conception of the decisive naval battle. The elegist also creates a myth of Actium in his hymn to Apollo, but the

---

20. Quinn, *Virgil's Aeneid*, 197.

battle is neither heroic nor impressive. The myth fails to convince, and Propertius ignores, or rather stubbornly refuses to recognize, the grave consequences and much hailed rewards of Actium. The public perception of the naval battle has changed; Actium belongs no longer to the distant horrors of a tainted past, but to the promise and beginning of a more glorious future.

The limitations inherent in any book have excluded certain areas of study from consideration; their exclusion should not be understood necessarily as a reflection on their significance. The most conspicuous omission in the assessment of contemporary historical evidence involves what I would call the "private" artwork that commemorated the Actian victory. An assortment of stone reliefs, ornate gemstones, and decorated cups and lamps may allude to Octavian's role in the battle.[21] Interpretation of such artwork,

---

21. In a series of related discussions, Tonio Hölscher assembles an imposing, though at the same time selective and motley collection of commemorative artwork, which he interprets as the "Denkmäler der Schlacht von Actium." See Hölscher, "Beobachtungen zu römischen historischen Denkmälern," *AA* 94.2 (1979): 337–48; "Actium und Salamis," *JDAI* 99 (1984): 187–214; *Staatsdenkmal und Publikum. vom Untergang der Republik bis zur Festigung des Kaisertums in Rom* (Konstanz, 1984); "Denkmäler der Schlacht vom Actium," *Klio* 67 (1985): 81–102; and "Historische Reliefs," in *Kaiser Augustus*, 351–400. The evidence consists primarily of fragmentary temple friezes, broken marble reliefs, gemstones, and decorated lamps. An example of the problems and limitations of any interpretation of these works might be found in one of the better known specimens, the sardonyx cameo now in the Museum of Fine Arts in Boston (cf. also the discussion by Zanker, *Power of Images*, 97–98). Hölscher, "Denkmäler der Schlacht vom Actium," 97, confidently identifies an "Actium-Motive" on the cameo's relief. A male youth, naked except for a flowing chlamys wrapped around his upper arms, holding a trident in his left hand, drives a quadriga of sea horses amid a swirl of billowing waves. The fine details (wavy hair and beardless face) may bear some resemblance to Augustus, who assumes the role of the god Neptune as he leads his team across the waters in triumphal fashion. If the figure is meant to represent Augustus, the divine imitation may presume a period after Actium and may even allude to the victory in the decisive naval battle, but the allusion would, in any case, be vague and indirect. The head and nude upper torso of a male figure emerging from the waves is probably a Triton or some marine deity, as Gisela Richter has plausibly suggested (see G.M.A. Richter, *Engraved Gems of the Greeks, Etruscans, and Romans*, vol. 2, *Engraved Gems of the Romans: A Supplement to the History of Roman Art* [London, 1971], 101, no. 483), not Antony, as Hölscher and Zanker, who is in doubt whether the swimming figure is Antony or Sextus Pompey, have indicated. Furthermore, however much the cameo may reflect the political consequences of Actium, the artwork should not be understood as a commemoration of the victory per se and provides no useful or reliable indication of how Augustus endeavored to shape the public perception of his military achievement. An exact date of the cameo, which is claimed to have been found at Hadrumetum, a coastal town in Tunisia, cannot be ascertained, and it is imprudent to insist on a fixed period immediately after Actium. A youthful representation of Augustus does not preclude a later date. An inscription POPIL(ius) ALBAN(us) presumably identifies the owner of the cameo with a name otherwise not known, though the gens Popil(l)ia is an ancient and distinguished patrician family. Similarly, the almost ubiquitous

however, is fraught with difficulty and uncertainty. Two factors frustrate scholarly efforts. First, the pieces often cannot be securely dated. "Actian" motifs should not be restricted to a limited span of years. The reputation of Actium survived long after the Augustan Age and continued to be cherished (perhaps even more so) in subsequent generations, as the memory of Rome's first princeps left an exemplary model of imperial rule and glory. And even when the dating can be fixed to the contemporary period, it must be kept in mind that forty-five years separate the victory at Actium from the death of Augustus. The image of a ship's prow or rudder is not always an allusion to Actium; nor need it even convey a political message. The frequent appearance of such motifs on private artwork throughout the Augustan period only suggests that aesthetic and personal concerns outweighed politics and public ideology. Sometimes a naval prow is just a naval prow.[22]

I have limited my examination of the contemporary literature to Latin authors. The evidence of the Greek poets who celebrated the victory at Actium demands special attention as a subject that has not yet been explored in any serious fashion.[23] Nevertheless, the praise of Crinagoras or the anonymous author of the epigram to Apollo Actius, who compares the victor at Actium to Zeus Eleutherios, cannot be placed beside an ode of Horace or an elegy of Propertius. Contemporary Roman poets other than Horace, Vergil, and Propertius—most notably, Ovid, Manilius, and the unknown poet of the *Elegiae in Maecenatem*—also make reference to Actium in their works.[24] The references, however, are brief—often no more than a couplet to identify the battle—and, for the most part, belong to the final years of the Augustan Principate or later. It is difficult to assess the value of these remarks. A papyrus fragment from Herculaneum offers the remains of a Latin epic poem most often identified as the *Carmen de Bello Actiaco*. The title is modern and misleading. The few surviving fragments deal with the fighting

---

representations of winged Victory on Augustan art and coinage, where the goddess stands on a globe and holds at times an *aplustre*, a laurel wreath, the *corona civica* or the *clipeus virtutis*, do not constitute a glorification of Actium; the goddess offers instead a well-established Republican (and later imperial) image of Roman conquest over the world, and when joined with allegorical representations and symbols of Augustan honors, Victory promotes the virtues of Rome's military leader and ruler, not the memory of a specific battle.

22. Cf. the comments by Zanker on the private and aesthetic exploitation of political motifs in his discussion, "The Final Stage: From Internalization to the Private Message," in *Power of Images*, 274–78.

23. For the evidence of the Greek epigrammatists on Actium, see *anth. Palat.* 6.236, 6.251, 9.553; and D.L. Page, ed. and trans. *Select Papyri*, vol. 3, *Literary Papyri: Poetry*, Loeb Classical Library 360 (Cambridge, Mass., 1941; reprinted 1970), 468–71, no. 113.

24. Ovid *Fasti* 1.711–12; *Meta.* 13.715, 15.826–28; *Tr.* 3.1.41–42; Man. 1.914–18, 5.52–53; *Eleg. in Maecen.* 1.45–52.

in Egypt and the final hours of Antony and the queen. It is impossible to determine the role or importance of Actium in the poem. The date and author of the poem are also uncertain. The obscure Rabirius, whom Velleius Paterculus singles out in his list of eminent Augustan authors immediately after Vergil, the *princeps carminum* (2.36.3), is known to have composed verses that included an account of Antony's death and consequently has been thought to be the poet who celebrated Actium in epic verse.[25] It is a tempting possibility, but the *carmen* may belong to another author and another era; perhaps it is the work of an unknown Neronian or early Flavian poet.[26]

There remains the verdict of the historians. Livy's treatment of the Actian battle unfortunately survives only in summary. The single reference to Actium in his extant books links the victory with the closure of the temple doors of Janus.

> post bellum Actiacum ab imperatore Caesare Augusto pace terra marique parta . . . (Livy 1.19.3)

> [after the battle at Actium peace was secured on land and sea by Imperator Caesar Augustus . . .]

The works of the biographer Nicolaus of Damascus, the censured Timagenes, and, more importantly, the Roman historians Pompeius Trogus and Asinius Pollio are not extant. The direct testimony of the victor would be more telling. Though the Augustan *Memoirs* are lost, the *Res Gestae* duly records the military campaign that resulted in the naval success at Actium.

---

25. Whether the subject of Rabirius' poem was the civil war between Octavian and Antony is far from certain. For the meager evidence on this point, cf. Sen. *de Ben.* 6.3.1, who cites Antony's dying words in a poem by Rabirius (*hoc habeo, quodcumque dedi*, Courtney, *FLP*, 332, frag. 2).

26. Attributions vary. Courtney, *FLP*, 334, suggests that the so-called *Carmen de Bello Actiaco* may, in fact, belong to the *Res Romanae* of Cornelius Severus, the author of the *Bellum Siculum* and a friend of the poet Ovid. H.W. Benario, "The *Carmen de Bello Actiaco* and Early Imperial Epic," *ANRW* II.30.3 (Berlin and New York, 1983), 1656–62, provides a readable text of the fragmentary epic poem with translation and briefly reviews the scholarly debate. G. Zecchini, *Il Carmen de bello Actiaco. Storiografia e lotta politica in età augustea*, Historia Einzelschriften 51 (Stuttgart, 1987), offers a stimulating argument that the work is a product of Augustan political opposition, whose author sympathized with the ambitions of Iullus Antonius, the younger son of Mark Antony and Fulvia, who also wrote an epic poem, the *Diomedea*, and was executed in 2 B.C.E. because of a conspiracy with Julia the Elder, the daughter of Augustus. The extremely mutilated condition of the work, however, prohibits any cogent interpretation of the poem and its specific literary (or political) context.

Iuravit in mea verba tota Italia sponte sua, et me belli quo vici ad
Actium ducem depoposcit; iuraverunt in eadem verba provinciae Gal-
liae, Hispaniae, Africa, Sicilia, Sardinia. Qui sub signis meis tum mil-
itaverint fuerunt senatores plures quam DCC, in iis qui vel antea vel
postea consules facti sunt ad eum diem quo scripta sunt haec LXXX-
III, sacerdotes circiter CLXX. (*RG* 25.2–3)

[The whole of Italy of its own will swore oaths of allegiance in my
words and in the war in which I was victorious at Actium demanded
me as the leader. The provinces of the Gauls, the Spains, Africa, Sicily,
and Sardinia swore to the same oaths. Those who served under my
standards at that time were more than seven hundred senators, among
whom were eighty-three who previously or later were declared consuls
up to this day when this document was written, and about one hundred and seventy were priests.]

What is significant here is not the attention directed toward the accomplished victory at Actium, which is slight, but the emphasis on the avowed
support of Italy, the provinces, and the representative figures of Roman
authority—the senators, consuls (former consuls, since the two consuls in
the previous year had already fled to Antony), and priests. The passage reads
more like a defense of the Actian campaign than a celebration or glorification of victory. Acknowledgment of the enemy (neither Roman nor foreign)
is absent. More than thirty years after the naval battle, Augustus, now
proclaimed Pater Patriae (father of his country), still felt compelled to justify
his earlier actions, much like his condensed and obfuscated accounts of the
battles of Mutina, Philippi, and Naulochus. Furthermore, he makes no attempt to define the struggle in the broad cultural or national terms evident in
Vergil's treatment of Actium and generally assumed to be part of an official
version of the war.

More surprising and telling in this clipped, but pointed, reference to
Actium is the exclusion of the public rewards and consequences of the naval
engagement. The frequent boasts of military conquest and territorial expansion (*RG* 27), the solemn declaration of peace on land and sea (*RG* 13), and
the formal proclamation of the end of the civil wars and the beginning of a
new political regime (*RG* 34) recur in the Augustan chronicle of deeds, but
these proud claims are not linked with the victory over Antony and Cleopatra. The judgment on Actium Augustus left to subsequent generations;[27]

---

27. Syme's concluding remarks in *The Roman Revolution*, 524, are appropriately concise
and cogent: "Like Augustus, his *Res Gestae* are unique, defying verbal definition and explain-
ing themselves."

contemporaries had already formed their own opinions. What follows in this book is an effort to perceive more clearly the Augustan image of Actium, a mixed portrait of victory and defeat, joyful celebration and bitter sorrows, a public ideology, slow, if not reluctant to emerge, and a wondrous and inspiring myth shaped more by the verses of individual poets, elated, angry, and at times indifferent, than by the concerted actions and directives of an imperious and vainglorious ruler.

Chapter One

"The Imperious Show of the Full-Fortun'd Caesar": Celebration in Rome and the Monuments of Victory

The Triple Triumph Ceremony

Nearly two years had passed since the naval victory at Actium before Octavian's triumphant return to Rome in the summer of 29 B.C.E. Despite the destruction of their fleet, the surrender of nineteen legions, and the subsequent betrayal by their allies, both Roman and foreign, Antony and his queen had managed to survive the disastrous affair in the Ambracian Gulf. Vanquished in battle, but not subdued in spirit, the pair withdrew to the safe confines and distance of Alexandria. Supported by the treasury of the Ptolemies, the Roman triumvir and the Egyptian queen still remained a serious concern for the Actian victor, if not a real danger. Antony's ambition to launch another campaign, however, was in vain, and Cleopatra's plot to escape beyond the reach of Octavian and the authority of Rome was ultimately frustrated.

Following his capture of Alexandria and the opportune suicides of his enemies, the victor was free to settle affairs in the East and to prepare for his late and much awaited return to Italian shores. Anticipation, anxiety, and, above all, uncertainty must have preceded Octavian's arrival. A formal triumphal celebration had already been planned, but many in Rome must have wondered how Octavian would celebrate his triumph over the man who was once his sister's husband, his colleague in power, and a fellow citizen. Even though the harsh rhetoric of Octavian, echoed in the imperious decrees of the senate, had declared Cleopatra the public enemy, and though the riches of Egypt decked the streets and temples of Rome and supplied the spoils of victory, the specter of civil war must have haunted the preparations for the triumphal occasion.

Prior studies have failed to consider the spectacle of Octavian's triple

---

Chapter title is taken from W. Shakespeare, *Antony and Cleopatra* 4.15.23–24.

triumph in a detailed or critical manner or to regard the occasion as anything more than an impressive display of a victor's propaganda and the
glorious celebration of the naval battle at Actium. To be sure, narratives of
the event, both dramatic and imaginative, can be found in the plethora of
Augustan biographies or in the general discussions on Roman triumphs.[1]
Most accounts, however, are merely descriptive and fail to consider the
purpose or effects of the manner in which Octavian represented and celebrated his victory at Actium. In this chapter, I address the triple triumph
ceremony of 29 from two perspectives.

First, the tradition of the Roman triumph. There were no fixed rules, no
standard procedures to maintain for celebrating a triumph. The victorious
general himself decided on the arrangements of the exhibits and the length of
his triumphal procession. Great victories demanded something special and
extravagant if an audience was to believe the claims of greatness. Grand
displays of foreign treasures and spoils, glaring spectacles, and sensational
parades of conquered peoples and nations exalted the prestige of the victor.
The triumphal celebrations of Julius Caesar offer an interesting comparison.
Both Caesars faced a similarly difficult predicament following their decisive
victories over their rivals. But success in civil war could not be the occasion
for a Roman triumph, at least not officially or openly.[2] Only the subjugation
of foreign enemies and the conquest of new lands merited the reward of a
triumph and the solemn procession along the Sacra Via. In the summer of 46
B.C.E., Julius Caesar chose to celebrate four triumphs held on different days
extending for about one month.[3] The triumphs commemorated foreign conquest; the battles at Pharsalus and Thapsus received no official recognition.
Octavian instead honored the victory at Actium with its own triumph. This
decision might at first suggest the special nature and prominence of Actium,

---

1. Historians and biographers of Augustus have usually referred to the triple triumph of 29
with simply a passing remark. For a more descriptive account, see R. Payne, *The Roman
Triumph* (London, 1962), 146–48. For an informative compilation of the ancient sources and
discussion on this subject, see V. Gardthausen, *Augustus und seine Zeit*, 2 vols. (Leipzig, 1891),
1:471–77.

2. On this matter, cf. the pertinent remarks of Val. Max. 2.8.7: *lauream nec senatus
cuiquam dedit nec quisquam sibi dari desideravit civitatis parte lacrimante.*

3. The four triumphs were officially proclaimed *ex Gallia, ex Aegypto, ex Ponto,* and *ex
Africa*. For the ancient sources regarding the triumphs of Caesar, see *RE* 10.1 (1918): col. 245;
Degrassi, *Inscr. Ital.* XIII, 567; Livy *Per.* 115; Vell. 2.56; Flor. 2.13.88; Suet. *Caes.* 37, 49, 54,
80; *Aug.* 8.1; Dio 43.14.3, 43.19.1; Plut. *Caes.* 55; Pliny *NH* 9.171, 14.97, 19.144; Appian *BC*
2.101; Oros. 6.16.6; Zon. 10.10. For an excellent discussion of Julius Caesar as triumphator,
see S. Weinstock, *Divus Julius* (Oxford, 1971), 60–79. The articles by M.E. Deutsch still merit
attention: "The Apparatus of Caesar's Triumphs," *PQ* 3 (1924): 257–66, and "Caesar's Triumphs," *CW* 19 (1926):101–6.

but Octavian's careful arrangement of the ceremonies reveals something quite different.

Second, the order and orchestration of the triple triumph. Unlike Caesar, Octavian chose to celebrate three triumphs, held on consecutive days. The first day commemorated former victories in Illyria; the second, the naval success at Actium; and the third, the conquest of Egypt. The Alexandrian campaign for which the third triumph had been awarded was more a matter of rhetoric and invention than any battle of consequence; yet the magnitude of its celebration on the last day of the proceedings far exceeded the attention directed to Actium. On the final day, the rich spoils of Egypt upstaged the naval beaks of Actium. This impression must surely have been part of Octavian's design and calculations. It is the aim of this section to examine the triumphator's careful staging of the ceremonies of the three-day affair to assess the role that the celebrations in 29 played in shaping the public image of the new Caesar and conqueror in Rome.

The ambition of every victorious Roman general was the honor and glory of a triumphal procession. The origins of this solemn ceremony and religious rite are obscure,[4] but antiquity credited Romulus with its institution and first celebration in Rome. Lacking the pomp and pageantry that so often characterized the triumphal displays of the late Republic and Empire, the celebration of victory in Rome's early years was probably little more than the simple procession of soldiers marching in line with their conquering general. There was no chariot or team of splendid white horses; the victor walked into the city proudly, but on foot. The spoils of victory were few and unimpressive, probably no more than the weapons of the captured enemy. The celebration ended with public sacrifices and thanksgiving to the gods.

Foreign victories and the conquest of the Mediterranean world profoundly changed the purpose and nature of the Roman triumph. Already by the second century B.C.E. the triumph ceremony had become more lavish, sensational, and political. The magnitude and consequences of the success on the battlefield were sometimes secondary factors in the bestowal of a triumph. The victor's political connections in Rome and his resources for bribery became equally powerful determinants. As the awards and celebration of triumphs multiplied, the prestige and distinction of the honor inevita-

---

4. For a provocative discussion and extensive bibliography on this matter, see H.S. Versnel, "Triumphus: An Inquiry into the Origin, Development and Meaning of the Roman Triumph" (Ph.D. diss., Leiden, 1970).

bly diminished. The rivalry shifted to the actual ceremonies of the triumph, to the demands of a public spectacle and urban entertainment. Each triumphator sought to surpass his predecessors by staging a show that would overwhelm the spectators with lavish displays of spoils and booty; representations of conquered cities, mountains, and rivers; and an impressive array of captives, sometimes crowned by a royal prisoner in chains. The triumphator yearned for a ceremony that Rome would never forget.

Fifteen years after Pompey celebrated his third and last triumph in 61 B.C.E., Julius Caesar, victorious in civil war, returned to Rome to celebrate his first. Not suffering to be surpassed by his conquered rival, Caesar claimed not one but four triumphs as the rewards of his victory, although the celebration of multiple triumphs in the same year by one man was without precedent. For a more impressive display of his spoils and supreme power, Caesar also arranged for the festive occasion to extend for almost one month. The interval of days between the celebrations gave individual attention and importance to each victory. Each day had its own processions of soldiers, elaborate spectacles, and surprises.

The first triumph was held at the end of June in 46. It honored the long campaign that had resulted in the conquest of Gaul, accomplished in the years before the conflict with Pompey. Because of the troubled political situation and civil conflict, the triumph had been long postponed. The captive Vercingetorix lingered in confinement during the struggle for power between the Roman rivals. When at last it came time to celebrate Caesar's achievement in Gaul, the once formidable opponent was not forgotten. Placed at the head of a long array of Gallic chiefs and prisoners, the still defiant captive overshadowed all the spectacles that had preceded him and served as the triumphator's most fearsome display.

Arsinoë, the Egyptian princess and younger sister of Cleopatra, assumed the role of chief captive in Caesar's second triumph for his victory over Ptolemy and Egypt. Her appearance in the triumphal procession, however, produced an unexpected reaction in the Roman audience. The young girl, about thirteen years of age, loaded with chains and forced to walk at the head of a procession of captive prisoners, surprisingly evoked sympathy from the usually boisterous throng of Roman citizens. Dio (43.19.3–4) remarks that the sight of the helpless captive, escorted by an imposing array of lictors, "pained the Romans terribly" and "aroused much pity, and with this as an excuse they bemoaned their own misfortunes." Dio adds that Rome had never before seen a woman once called a queen led in chains in a triumphal procession, and we may wonder if Cleopatra, more than fifteen years later, thought back to the plight of her sister when she resolved to take her own life rather than adorn Octavian's parade.

Caesar celebrated his third triumph over Pharnaces, the king of Pontus, the son of a more dangerous and successful opponent of the Romans, Mithridates. Unlike the reaction to Arsinoë, the crowd responded with scornful laughter at the sight of Pharnaces, or rather at the representation of him. Pharnaces had been killed in his attempt to flee after defeat in battle, and the cowardice of his flight was humorously depicted on an enormous placard. For staging purposes of the triumph, if the defeated foes had been killed in battle or had committed suicide, a depiction of the manner and last moments of their deaths served as a common, though not always prudent, substitute for their presence. Romans laughed at the death of Pharnaces, but they reacted more somberly when, later in the African triumph, they witnessed depictions of fellow citizens who had decided to take their own lives rather than to await an uncertain verdict or the humiliating pardon of a merciful conqueror.

A difficult problem confronted Caesar as he prepared to celebrate his fourth triumph for his victories won over the armies led by Metellus Scipio and M. Porcius Cato. Juba, the king of Mauretania, had supported the cause of the Pompeians, but his role in the fighting was limited and insignificant. The true enemy had been the Roman citizens who chose to fight against Caesar at the battle of Thapsus, and many of those who survived the engagement were later slaughtered by the victor. To honor his achievement but avoid celebrating a victory in civil war in any ostentatious or obvious display, Caesar made Juba serve as the enemy. To support his claim that the enemy was more foreign than Roman, Caesar forced the son of the slain Juba, who was only five years old at the time of the triumph, to walk in front of the procession of captive prisoners. The victor, however, could not refrain from mocking his defeated opponents in the civil war, especially those who preferred suicide to pardon. Appian (*BC* 2.101) records that the triumphator took special care not to inscribe the names of any Roman citizens on the placards that adorned his four triumphs. But, while the names were absent, ghastly depictions portrayed the final moments of the most prominent Romans who fought against Caesar in the wars in Spain and Africa. The scenes were intended to be comic and to ridicule the suicides that some in Rome perhaps were already beginning to praise. Scipio was depicted stabbing himself in the chest as he jumped into the sea, Petreius was shown killing himself at a banquet,[5] and the most shocking of all was the representation of Cato tearing out his own insides like a wild animal.

---

5. Dio (43.8.4) records that Petreius and Juba fought in single combat and died together to avoid capture by Caesar, from whom they expected no mercy. For the depiction of Petreius' death in Caesar's triumph, see Appian *BC* 2.101.

Perhaps Caesar expected that the spectators of his triumphal show would respond with the same laughter that had greeted the depiction of Pharnaces during the previous triumph. Appian, however, reports that the scenes had a powerful effect on the Romans; although fear restrained many from showing any signs of open displeasure, the people groaned at the representations that served only to remind them of their own private misfortunes. Appian does not say if the public reaction produced any effect on Caesar. The triumphator undoubtedly assured himself that the sumptuous banquets open to the public, the generous gifts to his soldiers, and the spectacles of the gladiatorial and naval combats that followed his triumphal celebrations would assuage the pain and embarrassment. His assurance was misplaced. An audience is not so easily comforted.[6] Octavian rode beside the victor in his chariot during the African triumph,[7] and it is possible that the young man still remembered the groans of resentment on this occasion when later, as the victor at Actium, he staged his own triumphal show.

The similarities between the triumphs of Julius Caesar and his heir are obvious and striking. Both men celebrated multiple triumphs after a victorious struggle in civil war. Prior victories, not honored previously, initiated the days of festivities and provided at least the semblance of a traditional triumph celebrating victory over a foreign enemy. For the victories achieved over fellow Roman citizens, the two triumphators employed as the excuses

---

6. Caesar celebrated his fifth triumph in October of 45 for his victories over Pompey's son in Spain. The triumph was his least successful, marred by several incidents that revealed the resentment and spirit of defiance not quite extinguished in the Romans. Plutarch (*Caes.* 56.7) claimed that no other celebration troubled the Romans more than Caesar's final triumph. First, a tribune, Pontius Aquila, refused to stand to salute the triumphator as the ceremonial chariot passed in front of those seats reserved for the tribunes (Suet. *Caes.* 78.2). Caesar was reported to have been especially annoyed and to have shouted back, "*Repete ergo a me Aquila rem publicam tribunus!*" It was also during the games celebrated on this formal occasion that Decimus Laberius, the famous writer of mimes, had the last word when Caesar forced the aged playwright to deliver in person the work he had been commissioned to compose (Macr. *Sat.* 2.7.4 and Cic. *Fam.* 12.18.2). The request was intended as an insult, since Laberius belonged to the equestrian order and necessarily abandoned his rank to perform, though it was later restored. The verses of Laberius, however, did not fail to hit the mark: *porro, Quirites, libertatem perdimus*. But there were more serious signs of public dissatisfaction. The grand feast that traditionally followed the triumphal ceremony was less than expected; Caesar felt compelled to offer another feast only five days later. (Suet. *Caes.* 38.2). The triumphator also decided to permit his two lieutenants in this campaign, Q. Pedius and Q. Fabius Maximus, to hold their own triumphs at this time. The populace ridiculed the fact that these men were allowed to use only wooden representations of triumphal apparatus instead of the customary ivory (Dio 43.42.1–2). We do not hear in the sources how local Spanish chiefs assumed the role of the defeated foreign enemy to obscure the unpleasant fact that Romans fought against Caesar. Perhaps the victor no longer felt the need of such pretense. Although called *Hispaniensis* by official title, the name only signified the location of battle.

7. Suet. *Aug.* 8.1 and Nic. Dam. *Vita Caes.* 8.

for a triumph the foreign foes who either had supported their rivals or had been regarded as enemies to Rome. So Caesar declared triumphs over Ptolemy of Egypt, Pharnaces of Pontus, and Juba of Africa. Only in his fifth and last triumph does it seem that Caesar abandoned the illusion and deceit. Interesting as the similarities may be, the differences between the celebrations of Caesar and Octavian are more suggestive.

➤✖︎⬅

On August 13, 14, and 15 in 29 B.C.E., Octavian celebrated his triple triumph.[8] The first day of the celebration honored Octavian's victories in Illyria. From our own modern perspective, we are inclined to dismiss this campaign as minor and insignificant, the "hors d'oeuvre of the more splendid triumphs," as one scholar has fashioned it.[9] It is clear from his actions at the time that Octavian held a different opinion. No account of the formal ceremonies on this day survives in the ancient sources, but from scattered remarks about the victor's military campaign in Illyria, we may assume that Octavian's first triumph, like Julius Caesar's Gallic triumph, began the festivities on the proper note, established the mood for the three-day extravaganza, and contributed to the specious claims that the recent victory over Antony had been a foreign campaign.

The Illyrian campaign had lasted almost three years and, for the most part, was led personally by Octavian. Appian and Dio offer the most detailed accounts of Octavian's military actions in this region, probably derived from a common source, the *Memoirs* of Augustus.[10] The list of defeated tribes and peoples that Appian (*Illyr.* 16–17) records in his narrative numbers more than twenty-eight. The long and impressive catalog of names seems to suggest an official version and the evidence of a contemporary witness. Even the abridged versions of the later historians reveal all the ingredients that the dramatic narrative of a successful *commentarius* might contain: sudden ambushes, prolonged sieges, near defeats, a wounded commander, and a final and glorious victory.

Dio records that a triumph had been awarded for the victories over the Illyrians already in 34, but Octavian deferred its celebration.[11] The reason

8. Degrassi, *Inscr. Ital.* XIII, 76–78, 180, 248, 325; *RG* 4; Livy *Per.* 133; Dio 51.21.5–9; Strabo *Geo.* 12.3.6, 12.3.35; Vell. 2.89.1; Suet. *Aug.* 22, 41.1, *Tib.* 6; Flor. 2.21.10; Serv. *Comm. in Verg. Aen.* 8.714; Oros. 6.20.1; Macr. *Sat.* 1.12.35.

9. Payne, *The Roman Triumph*, 147.

10. Appian *Illyr.* 16–28 and Dio 49.34–38. Appian discloses that he derived his information on the Illyrian campaigns from Augustus himself (chap. 15 of the *Memoirs*).

11. Dio 49.38.1. Although Octavian deferred the honor of a triumph at this time, he granted public statues and special privileges for Livia and his sister (the right to administer their own affairs without a male guardian and the sacrosanctity that the tribunes enjoy). On the

for Octavian's decision not to accept the triumph, if indeed the honor had actually been bestowed, probably arose from the political situation in Rome and confrontations with Antony. Congratulations were premature. Octavian's most difficult campaign in Illyria still awaited him. The Dalmatians, a more bellicose tribe than the Iapydes and Pannonians whom Octavian had earlier defeated, had recently formed an organized rebellion that threatened to spread throughout the whole region and to destroy the newly established peace. This was only the latest example of their stubborn refusal to come to terms with the Romans. Dalmatian treachery and Roman defeats had characterized the relationship between Rome and Illyria during the last fifteen years. Earlier in 48, the Dalmatians had dared to attack the fifteen cohorts of Gabinius, slaughtering his troops and seizing the Roman standards. Although only a few years later the tribe agreed to pay tribute, the standards were never returned. The murder of Caesar, however, prompted the Dalmatians to take advantage of the unstable situation in Rome; they revolted and refused to deliver the required tribute. When five Roman cohorts were sent to exact payment, the Dalmatians again defeated the Roman troops and left few survivors.

After a long and difficult campaign where Octavian was seriously wounded and some of his own soldiers had to be punished for desertion, the besieged Dalmatians finally surrendered. The demands of the victor were severe: more than seven hundred children as hostages, the payment of all the tribute that had been refused for the ten years since the death of Caesar, and, most importantly, the return of the lost standards. Dio concluded that the spoils of the Illyrian wars enabled Octavian to build the library and portico dedicated to his sister (the Bibliotheca and Porticus Octaviae), but the historian has confused two structures of similar family names.[12] Octavian deposited the standards in the Porticus Octavia, which had originally been built by Cn. Octavius following his naval victory over Perseus of Macedon in 168 B.C.E.[13] The standards and spoils from the Illyrian campaigns adorned the portico of Cn. Octavius, about which Augustus would later make the boast that he allowed the structure to maintain its original name despite his own restoration (*RG* 19.1).

significance of these actions, see M.B. Flory, "Livia and the History of Public Honorific Statues for Women in Rome," *TAPA* 123 (1993): 287–308.

12. Dio 49.43.8. Appian (*Illyr.* 28) gives the correct location.

13. The Porticus Octavia, originally built by Cn. Octavius, stood between the Theater of Pompey and the Circus Flaminius. The Bibliotheca and Porticus Octaviae that honored the sister of Augustus, replaced the portico of Q. Caecilius Metellus and surrounded the Temples of Jupiter Stator and of Juna Regina in the southern part of the Campus Martius. Cf. Suet. *Aug.* 29.4; Livy *Per.* 140; Vell. 1.11.3; Plut. *Marc.* 30.6. For discussion of the confusion of the

The Illyrian triumph displayed the glory of Octavian's martial activities in this campaign and exaggerated the extent of his achievement. The grand assemblage of defeated tribes that Appian duly records in his monograph on the Illyrian Wars probably was inscribed on banners that proclaimed the number of different peoples defeated and the names of the cities captured. This display, of course, could not compare with the prodigious list Pompey was able to collect for his two-day triumphal procession, but it must have seemed impressive. Though the ancient sources refer variously to the first triumph as a victory either *ex Illyrico* or *Delmaticum*,[14] the *Fasti Triumphales Barberiniani* may provide an official boast: *de Dalmatis triumphavit.*

The choice of the Dalmatians as the chief enemy for which the triumph had been awarded is understandable. It was this Illyrian tribe that proved the most formidable and from whom the standards were returned and later ceremoniously deposited by the triumphator. But Dio (51.21.5) includes a longer and more distinguished assemblage of conquered enemies. He records that the triumph celebrated victories over the Pannonians, Dalmatians, Iapydes, their neighbors, and some Germans and Gauls. The inclusion of the more northern Germans and Gauls is probably not the historian's invention or confusion. The conquest of these peoples (or at least the claims of conquest) may have resulted from Octavian's aborted expedition into Britain in 34 B.C.E.[15] In any case, the lengthy catalog of defeated peoples probably faithfully reflects the victor's claims throughout the celebration of his Illyrian triumph.

In the euphoria of a triumphal celebration, the magnitude alone of the number of the vanquished and captured can obscure the actual consequences and significance of the victory. A dazzling spectacle and a long parade of prisoners—which the display of the returned standards and the procession of the many Illyrian captives and hostages must have provided—can also contribute to the claims of a great victory. The sources do not reveal any Illyrian chieftain who might rival the fame of an individual like Vercingetorix of Caesar's Gallic triumph, but it is likely that some prominent captive was found to serve the role of the worthy adversary, noble and fearless. In the *Res*

---

structures of similar names and recent bibliography, see E. Nash, *Pictorial Dictionary of Ancient Rome*, 2 vols. (New York, 1962; reprinted 1981), 2:254, and L. Richardson, jr, *A New Topographical Dictionary of Ancient Rome* (Baltimore, 1992), 317–18.

14. Livy *Per.* 133 records the first triumph as *ex Illyrico*, and Suet. *Aug.* 22 labels it as *Delmaticum (triumphum).*

15. Dio (49.38.2) states that in emulation of his father, Octavian ventured an expedition into Britain in the early part of 34. He had already advanced as far as Gaul when trouble broke out in Illyria again and he was forced to abandon his plans. For a modern assessment of Octavian's motives in Illyria, cf. R. Syme, *Danubian Papers* (Bucharest, 1971), 17, 137; J.J. Wilkes, *Dalmatia* (London, 1969); and W. Schmitthenner, "Octavians militärische Unternehmungen in den Jahren 35–33 v. Chr.," *Historia* 7 (1958): 193–200.

Gestae (4.3), Augustus records that nine kings or children of kings adorned his triumphs. After his triple triumph ceremony, Augustus refused to accept the honor for himself again but allowed members of his family to receive it. Consequently these nine must belong to the three-day celebration. Six of these can be identified from various remarks in the ancient sources. Their names and roles in the ceremonies will be more closely examined in connection with the Actian and Egyptian triumphs. Perhaps some, if not all, of the remaining three served as the royal prisoners that adorned the Illyrian triumph.

The triumph in honor of the Actian victory occupied the middle of the three-day celebration. This fact should not lead us to assume that it held the center of attention or somehow acted as the climax of the triple triumph ceremonies. Placed between the other two triumphs—the first distinguished by a long parade of defeated enemies and the glory of standards returned, and the last adorned with the riches of Egypt and the dramatic representation of the dead queen—the Actian victory was upstaged. This was not an unforeseen event or some act of indifference by Octavian but a shrewd and deliberate manipulation of an audience by the showman of Rome par excellence.

For the most part, only speculation can reconstruct the nature of the celebration on the second day of Octavian's triple triumph. We are able to make a few assumptions, however, with a degree of confidence. Above all, the manner in which the victory was represented avoided any suggestion of civil war. Unlike Julius Caesar, who had dared to decorate his African triumph with unseemly representations of the suicides of fellow Roman citizens, Octavian did not allow personal animosity or vengeance to adorn his triumphs. Antony and the Romans who supported his cause were found nowhere in Octavian's triumphs. And if the effigy of Cleopatra was reserved for the final and climactic third day, worthy substitutes were required to perform the roles of the defeated. For this problem, Octavian shrewdly decided to exalt the foreign client kings of the East who had supported Antony and supplied troops for the battle at Actium. Their assistance was minimal. Several allies deserted Antony even before the naval engagement, and many were later pardoned and restored to their former power when they abandoned Antony shortly after the naval disaster.[16] Octavian made an exception of two kings, whom he retained in custody after Actium for the purposes of his triumphal procession, and whom he later executed.

16. For the desertion of Philadelphus, king of Paphlagonia, see Dio 50.13.5–6. For the support of the dynast Lycomedes, see Dio 51.2.3. Antony killed Iamblichus, a king of one of the tribes of the Arabians whom he suspected of treachery (Dio 50.13.8). The victor spared at least Amyntas, king of the Galatians, and Archelaus, who had chosen to abandon Antony before Actium (Dio 51.2.2–3). For a terse, yet informative, discussion of Octavian's policy in the East after the capture of Alexandria, see G.W. Bowersock, *Augustus and the Greek World* (Oxford, 1965), 42–61.

Adiatorix, the son of Domnecleius, was tetrarch of the Galatians in the province of Pontus. When hostilities broke out openly between the two Roman rivals and war threatened, Adiatorix lent his support to Antony. Shortly before the battle at Actium, the Galatian king led a surprise attack on Octavian's camp during the night and slaughtered a number of Romans. Even the claim that Antony had ordered the attack did not save Adiatorix. Led as a captive in Octavian's triumph, the enemy later paid the extreme penalty of his life for his nocturnal raid. Strabo (*Geo.* 12.3.35) mentions that Adiatorix's wife and two sons were also part of the triumphal procession. He does not specify the name of the triumph, but it was probably the Actian triumph. Alexander of Emesa, a king of one of the tribes in Arabia, also incurred the vengeance of the victor at Actium. Antony had tortured and killed his brother, Iamblichus, whose loyalty had been suspected in the desperate days before the battle. Alexander, who was responsible for the accusations that condemned his brother, received the throne from Antony. The victorious Octavian, however, did not spare the ambitious informer. Before his execution, Alexander was led in the triumphal procession (Dio 51.2.2). Again we do not learn what triumphal procession the client king adorned, but the Actian triumph seems likely.

The final day of celebration proclaimed the conquest of Egypt and the capture of the queen. In its lavishness and cost, the concluding triumph far surpassed those of the prior two days and became a fitting climax to the three-day extravaganza. The wealth of conquered Egypt was paraded throughout the city and adorned the temples. The hippopotamus and rhinoceros, African creatures never before seen in Rome, moved slowly along the Sacra Via for the entertainment of the crowd. A representation of the billowy Nile, complete with its seven mouths, was also exhibited. The city had never witnessed such a triumph, so superbly and richly orchestrated to captivate and deceive its audience. The defeated enemy had been dead for almost a year, but an effigy of the queen (presumably a painting or portrait of some sort) was substituted. From the words of Propertius, we know that the peculiar manner of her death was not ignored.[17]

bracchia spectavi sacris admorsa colubris,
    et trahere occultum membra soporis iter.

(3.11.53–54)

---

17. Whether the number of asps that killed the queen was one or two is a matter of some dispute among scholars. Cf. M.A. Levi, "Cleopatra e l'aspide," *PP* 9 (1954): 293–95; J. Gwyn Griffiths, "The Death of Cleopatra VII," *JEA* 47 (1961): 113–18; B. Baldwin, "The Death of Cleopatra VII," *JEA* 50 (1964): 181–82; J. Gwyn Griffiths, "The Death of Cleopatra VII: A Rejoinder and a Postscript," *JEA* 51 (1965): 209–11.

[I saw her arms bitten by the sacred asps
and her limbs take in the hidden journey of sleep.]

The ancient sources maintain that Cleopatra had been destined for Octavian's triumph, and his ambition to lead the queen in chains is often repeated.[18] But his failure to keep her alive after her capture raises some cause for doubt.[19] Surely if Octavian truly desired the queen alive for the glory of a triumph, security precautions, however severe and perhaps inhumane, could have prevented any suicide attempt. Perhaps he did not anticipate the resolve and courage of the queen. In any case, Rome certainly must have expected, if not demanded, the hated queen to adorn the triumph. Arsinoë, who had provoked an unexpected outpouring of sympathy in Julius Caesar's Egyptian triumph, was a young and innocent victim of circumstances. No one could believe that this girl posed any threat to the mighty Caesar. Arsinoë's sister, however, was neither young nor innocent at the time of her defeat. No enemy since Hannibal had caused such fear and hatred in Italy. Whether these emotions were justified or merely fabricated by the rhetoric of Octavian does not alter the situation. Octavian's prewar propaganda had succeeded so well, in part, because popular sentiment had seen the Egyptian queen as the cause of the civil conflict or at least had preferred to blame her. On the final day of the triumphal show, the crowd had to be content with a likeness of the dead queen. And the triumphator publicly expressed his annoyance, and admiration.[20]

Florus aptly remarks on the absence of any formal recognition of Julius Caesar's major victories in his triumphs.

Pharsalia et Thapsos et Munda nusquam. et quanto maiora erant,
de quibus non triumphabat!

(2.13.89)

---

18. Plut. *Ant.* 85–86; Dio 51.14.1–6; and the evidence of Livy reported by pseudo-Acron on Horace *Odes* 1.37.30: *Augusto invidens, ne captivitas sua illi speciosiorem faceret triumphum. nam et Livius refert Cleopatram, cum de industria ab Augusto capta indulgentius tractaretur, dicere solitam: Non triumphabor.* Cf. Livy *Per.* 133; Vell. 2.87.1; Flor. 2.21.10; Strabo *Geo.* 17.1.10.

19. Others have voiced such doubts on this matter. Cf. E. Groag, "Beiträge zur Geschichte des zweiten Triumvirats," *Klio* 14 (1915): 65–66; W.W. Tarn, "The War of the East against the West," *CAH* 10 (1934): 109–10; reprinted in *Octavian, Antony and Cleopatra*, by W.W. Tarn and M. Charlesworth (Cambridge, 1965), 138–39; and W.R. Johnson, "A Quean, a Great Queen? Cleopatra and the Politics of Misrepresentation," *Arion* 6 (1967): 393–94.

20. On the ancient evidence for Octavian's vexation over the queen's suicide and at the same time his begrudging admiration for her noble spirit, see especially, Plut. *Ant.* 86.4 and Dio 51.14.6.

[Pharsalus and Thapsus and Munda were nowhere. And how much greater those deeds were for which he did not celebrate any triumphs!]

While Caesar did not refrain from mocking the fellow citizens against whom he had waged a civil war by exaggerating their death throes on painted placards and parading these images down the Sacra Via, officially, at least, he chose to celebrate triumphs over foreign enemies. The victories at Pharsalus, Thapsus, and Munda did not merit their own triumphal glory. But Octavian chose to celebrate Actium by its own triumph. There is no precedent as far as I know for such a decision, for an individual battle, however decisive, to become the formal occasion and *nomen* of a triumph. And if, as I have argued, the victor had really endeavored to suppress any recollection of civil war and to downplay the success at Actium, why did he defy tradition and distinguish the naval battle by its own triumph? More importantly, under what circumstances and by what title was the Actian victory honored?

Dio's narrative (51.19.1–7) relates how the Senate responded to the initial news of the Actian victory with a plethora of honors that included a triumph. The triumph was granted, as Dio adds, "as if over Cleopatra." Later sources, however, refer by name to Actium.[21] Contemporary evidence is more telling. The *Fasti Triumphales Barberiniani* duly record the triumphs of Octavian in August of 29.

IMP • CAESAR • DE DALMA[TI]S • EID • SEX
   TRIVMPH • PALMAM• DEDIT
IMP • CAESAR • [EX • AEGY]PTO • XIIX • K • SEPT
   TRIVMP{H}AVIT

[Imperator Caesar triumphed over the Dalmatians
   on the Ides of Sextilis. He offered a palm branch.
Imperator Caesar triumphed over Egypt
   on the eighteenth day before the Kalends of September.]

The omission of the second day, the triumph in honor of Actium, is curious. No breakage in the fragment, no evidence of an apparent erasure or space can restore the missing triumph. Scholars long ago observed the remarkable absence in the *Fasti*; two obvious explanations have been suggested.

Theodor Mommsen argued the easiest and often the most common solu-

---

21. Livy (*Per.* 133) calls the triumph *ex Actiaca victoria*; Suet. (*Aug.* 22) refers to it as *Actiacum*.

tion to such problems: a careless error by the engraver of the inscription.[22] The triple repetition of IMP CAESAR might have caused the person responsible for marking the stone to omit the second line. Such mistakes are not unknown in epigraphical documents, and the absence of the Actian triumph may be nothing more than this. Such a mistake, such an omission, however, becomes unlikely if we consider the prestige of the triple triumph, the importance of the victor, and the probable contemporary date of the engraving.[23] The original editor of *CIL* I (and its revised edition, *CIL* I²) offered a more subtle argument to account for the single mention of the Egyptian triumph.[24] He suggested that the two victories, the naval battle at Actium and the capture of Egypt, were so closely associated in public opinion that for the sake of brevity (*brevitatis gratia*) the engraver compressed the two ceremonies into one. In support of this claim, the editor cited the *Fasti Antiates*, where a record of the Augustan triumph is found (*August. triump.*), but only for the 14th of August (XIX *Kal. Sept.*). Mommsen discounted this evidence, since the principal day of triumphs extending for two days is the last day, not the first.[25] The record of the *Fasti Antiates*, however, neither denies nor supports the interpretation, which Mommsen seems to have either misunderstood or misrepresented. The editor of *CIL* I did not seek to claim that the Actian and Egyptian triumphs were formally one triumph celebrated over the period of two days, as, for example, Pompey's third triumph in 61; he suggested instead that public opinion (or official policy; on this point he is somewhat vague) associated the two events so closely that they seemed to be part of the same ceremony and thus could easily be compressed into one on public documents.

However attractive, the argument for "brevity" is not convincing. More compelling is the suggestion that the Actian and Egyptian triumphs were closely associated in public opinion. We may suppose that in the rush of emotion when the first news of the Actian victory reached Rome, the Senate responded quickly with the formal award of a triumph (Dio 51.19.1). Since Cleopatra officially had been proclaimed the enemy before the actual fighting began (and there was no mention of Antony's involvement),[26] the tri-

---

22. Th. Mommsen, ed., *Res Gestae Divi Augusti*, 2d ed. (Berlin, 1883), 10.

23. The editor of *CIL* I² explains that an inspection of the size of the lettering on the inscription suggests that the triumphs after 40 B.C.E. were recorded as they occurred.

24. *CIL* I¹, p. 479 (Tabula Triumphorum Barberiniana, A.U.C. 725); *CIL* I², p. 78.

25. Mommsen, *Res Gestae Divi Augusti*, 10.

26. For discussion of the political tactics of Octavian at this time and an interesting, though speculative, examination into the formal and legal arguments that may have been employed in the declaration of war against Cleopatra, see M. Reinhold, "The Declaration of War against Cleopatra," *CJ* 77 (1981–82): 97–103.

umph served to continue this deceit. This triumph could well have celebrated the defeat of the queen and the conquest of Egypt. It is significant, however, that a second triumph was awarded and accepted after the capture of Alexandria. The foundation of a victory city and the establishment of games at the site of this final battle suggest that the victor himself sought to bolster his claims about the subjugation of this foreign land. When it came time to celebrate the triumphal show, Octavian formally accepted three curule triumphs but orchestrated the ceremonies to exaggerate the magnitude of his foreign conquests and perhaps at the same time to make the boast of universal peace. Early in the same year as Octavian's triumphant return to Italy, the Senate decreed the doors of the Temple of Janus to be closed, the symbolic and sacred action that publicly proclaimed the end of all wars throughout the empire. Dio (51.20.4) reports this honor as part of the accumulation of decrees voted after the arrival of Octavian's letter concerning the Parthians. The historian also records that no other decree pleased the victor more. There is no ancient testimony about the date of the formal closing of the temple's doors. Livy (1.19.3) linked the Actian victory with this sacred act. Perhaps the ceremony was postponed until Octavian's return to Rome and the celebration of his triumphs.

Unlike Julius Caesar, who extended his triumphal celebrations for one month and bestowed individual prominence to each victory, Octavian accepted three triumphs celebrated on consecutive days. On the final day of the lavish three-day ceremony, Octavian rode along the Sacra Via as conqueror of the world. The implications were clear. The defeat of the Illyrian tribes—augmented by the inclusion of Germans and Gauls—the naval success at Actium over Cleopatra and the foreign client kings, and the subjugation of Egypt were not extolled as separate or distinct military accomplishments. The *Fasti Triumphales Barberiniani* list only one palm of victory bestowed on this occasion. The evidence of the *fasti*, where recognition of the Actian triumph is absent, suggests that public opinion (or at least the engraver) was unsure of the formal distinctions between the second and third triumphs. The disparity of the titles for the "Actian" triumph found in the ancient literary sources perhaps reflects this uncertainty. There was no uncertainty, however, about what Octavian had achieved. The triple triumph celebrated the might of the victor who waged wars on land and sea and restored peace, symbolized by the closure of the temple doors of Janus in the same year.

Following the triumphal celebration, Octavian dedicated the new Senate chamber, the Curia Julia, and the temple consecrated to his deified father. In the former, he placed a statue of Victory, richly adorned with the spoils of Egypt. The naval beaks of Actium decorated the recently completed Temple of Divus Julius. The public ceremonies and gestures reveal that Octavian still recognized his debt and devotion to his adoptive father, Julius Caesar. The triumphal occasion represented a symbolic, and what proved to be historical, end to the relentless cycle of Roman civil war, renewed by the political assassination fifteen years earlier. The success at Actium was an impressive and decisive victory in the war against the Egyptian queen and her foreign allies, and the Actian triumph served as only one act in the conqueror's "imperious show." But Octavian was no Julius Caesar. The former's military victories in his civil war with Antony were few and, apart from the episode at Actium, insignificant. The triumphator of 29 B.C.E. exaggerated the claims of his military prowess and success but shrewdly chose not to exalt his individual campaigns by the interval of days to distinguish his triumphs. Much more than the celebration of Actium or the defeat of the queen, Octavian's triple triumph ceremony boasted the consequences of his victories, namely, the conquest of the world and the restoration of peace.

At the end of the eighth book of the *Aeneid*, Vergil closes his description of the shield of Aeneas with scenes from the celebration of the Augustan triple triumph.

> At Caesar, triplici invectus Romana triumpho
> moenia, dis Italis votum immortale sacrabat,
> maxima ter centum totam delubra per urbem.
> laetitia ludisque viae plausuque fremebant;
> omnibus in templis matrum chorus, omnibus arae;
> ante aras terram caesi stravere iuvenci.
> ipse sedens niveo candentis limine Phoebi
> dona recognoscit populorum aptatque superbis
> postibus; incedunt victae longo ordine gentes
> quam variae linguis, habitu tam vestis et armis.
> hic Nomadum genus et discinctos Mulciber Afros,
> hic Lelegas Carasque sagittiferosque Gelonos
> finxerat; Euphrates ibat iam mollior undis,
> extremique hominum Morini, Rhenusque bicornis,
> indomitique Dahae, et pontem indignatus Araxes.
>
> (8.714–28)

> [But Caesar in threefold triumph rode within the Roman
> walls and consecrated his eternal vow to the Italian gods,
> three hundred mighty shrines throughout the whole city.
> The streets resounded with joy, games, and applause.

In every temple stood a chorus of mothers, in every temple, altars.
And before the altars slaughtered bullocks strewed the ground.
He himself sat on the snowy threshold of shining Phoebus
and viewed the gifts of the nations and fitted them to the proud
doorposts; the conquered races passed in long array,
varied in languages as in their style of dress and arms.
Here the tribe of Nomads and ungirdled Africans,
here the Leleges and Carians and quivered Gelonians, Mulciber
had fashioned; the Euphrates went by, with waves already tamed;
the Morini, the most distant of men; the Rhine of two horns;
the unconquered Dahae; and the Araxes, indignant at its bridge.]

Censorious modern critics rebuke the exaggeration, anachronisms, and deceit of the epic poet. No race of Nomads, ungirted Africans, or arrow-bearing Gelonians walked in chains in the Augustan triumphal parade. Depictions of the mighty Euphrates, Rhine, and Araxes rivers did not adorn the victor's placards. Triumph in the East (or what was later proclaimed as such by the return of the captured standards from the Parthians) was still almost ten years away. The formal procession of vanquished nations and peoples did not pass by the Temple of Apollo on the Palatine, a monument formally dedicated in October of 28 B.C.E., more than a year after Octavian's triumphal ceremony.

But the final scene on the hero's divine shield derives not only from a poet's fancy or patriotic zeal. The impressive and boastful claims of Augustan triumph were not exaggerated public rhetoric or political propaganda but represented to Vergil the fulfillment of hopes and the destiny of Trojan Aeneas. Vergil prophesied Roman victory and a conquered world where Augustus would bring back the Golden Age to Latium. The repeated succession of civil wars would at last be halted, and the temple doors of Janus would stand closed, an imposing symbol of restored peace and the confinement of *impius Furor*. In the years following Actium, when he began to compose his epic poem, Vergil still dreamed of the comforting image and grandeur of Augustan triumph and rejoiced, but the painful memories and reality of civil conflict threatened to darken the bright illusion. The poet's vision of the Actian battle and triumphal parade revived and served to reshape the past. Modern historians who seek to interpret and judge the political evidence of the Augustan poets must be careful that they do not usurp the prerogatives and ambitions appropriate to the poet. What Vergil fashioned on the shield of Aeneas may reflect to some degree a mixture of fact and falsehood. But the epic endeavor may have also anticipated and inspired an Augustan political ideology. In chapter 5, I argue more fully how Vergil's *Aeneid* shaped a public consciousness of Actium and created a myth of battle. But it is a difficult, if not a useless, task to distinguish too closely between poetry and politics, to make sharp demarcations where one begins and the other ends. The dramatic scenes of glorious struggle, foreign conquest, and Augustan triumph represent how the epic poet viewed the Roman world after Actium and how he accepted (or at least sought to accept and come to terms with) its political hegemony and moral responsibilities.

The "Actian" Arch

Until the archaeological excavations in the Roman Forum in the early 1950s, the evidence to substantiate the claim that an arch had been erected to commemorate the Actian triumph was sparse and indecisive:[27] the brief notice by the Greek historian Dio Cassius (51.19.1), who cites the senatorial decree for an arch to the victor at Actium but nothing on its actual erection; a denarius issue of Octavian (*RIC*[2] 267) that depicts an arch of a single span with the legend IMP(erator) CAESAR inscribed on its enlarged architrave; and the record of an inscription (*CIL* VI, 873) that has been proposed as the formal dedication statement for the monument, although the inscription's reported size (the stone is now lost) is too small for an arch's architrave. The archaeological discoveries of Riccardo Gamberini Mongenet in 1950–52 subverted earlier opinions about the Augustan arch, its construction, location, and number of vaulted spans.[28] The excavations uncovered the remains of the foundation piers from what seems to have been an arch of a single span that once stood immediately in front of the triple arch, generally regarded as the structure built by Augustus in 19 B.C.E. to commemorate the return of the military standards by the Parthians. Because of the peculiar position, one arch set directly in front of the other, the two structures could

---

27. For earlier discussions on the subject of the "Actian" arch, see L.B. Holland, "The Triple Arch of Augustus," *AJA* 50 (1946): 52–59, and "The Foundations of the Arch of Augustus," *AJA* 57 (1953): 1–4. For a more recent and comprehensive review of the archaeological discoveries and opinions surrounding the Augustan arch(es) erected beside the Temple of Divus Julius, see E. Nedergaard, "Zur Problematik der Augustusbögen auf dem Forum Romanum," in *Kaiser Augustus*, 226–30.

28. Gamberini Mongenet conducted the most recent excavations in the area of the Forum where the remains of a triple arch had been discovered in the previous century. The results of his findings and opinions were never published, but a preliminary report was written by B. Andreae, "Archäologische Funde und Grabungen im Bereich der Soprintendenzen von Rom 1949–1956/57," *JDAI* 72 (1957): cols. 144–63. Cf. G. Carettoni, "Excavations and Discoveries in the Forum Romanum and on the Palatine during the Last Fifty Years," *JRS* 50 (1960): 194–95, and Nash, *Pictorial Dictionary of Ancient Rome*, 2:92–101.

not have stood at the same time. The more elaborate triple arch seems to have replaced the smaller one of a single span. It has now become generally accepted that an *arcus Actiacus* had been erected sometime after 30, that it was simple in design with a single span, and that about ten years after its construction, the arch was removed to make room for the larger and more richly decorated triple arch that commemorated the military success in the East.[29] The new evidence might seem compelling,[30] but former doubts about the erection of an "Actian" arch should not be abandoned so quickly. The subject of the Augustan arch demands further scrutiny.

The "Triumphal" Arch

The term "triumphal arch" is more modern than ancient.[31] The identification of an arch as *triumphalis* first occurs in extant Latin literature only near the end of the fourth century of this era.[32] Triumphal celebrations had occasioned the erection of arches before this late date, but the massive marble monument, surmounted with gilded statues and richly adorned with sculptural reliefs and decorations, a sight familiar to any visitor to the Roman Forum today, does not belong to the grand triumphal celebrations of the Republic; instead, the arch developed more from the impressive building

---

29. With few exceptions (see n. 30), scholars have maintained the conclusions of Andreae, "Archäologische Funde und Grabungen," cols. 152–53; Carettoni, "Excavations and Discoveries in the Forum Romanum," 195; Nash, *Pictorial Dictionary of Ancient Rome*, 2:92–101; H. Kähler, *The Art of Rome and Her Empire*, trans. J.R. Foster, rev. ed. (New York, 1965), 61–63; F.S. Kleiner, *The Arch of Nero in Rome: A Study of the Roman Honorary Arch before and under Nero* (Rome, 1985), 24–26; and P. Zanker, *Forum Romanum. Die Neugestaltung durch Augustus* (Tübingen, 1972), 15–16.

30. The most recent discoveries by Elisabeth Nedergaard, "Zur Problematik der Augustusbögen," seriously call into question the conclusions of Gamberini Mongenet's excavations. From a comparative study of the various architectural fragments discovered in the area (or at least reported to have been discovered in the area) and an inspection of the foundation piers of the arches and steps of the adjoining temples (the Temple of Divus Julius and Temple of Castor and Pollux), Nedergaard concludes that only one arch stood between these two temples in the Roman Forum—most probably the triple arch, which once commemorated the Parthian victory—and that the foundation piers excavated by Gamberini Mongenet and identified as belonging to the "Actian" arch, were dug in two different phases and are unlikely to have been used for the construction of an arch. What Gamberini Mongenet had conjectured to be supporting walls for the arch are thought by Nedergaard to be too large for this purpose. Nedergaard offers no suggestion for what purpose the piers and supporting walls may have served. The "Actian" arch may have stood in another site, not yet excavated; but Nedergaard's conclusions, if accepted, compel archaeologists to abandon long-standing assumptions about the arch and to begin the search anew.

31. Cf. remarks by C.D. Curtis, "Roman Monumental Arches," in *Supplemental Papers of the American School of Classical Studies in Rome* (New York and London, 1908), 2:27.

32. Am. Marc. 21.16.15. Inscriptions from North Africa, also late, provide the first appearance of the term in nonliterary sources: *CIL* VIII, 7094–98, 14728, and 14817.

projects of a later age and the conceit of emperors. Before the imperial age, the arch performed a varied array of functions, unrelated to official triumphs or military victories; arches served as formal entrance gates, ornamental headpieces for bridges, and memorials to honor the dead. The number of arches built before the Principate of Augustus is remarkably small, and our knowledge about their commemorative purposes is meager and limited.

On his victorious return from Spain in 196 B.C.E., Lucius Stertinius erected three arches in Rome: two in the Forum Boarium before the Temples of Fortuna and Mater Matuta, and one in the Circus Maximus (Livy 33.27.4–5). Although these are the earliest Roman arches about which we have any knowledge, it is not likely that they were the first honorary arches to be erected in the city.[33] Livy certainly adds no comment that the arches of Stertinius constituted something new. More importantly, the simultaneous construction of three arches would seem to suggest that Stertinius was only following an established, though perhaps recent, tradition where a victor could celebrate his military success by the erection of an arch. It is significant, however, that these arches were not part of any triumphal occasion (Stertinius, in fact, spurned the honor of a triumph, *ne temptata quidem triumphi spe*), and that the arches were erected at private expense. From Livy's remark that the returning victor deposited fifty thousand pounds of silver in Rome's treasury, it seems that the ample booty from Spain enabled Stertinius to erect these arches that exalted his name and commemorated his victories.

Only a few years later, Publius Cornelius Scipio Africanus erected a fornix on the Capitoline hill. Livy (37.3.7) again is the source for this information, and we learn that the structure displayed an impressive statuary group (*septem signa aurata* and *duo equos*) on its attic. Again there is no connection with a formal triumph; the fornix was not even built from the spoils of victory. Scipio erected the arch before he departed for Syria. One scholar has understood the fornix as a "votive, rather than a triumphal, monument,"[34] but Livy does not make this claim. The erection of the fornix may have held no relation to Scipio's planned departure to the East; it may have celebrated an earlier victory.

Scholars are more inclined to view the Fornix Fabianus, first erected *circa* 120 B.C.E. and later restored or rebuilt in 56, as the first triumphal arch in

---

33. For an informative and comprehensive discussion of Roman arches before the Age of Augustus, see Kleiner, *The Arch of Nero in Rome*, 11–19.

34. Kleiner, *The Arch of Nero in Rome*, 16.

Rome, and perhaps a model for the Actian arch.[35] Erected on the Sacra Via at the eastern entrance to the Forum near the Regia, the arch has claimed this honor, since it has been assumed to have been part of the triumph of Q. Fabius Maximus over the Allobroges. There is no reliable evidence to confirm the accepted opinion that the arch had any direct association with the Senate's decree or formal ceremony of the triumph. That the arch honored the victor's military success, exalted by the celebration of a triumph, is both plausible and probable, but this should not mean that the award of a triumph occasioned the erection of the arch. And when viewed in the tradition of Roman arches, this possibility seems even less likely. In fact, there survives no arch from the Republican age that can be linked with the formal declaration or ceremonies of a Roman triumph. Finally, it should be noted that none of the great men who celebrated triumphs in the late Republic, in particular, Pompey and Julius Caesar (who have eight triumphs between them), is said to have erected a commemorative arch to extol his prowess and success on the battlefield. If the initial erection of the Fornix Fabianus or its later restoration must be taken as a sign that the arch was becoming a more familiar monument and associated with triumphs, it is surprising that we do not possess any record that the Senate granted this honor to Julius Caesar. The commemorative arch, whether or not it merits the title "triumphal," has rightly been called the "creation of the Augustan age."[36]

The Evidence for the "Actian" Arch

Dio (51.19.1) records the ancient literary evidence for the "Actian" arch. The initial news of the victory at Actium prompted the solicitous Senate to decree two arches to be erected: one in the Roman Forum, a second in Brundisium. It is generally assumed that both arches were built in hasty preparation for the festivities that officially welcomed the returning victor back to Italy when he first disembarked at Brundisium and later entered Rome. Dio also reports a resolution at this time that instructed the Vestal Virgins, senators, and citizens of Rome, joined by their wives and children, to go out to meet Octavian as he entered the city. Dio adds later that Octavian expressly stated that of all the honors the Senate bestowed on the victor, only the proposal that the whole population of Rome should greet his triumphant arrival should not be allowed. Dio offers no reasons for this

---

35. Kleiner, *The Arch of Nero in Rome*, 16–17, and especially n. 16, documents the past scholarship and reiterates the claim that the first arch "incontestably connected with a triumph" is the Fornix Fabianus.

36. Kähler, *The Art of Rome and Her Empire*, 59.

decision by the victor, and we do not know if it had any effect on the decree to erect a commemorative arch. Perhaps more important, however, is that Dio does not remark that an arch (either at Brundisium or Rome) was actually built, and when the historian narrates the formal ceremonies of Octavian's triple triumph, he fails to include any mention of an arch. Apart from the brief citation in Dio, no other ancient literary text offers evidence of an arch erected in honor of the Actian victory. In later years, the arch became a customary addition in the plethora of honors awarded to a victorious emperor or member of his family.[37] At the time of the Actian victory, however, the honor of an arch would have been something of a novelty in Rome.

Numismatic evidence seems to confirm the testimony of the historian on the erection of an arch after Actium. A denarius issue of Octavian (*RIC*[2] 267, plate 4) depicts an arch for the first time on Roman coinage. The engraver of the coin has emphasized and exaggerated at the expense of any realistic detail the statuary group on the attic and the dedicatory inscription. The legend reads simply the honorific title IMP CAESAR, which was prominently displayed in the arch's out-of-scale architrave. The arch itself seems little more than a massive stone mantelpiece for the victorious quadriga of Octavian. The visible disproportions in the design of the arch, far from evidence of poor artistry, serve to bolster the impressive claims of a victor. This accords well with a remark by the elder Pliny, who identifies the commemorative monument as still a recent innovation (*novicium inventum*) in his own time, almost a century after Actium.[38]

The date of the denarius issue is uncertain. Numismatists have not always been so confident and precise about the chronology of Octavian's earliest issues. Editors once preferred to assign Octavian's two groups of coinage, issues that were identified only by the legends CAESAR DIVI F and IMP CAESAR, to a more indefinite span of years, the period of 36 to 27 B.C.E., from Octavian's victory at Naulochus to the assumption of his new title and

---

37. The suggestion by Tacitus that the arch voted to honor the memory of the emperor Tiberius' son, Drusus, was customary (*effigies principum, aras deum, templa et arcus aliaque solita*, *Ann.* 3.57.2) reflects the practices of his own day. The historian also records that four years earlier arches in memory of Germanicus were to be erected in Rome, on the bank of the Rhine, and on Mount Amanus in Syria (2.83.2). Arches in honor of the military victories of these two men had previously been voted. In 16 C.E., an arch, erected near the Temple of Saturn, honored the return of the Roman standards lost by Quinctilius Varus (2.41.1); and in 18 C.E., two arches, erected on each side of the Temple of Mars Ultor, displayed statues of Germanicus and Drusus.

38. Pliny *NH* 34.27: *Columnarum ratio erat attolli super ceteros mortales, quod et arcus significant novicio invento.*

solemn name, Augustus.[39] The depictions of a victor in military garb, naval trophies, and newly completed buildings in Rome (the Curia Julia or Temple of Divus Julius) on the reverse types of these issues cannot limit this large body of coinage to only the period after the success at Actium. Octavian's earlier victory at Naulochus (significantly a naval battle) may have occasioned coinage that proclaimed the rewards of the victory. Dio (49.15.1) records the formal decree of an arch after the success at Naulochus. Again there is no supporting evidence that the arch was ever built. Much is made about Dio's testimony of an "Actian" arch, but few scholars attach any credence to the record of an earlier arch. The momentous and profound consequences of Actium have overshadowed the events and boastful claims after Naulochus. But it must be kept in mind that the victor accepted an *ovatio* (a lesser honor owing to the lack of a foreign foe); that the day of his victory became an annual occasion for thanksgiving and was enrolled in the official state calendar; and that a *columna rostrata* was erected in the Forum, surmounted by a gilded statue of Octavian dressed in the ceremonial garb he wore when he entered the city. The inscription on the monument proclaimed the restoration of peace on land and sea.[40] Appian, who reports that the *columna rostrata* was built by official decree and at public expense, does not include the honor of an arch at this time, but if Dio's account is accepted, the denarius issue may represent this arch. In the next section, I discuss more fully the nature of the evidence that has long complicated the efforts to establish a more exact chronology for Octavian's war coinage and how the most recent numismatic studies have been presumptuous to claim an Actian motif where none can be substantiated. At this point the numismatic evidence must remain too inconclusive to identify with certainty an "Actian" triumphal arch. The depiction of an arch of a single span on an issue of Octavian may represent a commemorative monument (or the intentions to build such a structure) after the naval victory at either Actium or Naulochus.

Evidence for the actual erection of an "Actian" arch has also been found in an inscription (*CIL* VI, 873) that scholars have claimed to have been part of the arch's official dedication. The inscription is, in fact, a Renaissance transcription; the original stone has been lost since the sixteenth century. The text is a brief statement of formal dedication.

---

39. Two recent works have fixed Octavian's IMP CAESAR issues to a period shortly after the Actian victory: K. Kraft, *Zur Münzprägung des Augustus* (Wiesbaden, 1969), and C.H.V. Sutherland, "Octavian's Gold and Silver Coinage from c. 32 to 27 B.C.," NAC 5 (1976): 129–57. For arguments against this chronology, cf. my discussion in the following section in this chapter.

40. Appian *BC* 5.130.

SENATVS • POPVLVSQVE • ROMANVS
IMP • CAESAR • DIVI • IVLI • F • COS • QVINCT
  COS • DESIGN • SEXT • IMP • SEPT
REPVBLICA • CONSERVATA

[The Senate and the People of Rome
To Imperator Caesar, son of the divine Julius, consul for the fifth time,
  consul designate for the sixth, imperator for the seventh,
  because he rescued his country from danger.]

Octavian's titles place the inscription in an appropriate year for an erection of an "Actian" arch in 29, but this seems to be the only substantive or compelling reason to connect it with a commemorative arch.

The Renaissance scholars who duly recorded the inscription disagree over the exact place of its discovery. If one reflects on the large number of public buildings and commemorative monuments formally dedicated in this year (the Curia Julia in which Octavian placed a statue and altar of Victory, the Temple of Divus Julius, and the shrine to Minerva, also known as the Chalcidicum, and the various decorated columns that may have honored the naval victory at Actium),[41] the disagreement over the location of the inscription's discovery becomes rather important. Testimony varies, placing the inscription inside the building to which the *Fasti Capitolini* belonged; near the columns of the Temple of Castor; or before the portico of Faustina.[42] The general location in the Roman Forum is fixed, but we may begin to suspect the confidence that once led scholars to link the inscription conclusively with an "Actian" arch. The size of the inscription, as it has been reported, raises further, serious doubts over its actual placement on the architrave of an arch. The Renaissance scholars recorded an approximate measurement for the inscription as nine feet wide by three feet high and two feet in thickness.[43] Archaeologists have discounted the possibility that the inscription could have served as the principal dedicatory statement for either the triple arch, whose central passageway was more than thirteen feet or an earlier arch of a single span. It has thus been proposed that the transcribed inscription is "a miniature copy of the original inscription," though a per-

---

41. For the ancient references to the public monuments dedicated in 29, see F.W. Shipley, "Chronology of the Building Operations in Rome from the Death of Caesar to the Death of Augustus," *MAAR* 9 (1931): 49.

42. For a citation of these sources, see A. Degrassi, "L'edificio dei Fasti Capitolini," *Rend-PontAcc* 21 (1945–46): 80–81, 97.

43. See Degrassi, "L'edificio dei Fasti Capitolini," 97 n. 182.

suasive explanation is lacking for the double inscription.[44] Since this problem concerns the structure of the arch itself, it is necessary at this point to consider the archaeological excavations in the area.

In 1888 Otto Richter discovered the foundations of a triple arch on the south side of the Temple of Divus Julius in the Roman Forum. The size of the foundations and the distance between the piers indicated an unusual triple structure where the central span of the arch was considerably larger than the two arches on each side. In his discussion of his excavations in the following year, Richter identified the foundations with the arch that commemorated the victory at Actium.[45] Subsequent excavations in 1904, failing to find any remains for an arch on the north side of the Temple of Divus Julius, led Richter to amend his identification and maintain that the remains of the triple arch belong to the monumental structure that Augustus built to celebrate the return of the standards from the Parthians. The evidence, both literary and numismatic, seems to confirm this identification. Dio (54.8.3) reports the decree of the arch following the return of the standards in 20, and the Veronese scholiast to Vergil's *Aeneid* 7.606 (*Parthosque reposcere signa*) locates the arch at this site (*huius facti Nicae repraesentantur in arcu qui est iuxta aedem divi Iuli*). Coins minted in Spain and dated to 18–17 B.C.E. (*RIC*[2] 131–37) depict a triple arch with an inscription that confirms an association with the return of the standards: CIVIB(us) ET SIGN(is) MILIT(ibus) A PARTH(is) RECUP(eratis). A denarius issue of L. Vinicius, minted in Rome in 16 B.C.E. (*RIC*[2] 359), also offers the representation of a triple arch with architectural features conforming exactly to the peculiarities of the foundations in the Forum—a central arch much larger and more richly decorated than the flanking arches of a lesser height on each side, although the details of the design differ. Even though no inscription can

---

44. Andreae, "Archäologische Funde und Grabungen," col. 152. Andreae also suggests that Gamberini believed that the Parthian triple arch employed architectural material from the earlier arch in its construction. Apart from the dedicatory inscription, Andreae does not give any other evidence to support this view and fails to explain how such a suggestion can be verified. Carettoni, "Excavations and discoveries," 195, and Kleiner, *The Arch of Nero in Rome*, 25–26, have been too quick to reiterate this unlikely suggestion in a tone that makes it seem a matter of fact that the Parthian arch incorporated building material from the earlier arch. Now it is certainly plausible that the same Corinthian pilasters and engaged columns of an "Actian" arch adorned the central passageway of the more intricate triple structure (although Andreae did not explain how this suggestion can be proved from the few scattered and broken fragments that survive), but there is no compelling reason for us to associate the inscription formerly attributed to the "Actian" arch with the remains of the newly discovered foundation piers. For a convincing refutation of Gamberini's speculative remarks, see now Nedergaard, "Zur Problematik der Augustusbögen," 233–35.

45. O. Richter, "Die Augustusbauten auf dem Forum Romanum," *JDAI* 4 (1889): 137–62.

clearly identify the arch (an exaggerated architrave above the central arch reads only SPQR IMP CAE), the coin is likely to represent the Parthian arch.[46] While details differ slightly (on the Spanish issues, the arches are more uniform in size, and no inscription decorates the central architrave), it would seem likely that both issues represent the same commemorative structure.

In the excavations of the Roman Forum in 1950–52, Gamberini Mongenet uncovered the vestiges of two large foundation piers situated 6.8 meters apart immediately before the side passageway at the northern end of the remains of the triple arch, long accepted as the Parthian arch. The discovery of the two piers suggested the existence of an earlier structure of a single span at this location, but the odd placement of the two arches, one directly in front of the other, led to the conclusion that the arch of a single span, assumed to have been erected after 30 to honor the victor at Actium, was later replaced by a more elaborate triple arch that commemorated the return of the standards from the Parthians. The reasons for the earlier arch's removal have never been fully or adequately explained in the modern discussions of the arch. It has been maintained that the removal or destruction of the "Actian" arch must have held political associations. The underlying presumption to this view is that Octavian (and later as Augustus) exalted his victory in civil war in the early years of his Principate and sometime thereafter chose to abandon this public image. The scenario envisioned is of a boastful victor who supports his incipient political regime on the military glory of Actium and the conquest of Egypt. A monumental arch of a single span stood as a reminder of the triumphal occasion celebrated in the summer of 29 when the victor returned to Rome. Ten years later, however, when he was firmly established in power, Augustus, no longer calling himself simply Caesar and the son of the deified Julius, sought to enhance his past record and to remove the unpleasant reminders of earlier civil strife. The Actian monument was thus removed and replaced by a larger and more ornate triple arch that celebrated the proclaimed victory in the East over the Parthians. The memory of Actium yielded to the new political climate. Serious and substantial difficulties, however, confront such an assumed sequence of events and political motivations. Surely the reasons that might have led Augustus in 19 "to deemphasize his civil war victory and celebrate instead his success on behalf of Rome against a foreign foe,"[47] as one scholar has maintained, were as strong or even stronger ten years earlier

---

46. Cistophori issues from Pergamum, dated to 19 B.C.E. (*RIC²* 508–10) also herald the victory proclaimed over the Parthians, S P R SIGNIS RECEPTIS and IMP IX TR PO(T) IV (and V). Although these issues depict an arch of a single span, they probably represent an arch that had only recently been awarded to the victor and not yet erected.

47. Kleiner, *The Arch of Nero in Rome*, 26.

when the victor sought to exalt his success over Antony and Cleopatra. It is more prudent to avoid seeking "political" motivations before a closer assessment of the archaeological evidence.

Bernard Andreae's summary of Gamberini Mongenet's excavations contains a report that the southern foundation pier of the single span arch seemed to have been supported by a complex system of bracing walls and underground props built to prevent a crack from developing in the pier.[48] But it is also possible, if not more likely, that the support system had been added only after a crack had become visible and had threatened the foundation of the arch. It is thus plausible that the attempts to save the arch were in vain and that the decision was then made to replace the older structure with a larger and more elaborate triple arch, an arch that commemorated the acclaimed, though not formal, triumph over the Parthians. Though we may infer that the decision to build an arch to celebrate the diplomatic success reflects contemporary propaganda, this should not lead us to suppose that the removal of an arch—in this case, an arch for which there is evidence of structural problems—was somehow arranged as part of an official policy and direction to remove from public view any unfavorable past associations.[49]

New archaeological finds have changed old assumptions about the "triumphal" arches of the Augustan age,[50] but historians are unwilling to be-

---

48. Andreae, "Archäologische Funde und Grabungen," cols. 151–52.

49. Kähler, *The Art of Rome and Her Empire*, 62, suggested that the pillars were threatening to sink into marshy ground. This explanation is derived in part from Andreae's report of underground channels near the southern pier and the presence of the Puteal Libonis in the immediate vicinity. But if this were true, it seems unlikely that Augustus (or his architects) would have chosen to build another arch in almost the same location. If we accept the most recent findings by Nedergaard, "Zur Problematik der Augustusbögen," 236, who concluded that the foundation piers were dug in two different phases, we may conjecture that the initial efforts to erect an arch at this site (whether in 36, 30, or 19 B.C.E.) were unsuccessful because of the conditions of the soil or that the architects of the *novicium inventum* revised their dimensions of the arch's span(s) before the monumental edifice was completed.

50. In a recent survey of the architecture of the Roman Forum, F. Coarelli, *Il Foro Romano*, 2 vols. (Rome, 1985), 2:258–308, located all three "triumphal" arches from the ancient and Renaissance testimonia. In his reconstruction, Coarelli attempted to resolve all the loose ends and to present a coherent order to the erection of the Augustan arches. He proposes that Octavian built an arch of a single span to commemorate his naval victory at Naulochus. The victor's denarius issue (*RIC*[2] 267) commemorated this structure. More than fifteen years later, the arch was removed as part of the recent efforts to downplay Octavian's tainted association in civil war. The triple arch that has generally been regarded as the Parthian arch is, according to Coarelli's opinion, the "Actian" arch depicted on a denarius of L. Vinicius (*RIC*[2] 359). The Parthian arch was built in 19 and located on the opposite side of the Temple of Divus Julius where scholars have generally identified the site of the Porticus of Gaius and Lucius, the grandsons of Augustus. The reconstruction is elaborate and ingenious but speculative and contrary to the literary and numismatic evidence.

lieve that the victory at Actium did not demand such a commemorative monument in Rome:

> It is impossible, however, to think that after 19 B.C. no monument commemorated the Battle of Actium. It was the great victory over Eastern despotism and about it revolved the foundation myth of the imperial principate. It is unlikely that Augustus would ignore such a victory while he glorified the comparatively (in comparison to Actium) insignificant achievement of regaining standards by diplomatic means.[51]

This prevailing opinion on an "Actian" arch and its later removal must be abandoned. The numismatic, literary, and archaeological evidence is inconclusive and uncertain. A denarius issue confirms that Octavian erected (or at least intended to erect) an arch of a single span to extol his name and military glory. Victory in civil war, against Antony and the Egyptian queen in 31 or against Sextus Pompey only five years earlier, may have occasioned an impressive dedicatory monument. Octavian's arch, nonetheless, would surely not have been an "Actian" monument, at least not if this would mean that the stone structure commemorated the fame of the naval victory. As Pliny described the recent innovation in Roman architecture, the arch (and likewise bronze statues surmounted on columns) exalted the honored figure *supra ceteros mortales*. Whatever formal inscription might have adorned the massive attic of the arch, the message would have proclaimed the military prowess of the victor, the establishment of peace, and the salvation of the state. Actium would have received no official or overt recognition on Octavian's arch. Less than ten years later, a larger and more ornate arch may have replaced the earlier structure. The richly decorated keystone of the triple arch, flanked by figures of winged Victories, subjugated enemies, and Roman standards, exhibited an image of Augustus as victor over a foreign foe, the Parthians. Though he declined the honor of a formal triumph, he accepted public sacrifices in honor of his achievement and the dedication of an altar to Fortuna Redux. The replacement of the single arch was not a restatement or change of political ideology. The enlarged arch stood as the fulfillment of the proud boasts of the triple triumph celebrated more than ten years earlier. Much more than the modest arch of a single span that may have been erected shortly after Actium (or perhaps earlier) and at some later time removed, the Parthian monument, with its triple marble span and

---

51. J.R. Johnson, "Augustan Propaganda", 136.

elaborate artwork, glorified the Roman triumphator and, perhaps more than any other Augustan monument, marked the beginning of the imperial age.

The Coinage of the Victor

Two large groups of gold and silver issues, identified by the nonspecific legends CAESAR DIVI F(ilius) and IMP(erator) CAESAR, served to commemorate the naval victory at Actium and herald the triumphant arrival of the new ruler in Rome. Such is the prevailing consensus of numismatic opinion since Harold Mattingly's *Coins of the Roman Empire in the British Museum* first appeared in 1923. Earlier editors of catalogs had not been so bold or certain but had preferred to assign issues from either one or both groups to a more indefinite span of years, from Octavian's naval victory over Sextus Pompey at Naulochus in 36 to his adoption of the title Augustus almost ten years later in 27. In recent decades, two important studies have sought to establish a more rigid chronology and location of mintage for the two series: Konrad Kraft's analysis of the varied reverse types in his monograph *Zur Münzprägung des Augustus*, and C.H.V. Sutherland's die study of the obverse portraits of Octavian in his article "Octavian's Gold and Silver Coinage from c. 32 to 27 B.C."[52] Through his illuminating, but more often imaginative, interpretation of the divine figures, symbols, and images depicted on the coins' reverse types, Kraft attributed and restricted the two large series to Octavian's victory coinage (Siegesprägung) issued after Actium. Similarly, Sutherland, who examined the new and strikingly different style of Octavian's portraiture on the two series through a close analysis of obverse dies, identified two distinct styles of portraiture and argued that the decisive military success at Actium motivated, if not necessitated, the stylistic (and political) changes of representation. Subsequent scholars, almost without exception, have been quick to accept these interpretations.[53]

---

52. Kraft, *Zur Münzprägung des Augustus*, 1–25; Sutherland, "Octavian's Gold and Silver Coinage," 129–57.

53. The voices of scholarly dissent are few, brief, and intermittent. Throughout his discussions of Octavian's coinage, M. Grant reiterated his claim that the CAESAR DIVI F series (he followed Mattingly's chronology for the IMP CAESAR series) belonged to 36 or even a year or two earlier. See Grant, *From Imperium to Auctoritas: A Historical Study of Aes Coinage in the Roman Empire 49 B.C.–A.D. 14* (Cambridge, 1946), 49–50 n. 14; *Roman Anniversary Issues: An Exploratory Study of the Numismatic and Medallic Commemoration of Anniversary Issues 49 B.C.–A.D. 375* (Cambridge, 1950), 16–18; and *The Six Main Aes Coinages of Augustus: Controversial Studies* (Edinburgh, 1953), 65. In his review of Kraft's *Zur Münzprägung des Augustus*, in *JRS* 64 (1974): 246–47, M.H. Crawford raised serious objections to Kraft's

Recent attempts to impose a more exact and fixed chronology on the issues and to identify a predominant "Actian" motif throughout the two series are unwarranted. The reasons that once led numismatists to prefer a longer period of mintage for the two groups should not be rashly rejected. The absence of any specific titulature on the coinage, the ambiguous depictions of symbols and monuments of victory—equally appropriate to commemorate the naval success at either Actium or Naulochus—and the disputed identification for the coin types that have been claimed to allude to the Actian victory suggest that there still remains sufficient reason to question the current confidence in the chronology.

Plates 1 through 4 offer a composite view of the two series. Twenty-two distinct coin types comprise the two large groups.[54] Unlike previous coinage of the triumvir, a bare portrait of Octavian, conspicuous by the total absence of any long or specific titulature, appears on the obverse of seven issues in each group. Following a standard practice of Republican coinage, the remaining obverse types offer a pantheon of various Roman deities: among the CAESAR DIVI F group, Venus (RIC^2 251), Pax, Fortuna, or Concordia (RIC^2 253),[55] and Victory (RIC^2 256); among the IMP CAESAR issues, Apollo

---

methodology and interpretations and accused Kraft of forcing the evidence to find Actian motifs or references. F. Prayon, "Projektierte Bauten auf römischen Münzen," and D. Mannsperger, "Annos undeviginti natus. Das Münzsymbol für Octavians Eintritt in die Politik," in *Praestant Interna. Festschrift für Ulrich Hausmann*, ed. B. von Freytag gen. Löringhoff et al. (Tübingen, 1982), 322–25 and 331–32, respectively, also questioned the standard view that both groups were issued after the victory at Actium and suggested an earlier date and a connection with Naulochus for several issues of the CAESAR DIVI F group and IMP CAESAR series, a claim later dismissed by J.-B. Giard, "La monnaie coloniale d'Orange. une attribution en question," *RevNum* 26, ser. 6 (1984): 79 n. 7, as "ingénieuse mais mal fondée." Giard, editor of *Bibliothèque Nationale. Catalogue des monnaies de l'empire romain*, vol. 1, *Auguste* (Paris, 1976), followed Kraft's dating of the coins and placed both series in 29, the year of the triple triumph ceremony. W. Trillmich, "Münzpropaganda," in *Kaiser Augustus*, 507, who identified the Augustan coinage in the catalog for the Berlin exhibition of 1988 and discussed the propagandistic purposes of the issues, acknowledged the sporadic doubts about the fixed dating of the two series but tentatively assigned the individual issues represented in the exhibition to the years 29/28, though his uncertainty was indicated by a question mark. And in a systematic and judicious study of divine appropriations ("assimilation" and "imitation") on official coinage from the *asses* of Sextus Pompey in the late 40s to the aurei and denarii of senatorial moneyers from 19 to 13 B.C.E., John Pollini, "Man or God: Divine Assimilation and Imitation in the Late Republic and Early Principate," in *Between Republic and Empire*, 342 n. 33, briefly reviewed the dating of the two groups and concluded that the issues probably belonged to the period just after Actium ("Prior to 31 Octavian seems to have projected officially an image that would not give open offense to old republican sensibilities," p. 336).

54. Only one coin type (RIC^2 263 and 264), with Victory standing on a ship's prow on the obverse and a victorious quadriga on the reverse, actually connects the two groups with the same obverse and reverse types except for the distinguishing legends.

55. The figure holds an olive branch and cornucopia in her hands. Depictions of the goddess Pax are not common in prior Roman coinage. Crawford, *RRC* 480/24 (44 B.C.E.) offers a

(*RIC*² 272), Diana (*RIC*² 273), Mars (*RIC*² 274), and a bust of a herm, interpreted by Kraft to be the god Terminus associated with Jupiter Capitolinus (*RIC*² 270).[56] Only one obverse type portrays the same representation in both groups, a figure of Victory standing on a ship's prow (*RIC*² 263 and 264).

The reverse types offer an unusually rich variety of depictions. Of the CAESAR DIVI F group, four issues show Octavian in a military pose—riding on horseback (*RIC*² 262), holding a spear with his one hand extended (*RIC*² 251), raising his right hand in address to his soldiers (*RIC*² 253), and driving a victorious quadriga, a four-horse chariot (*RIC*² 263). Two issues depict the goddess Victory; on one she holds a crown and palm branch in her hands as she stands on a globe (*RIC*² 254a–b and 255), and on the other she is driving a biga, a two-horse chariot (*RIC*² 260 and 261). An aureus issue (*RIC*² 258 and 259) offers a quadriga, but without any rider depicted. Five reverse types show Roman deities in full-length representations, three of which have been claimed by Kraft to be the matching pairs of portrait depictions on obverse types:[57] Venus, standing, adorned with helmet, spear, and shield (*RIC*² 250a–b); Pax, Fortuna, or Concordia, standing with olive branch and cornucopia (*RIC*² 252); a herm (*RIC*² 269a–b), interpreted by Kraft as the full-length counterpart to the obverse of *RIC*² 270; a naked male deity, who holds the ornamented post of a ship's stern (*aplustre*) in his right hand and a spear in his left as he places his right foot on a globe, and who is assumed to be either Neptune or Octavian in the guise of this god (*RIC*² 256); and a seated male divinity playing the lyre, who has been

---

certain depiction; the legend reads PAXS. Less likely is the depiction on the denarius from the following year (Crawford, *RRC* 485); the female figure with the cornucopia and scepter is probably Venus. Fortuna appears on several issues from 44 to 40 (Crawford, *RRC* 480/25, 494/32 and 33, 525/1). Her attributes are the cornucopia and a symbol of victory (a rudder or scepter). Concordia also appears in a number of issues from 62 to 39 (Crawford, *RRC* 415, 417, 429/2a, 430, 494/41 and 42, 529/4). All but the quinarius issue from 39 (529/4) display a legend that clearly identifies the goddess. Her attributes are usually the veil and diadem.

56. Kraft, *Zur Münzprägung des Augustus*, 10, unconvincingly argues that the god Terminus was involved in Octavian's war of propaganda against Antony and Cleopatra to assert Roman dominion over the lands that Antony had bestowed on the queen in 34. The ancient evidence for Kraft's contention derives almost exclusively from a passage in Augustine (*Civ. Dei* 4.29) that explains that Terminus was a symbol of Rome's refusal to yield land in their possession: *nemini locum, quem teneret, daturum.*

57. See Kraft, *Zur Münzprägung des Augustus*, 6–11, for his discussion of the issues that he places in pairs. In his review of Kraft's thesis, Crawford rightly points out that the existence of such groupings need not imply that the matched pair were designed and minted at the same time. Kraft also fails to explain why only two issues (*RIC*² 252 on all specimens and 253 on only some) display a border of pearl dots while all other issues in the two groups are distinguished by the line border. The difference in design is difficult to understand if the pairs were issued and conceived at the same time, as Kraft maintains.

identified most recently as Apollo, and who has been given the distinctive epithet Leucadius or Actius (*RIC*[2] 257).

Several issues from the IMP CAESAR group depict commemorative monuments: a colonnaded temple generally assumed to be either the Curia Julia or Temple of Divus Julius (*RIC*[2] 266); a "triumphal" arch of a single span (*RIC*[2] 267); a temple in which a naval trophy is depicted (*RIC*[2] 273); and a *columna rostrata* surmounted with a statue (*RIC*[2] 271). One issue depicts a veiled figure driving a team of oxen, recently associated by Kraft with the foundation of Nicopolis (*RIC*[2] 272);[58] another depicts Octavian seated in a curule chair as he holds a miniature winged Victory in his hand (*RIC*[2] 270). A round shield appears on the issue whose obverse depicts Mars (*RIC*[2] 274). A figure of Victory who stands on a globe, facing front (*RIC*[2] 268), has been associated with a statue of Victory from Tarentum that Octavian set up in the new Senate chamber, the Curia Julia, in 29.

Earlier Doubts and Controversy

The early numismatic opinion on Octavian's coinage is indicative of the problems involved in the efforts to associate the two groups by chronology and location of mintage. The editors of the standard catalogs from the end of the nineteenth century refrained from any exact chronology for the CAESAR DIVI F and IMP CAESAR series. Henry Cohen and Ernest Babelon preferred an extended and somewhat indefinite period from ca. 36 to 27.[59] H.A. Grueber, the original editor of *Coins of the Roman Republic in the British Museum*, was the first scholar to distinguish the two groups by their legends; while Grueber extended the mintage of the CAESAR DIVI F series for a span of seven years (36–29), he restricted the issues from the IMP CAESAR series to a shorter, two-year period of mintage (29–27).[60] Subsequent scholarship has maintained this chronological sequence for the two series, although the reasons that first led Grueber to make this authoritative judgment are subject to serious objections.

Grueber based his chronology for the IMP CAESAR series almost solely on the testimony of Dio Cassius (52.41.3–4) that Octavian assumed the title of imperator as a praenomen officially in 29.[61] Relying on this statement of the historian, Grueber contended that the Senate's formal decree prompted an

---

58. Kraft, *Zur Münzprägung des Augustus*, 11–14.

59. H. Cohen, *Description historique des monnaies frappées sous l'Empire romain communément appelées médailles impériales*, 9 vols., 2d ed. (Paris, 1880; reprinted Graz, 1955), vol. 1, and E.A. Babelon, *Description historique et chronologique des monnaies de la République romaine vulgairement appelées monnaies consulaires*, 2 vols. (Paris, 1885; reprinted Bologna, 1963), vol. 1.

60. Grueber, *BMCRR* II, 13–14 n. 1, 18 n. 1.

61. Grueber, *BMCRR* II, 4.

RIC²250a

RIC²252

RIC²255

RIC²251

RIC²256

RIC²253

RIC²251

Plate 1

RIC²259

RIC²257

RIC²262

RIC²261

RIC²263

Plate 2

RIC²269a

RIC²271

RIC²270

RIC²264

RIC²268

Plate 3

RIC²267

RIC²266

RIC²265a

RIC²273

RIC²272

RIC²274

Plate 4

RIC²257

RIC²276

RIC²275a

Plate 5

RIC² 255, 252, 253, 256, 251, 259, 257, and 262 reproduced courtesy of The American Numismatic Society, New York.
RIC² 250a, 261, and 263 reproduced courtesy of the Trustees of the British Museum, London.

RIC²	Giard, BNC	Denom.	Obverse	Reverse
269a [BMCRE 628–29]	49–51	DEN	Head of Octavian (r.)	Ithyphallic terminal figure, placed on winged thunderbolt IMP CAESAR
271 [BMCRE 633–36]	68–71	DEN	Head of Octavian (r.), laureate	Rostral column surmounted by male figure, holding spear and *parazonium* IMP CAESAR
270 [BMCRE 637]	43–47	DEN	Terminal head (r.), winged thunderbolt behind	Octavian, togate, seated (l.) on curule chair, holding Victory IMP CAESAR
264 [BMCRE 617–19]	98–104	DEN	Victory, standing (r.) on prow, holding wreath and palm	Octavian, standing (r.) in ornamented quadriga IMP CAESAR
268 [BMCRE 622–23]	85–86	AUR	Head of Octavian (r.)	Victory on globe, holding wreath with vexillum over shoulder IMP CAESAR

RIC²	Giard, BNC	Denom.	Obverse	Reverse
267 [BMCRE 624]	66	DEN	Head of Octavian (r.)	Arch surmounted by quadriga IMP CAESAR on architrave
265a [BMCRE 625]	57–63	DEN	Head of Octavian (r.)	Military trophy, with rudder and anchor, set on prow IMP CAESAR
266 [BMCRE 631]	52–55	DEN	Head of Octavian (r.)	Colonnaded structure, with Victory on apex of pediment IMP CAESAR on architrave
272 [BMCRE 638–40]	92–96	DEN	Bust of Apollo (r.), laureate, with long curls falling down neck	Male figure, veiled (r.), ploughing with yoke of oxen IMP CAESAR
273 [BMCRE 643]	91	AUR	Bust of Diana (r.), draped, shoulder bare, bow and quiver behind	Temple with naval trophy, triskelion in pediment IMP CAESAR on architrave
274 [BMCRE 644–45]	87–90	DEN	Bust of Mars (r.), bearded, with helmet IMP below	Round shield, star with eight rays in center CAESAR on rim of shield

RIC² 269a, 271, 270, 264, 268, 267, 265a, 266, 272, and 274 reproduced courtesy of The American Numismatic Society, New York. RIC² 273 reproduced courtesy of the Trustees of the British Museum, London.

RIC²	Giard, BNC	Denom.	Obverse	Reverse
257 [BMCRE 596–98]	73–76	DEN	Not shown	Enlargement of coin Mercury on rock, holding lyre, with petasus and *talaria* CASESAR DIVI F
276 [BMCRE 647–49]	899–903	QUIN	Head of Octavian (r.) CAESAR IMP VII	Victory, holding wreath and palm, standing (l.) on *cista mystica* between two snakes ASIA RECEPTA
275a [BMCRE 650–51]	905–6	DEN	Head of Octavian (r.), lituus behind CAESAR COS VI	Crocodile, standing (r.) AEGVPTO CAPTA

RIC² 257, 276, and 275a, reproduced courtesy of The American Numismatic Society, New York.

immediate change in the nomenclature on Octavian's coinage. The issues from the IMP CAESAR group are thus to be understood as the new recognition of Octavian's extraordinary title. Even if Dio's authority can be trusted in this matter,[62] prior coinage of the triumvir refutes the significance of the senatorial decree. From as early as an issue of Marcus Agrippa (Crawford, RRC 534), generally assigned to 38 or 37, the initial position for Octavian's honorific title of imperator becomes a regular feature in his coinage.[63] The legend on the obverse of the Agrippa issue reads IMP CAESAR DIVI IULI F. No subsequent issue fails to place the title of imperator before Octavian's name. In short, the issues from the IMP CAESAR group should be seen only to continue this practice already adopted by the triumvir; the coin's legend can offer no reliable indication for a chronology and certainly does not indicate the fixed and widely accepted demarcation of 29.

Grueber's chronology for the IMP CAESAR series was accepted without much question, but scholars soundly rejected his attribution of the mintage of the two series to Rome. Laffranchi, Sydenham, and Mattingly dismissed the possibility that the senatorial mint of Rome continued in operation after 36, although no ancient sources can confirm their assertion. Laffranchi assigned both groups to the Bithynian mints at Nicomedia and Nicaea for 29–27.[64] Sydenham followed Laffranchi's chronology and general attribution to Asia Minor, but he preferred the cities of Ephesus and Pergamum, to which he also assigned the mintage for Octavian's large cistophori issues beginning in 28.[65] However, both Laffranchi and Sydenham, though they differed on the specific chronology and location of mintage, found no cause to distinguish the two groups, or, as Sydenham explained it, "no logical reason, either from the nature of the titles or from the style of the coins, why the legends CAESAR DIVI F and IMP CAESAR should not have been used simultaneously, since they clearly complement each other."[66]

---

62. Sutherland, "Octavian's Gold and Silver Coinage," 142, especially n. 3, rightly points out that we have only Dio's testimony to support the sequence of the two groups, distinguished by the year 29. He discounts the evidence from the hoards and the contemporary (and derivative) issues of L. Pinarius Scarpus (Crawford, RRC 546/4–8) that Crawford suggested might be useful in exacting the chronology for the two groups. Despite the lack of more convincing evidence, Sutherland, nonetheless, maintains the fixed chronology, originally proposed by Grueber.

63. The following issues continue this practice: Crawford, RRC 537/1–2, 538/1–2, and 540. On this matter, see R. Syme, "Imperator Caesar: A Study in Nomenclature," Historia 7 (1958): 172–88, who cogently argued from an examination of the epigraphical and numismatic evidence that Octavian assumed the title as early as 38.

64. L. Laffranchi, La monetazione di Augusto (Milan, 1919), 16.

65. E.A. Sydenham, "The Coinages of Augustus," NumChron 20, ser. 4 (1920): 21.

66. Sydenham, "The Coinages of Augustus," 22. More recently, Giard, "La monnaie coloniale d'Orange," 78–79 n. 7, objected to the attempts to distinguish the two groups by chronology.

Mattingly's *Coins of the Roman Empire in the British Museum* established a more exact and definite chronology of the series and fixed the location of mintage firmly in the East.[67] He maintained that the two groups belonged to only a short period of years that followed the victory at Actium. Again Dio's testimony constituted the evidence to bolster the significance of the year 29. Mattingly distinguished the two groups by chronology, placing the CAESAR DIVI F issues in 31–29 and all the IMP CAESAR issues in 29–27. But he allowed the possibility that the CAESAR DIVI F series may have continued after 29 and that issues from this group may have been issued simultaneously with the IMP CAESAR coins. Mattingly also argued that both groups were "certainly the work of Greek artists, and in part at least, of artists who worked after B.C. 27 at Ephesus and Pergamum."[68] As part of this view, he assumed that shortly after Actium, Octavian assembled a staff of Greek artists to design his coins. The results were immediate, visibly impressive, and politically advantageous: a large series of coins "mainly devoted to the commemoration of Actium" and a new and distinctive portrait style. These two particular features, the depictions of an "Actian" commemoration on the reverse types and the change in the portraiture of Octavian on the obverse types, have become chiefly responsible for the chronology generally accepted by recent scholarship and frame my arguments of refutation.

The Portraiture of Octavian

Of the twenty-two different types in the two groups,[69] thirteen depict a portrait of Octavian on the obverse, one with a laurel crown (*RIC*[2] 271). Two conspicuous features of design distinguish both groups: the total absence of epigraphy and the border of a thin line on nearly all the obverse types.[70] The most common style of design in Republican coinage displayed legends, often long titles of office, that encompassed the whole circumference of some coins. It is not at all certain whether aesthetic or political concerns motivated the change.[71] Nonetheless, the removal of the legend on the ob-

---

67. Mattingly, *BMCRE* I, cxx–cxxvii.

68. Mattingly, *BMCRE* I, cxx.

69. Although *RIC*[2] 263 and 264 are identical in both their obverse and reverse types, I have considered them separately because of their different legends.

70. There are few exceptions. *RIC*[2] 252 and 253 have dotted borders, and *RIC*[2] 274, obverse, displays IMP of the legend IMP CAESAR above the head of Mars.

71. Cf. the apt remarks by J. Liegle, "Die Münzprägung Octavians nach dem Siege von Actium und die augusteische Kunst," *JDAI* 56 (1941): 92, on the consequences and significance of the change. The function of Roman coin types and their role in an official "propaganda" has been much discussed. For a review of the scholarship on this subject, see the important discussion by A. Wallace-Hadrill, "Image and Authority in the Coinage of Augustus," *JRS* 76 (1986): 66–87.

verse left a visible and significant effect on the general appearance of the coin and, most particularly, on Octavian's profile. Extending the full vertical dimension of the coin, the head of Octavian became appreciably larger. The empty background on each side enhanced the overall visual impact. Octavian's prior issues had displayed in a circle around the obverse portrait the titles of consul, augur, and, most prominently, triumvir (III VIR R P C). The total absence of these official titles may suggest a new direction in Octavian's efforts to bolster his public image in Rome at this critical time without any change in his legal or political position—or without the presumptions of the consequences of Actium.

The change in Octavian's portraiture poses a difficult problem. Few sculptural representations of the adopted son of Caesar survive that can be assigned with any assurance to the crucial period of transition from the Triumvirate to the Principate. Most surviving works probably belong to the middle or later years of Augustan Rome; and many others are posthumous reproductions. The idealized, youthful portrait style that the princeps eventually chose for his likeness throughout the empire is well known and richly illustrated by surviving types, but the origins and early development of the change in style are unclear and poorly represented.

More than fifty years ago, Otto Brendel provided one of the earliest examinations into the various changes in the portrait styles of Augustus.[72] His classification of the "Typus B" has remained the standard for identifying the portrait style of Octavian as triumvir. Brendel based his identification on Octavian's early coinage from 43 to 36 that displayed a conspicuous beard of mourning. Brendel adhered to Mattingly's arguments of an Eastern mint and to his chronology for the CAESAR DIVI F and the IMP CAESAR series and thus concluded that the new style of portraiture that characterized the two groups must have derived from the Hellenistic influence that Octavian encountered as he lingered in the Greek East after the victory at Actium. As Brendel explained the change in Octavian's portraiture, the issues heralded a new ruler, whom he called the "Hellenisticher Augustus."[73]

More recently, Paul Zanker continued and expanded on Brendel's original work in Augustan portraiture.[74] Adopting Kraft as the numismatic authority on which to base his opinions, Zanker presumed a period of mintage after Actium for the issues that depicted Octavian's new portraiture. Zanker sought to find the origins of the new style, the "Actium-Typus," as it has

72. O. Brendel, *Ikonographie des Kaisers Augustus* (Nuremberg, 1931).

73. Brendel, *Ikonographie des Kaisers Augustus*, 41.

74. P. Zanker, *Studien zu den Augustus-Porträts*, vol. 1, *Der Actium-Typus* (Göttingen, 1973). Cf. also his epilogue in the unrevised 1978 edition and the informative reviews by W. Trillmich, *BJ* 174 (1974): 687–93, and W.-R. Megow, *Gnomon* 48 (1976): 699–705.

now been commonly named, from a close comparison with Hellenistic ruler portraits. His inclinations were sound. Taking special note of Octavian's forehead hair, Zanker argued that the style consciously imitated the youthful portraits of Alexander. The change was perhaps part of the victor's public efforts to associate himself with the greatest of the Macedonian kings, although Zanker was not willing to conclude that the new style implied any programmatic statement of a new political policy.[75] Nonetheless, the subtle allusion to the world conqueror would not be lost to contemporaries.

Efforts to evaluate the change in Octavian's portraiture require a new approach and terminology. Phrases like "Hellenisticher Augustus" and "Actium-Typus" are imprecise and anachronistic,[76] and the distinctions between *Hellenic* and *Hellenistic* that have been used by numismatists to describe the change in portraiture are minimal and subjective. The characteristic features of Octavian's profile—the thin neck with the visible, though slight, appearance of an Adam's apple; the strong cheekbones; the sharply protruding nose; and the penetrating glance of the eye—confer an imposing and austere dignity to the figure. More than anything else, the enhancement of detail in the portrait, perhaps only an indication of superior workmanship, distinguishes these issues from the prior coinage of the triumvir. While the new style can be seen as a conspicuous change, *Hellenistic* is too vague and general a term to explain the complex nature of the changes in style. Scholars often refer to Octavian's wavy locks of hair on the coinage. While this feature may resemble the distinct hairstyle in Alexander portraits, it alone cannot suffice to label the style Hellenistic. Even in this matter, there is substantial disagreement over the description. The whirling fashion of hair

---

75. Zanker, *Studien zu den Augustus-Porträts*, 39, explains that the "Actium-Typus" portraiture, influenced by Hellenistic ruler portraits and sculpture, nonetheless, suggested "keine programmatische Aussage."

76. Serious doubts about the appropriateness of the term "Actium-Typus" have already been voiced by B. Schmaltz, "Zum Augustus-Bildnis Typus Primaporta," *RömMitt* 93 (1986): 239–42, who, in a stimulating analysis of the Augustan Prima Porta-Typus, indicated the likelihood of a dating for the "Actium-Typus" before Actium and warned against the tendency of modern scholars to attribute and fix typological changes in sculptural portraiture to historical events. The cautionary note is prudent and well advised. As Zanker himself has demonstrated so persuasively, the origins and nature of the creative dynamics for the political ideology, arts, and literature in the Augustan Age are complex, indeterminate, and reciprocal. Rather than understanding the varied cultural and rich artistic productivity of this pivotal period in terms of a rigid imposition of a carefully planned and formally articulated ideology on poets and artisans (and here one should not exclude the engravers of coins), it is more profitable to see a convergence or confluence of ideas, symbols, and images, which borrow from and expand on traditional models, exhibit individual and creative impulses, and, most importantly, embrace multiple, and at times even contrary, interpretations and receptions.

has also been described as "Classical" and "Polykleitan."[77] Indeed, the Hellenistic or Classical influence cannot be restricted only to the period after the Actian victory. A distinct trend toward a more Hellenic style (the general "Hellenistic" and "Classical" are inadequate) had already begun to develop as early as the late Republic, though the evidence from the triumviral period is more reliable and compelling.[78]

In a new and illuminating study of a bust in the Museo Chiaramonti of the Vatican (XLVII.17, inv. 1977), previously identified to be the likeness of either Claudius Marcellus, the young nephew of Augustus, or Cn. Domitius Ahenobarbus, the father of the emperor Nero (neither identification is convincing), Sheldon Nodelman has argued for an earlier dating and has identified the bust as a portrait of Brutus, the assassin of Julius Caesar.[79] Rejecting the stylistic features of neoclassicism (particularly, the treatment of the figure's hair in comma-shaped locks and curls) as an irrefutable evidence of an Augustan date, Nodelman placed greater emphasis on the vibrant realism and emotion of the slightly damaged sculptural piece, on the striking twist of the neck, the contracted brow, and the penetrating force of the gaze—all more characteristic of what we generally label as Hellenistic art and its revival in late Republican Rome. Similar stylistic features, most often associated with the established traditions of Hellenistic ruler portraits, may also be found in surviving portraits of some of Brutus' contemporaries, such as Cicero, Cato the Younger, L. Domitius Ahenobarbus, Julius Caesar, Marcus Agrippa, and Octavian (namely, the so-called Typus B).[80] Nodelman has plausibly suggested the prominence and activity of an Attic-Roman atelier that seems to be responsible for the experimentation and change of portrait styles as early as the 40s and still strong in the 30s. The dramatic transformation in Octavian's portrait style, evident on his coins at this time, is thus reflective of a broader evolution of artistic style and is paralleled by develop-

---

77. M. Bieber, "The Development of Portraiture on Roman Republican Coins," *ANRW* I.4 (Berlin and New York, 1973), 889.

78. On this subject, see V. Poulsen, *Les Portraits Romains*, 3 vols. (Copenhagen, 1962), 1:12–15; D. Michel, *Alexander als Vorbild für Pompeius, Caesar und Marcus Antonius. Archäologische Untersuchungen*, Collection Latomus 94 (Brussels, 1967); J.D. Breckinridge, *Likeness: A Conceptual History of Ancient Portraiture* (Evanston, Ill., 1968), 186–89; Bieber, "Development of Portraiture on Roman Republican Coins," 871–98; and M. Hofter, "Porträt," in *Kaiser Augustus*, 291–343.

79. S. Nodelman, "The Portrait of Brutus the Tyrannicide," in *Ancient Portraits in the J. Paul Getty Museum*, vol. 1, Occasional Papers on Antiquities 4 (Malibu, 1987), 41–86.

80. Zanker, *Studien zu den Augustus-Porträts*, 1:38, and *Power of Images*, 8–11, himself has argued that surviving representations of Pompey, M. Agrippa, L. Domitius Ahenobarbus, and Antony display features characteristic of Hellenistic ruler portraits. Cf. also the discussion by Hofter, "Porträt," 294–98.

ments in other areas, such as architecture, painting, and decorative arts. Actium is not the impetus of these profound changes but rather portends an end of experimentation and variety. The almost rigid adherence to an idealized classicism, which would become emblematic of the subsequent age and the Principate of Augustus, both results from the stylistic inclinations and innovations in the preceding two decades and at the same time demarcates the final stage in this artistic period.

In his die study of the coinage, Sutherland observed two visibly distinct portrait styles.

> That of Group (1) shows mainly a "heroic" treatment with a tall Octavianic head of noble and "fine" proportions, strong yet delicate features, and totally confident expression. That of Group (2) shows a head that is square, more "realist," sometimes heavier, with features clearly less delicate and unheroized, and an expression that varies between the pensive and the purely natural. If one wished to impose loose concepts on these two dominant portrait-styles, one might call that of Group (1) the more Hellenizing (though certainly not Hellenic), and that of Group (2) the more purely Italic.[81]

Sutherland's terms of description are imprecise and subjective, and the subtle distinctions fail to convince. Nonetheless, his careful analysis clearly demonstrates that the same portrait styles are found within both groups. Die links between the portraiture closely connect the two groups; there are nine between the two groups but only one within the CAESAR DIVI F issues and two within the IMP CAESAR issues.[82] Sutherland, of course, does not comment on the problematic finding that the so-called Hellenizing style is found predominately among the CAESAR DIVI F issues that he has assigned to an earlier period, where five out of the seven representative types display this style. Only one in the allegedly later IMP CAESAR series (this issue actually displays both styles on surviving specimens) features what Sutherland prefers to call the "Hellenizing" style. While we may be able to observe more conspicuous distinctions in the portrait style of later Augustan coinage—for example, in the cistophori issues from Asia Minor (what Sutherland would call the "Hellenizing" style) and the silver and gold issues of Lugdunum (what he would call the "purely Italic" style)—distinctions are not as clearly defined and precise within the CAESAR DIVI F and the IMP CAESAR groups.

---

81. Sutherland, "Octavian's Gold and Silver Coinage," 144.

82. For this evidence, see Sutherland, "Octavian's Gold and Silver Coinage," table 3, the diagram of the die links.

Here we find only faint variations among the two styles Sutherland has identified. The portraits, lacking the so-called heroic treatment, are not actually "more realist," and the expressions do not range between the "pensive" and the "purely natural." What these portraits lack are only the fine quality, proportion of design, and superior workmanship that exemplify the other style. These variations intimate an active period of experimentation in Octavian's portraiture. The individuality of the die makers may also account for the differences and subtle distinctions. In any case, we should not presume that one style of portraiture succeeded and later replaced the other. It seems more likely that the two portrait styles, as Sutherland has distinguished them, were issued simultaneously and *before* Actium.

Reverse Types

In efforts to date the coins after Actium, more convincing than the change in Octavian's portraiture would seem to be the clear identification of conspicuous and commemorative allusions to the victory on issues from both groups: naval trophies; the globe, representing victory on land and sea; a *columna rostrata*; and a triumphal arch. Closer consideration of the depictions on the individual issues shows that "Actian" allusions are dubious and speculative; no specific reference to the Actian victory can be surely identified on any issue.

The appearance of naval trophies on Octavian's coinage demands more critical assessment. As I have already suggested, Octavian's earlier naval victory at Naulochus could have occasioned the coin types. The obverse type of an aureus issue from the IMP CAESAR group (*RIC*[2] 273) depicts the goddess Diana, who is identified by her bow and quiver. The reverse type depicts a temple, presumably the temple of the goddess on the obverse. The architrave of the temple shows the legend IMP CAESAR. No other inscription serves to identify the structure, but the depictions of two adornments in the temple make an association with Octavian's victory at Naulochus seem likely.[83] A naval trophy stands in the temple, and a triskelion,[84] symbolic of Sicily, appears in the pediment of the temple. Issues from the imperial mint at Lugdunum, more than twenty years after the battle, commemorate Diana's role at Naulochus.[85] The legend on these issues reads simply SICIL, in

---

83. For this interpretation, see Prayon, "Projektierte Bauten auf römischen Münzen," 323–25.

84. Grueber, *BMCRR* II, 15, no. 4355, also identifies an *aplustre* on the triskelion. The small scale of the depiction and the poor quality of the surviving specimens make it difficult to confirm this attribute.

85. *RIC*[2] 172 and 173a–b, 175, 181–83, 194a–b and 195, 196 and 197a–b, 204.

allusion to the naval battle off the coast of Sicily. It is tempting to conclude from later evidence that the issue from the IMP CAESAR group that features the triskelion and naval trophy in the temple of the goddess offers an early recognition for the association between Diana and Naulochus. The origins and nature of this association are uncertain.[86] Perhaps a temple of Diana stood near the site of battle. In any case, the aureus issue surely alludes to Octavian's victory at Naulochus.

The naval trophy on the reverse of *RIC*[2] 265a–b is perhaps another allusion to the victory over Sextus Pompey. It seems to be the same trophy as the one that stands in the Temple of Diana on the reverse of *RIC*[2] 273. Both issues belong to the IMP CAESAR group. Another issue from the IMP CAESAR group displays a *columna rostrata* (*RIC*[2] 271), the monument of a naval victory. A statue of a male figure, who seems to be wearing a cloak extending from his shoulders, and who leans on a spear with his right hand and holds a parazonium in his left, surmounts the column. It is generally believed that the statue represents Octavian as victor. The obverse may confirm this image of Octavian, since only here is he crowned by a laurel wreath. Among the various honors that Octavian received on his return to Rome after the victory at Naulochus, Appian (*BC* 5.130) lists a statue to be erected in the Forum, surmounting a *columna rostrata*. The historian records that the Senate voted that a golden statue of Octavian, dressed in the garb that he wore when he entered the city to celebrate his *ovatio*, was to stand on a column that was decorated by the beaks of the ships captured at Naulochus. Appian's evidence accords well with the representation of the cloaked and armed figure on the reverse of *RIC*[2] 271. The coin type could allude to this monument in Rome.

A male deity with long, flowing locks and a laurel crown appears on the obverse of *RIC*[2] 272. The figure has often been identified as Apollo. The reverse of this issue poses more serious problems. Kraft has interpreted the scene of the veiled man, who is leading a team of oxen, to be an allusion to Octavian's foundation of Nicopolis at the site of the Actian victory.[87] That the coin type alludes to Octavian's role as a founder of a city or colony is

---

86. Sometime during the triumviral period, L. Cornificius, who fought on Octavian's side in the war against Sextus, rebuilt the Temple to Diana on the Aventine (Suet. *Aug.* 29.5). The date is not certain, but perhaps it served to commemorate his role in the victory over Sextus. Cf. Shipley, "Chronology of the Building Operations in Rome," 28–30 and 48, who dates the rebuilding to 33 or 32 B.C.E. to associate it with the triumph that Cornificius celebrated *ex Africa* at that time.

87. Kraft, *Zur Münzprägung des Augustus*, 11–19. Giard, *BNC* 92–96, accepts this identification.

likely, although it cannot be certain.[88] And even if we accept that the type alludes to the foundation of cities, there is no compelling reason to assume a specific allusion to Nicopolis. Mattingly suggested that "we see Octavian as founder of cities, celebrated under the guise of the colonists' god."[89] Sutherland interpreted the veiled figure to be "Octavian as the founder or re-founder of urban communities."[90] The activities of the triumvir as the settler of veterans and founder of colonies is well attested in the ancient sources.[91] Both Appian (*BC* 5.129) and Dio (49.13–14) record the serious problems that faced the victor after Naulochus as he sought to discharge more than twenty thousand disgruntled veterans. Octavian established a number of colonies primarily in southern Italy and Sicily to accommodate his legions. The coin type on the reverse of *RIC*[2] 272 cannot and should not be restricted to the aftermath of the Actian victory. It reflects Octavian's activities as the founder of colonies throughout the turbulent period of the Triumvirate.

The identification of the deity on the reverse of *RIC*[2] 257 is a crucial point; scholars have wavered between Mercury and Apollo.[92] The naked god, facing right, is seated on a rock. He holds a lyre in his hand, and on his back a broad-brimmed hat, a petasus, is clearly visible. The lyre is the traditional attribute for either god (Mercury invented the instrument; Apollo played it), but the petasus belongs exclusively to Mercury. Recent scholarship has sought to establish the identity of the god more conclusively. It has been suggested that the seated figure is Apollo in his role as the protecting deity at Actium (either Apollo Leucadius or Actius). If this identification can be accepted, the depiction of Apollo would thus add more conviction to the view that the commemorative issues belong to the period after Actium.

Kraft identified the god with the lyre as Apollo Leucadius.[93] The depiction of the petasus complicates his identification. Kraft strains at great length to find in the ancient evidence associations of individuals other than

---

88. Laffranchi, *La monetazione di Augusto*, 16, had understood the scene to be an allusion to Octavian's extension of the *pomerium*.

89. Mattingly, *BMCRE* I, cxxiv.

90. Sutherland, *Coinage in Roman Imperial Policy 31 B.C.–A.D. 68* (London, 1951; reprinted New York, 1971), 30.

91. For discussion of this subject, see L. Keppie, *Colonisation and Veteran Settlement in Italy, 47–14 B.C.* (London, 1983), 58–73.

92. Liegle, "Die Münzprägung Octavians nach dem Siege von Actium und die augusteische Kunst," 108, speaks of the depicted figure on the coin as "Apollo-Merkur" and an "apollinischen Merkur." Giard, *BNC* 73–76, who rightly identifies the seated figure with the lyre as Mercury, gives no explanation for his choice and fails to include the *talaria* in his description of the god (see below for significance of this attribute).

93. Kraft, *Zur Münzprägung des Augustus*, 14–19.

Mercury with a petasus. Various heroes from Greek mythology, such as Jason, Perseus, Theseus, Peleus, and Oedipus, have been depicted in art and literature with this distinctive type of hat.[94] Kraft shows how the petasus should not be seen as the exclusive property of divine heads; it is the "headcoverings of sailors and fishermen."[95] As a common form of protection from the heat of the sun, it was often viewed as the sign of a traveler. Despite the impressive array of examples for the petasus in mythology and art, Kraft fails to find the confirmation that his interpretation demands, an example of Apollo wearing a petasus. Kraft identified the seated figure on Octavian's denarius issue as Apollo Leucadius without evidence of contemporary representations. An examination of the later coinage from Nicopolis by Peter Franke, however, reveals a much different iconography for the cult figure of Apollo Leucadius.[96] The issues from Nicopolis depict a god standing and holding a torch in his raised right hand and a bow in his left. Sutherland subsequently suggested that the figure on Octavian's issue be identified as Apollo Actius because of a noted similarity with the seated figure on the Budapest Relief.[97] The identification of the figure as Apollo, however, cannot be maintained.

A close inspection of the detail of the seated figure on the coin reveals the crude, yet clearly recognizable, shape of a feather that extends from his ankle and cuts across his garment, which is draped on the rock (for an enlargement of the coin, see plate 5). In a footnote that subsequent scholarship has ignored, H.A. Grueber had already explained his identification of Mercury for the seated divine figure because of his observation of the petasus and the winged sandal (*talaria*) on the coin.[98] The feathered wing, which is still recognizable on a few specimens, makes the identification certain. Grueber's original claim that the type "may refer specifically to the restoration of commerce to Italy after the battle of Naulochus" is still valid, although we need not presume a specific allusion. In any case, the coin type cannot be seen as an allusion to the god who secured the victory at Actium.

---

94. For ancient evidence, see *RE* 19.1 (1937): cols. 1119–24.

95. Kraft, *Zur Münzprägung des Augustus*, 15.

96. P.R. Franke, "Apollo Leucadius und Octavianus?" *Chiron* 6 (1976): 159–63. Franke concluded that the seated god should be understood as Mercury and that the denarius issue (*RIC*[2] 257) belongs to an earlier period, 36–31 or 34–31.

97. See Sutherland, "Octavian's Gold and Silver Coinage," 150–51, but the identification of the seated figure on the relief is disputed. For discussion, cf. E. Strong, *Scultura Romana* (Florence, 1923), 14–16; A. Hekler, *Museum der bildenen Künste in Budapest. Die Sammlung antiker Skulpturen* (Budapest, 1929), 116, pl. 107; H. Prückner, "Das Budapest Aktium-Relief," in *Forschungen und Funde. Festschrift für Bernhard Neutsch*, ed. F. Krinzinger et al. (Innsbruck, 1980), 357–66 (see 364 n. 1 for bibliography).

98. Grueber, *BMCRR* II, 11 n. 1.

The globe is prominently displayed on three issues from the two groups: the figure of Victory stands on a globe, facing left or right and holding a wreath and palm branch (*RIC*² 254a–b and 255); a naked male figure, facing left, places his right foot on a globe and holds a scepter and aplustre in his hands, with a sword hanging from his side (*RIC*² 256); and a second figure of Victory standing on a globe faces front and holds a wreath and vexillum (*RIC*² 268). Kraft doubts the possibility that this symbol of world dominion would have appeared on Octavian's coinage in the aftermath of his victory over Sextus Pompey.[99] He prefers a period after the Actian victory when Octavian returned from the East in 29. The appearance of the globe on Octavian's coinage, however, does not necessitate the historical background and circumstances after Actium.

Kraft remarked that the representation of Victory on the globe was not seen before on earlier Roman coinage.[100] The globe, however, is a familiar symbol on coins from the late Republic, especially issues by Julius Caesar and the triumvirs.[101] While no prior issue depicts Victory standing on a globe, deities such as the Genius Populi Romani, Roma, and Venus are often depicted either standing on or leaning against a globe.[102] It should not seem an extraordinary or peculiar development in the coin types or public ideology that the goddess Victory would assume this symbolic role representing Roman conquest and dominion over the world. Nonetheless, a formidable consensus of numismatic opinion (Grueber, Mattingly, Kraft, and Sutherland)[103] has argued that the Victory on the globe (*RIC*² 268) is meant to represent the statue of Victory that Octavian had set up in the Curia Julia in

---

99. Kraft, *Zur Münzprägung des Augustus*, 20 n. 5.

100. Kraft, *Zur Münzprägung des Augustus*, 20 n. 5.

101. The following issues display the globe: Crawford, *RRC* 393/1a–b, 397, 403, 409/2, 426/41, 449/4, 465/8a–b, 480/6, 480/15, 480/16, 480/17, 494/5, 494/39, and 520. For a discussion of the globe and its symbolic meaning, see A. Schlachter, *Der Globus. Seine Entstehung und Verwendung in der Antike* (Berlin, 1927); T. Hölscher, *Victoria Romana. Archäologische Untersuchungen zur Geschichte und Wesensart der römischen Siegesgöttin von den Anfängen bis zum Ende des 3. Jhs. n. Chr.* (Mainz, 1967), 6–47; and Weinstock, *Divus Julius*, 42–53.

102. Crawford, *RRC* 397 (Genius Populi Romani), 449/4 (Roma), 480/15 (Venus, who actually is leaning her elbow on a shield that rests on a globe). The reverse type of Crawford, *RRC* 494/5 depicts a curious winged male figure, with radiant crown, bow and quiver, caduceus, and cornucopia, standing on a globe with his right foot. The obverse shows a portrait of Antony. For discussion of the unusual type and possible identifications, see T.V. Buttrey, Jr., *The Triumviral Portrait Gold of the Quattuorviri Monetales of 42 B.C.*, ANSNNM 137 (New York, 1956), 9–10, esp. n. 40.

103. Grueber, *BMCRR* II, 14 n. 1; Mattingly, *BMCRE* I, cxxiii n. 4; Kraft, *Zur Münzprägung des Augustus*, 20 n. 5; Sutherland, "Octavian's Gold and Silver Coinage," 151, 154; Giard, *BNC* 52–56.

29. Support for this interpretation may be that the figure of Victory depicted on *RIC*² 268 is reproduced in miniature on the apex of the pediment of the colonnaded building on *RIC*² 266, which numismatists have identified as the Curia Julia. There are serious problems with either identification.

First, it is not at all certain that the building on *RIC*² 266 is the Curia Julia. Grueber and Mattingly identified the structure as the Temple of Divus Julius, vowed in 42 B.C.E., though not officially dedicated until Octavian's return from the East and his celebration of the triple triumph in 29.[104] Second, and more importantly, Dio (51.22.1–2) confirms neither that the figure of Victory on the globe is the statue from Tarentum nor that this statue was placed on top of the new Curia Julia as the coin depicts it. Rather Dio records that the statue was set up in the Senate chamber (*in* seems the easiest and most normal translation of the Greek preposition).[105] Dio also reports that the statue was adorned with the spoils from Egypt. The coin type displays no adornments to suggest conquest of Egypt. Though it is possible that the figure of Victory depicted on *RIC*² 266 is the same statue set up in the Curia Julia, the passage in Dio cannot be the evidence to maintain this opinion. Since no copy of the sculptural piece survives, and since no description of the Victory statue is found in the ancient sources, it seems that we should be less insistent on associating the coin's depiction with the Tarentine Victory statue and on assuming that the issue belongs to a period only after 29. Mattingly explained that the symbols of victory and universal peace represented on the various issues and, in particular, the appearance of the globe have "general reference to the conditions prevailing after Actium."[106] This possibility cannot be excluded, but the situation in the aftermath of the victory at Naulochus is equally appropriate.

The lavish celebration that greeted the victor after Naulochus when he returned to Rome established the precedent for his later triumphal ceremony in 29.[107] The Senate exalted Octavian with declarations of praise and gratitude; the formal ceremony of an *ovatio*, for which he was allowed to ride into the city on horseback; annual recognition of the day on which he won his victory; the erection of statues and the "triumphal" arch; and the privilege of the front seat at public occasions. Many of the commemorative issues from the CAESAR DIVI F and the IMP CAESAR groups that have been confi-

---

104. Grueber, *BMCRR* II, 14 n. 1, and Mattingly, *BMCRE* I, cxxiii n. 4.

105. Sutherland, "Octavian's Gold and Silver Coinage," 154 n. 19, claims that Dio's text (ἔν τε τῷ συνεδρίῳ) allows that the statue was set up either "on" or "in" the Curia Julia, although this ambiguity strains the regular usage of the Greek preposition.

106. Mattingly, *BMCRE* I, cxxiii.

107. Appian *BC* 5.130 and Dio 49.15.1–2.

dently assigned an "Actian" motif can be interpreted to allude to Octavian's victory over Sextus Pompey. After Actium, Octavian boasted of the restoration of peace on land and sea and recorded his boast (*pace parta terra marique*) on the monumental inscription erected at Nicopolis.[108] The solemn closure of the Temple of Janus echoed the same message. The rhetoric that broadcast Octavian's victory at Naulochus sounded very much the same.[109] In the public speeches that were also written down and circulated in pamphlets at that time, the adopted son of Caesar spoke often and proudly of the newly won peace and harmony in the state. The public inscription on Octavian's *columna rostrata* erected in the Forum read:

Peace, long disturbed, he reestablished on land and sea.

The gracious victor pardoned former enemies (except the assassins of Caesar) and claimed, however prematurely, that the civil wars were ended.

Sometime shortly after his victory over Sextus Pompey, Octavian promised to abandon his office and to dissolve the Triumvirate (Lepidus already had been removed after his failed conspiracy) as soon as Antony returned in triumph from the East.[110] It matters little that Octavian may have been neither sincere nor serious in his intentions. To give credence to his promise, Octavian may have decided to remove the title of triumvir from his coinage. If we exclude for the moment the CAESAR DIVI F and IMP CAESAR groups, few issues of Octavian date between Naulochus and Actium.[111] This conspicuous absence of coinage by Octavian in the years intervening between the

---

108. For a reconstruction of the dedicatory inscription of the Augustan monument, see W.M. Murray and P.M. Petsas, *Octavian's Campsite Memorial for the Actian War*, Transactions of the American Philosophical Society 79.4 (Philadelphia, 1989), 62–76. For text, see n. 116 in this chapter.

109. The chief sources for this period are Appian *BC* 5.130–32 and Dio 49.15.1–6. For discussion of Octavian's ambitions at this time, see Syme, *Roman Revolution*, 233–35.

110. Appian *BC* 5.132.

111. P.V. Hill, "From Naulochus to Actium: The Coinages of Octavian and Antony, 36–31 B.C.," *NAC* 5 (1976): 121–28, offers a brief discussion of the coinage from this period. Apart from a small and seemingly random selection from the CAESAR DIVI F group, Hill chooses three issues: Crawford, *RRC* 540 (aureus and denarius—obverse: head of Octavian, bearded, IMP CAESAR DIVI F III VIR ITER R P C; reverse: Temple of Divus Julius, with figure standing within, veiled and holding *lituus*, COS ITER ET TER DESIG); Sydenham, *CRR* 1339 (quinarius—obverse: galley with rowers sailing, IMP CAESAR; reverse: Victory, holding a wreath, palm branch, and rudder, DIVI F); and *BMCRE* I, 56–57, nos. 309–13 (denarius—obverse: head of Octavian, no legend; reverse: circular shield with boss in center and decorated with three concentric circles of dots, IMP CAESAR DIVI F). These issues may belong to the immediate aftermath of Naulochus, but they could not have constituted the coinage necessary to support the campaign against Antony.

two victories is rarely observed by numismatists, but it must be explained.[112] We should expect that the victor at Naulochus needed to pay the large number of veterans who served under him during this past campaign. In the following year, Octavian set off for Illyria. Initial victory was met with defeat, and the warfare continued for three years. Again we may assume the need to mint coinage. Finally, the preparations for the struggle against Antony and the Egyptian queen necessitated even more coinage. The vast number of issues that Octavian's rival minted in the year before Actium (Crawford, *RRC* 544/1–39) makes it all but certain that the triumvir, who preferred to call himself by the titles *Caesar divi filius* and *Imperator Caesar*, was also engaged in an extensive, and perhaps hurried, production of coinage.

Octavian's victory at Actium produced no immediate or visibly distinct change in his coinage. The issues that heralded the legends CAESAR DIVI FILIUS and IMPERATOR CAESAR continued in the aftermath of the naval success over Antony and the Egyptian queen. The coinage that initially financed Octavian's campaign against his Roman rival later commemorated his victory. But Octavian did not fail to recognize his victory on his coinage. On his triumphant return to Rome in 29 or perhaps shortly before, during his settlement of political affairs and administration in the Greek East, Octavian began to issue new types that celebrated his recent success. A silver quinarius, produced in large numbers and widely circulated (*RIC*² 276, plate 5), prominently depicts a figure of Victory on its reverse. Holding a crown and palm branch, she stands to the left on a *cista mystica*, embraced by two serpents. The legends on the coin commemorate Octavian's victory in the East and establish firmly the date of issue. The title CAESAR IMP VII on the obverse places the quinarius in 29; and on the reverse, the claim ASIA RECEPTA heralds the theme of the triple triumph. The more famous AEGYPTO CAPTA series (*RIC*² 275a, plate 5; 275b; and 544–45) that displays the crocodile on its reverse belongs in the same background. The issues are dated by Octavian's sixth and seventh consulships (28 and 27, respectively).[113] The boastful legend and the exotic image of a crocodile highlight the glory of Octavian's triumphal ceremonies, the conquest of Egypt.

112. Kraft's explanation, *Zur Münzprägung des Augustus*, 22, that there are similar periods of mint inactivity in the Roman Republic and later Empire is not convincing. Antony's prodigious and hurried mintage of his legionary issues in the late 30s documents the need to finance such military campaigns not only after the victory but in preparation of the war.

113. Sutherland (*RIC*² 546) also identifies another issue that offers a depiction of a hippopotamus (or head of a rhinoceros) instead of the crocodile. The obverse legend reads IMP CAESAR DIVI F AUGUST COS VII.

The numismatic evidence affords a rich and valuable contribution to the modern perception of the Augustan public image and even more important and crucial to historical studies, of how this image emerged and evolved throughout the long, often turbulent fifty years from Caesar's assassination to the succession of Tiberius. But matters of chronology, geographical attribution of the mintage, and identification of coin types pose serious obstacles to the sure application of this evidence. The two large groups of issues with the legends CAESAR DIVI F and IMP CAESAR, have suffered from the problems of interpretation. The rigid chronology that has been imposed on the two groups of Octavian's coinage, identified by the legends CAESAR DIVI F and IMP CAESAR, must be abandoned. The lack of a specific titulature allows more flexibility. The changes in Octavian's portraiture, evident on the coin types of both series, do not necessarily presume or indeed require the momentous consequences of Actium for explanation. Rather the varied and subtle differences among the obverse types suggest a somewhat extended period of experimentation and the development of a distinctive style, prompted undoubtedly by a bold and calculated effort to fashion a new political image in Rome in the aftermath of a great victory. The naval beaks, arch, and colonnaded temples prominently represented on the two series exalted Octavian's role as victor, though the coins were perhaps issued not only in the years after he won his greatest military success and secured supreme power in Rome but in the years before. The coinage must be understood and assessed in the political background of the Second Triumvirate, from the jubilant celebrations in Rome, architectural monuments, and exaggerated rhetoric following Octavian's defeat of the younger son of Pompey, to the fierce battle of propaganda and politics that preceded and contributed to the war against Antony and the Egyptian queen. The outcome at Actium only served to confirm what Octavian had already boasted after Naulochus.

Monuments in the East: Victory Cities and Actian Games

Quoque Actiacae victoriae memoria celebratior et in posterum esset, urbem Nicopolim apud Actium condidit ludosque illic quinquennales constituit et ampliato vetere Apollinis templo locum castrorum, quibus fuerat usus, exornatum navalibus spoliis Neptuno ac Marti consecravit. (Suet. *Aug.* 18.2)

[And to exalt the fame of his Actian victory and to perpetuate its memory, he founded the city of Nicopolis near Actium and established quinquennial games there. He enlarged the ancient temple of Apollo and adorned the area where he had set up his camp with naval trophies and consecrated it to Neptune and Mars.]

The Roman biographer Suetonius records the impressive memorials of the victory at Actium: the foundation of Nicopolis near the site of the naval battle; the establishment of athletic competitions in cyclical rotations; the enlargement of an ancient temple to Apollo; and the dedicatory monument of naval trophies on the campsite of Octavian. The new city, a synoecism of neighboring communities, which was founded by a treaty and granted the status of a *civitas libera*, became at once the political, economic, and social center of its provincial region and flourished more than a thousand years after the outcome of war was first decided in the Ambracian Gulf. The Actian games, officially designated by the honorific title Olympian, were performed every four years in the sacred precinct of the newly founded city and subsequently imitated in various cities throughout the Greek East. In gratitude to the god whose temple stood near the site of the naval battle, the Roman general dedicated as the first fruits of his victory a squadron of ten selected ships, a *dekanaia* that represented warships outfitted with from one to ten banks of oars, respectively.[114] The temple of the god was enlarged, and the local cult of Apollo Actius quickly emerged as a potent symbol of Augustan victory and a new world order. On the hillside site where he had pitched his military camp, overlooking the mouth of the Ambracian Gulf and just north of his victory city, Octavian erected a massive stone monument to commemorate his victory.[115] A stoa more than forty meters wide embraced an expansive open space on three sides. On a lower terrace, a long line of brazen warship rams, arrayed in generally increasing sizes from right to left, adorned the immense podium of the structure. A dedicatory inscription boasted of the victory "in the war waged on behalf of the republic" and consecrated the area to Neptune and Mars.[116]

---

114. The war memorial was short-lived. A fire had already destroyed not only the ten representative warships dedicated by the victor but even their naval stations when Strabo, a Greek historian and contemporary of Augustus, composed his account of the region in his *Geographica* (7.7.6).

115. For the most recent, comprehensive, and informative discussion of the structure, based on extensive work in the area and careful review and new assessment of the archaeological remains, see Murray and Petsas, *Octavian's Campsite Memorial.* This impressive study not only contributes to our previously limited, if not confused, understanding of Octavian's efforts to commemorate his victory in this region (what Murray and Petsas call "a mixture of Roman pragmatic simplicity and Hellenistic imperial grandeur") but offers important information on the size of the warships in the naval battle, the composition of Antony's fleet, and the subsequent propaganda and exaggerations of the victor.

116. For a sober reconstruction of the dedicatory inscription with full bibliography of earlier attempts, see Murray and Petsas, *Octavian's Campsite Memorial,* 62–76, who have

This boastful array of war memorials and monuments of victory, grandiose and long-standing, attests to Octavian's intentions to exalt his achievement at Actium and to the contemporary recognition and significance of the decisive naval battle. The celebration of Actian games and the newly established city broadcast an official message of Roman victory and imperial rule. No Roman general before him—neither Flamininus nor Aemilius Paullus, conquerors of Greece, and neither Pompey nor Julius Caesar, victors in Roman civil war—left such a legacy to the name and glory of an individual victory. This final section of chapter 1 examines the literary and archaeological evidence for these monuments and memorials founded near the site of the Actian battle, to assess the content, tone, and audience of the message of victory in the Greek East and to decide how this imperial message must be judged and distinguished from the extraordinary honors, decrees, and trophies voted by the Roman Senate and the grand triumphal celebration that awaited the victor's arrival in Italy.

The Foundation of a Victory City

Strabo of Amaseia, the author of a lost universal history in forty-seven books and the extant *Geographica* in seventeen books, is our only contemporary witness for the founding of Nicopolis near Actium. His narrative (*Geo.* 7.7.6) sets forth clearly the contributing factors that help to explain Octavian's establishment of what was in fact a synoecism formed from neighboring towns. Later historical accounts in Suetonius, Dio Cassius, and Pausanias[117] virtually ignore any motivations for the founding of the city apart from the Roman victor's ambition and pride to exalt and commemorate his military accomplishment. Strabo, however, informs us that already before the decisive battle, Ambracia and other cities in the immediate area had been devastated by the Macedonian and Roman conquerors in a long series of intermittent wars. The provincial administration had been slow, if not unable, to resolve the severe political and economic problems in the region.

---

pointed out that J.M. Carter, "A New Fragment of Octavian's Inscription at Nicopolis," *ZPE* 24 (1977): 227–30, misread one of the extant blocks at the site and mistakenly claimed a twenty-sixth block for the monument. According to their revised reconstruction, the dedication read:

vacat Imp • Caesa]R • DIV[i • Iuli •]F • VIC[toriam • consecutus
• bell]O • QVOD • PRO [• r]E[•]P[u]BLIC[a] • GES[si]T • IN • HAC •
REGION[e • cons]VL [• quintum • i]MPERAT[or • se]PTIMUM • PACE[•]PARTA
TERRA [• marique • Nep]TVNO [• et • Ma]RT[i • c]ASTR [• ex •] QVIBV[s •
ad • hostem • in]SEQ[uendum • egr]ESSU[s • est • navalibus • spoli]IS
[• exorna]TA • C[onsacravit *vacat*

117. Suet. *Aug.* 18.2; Dio 51.1.2–4; Paus. 5.23.3, 10.38.4.

The victor's decision to found Nicopolis may thus be understood as a practical endeavor, a deliberate and serious response to an urgent local problem, and "a natural culmination of a long development."[118]

Earlier attempts in Hellenistic times to found a major city in the vicinity around the ancient Temple of Apollo Actius had failed. Nicopolis, however, proved an immediate success. Strabo described the new city, only one generation after its founding, as rich, populous, and expanding. His praise was well deserved. The city and the environs under its local administration incorporated most of the territory that formerly had been part of the Acarnanian and Aetolian leagues. In fact, the synoecism was intended to replace these two formerly powerful political leagues. We know that Ambracians, Leucadians, Acarnanians, and Amphilochian Argives were forced to participate in the city's foundation. Almost the whole of Aetolia suffered from the decision to form the synoecism, when large numbers of the area's population were uprooted and moved.[119] Politically, Nicopolis was declared a free city (*civitas libera*) by a formal treaty (*foedus aequum*) and sent six delegates to the revived Amphictyonic League.[120] Its role and power in this new, effective, and tightly controlled confederation of Greeks is confirmed by the number of delegates sent from Nicopolis (only the Macedonian and Thessalian leagues had as many) and its regular attendance at every meeting. Scholars have generally dismissed the notion that a Roman colony was settled in the immediate area, though both Pliny the Elder (*colonia Augusti Actium cum templo Apollinis nobili ac civitate libera Nicopolitana, NH* 4.5) and Tacitus (*Nicopolim Romanam coloniam ingressus, Ann.* 5.10) attest to the existence of such a colony.[121] In an effort to explain the contradiction within the sources, it has been plausibly suggested that some form of "double commu-

118. On this matter, see U. Kahrstedt, "Die Territorien von Patrai und Nikopolis in der Kaiserzeit," *Historia* 1 (1950): 549–61, and N. Purcell, "The Nicopolitan Synoecism and Roman Urban Policy," in *Nicopolis I*, 73. Purcell's discussion belongs to an important collection of papers from the first international symposium on Nicopolis held in 1984 (see the Abbreviations for full bibliography). For reviews of the thirty-two papers on subjects ranging from the earliest Greek settlements in Epirus to nineteenth-century travel literature of the city, see J.M. Carter, "Nicopolis," *CR* 40 (1990): 387–89, and P.N. Doukellis, "Actia Nicopolis: idéologie impériale, structures urbaines et développement régional," *JRA* 3 (1990): 399–406.

119. Paus. 5.23.3 and 10.38.4.

120. Paus. 10.8.4. For discussion, see D. Kienast, *Augustus. Prinzeps und Monarch* (Darmstadt, 1982), 373–77.

121. Perhaps most significantly, Strabo fails to mention the establishment of a Roman colony at Nicopolis. Archaeological discoveries so far have not found a site for the colony, and local epigraphical remains offer no evidence of veterans in the area. For the controversy with full bibliography, see Kahrstedt, "Die Territorien von Patrai und Nikopolis in der Kaiserzeit"; Th. Sarikakis, "Nicopolis d'Épire était-elle une colonie romaine ou une ville grecque?" *Balkan Studies* 11 (1970): 91–96; Purcell, "Nicopolitan Synoecism and Roman Urban Policy," 71–90.

nity" existed at Nicopolis, not unlike the synoecism of Roman veterans and Greek citizens at Patras, also founded by Augustus.[122] In any case, Nicopolis was, above all, a Greek city with Greek institutions. Its local government, coinage, and public inscriptions were Greek.[123] From Strabo's testimony regarding the long-standing and serious economic problems of the region, it seems unlikely that the new synoecism was an immediate or impulsive reaction to the military success at Actium. Although Greece soon fell into Octavian's control after Antony's retreat from the debacle in the Ambracian Gulf, serious plans for reorganization and administration of the region probably began only after the capture of Alexandria in 30, when the victor was freed from the burden of military operations in the Eastern Mediterranean. Later events at Alexandria—unrelated to, and perhaps more important than, local concerns—may also have influenced the decision to found a Nicopolis near Actium.

The founding of victory cities, whether in one's own name or in honor of a recent military success, is a Hellenistic development that goes back to Alexander the Great and his reputation as the founder of at least twelve cities throughout the conquered territory of the Persian Empire.[124] Roman conquerors in the Hellenistic East had not often imitated this practice. The traditional Roman method was to establish a colony, which often adopted the name of its founder and honored him as the official patron of the city. Veteran soldiers and Roman citizens settled in the newly founded communities to establish political and economic security in the region. Antony, the victor at Philippi, had founded a colony at the site of battle (*colonia Antonia victrix*), which later abandoned its patron and changed its name to the *colonia Iulia Augusta Philippensium*. For Octavian's decision to found a victory city instead of a more traditional Roman colony, however, Pompey offers the only Roman precedent. At least seven cities (including a Nicopolis and a Pompeiopolis) are known to have been founded by the Roman general during his extended and much celebrated campaign in the East.[125] In each of

---

122. For this view, see Purcell, "Nicopolitan Synoecism and Roman Urban Policy," 88–90.

123. For the coinage of Nicopolis, of which little survives that can be securely dated to the Augustan Age, see M. Karamessini-Oikonomidou, Ἡ Νομισματοκοπία τῆς Νικοπόλεως, Βιβλιοθήκη τῆς ἐν Ἀθήναις Ἀρχαιολογικῆς Ἑταιρείας 79 (Athens, 1975), and reviews by C. Kraay, *NumChron* 16, ser. 7 (1976): 235–47, and W.E. Metcalf, *Gnomon* 49 (1977): 632–33. For a new reassessment of the coinage, see *RPC* 1.1:272–73, nos. 1363–67 (and introductory comments).

124. For the evidence on the first Nicopolis, founded by Alexander to commemorate the battle of Issus, and for an informative discussion on the subject of victory cities in antiquity, see J.E. Jones, "Cities of Victory—Patterns and Parallels," in *Nicopolis I*, 99–108, esp. 106 n. 33.

125. Pompey founded a Nicopolis on the border of Armenia Minor to celebrate his victory over Mithridates. Cf. Strabo *Geo.* 12.3.28; App. *Mithr.* 105, 115; Dio 36.50.3, 49.39.3;

these cities, Pompey must have been worshiped as the founder, and cults in his name were established. The founding of these cities seems to be connected with his efforts at this time to be seen throughout the Greek East as the new Alexander.[126] Little is known about Pompey's activities in these cities apart from their initial founding. It is doubtful that the Roman victor had any direct involvement in the cities after his departure. His involvement, in any event, was unnecessary. It was the initiative and responsibility of locals to maintain his cult. Similar motivations to associate himself with the great Macedonian conqueror may have prompted Octavian to found the victory city at Nicopolis.[127] Events at Alexandria support this view.

When Octavian entered Alexandria on the first day of August, Antony had just committed suicide, and the last ruler of the Ptolemies was a captive in her own palace. Plutarch (*Ant.* 80.1) informs us that Areius the philosopher accompanied the victor as he toured the conquered city. When the two entered the gymnasium, Octavian ascended a tribunal that had been erected for the special occasion. Here the Roman conqueror addressed the fearful Alexandrians in a speech that pardoned their city and themselves of all blame in the past conflict with Antony and their queen. Most remarkable about the address was not the benevolent tone or content of the speech but the choice of language. Octavian delivered his words in Greek (Dio 51.16.4). The rhetorical exercise was neither perfunctory nor easy for the Roman victor. Among interesting bits of personal information and gossip about Augustus, Suetonius (*Aug.* 89.1) tells how he never acquired the ability to converse or to compose in the Greek tongue without great difficulty. Whenever he used the language, the Roman biographer adds, he first wrote what he had to say in Latin and then gave it to someone else to translate. We might then wonder why Octavian took the trouble to address the Alexandrians in Greek at all.

Dio supposed that the Roman victor spoke his address to the Alexandrians in Greek because he wanted his audience to understand his gen-

---

Oros. 6.4.7. For the political ambition of Pompey and the practical purpose in the choice of the city's site, see P. Greenhalgh, *Pompey: The Roman Alexander* (London, 1980), 152–53. Other cities founded by Pompey included Pompeiopolis, Neapolis, Magnopolis, Diospolis, Zela, and Megalopolis. See A.H.M. Jones, *The Cities of the Eastern Roman Provinces*, 2d ed. (Oxford, 1971), 157.

126. For Pompey's association with Alexander the Great, see Greenhalgh, *Pompey: The Roman Alexander*, esp. 122–46 and 242 (bibliography).

127. D. Kienast, "Augustus und Alexander," *Gymnasium* 76 (1969): 430–56, has presented a strong and cogent case for the contemporary association between Augustus and Alexander. See also Kienast, *Augustus. Prinzeps und Monarch*, 377, and E.S. Gruen, "Augustus and the Ideology of War and Peace," in *Age of Augustus*, 68–72.

erous words of pardon. This explanation only partially suffices. Certainly if Octavian wished to address the citizens of Alexandria in their native tongue, he could have just as easily allowed another individual—a Roman representative, a local dignitary, or his friend Areius—to declare the words of pardon in the Greek tongue, avoiding either embarrassment or serie is misunderstanding. His choice to make the address in person and in a language rather difficult for him to speak must have been deliberate and meaningful. It was not merely a ceremonious display of clemency. Through his actions and words at the time, Octavian had in mind a much larger audience than the local inhabitants of Alexandria.

Both Plutarch and Dio conclude that the Roman victor's ambition to associate himself with Alexander led to his decision to pardon the city originally founded by the Macedonian conqueror.[128] Plutarch lists this motivation as most important; Octavian's admiration for the city's great size and beauty and his friendship with Areius were secondary factors. Octavian probably made some mention of Alexander in his formal speech that pardoned the city. But this is not his only association with the Macedonian at this time. After his generous words of pardon, Octavian visited the tomb of Alexander and, in a public and symbolic gesture, touched the mummified nose. Whether it is true or not, the story circulated that a piece of the nose broke off, an occurrence that might imply some transference of the special nature and character of the former Greek conqueror of the East to his later Roman successor. That such a tale survives suggests that Octavian wished others to believe it. Octavian's intention to place himself as the equal of the Macedonian king is further seen by his curt response to the Alexandrians when they attempted to show him the tombs of the Ptolemies: "I wished to see a king, not corpses."

A far more important and visible sign of the connection with Alexander at this time was the seal of Octavian's signet ring.[129] Octavian first used Caesar's ring, later the sphinx as his own seal. During the war with Cleopatra, the sphinx as a symbol of authority must have seemed a strange irony and embarrassment for the Roman who claimed to be leading Italy against the threat from Egypt. Probably shortly after the capture of Alexandria, Octavian chose to replace the sphinx with the image of the city's founder.[130] The seal served on all official and private documents of Octavian and visibly associated the Greek conqueror of the East with the new leader in Rome.

---

128. Plut. *Ant.* 80.1 and Dio 51.16.4.

129. The best discussion on this subject is H.U. Instinsky, *Die Siegel des Kaisers Augustus. Ein Kapitel zur Geschichte und Symbolik des antiken Herrschersiegels* (Baden-Baden, 1961).

130. For ancient evidence, see Pliny *NH* 37.10 and Suet. *Aug.* 50.

The conquerors had much in common: youth, military glory, and supreme political power. But Augustus' fascination with Alexander was not unbounded. At some later time, the image of the Macedonian conqueror was replaced. The portrait of Augustus signed all imperial epistles and decrees.

On the site where he claimed victory over Antony in what was no more than a mere skirmish of forces just outside Alexandria and a final, desperate effort to thwart the encircling armies of the invading Roman generals, Octavian built a victory city and established quinquennial games. That Octavian built two victory cities is not well known, rarely mentioned, but particularly significant for an assessment of the motivations behind the foundation of the victory city near Actium and its role in Augustan propaganda and politics. The Nicopolis of Alexandria most often appears in relation to its more famous sister city as the later and "other" Nicopolis of Augustus. The reasons for its inferior status are not difficult to understand. Both as a city and as a monument, the Egyptian Nicopolis was a failure; and the city has left little evidence of its existence either in the ancient sources or at its actual site. What prompted Octavian to imitate his actions at Actium and found a victory city near Alexandria, and how should this decision affect an assessment of the role of Actium in the imperial ideology circulated in the Greek East?

The sparse information that survives in the ancient sources about the city can be briefly cited. The victor founded a city on the very site of his victory over Antony and the Egyptian queen and bestowed on it the same name and similar games as those he bestowed on the city he had earlier founded at Actium (Dio 51.18.1). The new settlement was on the sea, "no smaller than a city," the distance of thirty stadia from Alexandria. Because of the construction of the new and grandiose buildings at Nicopolis, including an amphitheater and stadium where the quinquennial games were performed, the Serapium and other ancient sacred precincts were quickly abandoned, and the buildings in the area fell into neglect (Strabo *Geo.* 17.1.10). Unlike the Actian Nicopolis, the victory city at Alexandria does not seem to have addressed any local concern or problem. In his charming history and instructive guide to the ancient Egyptian city, E.M. Forster opined that the boastful Roman victor founded Nicopolis because of a personal dislike of Alexandria.[131] More recent scholars have claimed that Octavian's foundation of Nicopolis was intended to rival the splendid city Alexander had planned but had never seen.[132] Since Augustus does not seem to have taken

---

131. E.M. Forster, *Alexandria: A History and a Guide*, 3d ed. (New York, 1961), 48.
132. See Kienast, *Augustus. Prinzeps und Monarch*, 374.

any serious or overt steps to weaken the prestige or political position of Alexandria (Plutarch stated that Augustus admired the size and beauty of the city founded by the Macedonian conqueror), it seems another explanation for this city is warranted.

Strabo's comment that the Serapium and other ancient sacred places in Alexandria had already become abandoned in his own time because of the construction of Nicopolis is perhaps indicative of Octavian's intentions to replace the antiquated Egyptian rituals with the worship of his own divinity. From the geographer's report of the city and its architecture, it is plausible that Nicopolis was designed not to rival the Egyptian capital but to serve as some kind of suburb to Alexandria—as, for example, the Necropolis.[133] The "city," which Strabo described as "no smaller than a city," may then have been intended to be the sacred area for the celebration of the games in honor of Octavian's Alexandrian victory[134] and perhaps also for a local cult of the victor. This view seems to explain the origins of Nicopolis more reasonably than to claim it as a rival city to Alexandria. Like the ancient sacred precincts, the newly established Nicopolis may have later lost prominence and fell into neglect. The victory city at Alexandria probably lost its original name in the next century, since the elder Pliny (*NH* 6.102) mentions a Juliopolis that was situated on the same canal and at just about the same distance from Alexandria.

In sum, the two victory cities, founded near the site of battles at Actium and also Alexandria, must be understood as closely related, and perhaps even coordinated, events. The decision to build a Nicopolis in northwestern Greece may have been influenced by the victor's prolonged stay in Alexandria (he had entered on the first day of August and may not have left the city until late fall), where he attended to the details and problems of local administration after the death of Cleopatra, collected the riches and jewels from the holiest shrines and the queen's vast treasury as spoils of his victory and adornment for his triumph in Rome, and even spent time clearing out and redigging the canals that interlaced and connected the Egyptian city on the sea. The Roman victor's admiration and emulation of the youthful Macedonian conqueror, the founder of Alexandria, must also have contributed to the ambition of founding his own victory city. Despite Dio's assertion (51.18.1) that Octavian founded the Nicopolis at Alexandria in imitation of his action at Actium, it is plausible that the so-called other Nicopolis

133. For a description of Nicopolis as a suburb, see P.M. Fraser, *Ptolemaic Alexandria*, 3 vols. (Oxford, 1972), 1:28, 2:92 n. 204.

134. For the argument that the games celebrated at Alexandria were not "Actian" as scholars have suggested, see discussion in n. 151 in this chapter.

prompted the "first" and more famous victory city. In any case, it is significant that the Roman conqueror chose to celebrate with similar and equal
honors (a Nicopolis and quinquennial games) two victories over Antony and
the queen, even if the second battle was a halfhearted effort to defend the
Egyptian city from the invading Roman armies. We must consider the nature
and function of the "Actian" games before we may reach any final conclusions about Octavian's intentions in the region that his fellow triumvir,
political rival, and later enemy controlled for more than ten years before the
military outcomes at Actium and Alexandria.

Actian Games

The establishment of festivals and games in honor of Octavian was closely
and conspicuously linked with the institution and practice of his worship in
the cities of the Greek East.[135] In fact, they were part of the same system. The
origins for many of these solemn and festive rituals, known only through the
names of priests and victors on scattered inscriptions, are difficult to assess.
The evidence suggests, however, that the princeps in Rome had little direct
influence on or even knowledge of the supervision of the usual Greek cus-
toms and institutions.[136] For the most part, the organization, maintenance,
and control remained firmly in the hands of local dignitaries. The Actian
games, however, seem to offer a different pattern. Their origin, name, and
status attest to a special interest of Octavian.

The exalted Actian games, celebrated beside the sacred grove of Apollo at
the southern entrance of the Ambracian Gulf, lacked a poet of Pindaric
stature to record the names and deeds of their illustrious competitors. What
survives today of these athletic and musical competitions is only a meager
and inglorious assortment of names and titles that can be gathered from
fragmentary records inscribed on the tombstones of long-forgotten winners.
Our ignorance of the most important aspects of the games is far greater than
any knowledge we possess. And to what little we know we must apply
special caution, in particular, in our assessment and use of the epigraphical

---

135. On the role of the imperial cult in the Greek East, see S.R.F Price, *Rituals and Power:
The Roman Imperial Cult in Asia Minor* (Cambridge, 1984), esp. chap. 5, "Festivals and
Cities," 101—132. Still useful, though some of the conclusions have been refuted by new
epigraphical finds, is the discussion by L.R. Taylor, *The Divinity of the Roman Emperor*
(Middletown, Conn., 1931), esp. chap. 8, 205–23. Cf. also the prudent remarks on the imperial
cult in the Age of Augustus in Bowersock, *Augustus and the Greek World*, 112–21.

136. For a sober discussion of the limited involvement of Augustus in Greek athletic games,
see H. Langenfeld, "Die Politik des Augustus und die griechische Agonistik," in *Monumentum
Chiloniense. Studien zu augusteischen Zeit. Kieler Festschrift für Erich Burck zum 70. Geburtstag,* ed. E. Lefèvre (Amsterdam, 1975), 228–59.

evidence. Virtually nothing of significance has been found in the area of Nicopolis to assist inquiry in this matter; a more revealing excavation of the city still awaits.

Scholarly interest in the Actian games has focused almost exclusively on one point of dispute of dubious significance, namely, the year for the first celebration of the games at Nicopolis. Strabo informs us that Octavian conferred Olympian status, or more specifically an "isolympic status," on the Actian games.[137] The exalted status of the games led Jean Gagé to posit the year 28 B.C.E. as the date for the first official performance of Octavian's "Actian" games and to assume that Octavian intended to rival the fame of the Olympian competitions by the institution of his own games in honor of his victory at Actium.[138] For Gagé, the known occurrence of Olympian games in 28 fixed the date of the Actian games to the same year. Brenda Tidman, however, argued more persuasively that the phrase in Strabo has a technical meaning that refers to the types of competitions, age categories, or prizes[139] and should not be seen as evidence to suggest that Octavian desired to replace the more famous Olympian games. Tidman preferred the following year for the first celebration of the Actian games. And in a valuable study of the various games inaugurated in honor of Augustus, Rudolf Rieks supported Tidman's arguments and also assigned the first celebration of Actian games to 27.[140] In their efforts to assign a specific year to the first celebration of the Actian games at Nicopolis, scholars have been guided by two plausible, but unsubstantiated, suppositions: (1) that the initial celebration of Actian games was closely linked with the official dedication ceremonies of

---

137. Strabo Geo. 7.7.6.

138. Gagé, "Actiaca," 92–100. See also his discussion in Apollon Romain. Essai sur le culte d'Apollon et le développement du "ritus Graecus" à Rome des origines à Auguste, BEFAR 182 (Paris, 1955), 512–13.

139. B. Tidman, "On the Foundation of Actian Games," CQ 44 (1950): 123–25. Other imperial festivals also received the status "isolympic", such as the Sebasta, established by Augustus in Naples. A fragmentary inscription (IvOlympia 56), which records the official title and regulations for the Sebasta festival in Naples, indicates, however, that the Augustan games differed from its Olympic model in events (musical and dramatic competitions were not held at Olympia) and in age categories (a three-tier system of παῖδες, ἀγένειοι, and ἄνδρες was not established at Olympia). For reconstructions of this text and recent bibliography, see SEG XXXVII, 356.

140. R. Rieks, "Sebasta und Aktia," Hermes 98 (1970): 96–116. The most compelling argument, however, is the evidence of Statius (Silv. 2.2.6–12), who speaks of the celebration of Actian games shortly after the Sebasta Romaea in late July or early August of the same year. Since the cycle of the games in Naples can be affirmed by external evidence, Actian games can be assumed to have occurred in a cycle that goes back to 27 B.C.E. On the importance of this evidence, cf. also Tidman, "On the Foundation of Actian Games," 124–25 and R.M. Geer, "The Greek Games at Naples," TAPA 66 (1935): 208–21.

Nicopolis and (2) that the games at Nicopolis were directly influenced by political events and decisions across the Adriatic. The second supposition is potentially more serious—and dubious. Gagé rightly criticized those who sought to call the games of the quinquennial festival, first celebrated during the dedication ceremonies for the Temple of Apollo Palatinus in Rome in 28, by the formal title Ludi Actiaci.[141] Nonetheless, Gagé suggested at least an indirect connection between the ceremonies at Nicopolis and Rome, because he believed the games shared the same cyclical celebration.[142] Others assumed an even greater association. Rieks asserted that the politically significant events of 27 in Rome, namely, the so-called restoration of the Republic and the assumption of the name Augustus, bolster the claim that the official foundation of Nicopolis and the first celebration of Actian games occurred in the same year.[143] Langenfeld speaks of an orchestrated political program in the foundation activities at Nicopolis that Augustus did not pursue elsewhere in the East.[144] These claims require serious reassessment.

The most significant fact known about the Actian games is that they were not an Augustan innovation. The testimony of the only contemporary witness is instructive. Strabo (*Geo.* 7.7.6) informs us that "Actian" games had been traditionally celebrated in honor of the local god by inhabitants of the surrounding area. It is not certain whether the local Actian games were still being performed during the period of the late Republic. It is possible that the institution had fallen into neglect because of the economic and military devastation of the surrounding area. Nonetheless, it is equally possible that the games sacred to Actian Apollo still continued from ancient times into the contemporary Roman period.[145] If the games were still being celebrated at the time of the outbreak of civil war between Antony and Octavian, the solemn and festive rites may have coincided with the clash of the two rivals and their mighty forces in the Ambracian Gulf in 31. We do not know the actual date of the ancient games, but like most athletic contests in the Greek world, they were held in the summer. The encampment of the two armies at Actium during the long month preceding the naval battle perhaps cancelled or postponed the celebration. The local inhabitants may have responded to the victory with the customary celebration (or perhaps renewal) of the an-

---

141. These games of 28 were celebrated in connection with the formal dedication of the Temple of Apollo on the Palatine. For the significance of these games, which were not "Actian" games in either name or type of events, see discussion in chap. 2: "The Temple of Apollo."

142. Gagé, "Actiaca," 96, and *Apollon Romain*, 512–13.

143. Rieks, "Sebasta und Aktia," 110.

144. Langenfeld, "Die Politik des Augustus und die griechische Agonistik," 258.

145. For the evidence of ancient Actia, see Habicht, "Eine Urkunde des Akarnanischen Bundes," *Hermes* 85 (1957): 98–109.

cient games in special honor of Octavian. The occasion of the games may have prompted the victor to bestow his gratitude on the local god. In any event, Octavian must surely have learned of the existence of the sacred games dedicated to Actian Apollo during his stay in the area. As part of his public recognition and offering to the god for his success over Antony, we know that Octavian enlarged the Temple of Apollo and dedicated spoils of his victory. He endowed the ancient games with greater prestige by granting them an "isolympic" status.[146] The local festival now became Panhellenic and quinquennial, joining the roster of competitions and games frequented by every serious athlete and musician in the Greek world.

A large collection of agonistic inscriptions documents the immediate prestige and popularity of the Augustan Actia.[147] Philippus Glyco of Pergamum is the earliest known victor of the recently exalted games in Nicopolis, the winner in perhaps three athletic contests: boxing, wrestling, and the pancratium.[148] The marble stele dedicated to the victor by his native city records the prominence of the Actia where the Augustan games are listed third in order, subsequent only to the Olympian and Pythian games, the most distinguished of the older Panhellenic games. Other inscriptions that can be dated to the Augustan era also place the Actia before the Nemeia, the Isthmia, the Heraia at Argos (often called the Shield), and the Sebasta Romaea of Asia.[149] Some scholars have even suggested that the Actia were almost immediately made part of the traditional *periodos*, the circuit of the

---

146. Strabo (*Geo.* 7.7.6) also tells us that Octavian gave the supervision of the Actian games to the Lacedaemonians, not to the local inhabitants of his new city. The decision may have been designed as a public gesture of gratitude to the newly recognized ruler of Sparta, Eurycles, one of the few Greek mainlanders to support Octavian before Actium. During the battle at Actium, the ship of Eurycles attacked and pursued one of the ships of Cleopatra, which had taken aboard Antony. When Antony demanded who it was that was pursuing him, Eurycles boldly answered his name and birth. For the career of Eurycles, see Bowersock, "Eurycles of Sparta," *JRS* 51 (1961): 112–18. But it is also possible that the control of the Actian games was conferred on the Lacedaemonians before the initial plans or the later dedication of the new community. This may suggest that the first celebration of the newly exalted Actian games may have preceded and may not have been directly related to the foundation and dedication of Nicopolis as scholars have assumed.

147. On the origins, nature, and organization of the Augustan Actia in Nicopolis, see the useful discussion by Th. Sarikakis, "Ἄκτια τὰ ἐν Νικοπόλει," *AE* 15 (1965): 145–62, and the recent summary of the evidence in M. Lämmer, "Die Aktischen Spiele von Nikopolis," *Stadion* 12–13 (1986–87): 27–38.

148. *IGRR* IV, 497; *SEG* XIV, 764; *IvPergamon* 535 (= Moretti, *IAG* 58, and Sarikakis, Ἄκτια 38). Cf. also *anth. Palat.* 7.692 (an epigram by Antipater of Thessalonica) and Hor. *Epist.* 1.1.30, who praises the *membra invicti Glyconis*.

149. *IGRR* IV, 1064 (= Moretti, *IAG* 60, and Sarikakis, Ἄκτια 43) and *CIG* 2723 (= Sarikakis, Ἄκτια 44).

four festivals during the Classical and Hellenistic periods: the Olympia, the Pythia, the Nemeia, and the Isthmia.[150] Epigraphical and numismatic evidence also testifies to the celebration of Actia in cities throughout the eastern Mediterranean, including Perinthus on the Propontis (later called Heraclea); Hierapolis in Phrygia; Neocaesarea in Pontus; Tyre, Damascus, and Antioch in Syria; and even Bostra in Roman Arabia.[151] Such festivals, named after and modeled on the traditional Panhellenic games—most often the Olympics and the Pythia, but later the Actia—are not uncommon during the imperial era and reflect the intense rivalry among Greek cities to attract foreign competitors for local athletic and musical contests. In the beginning of the third century c.e., an unknown flute player records a total of fifty-five victories in more than thirty different festivals, including Olympian games in four cities (Smyrna, Adana, Tarsus, and Anazarbus) and Pythian games in three (Tralles, Laodicea, and Troades).[152] The inscription from Delphi attests to the popularity and proliferation of such imitative festivals, but their origins and

---

150. N.M. Kennell, "ΝΕΡΩΝ ΠΕΡΙΟΔΟΝΙΚΗΣ," *AJP* 109 (1988): 239–51, argues that the itinerary of Nero's tour of Greece in 66/67 was chosen by the sites of the festivals belonging to the *periodos* of the time (Olympia, Pythia, Nemeia, Isthmia, Actia, and Heraia). The epigraphical evidence is not conclusive, and his claims that the Actia belonged to the *periodos* at this time are not persuasive. The inscription of Aurelius Septimius Irenaeus (*IGRR* III, 1012, lines 8–9) belongs to the third century c.e. and cannot be used as evidence for the time of Nero. The other inscription Kennell cites (*IvOlympia* 230) is of an uncertain date, although it probably belongs to the first century c.e. The unusual phrase καὶ τὴν λοιπὴν περίοδον σὺν Ἀκτίοσι in lines 2–3 documents that the Actia were highly regarded at this time, but it also suggests that the games were an addition to, not a formal part of, the traditional *periodos*. For this view, see I.E. Stephanis, "Ἀθλητῶν ἀπολογία," *Hellenica* 39 (1988): 270–90, who challenges the earlier assumptions on the *periodos* in the Roman imperial age by L. Moretti, *IAG*, p. 150, and J. Robert and L. Robert, "Bulletin Épigraphique," *REG* 67 (1954): 113–15. Stephanis offers compelling evidence that the Capitolia and Actia were not part of the *periodos* until probably the late second or early third century.

151. Reisch, *RE* 1.1 (1893): cols. 1213–14 (s.v. *Aktia*), also includes the cities of Thessalonica, Ancyra, Nicomedia, and Sardis, but I have found no epigraphical or numismatic evidence to support these claims. Alexandria celebrated a quinquennial festival, which Augustus had established (Dio 51.18.1), but despite the historian's assertion, it probably did not include Actian games. An inscription from the beginning of the second century c.e. (*IG* XIV, 747 and *IGRR* I, 446 = Moretti, *IAG* 68, and Sarikakis, Ἄκτια 40) records that the games in Alexandria, at least at this time, were not Actian by name, τὸν ἐν Ἀντιοχείαι ἱερὸν πεν[ταετηρικὸν ἀγῶνα]. Scholars have been confused by the mention of the victory in the age category of the παῖδες Ἀκτιακοί. For discussion of this obscure age-group (similarly, παῖδες Πυθικοί, Ἰσθμικοί, and Κλαυδιανοί), see Moretti, *IAG*, p. 159 and, more recently, P. Frisch, "Die Klassifikation der παῖδες bei den griechischen Agonen," *ZPE* 75 (1988): 179–85, who argues that the categories may have been determined not strictly by the contestant's age but by his physical size.

152. *FD* III, 1, 550 (= Moretti, *IAG* 81, and Sarikakis, Ἄκτια 50). "Olympian" and "Pythian" games were held in more than twenty-five different cities of the Greek East. For the epigraphical evidence and a list of these cities, see index 2, Agoni, in Moretti, *IAG*, pp. 278–79.

character are unknown. Some may have been established at the outset as "talent" festivals, where victors would receive substantial monetary prizes, and may have been elevated to the "sacred" rank at a later time by imperial action. Others may have acquired the rights and name of the traditional festivals directly from the original cities, perhaps by the personal intervention of an emperor. For example, Claudius granted the formal petition to establish Olympian games in Antioch when the quinquennial games, which had previously been founded in the city by Sosibius, a local senator and friend of Augustus, were discontinued because of improper administration and corruption.[153] Later, Hadrian founded Olympian games in his honor at Athens, and Commodus established an obscure festival known as the Olympia Comodeia at Sparta.[154]

The establishment of Actia in cities other than Nicopolis may derive from similar circumstances of imperial involvement or approval. Yet, though scholars are inclined to believe that Actian games were founded in Greek cities during the Augustan Age either by the actions of the princeps or by local officials to flatter the new conqueror of the East, it is more likely that the later prestige of the athletic and musical contests, not the glory of the Actian battle or Augustus himself, encouraged cities to imitate the Actia and establish their own games. The evidence from agonistic inscriptions and coins indicates that the Actia in Greek cities other than Nicopolis took place much later than the Augustan Principate and perhaps were not founded in cities until the second and third centuries of this era. The active role of later emperors, particularly Trajan, Hadrian, and Commodus, in the establishment of new festivals and in the imitation of older, traditional festivals in new cities is well documented. For the celebration of Actia in cities other than Nicopolis, the earliest known honorific inscription for a victor belongs to the second half of the second century of this era.[155] Among his multiple victories in the pentathlon, an athlete from Ephesus includes the Actia in Perinthus.[156] More inscriptions have been found from the first half of the third century, when the celebration of such games reached its height during

153. For discussion of these games, see A. Schenk von Stauffenberg, *Die römische Kaisergeschichte bei Malalas. Griechischer Text der Bücher IX–XII und Untersuchungen* (Stuttgart, 1931), 412–43, and C. Millon and B. Schouler, "Les jeux olympiques d'Antioche," *Pallas* 34 (1988): 61–76. The quinquennial games that Sosibius had founded from the generous bequest of his will to his native city were not Olympian.

154. For discussion and evidence of these Olympic games, see A.J.S. Spawforth, "A Severan Statue-Group and an Olympic Festival at Sparta," *ABSA* 81 (1986): 327–31.

155. IvEphesos 2072 (= Moretti, *IAG* 75, and Sarikakis, Ἄκτια 48).

156. The Actia in Perinthus are also known from an inscription from Ancyra (*SEG* XXVII, 843) for the athlete Q. Iulius Dionysius. The date of the inscription is third century, after the death of Caracalla in 217. The marble block breaks off with the listing of Actia in Antioch.

the Severan dynasties.[157] It is also suggestive that the phrase Ἄκτια ἐν Νεικοπόλει becomes common in the epigraphical evidence only after the first century C.E.; inscriptions from the Julio-Claudian and Flavian periods regularly record only the title Ἄκτια, without any specification of a city.[158] Agonistic titulature varied but the regularity of the identifying phrase ἐν Νεικοπόλει from later inscriptions supports the view that the Augustan Actia had many imitators at this time. The numismatic evidence on this subject is less reliable. Coins from Neocaesarea, Hieropolis, and Bostra that depict either the god Apollo Actius or trophies of athletic competitions with the legend AKTIA only date from the beginning of the third century.[159]

Sometime in the late second or early third century, the Actia in Nicopolis began to lose their prestige. The competition was fierce among cities to attract popular athletes to their local festivals, and the imperial "sacred" festivals also increased in number. While the Greek games in Rome, the Neronia, did not survive their eponymous founder, the Capitolia, also held in Rome, in honor of Jupiter Capitolinus, maintained their prestige even after the death and disrepute of Domitian. Later, the Eusebeia at Puteoli, established by Antoninus Pius in memory of Hadrian, challenged the supremacy of all games except the Capitolia and the four traditional Panhellenic games. The honorific inscription of the herald Valerius Eclectus in the third century lists the Actia in Nicopolis below all later imperial games, even the Augustan Sebasta in Naples.[160] A century later, the triumph of

---

157. *FD* III, 1, 555 (= Moretti, *IAG* 87, and Sarikakis, Ἄκτια 51) lists Actia in Neocaesarea, Tyre, and probably Damascus (Φιλίππια Ἄκτια ἐν τῇ πατρίδι). If the Philippia Actia refer to Philip the Arabian (on this, see L. Robert, "Études d'épigraphie grecque," *RevPhil* 4, ser. 3 [1930]: 52), the inscription dates from the middle of the third century. *IG* II² 3169/70 (= Moretti, *IAG* 90, and Sarikakis, Ἄκτια 32) records the victories of the herald Valerius Electus (Ἄκτια ἐν Νεικοπόλει, line 17, and Ἄκτια ἐν Τύρῳ, line 29), whose agonistic career belongs to the middle of the third century.

158. Two inscriptions from the Augustan era provide an official title for the Actian games, Ἄκτια τὰ μεγάλα Καισάρηα: *Milet* 369, lines 9–11 (= Moretti, *IAG* 59, and Sarikakis, Ἄκτια 42) and *IGRR* IV, 1064, line 3; *SGDI* 3660; *ICos* 104 (= Moretti, *IAG* 60, and Sarikakis, Ἄκτια 43). Until the second century C.E., all other inscriptions record only the title Ἄκτια.

159. Frère G. von Papen, "Die Spielen von Hierapolis," *ZN* 26 (1907): 177–81, examines the coin types with the legend AKTIA minted by various cities of Asia Minor. For the coins of Hieropolis, see T. Ritti, *Fonti letterarie ed epigrafiche. Hierapolis. Scavi e Ricerche*, Archaeologica 53 (Rome, 1985), 83–84. For the ancient evidence of the *Actia Dousaria* (or *Dousaria Actia*), Actian games celebrated in Bostra, see M. Sartre, *Bostra. Des origines à l'Islam* (Paris, 1985), 156–58. Sartre, who is reluctant to believe that the games are of Augustan origins, concludes that there is no reliable evidence that the games existed before the beginning of the third century. A Latin inscription from Ostia also testifies to the games (ACTIA APUT BOSTRAM II, *CIL* XIV, 474), but it cannot be dated with more accuracy than after the early second century.

160. *IG* II² 3169/70 (= Moretti, *IAG* 90, and Sarikakis, Ἄκτια 32).

Christianity portended an end to the celebration of pagan festivals in many Greek cities. The sacred games to Apollo had probably already fallen into neglect, for the attempts by the emperor Julian to reestablish the old religion and imperial glory in Nicopolis were short-lived.[161] The Actian games had become a distant memory of athletic prowess and proud competition, and the city of Nicopolis began a slow, long decline until its reemergence in the Byzantine period.

In Augustan Rome, the building of victory cities and the establishment of Actian games must have attracted little attention. No Roman author makes mention of them, and few citizens probably visited the site of victory or witnessed the quinquennial celebration. But Vergil alludes to the future Nicopolis and Actian games in the third book of the *Aeneid*, where Aeneas and his men celebrate Trojan games on the Actian shores.

> mox et Leucatae nimbosa cacumina montis
> et formidatus nautis aperitur Apollo.
> hunc petimus fessi et parvae succedimus urbi;
> ancora de prora iacitur, stant litore puppes.
> ergo insperata tandem tellure potiti
> lustramurque Iovi votisque incendimus aras,
> Actiaque Iliacis celebramus litora ludis.

(3.274–80)

> [Thereafter the cloudy peaks of the Leucadian mount
> and Apollo, feared by sailors, come in our view.
> Here we wearily seek and approach the little town;
> anchors are cast from the prow; sterns rest on the shore.
> Then at last we gain land beyond our expectations,
> we pour libations to Jove and kindle altars with vows,
> and on the Actian shore we celebrate Trojan games.]

Scholars have been troubled by the particulars of Vergil's passage that do not seem to correspond to local geography, literary tradition, and Augustan

---

161. Mamertinus *Grat. Actio Iuliano* 9.2–3: *Urbs Nicopolis, quam divus Augustus in monumentum Actiacae victoriae trophaei instar exstruxerat, in ruinas lacrimabiles prope tota conciderat. . . . Certamen ludicrum lustris omnibus solitum frequentari intermiserat temporis maesti deforme iustiti[ci]um.*

political ideology.[162] First, the epic poet mentions Apollo Leucadius, not Apollo Actius, the local god to whom Augustus attributed his victory in the naval battle. The cult of the Apollo on the island of Leucas, located just south of the mouth of the Ambracian Gulf, was famous in antiquity, but for its dangers to sailors and its attraction to suicidal lovers.[163] Second, the Trojans seem to land here, even though some would prefer either Ambracia, Actium, or the future site of Nicopolis as the "little town" to which Vergil refers. Finally, Actian Apollo is slighted again when the Trojans perform games on Actian shores but offer a lustration to Jove, and not Apollo. Solutions to these problems, if these poetic deviations from tradition are indeed problems, may be found in the specific context of Vergil's epic. The escape from the stormy heights of Leucas (*nimbosa cacumina montis*) belongs to the hurried flight of the Trojans from the Strophades, the islands of the Harpies. In the immediately previous verses, the followers of Aeneas pass safely by the *Neritos ardua saxa* (271) and the *scopulos Ithacae, Laertia regna* (272). The lustral sacrifice to Jove fulfills the prior thanksgiving to the god that had been interrupted by the appearance of Celaeno (222–24). Whatever ancient site Vergil actually had in mind, the "little town" of verse 276 surely must look forward to the mighty Augustan Nicopolis, much like the rustic simplicity of Evander's Pallanteum later gives way to the urban sophistication of Rome. Here Vergil links the wanderings of the Trojans with the fate of Rome and, above all, associates the hero of his epic with the Roman ruler of the world. The passage anticipates the description of the naval battle on the shield of Aeneas at the end of the eighth book. A critical assessment of Vergil's attitude toward Actium and the consequences of the Augustan victory has been postponed until a full treatment of that passage in chapter 5, but the poet's allusion to Nicopolis and the Actian games, though it should not be ignored or discounted, is not evidence to support the claims that Vergil composed the verses from "first-hand knowledge" of games in Rome and that these games celebrated Actium and imitated the model at Nicopolis.[164]

More significant than the poet's allusion is the absence of ancient testi-

---

162. For discussion of the controversy and bibliography, see R.B. Lloyd, "On *Aeneid*, III, 270–280," *AJP* 75 (1954): 288–99, and M. Paschalis, "Virgil's Actium-Nicopolis," in *Nicopolis I*, 57–69.

163. For the confusion between Apollo Leucadius and Apollo Actius, see P.R. Franke, "Apollo Leucadius und Octavianus?" *Chiron* 6 (1976): 159-163 and M. Paschalis, "Virgil's Actium-Nicopolis," in *Nicopolis I*, 67 n. 54. Paschalis cogently argues that the Augustan poets were not confused about matters of geography or cult titles of Apollo. See also discussion in chap. 4: "The Elegist's Defense: Rome's Fear and the Shame of Civil War."

164. For such claims, see Lloyd, "On *Aeneid*, III, 270–280," 297–98.

mony to the active involvement of the princeps in the foundation of Nicopolis or in the organization of the Actian games. Even the Augustan victory city relied on the support of local patrons. Josephus (*Ant. Iud.* 16.148) reports that it was left to the generosity of King Herod to finance the greater part of the public buildings of Nicopolis.[165] Imperial visits to the area are not recorded, and unlikely.[166] Furthermore, no city in Italy or the West, not even those cities with Greek origins and connections, established Actian games. When Augustus later instituted Greek games in Italy (2 C.E.), the games in Naples were officially called the Italica Romaea Sebasta Isolympia, honoring the name and glory of Augustus, not the memory of his earlier victory.[167] The author of the *Res Gestae* makes no mention of these Greek games or his "Actian" commemorative acts or memorials. Their omission is more suggestive than surprising. In contrast, the triumphal celebration and the honors awarded at the time of his victory are amply recorded and offer a better understanding of what steps Augustus had taken in Rome to exalt his success in the naval battle. The proud victor lists his triple triumph and the

---

165. On this subject, see E. Netzer, "Herod the Great's Contribution to Nicopolis in the Light of his Building Activity in Judea," in *Nicopolis I*, 121–28.

166. Despite some elaborate speculations by Rieks, "Sebasta und Aktia," 112, there is no evidence to suggest that Augustus ever returned to the site that gave him victory and established him as sole ruler in Rome. One might expect such a visit to be recorded among the many anecdotes and stories in the life of Augustus. No such visit is mentioned in the sources. Cf. Langenfeld, "Die Politik des Augustus und die griechische Agonistik," 240–41, who is willing to admit that Augustus may have stopped at Nicopolis in 19 B.C.E. on his triumphant return from the East, but who infers from the total silence of the ancient sources that such a visit must not have been exploited for political purpose in official propaganda. Tacitus (*Ann.* 2.53) records a visit to Actium by Germanicus in 18 C.E., but its significance has been misunderstood. As Tacitus relates the story, the visit had little to do with the Actian games, and since the date of the visit was in January (that he entered the consulship at Nicopolis confirms this), it is most improbable that games were held at this time. It is irrelevant and coincidental, if the visit by the new consul occurred in the same year as the games' celebration according to the chronology proposed by Rieks. The coast of Epirus, in particular the area around the Ambracian Gulf, was a regular stop for Romans traveling from Greece to Italy (cf. the evidence collected by Purcell, "Nicopolitan Synoecism and Roman Urban Policy," 74–75). Germanicus was in the area to fit his ships, not to officiate at any ceremony. Also, the suggestion by R. Seager, *Tiberius* (Berkeley and Los Angeles, 1972), 99, that Tiberius had recently sanctioned an act in Rome commemorating the fiftieth anniversary of the battle and that the visit by Germanicus was in some way to herald this celebration, is unfounded. The claim by Grant, *Roman Anniversary Issues*, 58, 61, for the numismatic celebration of the half-centenary of Actium and *Aegypto capta* on Roman coinage is speculative and unlikely. In any event, the fiftieth anniversary would have been two years later in 20 C.E., and even if it had received public recognition, it could bear no relation to the visit by Germanicus. For discussion of the visit in the East by Germanicus and its impact in Rome, see E. Koestermann, "Die Mission des Germanicus im Orient," *Historia* 7 (1958): 331–75, esp. 339; Seager, *Tiberius*, 99; and B. Levick, *Tiberius the Politician* (London, 1976), 154–55.

167. On the establishment and nature of these games, see Geer, "Greek Games at Naples."

number of royal captives whom he led before his chariot (*RG* 4.1 and 4.3); the insertion of his name in the *carmen saliare* (*RG* 10); and the formal closure of the doors of the Temple of Janus (*RG* 13). When Augustus lists the quinquennial vows and games held in Rome for his welfare (*pro valetudine*), voted in the aftermath of his victory over Antony and Cleopatra, there is no association with Actium (*RG* 9). Similarly, when Augustus boasts of his acts of piety toward the gods by the restoration to the temples of the cities in Asia of all the sacred objects and ornaments that Antony (whom he conspicuously does not name: *is cum quo bellum gesseram*) had seized for private gain (*RG* 24), he fails to mention his devotion or offerings to Apollo Actius, the very god to whom he attributed his victory in this war.

In the Greek world under Roman dominion, Octavian's victory at Actium meant the substitution of one ruler for another. The subject peoples of the former Hellenistic kingdoms had long been accustomed to foreign domination and changes in authority even before the Roman expansion and conquest in their territory. The most recent intruder only increased the number and frequency of the changes in authority. The result was a long succession of conquering generals, an annual rotation of governors, and, in the most recent past, a ruinous extension of civil discord from Italy into the East. The Roman governing officials assumed the roles and the privileges of the former kings, dynasts, and rulers, with few changes in the existing system in place, changes that were more superficial than substantial. Octavian inherited what Antony and others before him had accepted to facilitate administration of this vast area. Celebration of victory in the Greek East had a well-established tradition of cults, festivals, and rituals that the victor at Actium adopted. Athletic games and victory cities played an important role in the public actions to herald the name and glory of a new ruler. The exaltation of Octavian's name and his Actian victory served the victor well in his reorganization and settlement of authority in the Greek East; the official recognition and glorification of Actium in this area, however, should not be associated with or mistaken for the consolidation of power and the shaping and reception of the princeps' public image in Rome. The East, with traditions and institutions of homage to a ruler distinct from those practiced in Rome, incorporated the victory at Actium into its own experience and transmitted it in its own manner.

The Augustan Actian monuments—the victory city and the quinquennial games—served imperial priorities and political ambitions, articulating a sharply defined and powerful message of the new leadership in Rome. The Hellenistic world of the eastern Mediterranean once again endured and welcomed a new conqueror and, twice within thirty years, a new Alexander.

The serious and considerable distinctions between the Greek-speaking East and the Latin-speaking West remained, and perhaps increased, during imperial Roman rule. What Augustus initiated, modified, or tolerated in the tradition of Roman and Hellenistic precedents in this region was not transferred to Rome. Or at least not officially recognized. And yet, when it had seemed for a brief moment that the Roman Empire might split apart during the struggle for power between two generals, a hurried naval battle, the defeat of a foreign queen, and the political ambition and foresight of the victor secured a union that endured unimpaired until the violent upheavals of the third century and the reforms of Diocletian. Throughout these long years of stability and sporadic civil strife, the memory of Actium was never forgotten. Transformed into a political myth, ever potent, useful, and attractive, the victory of Augustus constituted the beginnings of imperial rule and bestowed the glory and exalted status of its founder on his successors.[168]

---

168. Of the successors of Augustus, only the emperor Gaius (Caligula) publicly maligned the memory of Actium. He forbade the consuls to perform the officially recognized annual sacrifices on the anniversaries of the naval battles at Actium and Naulochus (September 2 and 3, respectively), because both days exalted the glory of Marcus Agrippa, and because the former battle, in particular, celebrated the ignominious defeat of Antony, his paternal great-grandfather (Suet. *Cal.* 23.1). Of course, the victors were equally his relatives: Augustus, his maternal great-grandfather, and Marcus Agrippa, his maternal grandfather.

Chapter Two

Tuus iam regnat Apollo: Octavian, Apollo, and the Temple on the Palatine

Octavian and Apollo

On the ninth day of October in 28 B.C.E. Octavian dedicated the Temple of Apollo on the Palatine Hill.[1] More than a year had passed since the victor's return from the East and the formal celebration of his triple triumph in Rome. And it had been almost eight years since Octavian defeated Sextus Pompey at Naulochus and expressed his intent to erect the temple to Apollo. Whatever motivations or events (public and private) originally led Octavian to this vow are now widely assumed by scholarly opinion to have yielded to an emergent political ideology following Actium. It has been maintained that at the time of the temple's dedication, the decisive outcome of battle in the Ambracian Gulf inevitably and fundamentally changed the contemporary perception of the new Palatine sanctuary and its divine inhabitant. Octavian, who had earlier shown his personal devotion to Apollo, later desired his temple to be seen as a public offering of gratitude for the god's role in the recent naval confrontation. Although first vowed as early as 36, the Temple of Apollo on the Palatine would become the most conspicuous and prominent testimonial in Rome to Octavian's victory at Actium.

Such is the modern verdict on the public perception and political significance of the temple and its vow, advanced and supported by an impressive array of scholars. The author of the original chapter on the art of the Age of Augustus in the *Cambridge Ancient History* asserted that Octavian dedicated the temple "in thanksgiving for the victory of Actium won by the grace of the god," mistakenly placing the dedication of the temple in the same year as Octavian's celebration of his triple triumph (29 B.C.E.).[2] Perhaps no more than a careless error of chronology, but it may help to explain why so many other scholars have been inclined to associate the temple with the Actian

---

1. VII *Id. Oct.*: *Fasti Arvalium* (CIL I², p. 214); *Fasti Amiternini* (CIL I², p. 245); *Fasti Antiates* (CIL I², p. 249).
2. E. Strong, "The Art of the Augustan Age," *CAH* 10 (1934): 574–75.

victory. Jean Gagé expressed a similar opinion about the public recognition of the Palatine temple at the time of its dedication. In his exemplary study on the introduction of the originally Greek cult of Apollo to Rome and its later development, Gagé examined the historical background of the triumvir's vow of the Palatine temple and explored the significance of the chosen date of its dedication. Giving support to earlier assertions, Gagé declared that the temple to Apollo was perceived by contemporaries in Rome as the most beautiful votive offering of the victory at Actium.[3]

More recently, as a result of the excavations of the temple site in the Palatine area, Paul Zanker was able to explore the political dimensions of Octavian's bold decision to erect a public temple of Apollo beside and adjoining his private residence.[4] The traces of a ramp that directly connected the residence to the court of the temple have been discovered. Through his plans for his private residence on the Palatine and his family mausoleum on the Campus Martius, Octavian already was acting the part of the Hellenistic monarch in Rome. From an examination of the temple's artwork and his interpretations of the choice of statues, style of decoration, and subjects of sculptured reliefs, documented unfortunately more from literary texts than physical remains, Zanker argued that a subtle political message ("veiled metaphors for the defeat of Antony")[5] pervaded the sumptuous temple and its surrounding complex. Though Octavian's new sanctuary to Apollo, as Zanker himself conceded, was not a victory monument, and though the victor was nowhere to be found, the Apollo of the Palatine temple was the Apollo of Actium—an agent of political vengeance, the redemptor of civil war, and the guarantor of peace.

Modern opinion of the relationship between Octavian and Apollo before Actium prejudges the temple on the Palatine. The chief points of the scholarly consensus on this matter can be summed up briefly. During the often contentious period of the Second Triumvirate, Octavian exploited for political advantage a close and personal connection with Apollo. Because of this already well-established relationship and the opportune presence of a local cult to the god at the site of the Actian battle, Octavian recognized the support and allegiance of Apollo in his victory over Antony and the Egyp-

---

3. Gagé, *Apollon Romain*, 524: "le plus bel ex-voto de la victoire d'Actium."

4. P. Zanker, "Der Apollontempel auf dem Palatin. Ausstattung und politische Sinnbezüge nach der Schlacht von Actium," in *Cittá e Architettura nella Roma Imperiale. Atti del Seminario del 27 Ottobre 1981 nel 25° Anniversario dell'Accademia di Danimarca*, Analecta Romana Instituti Danici Supplementum 10 (Copenhagen, 1983), 21–40, and *Power of Images*, 50–53 and 85–89.

5. Zanker, *Power of Images*, 85.

tian queen. The god's temple was refurbished at the site of battle, a victory city built, and quinquennial games celebrated. On his triumphant return to Rome, the victor bestowed a new honor and epithet of the god on the temple that he was about to dedicate on the Palatine.

Speculation on Octavian's ambitions after Naulochus has distorted the interpretation of the temple's vow and its formal dedication eight years later. My inquiry in this chapter aims to dismantle the foundations that have long supported the prevalent assumptions of the so-called political and religious policies of the young triumvir. In the first of two sections, I refute the widely held notion that Octavian was involved at this time in a carefully orchestrated campaign of propaganda to promote a special relationship with Apollo as part of his public image in Rome. Octavian may certainly have acquired a personal attachment to the god at a very early time, but this attachment, whatever its nature and its origin, does not imply that the adopted son of Caesar endeavored to exploit this connection with Apollo to political advantage in Rome during the period of the Second Triumvirate.

The second section of this chapter addresses the circumstances leading to the vow of a new temple to Apollo in 36 and the eventual ceremony of dedication. The decision to erect the sanctuary has often been linked with the naval victory over Sextus Pompey, although no ancient evidence survives to confirm this connection. In any case, it has generally been assumed that the significance of Actium later surpassed the recognition of Naulochus. A publicly recognized and fostered association with either victory, however, is dubious. The date of the temple's dedication in October of 28 suggests that Octavian did not seek to connect the temple or its god in any direct or conspicuous manner with the victory at Actium. I argue that the often repeated claim that "Actian" games accompanied the temple's formal dedication cannot be maintained.

In the years immediately following the Actian victory, it seems that Octavian did not seek to establish or promote the cult of Apollo Actius in Rome. Numismatic evidence reveals official recognition of and perhaps an exalted role for the god in imperial ideology, but the issues that feature a depiction of Apollo Actius (and also of Diana Siciliensis, in allusion to the victory at Naulochus) first circulated more than fifteen years after the naval battle at Actium.[6] The significance of these select coin types must be viewed and

---

6. A depiction of Apollo Actius first appears on an issue of C. Antistius Vetus, one of the *triumviri monetales* of 16 B.C.E. The coin (*RIC*[2] 366, plate 6) depicts the bust of Augustus on the obverse with the legend IMP CAESAR AUGUS TR POT IIX. The reverse depicts the god in a long robe, standing on a platform that is ornamented with what seems to be the beaks of ships and anchors. In his left hand, the god holds a lyre, and in his right hand, he makes a sacrifice from a

judged in the context of the political events and position of Augustus in Rome after 16 B.C.E., when the issues first appeared. The somewhat belated appearance of Apollo Actius on Augustan coinage may indicate a new and more glorified status of the naval victory in the shaping of a public image of the princeps at this time. I explore this suggestion in the epilogue of this book. Nonetheless, these late issues do not support the modern opinion that Octavian sought to exploit the fame of his military success in the formation of his new political regime in the immediate aftermath of Actium or that he associated his defeat of Antony and the Egyptian queen with his newly built temple to Apollo on the Palatine.

Before the end of the first century B.C.E., Apollo had been a god of inconsiderable attention and minor significance in Rome. More than any other member of the Roman pantheon, Apollo maintained his distinctively Hellenic character and proclaimed his origin and legacy through the retention of his Greek name. The first temple to the god in the environs of Rome was erected in the late fifth century when an epidemic spread into the city and surrounding areas. Livy (4.25.3) records the original role and function of the deity by the vow of the new temple.

> Aedes Apollini pro valetudine populi vota est

> [A temple to Apollo was vowed on behalf of the public health]

The Vestal Virgins thereafter invoked the god under the name "Apollo Medicus, Apollo Paean."[7] His temple, built in the Campus Martius, stood just beyond the Porta Carmentalis and outside the *pomerium Romuli*. The "foreign" god could not be allowed in the formal boundaries of the city. In 212 B.C.E. Apollo was honored by the first celebration of the Ludi Apollinares, and three years later the ritual was formally enrolled in the pontifical calendar.[8] Despite the public attention of these games, Apollo remained a

---

patera over an altar. The legend placed above and below the platform offers a dedicatory inscription (APOLLINI ACTIO); In the following year, the mint at Lugdunum circulated issues that included depictions of Apollo Actius and Diana Siciliensis. The double issues continued until 12 B.C.E., dated by the legends IMP X and IMP XII (*RIC*² 170, 173a, 192a, and 196, plate 6). For the significance of the types and the controversy over the identification of Apollo Actius, whether it represents the cult statue of the god's temple near the site of battle or a statue set up in the temple of Apollo on the Palatine, see my discussion in the epilogue.

7. Macr. 1.17.15.

8. For the definitive treatment on the origin and significance of the Ludi Apollinares, see Gagé, *Apollon Romain*, 257–418. Weinstock, *Divus Julius*, 13–14, attributes the rise of

minor deity in Rome until the dedication of his new temple on the Palatine and the emergence of the Augustan Principate.

Sextus, Antony, and Octavian

The special favor that Augustus later bestowed on Apollo is well known and has been much discussed.[9] Most scholars have assumed that a well-established connection already existed between the two long before that momentous day in September of 31. The "miracle d'Actium," as Gagé once called it, was only the final, but most decisive, confirmation to Octavian in his acceptance of this divine patron.[10] The beginnings of this long and famous relationship have been located in the fiercely contested struggle of politics and propaganda that characterized the turbulent ten-year period from Philippi to Actium. During this time, the chief actors in the political drama in Rome were playing various divine roles to satisfy their ambitions and to justify their causes.

For almost six years since the bitter defeat of the Republican cause in 42, Sextus Pompey endeavored to win public support and favor in Italy as the son of Neptune, and his efforts met with considerable success.[11] His coinage in these years preserves his boastful claims. The god and his familiar attribute, the trident, were prominently depicted on issues that displayed Sextus' name and the names of his more distinguished father and older brother.[12]

Apollo's prestige in Rome to Sulla, who credited the god with his victories, most notably, at the Porta Collina in 82 B.C.E., and who carried the god's image with him at all times (Plut. *Sulla* 29.6–7). But as even Weinstock points out, when Sulla founded games in commemoration of his victory and built a temple, Apollo received no public attention. The games were called the Ludi Victoriae, and the temple was in honor of the goddess Venus. Caesar, whose family had ancestral ties with Apollo, also did little to advance the god's recognition in Rome. Such contemporaries as Catullus, Lucretius, and Cicero rarely mention the god, and as Weinstock admits, Apollo appears mostly as a Greek god.

9. On this subject, see O. Immisch, "Zum antiken Herrscherkult," in *Aus Roms Zeitwende. von Wesen und Wirken des augusteischen Geistes*, ed. O. Immisch et al. (Leipzig, 1931), 1–36; W. Deonna, "Le trésor des Fins d'Annecy," *RevArch* 11, ser. 5 (1920): 112–206; L.R. Taylor, *Divinity of the Roman Emperor*, 118–21, 131–34; P. Lambrechts, "La politique 'apollinienne' d'Auguste et le culte impérial," *NouvClio* 5 (1953): 65–82; Gagé, "Apollon impérial, Garant des *Fata Romana*," *ANRW* II.17.2 (Berlin and New York, 1981), 561–630; and E. Simon, *Die Portlandvase* (Mainz, 1957), 30–44.

10. Gagé, *Apollon Romain*, 480.

11. See discussion by Taylor, *Divinity of the Roman Emperor*, 120–21, for a list of the references in the ancient sources in regard to the claim of Sextus. Cf. also appendix 2 in A. Gowing, *The Triumviral Narratives of Appian and Cassius Dio* (Ann Arbor, Mich., 1992), 309–10. For an assessment of Sextus Pompey and his activities at this time, see full treatments by M. Hadas, *Sextus Pompey* (New York, 1930) and B. Schor, *Beiträge zur Geschichte des Sextus Pompeius* (Stuttgart, 1978). Cf. Syme, *Roman Revolution*, 227–42.

12. On the coinage of Sextus Pompey, see the study by J. DeRose Evans, "The Sicilian Coinage of Sextus Pompeius (Crawford 511)," *ANSMN* 32 (1987): 97–157.

Sextus' virtual occupation of Sardinia and Sicily, his pirate raids along the coast of southern Italy, and his frequent interception of the grain supplies to Rome offered encouragement and refuge for all those who still resisted the established government in Rome—the rebellious, the poor, and the disenfranchised. Attired in a sea-green cloak, Pompey publicly attributed his naval victories and his unchallenged command of the Mediterranean to the favor of Neptune. Dio remarks that Sextus enjoyed such popularity and such a close association with Neptune in the public mind that the triumvirs refused to lead out the god's statue in the procession for the games in 40, because prior occasions had provoked loud applause and manifest signs of approval for Sextus.[13] Their calculated decision to exclude Neptune from the games was a vain attempt to silence the supporters of Sextus; it only infuriated the crowd of urban spectators. An angry and violent mob attacked the magistrates with stones and tore down the statues of Antony and Octavian. Four long years of civil strife in Rome, broken agreements between the rivals for power, and indecisive battles on land and sea followed before the successful outcome at Naulochus and the final blow to the divine claims of Pompey's son.

Unlike Sextus, Antony inherited his first connection with a god. According to an old family tradition of the Antonii, Anton was the legendary son of Hercules, and through him, his descendants in Rome traced their descent.[14] Plutarch reports that Antony enhanced and promoted his resemblance to his fabled ancestor by his manner of dress and by his fondness for jests, wine, and women. Plutarch's account may be authentic, but there is little evidence that suggests Antony sought to gain much political advantage from it in the early years of the Triumvirate. Such claims of divine or legendary ancestors were well established and common among a select group of Roman families. Antony's actions may have been conspicuous in Rome, owing to his personality and prominence, but they should not be seen as politically motivated except to the extent that they added greater prestige and public attention to his name. In this, however, Antony was following an accepted and long-practiced Roman tradition. The numismatic evidence suggests the same conclusion; his early coinage alludes to his distinguished heritage in only one issue.[15] While the coinage attests to his family's well-known association

---

13. Dio 48.31.5.

14. Appian *BC* 3.16, 19; Plut. *Ant.* 4.1–3, 36.4, and 60.3. On Antony's efforts to associate himself with Hercules, see C.B.R. Pelling, ed., *Plutarch: Life of Antony* (Cambridge, 1988), 124, who suggests that the Greek biographer may have exaggerated Antony's "Herculean behaviour" to suit his own narrative construct and themes.

15. Crawford, *RRC* 494/2 (42 B.C.E.) is the only example of a direct association of Antony with Hercules on his coinage. The majestic lion with the sword in his paw on the reverse of

with the god, its evidence cannot allow us to maintain that Antony promoted unprecedented associations with a god at this time.

Following the victory at Philippi, Antony traveled to Ephesus, and there established a new and more powerful alliance with Dionysus—the Hellenistic East had long been accustomed to the deification of earthly kings.[16] Later, in Athens, Antony, in the company of his wife Octavia, was called the New Dionysus, and the Panathenaic festival was named in his honor.[17] Finally, in Alexandria, Antony played a similar role, though now in the union with the foreign queen. Once settled in the Hellenistic East, Antony exploited for his political advantage the past tradition of Roman governing officials in this region and received the excessive adulation of a subject people. If Antony surpassed the precedents of former Roman generals— beginning with Flamininus, victor over Philip of Macedon in the second century B.C.E.—it must be admitted that no Roman before Antony, neither Caesar nor Pompey, had held such absolute power in this wide expanse of land, established virtual residence there, and directed its administration for so long a period.[18]

In Rome, Octavian was in a different and more difficult position. From the start of his political career, Octavian realized that his future position depended solely on his connection with Julius Caesar. Adopted posthumously in Caesar's will, the youth had neither a strong following nor an attractive reputation. The name of Caesar alone determined his chance for success and influence among the veterans and the urban population. His early military actions claimed their motivations, and sought justification, in vengeance.

Qui parentem meum trucidaverunt, eos in exilium expuli iudiciis legitimis ultus eorum facinus, et postea bellum inferentis rei publicae vici bis acie. (*RG* 2)

[Those men who slaughtered my father I drove into exile and avenged their crime through legal proceedings, and later I twice defeated them in battle when they brought war on our country.]

533/1 (ca. 38) may be some allusion to the god, but its type is extraordinary and is probably derived from Eastern influence.

16. Plut. *Ant.* 24.3–4, 26.1–3, 60.2–3, 75.3–4. For full citation of ancient sources and discussion, see comments by Taylor, *Divinity of the Roman Emperor*, 121–30. Cf. also Pelling, *Plutarch: Life of Antony*, 179–80, 304, and E.G. Huzar, *Mark Antony: A Biography* (Minneapolis, 1978), 194–96, 297 n. 20.

17. *IG* II², 1043, 22–23; Plut. *Ant.* 33.6–7; Dio 48.39.2.

18. For discussion of the divine honors awarded to Flamininus in Greece and other Republican precedents for the actions of Antony in the East, see Taylor, *Divinity of the Roman Emperor*, 35–57.

Only two years after the victory at Philippi, Octavian celebrated the capture of Perusia by the public execution of three hundred Roman senators and knights in a public ceremony in honor of Divus Julius.[19] Though the horrific account undoubtedly derives from a hostile tradition with literary embellishment and slanderous exaggeration, the story must derive from an actual incident.[20] A cult to his father had already been established in Rome, and a temple was planned. On all official documents since the deification of Julius, Octavian boasted of his paternal inheritance and proclaimed what was at that time the extraordinary and unprecedented title of *divi filius*. Many contemporaries were surely not impressed by the vaunting claims, but Octavian's ambitions and political steps to associate himself with the prestige and partisans of Caesar ultimately proved successful. Neither surviving inscriptions nor contemporary coinage indicate any prominence given to Apollo by Caesar's son at this time. Nonetheless, a connection between Octavian and Apollo is widely believed to have originated, developed, and prospered during this period. The problem can be framed succinctly in two questions: What constitutes the evidence for this relationship during the period? And how valid and reliable is this evidence, certainly influenced by the subsequent events and the verdict of posterity, for assessing Octavian's political ambitions and actions at this time?

Banquet of the Twelve Gods

In her monograph *The Divinity of the Roman Emperor*, Lily Ross Taylor briefly listed some early connections between Apollo and Octavian.[21] Though she asserted that Octavian was not actually claiming to be identified with Apollo at this time, her work has often been cited to support this view. The most well-known example of Octavian's early attempt to claim Apollo as his divine counterpart on earth involves the famous scandal of a private feast, known publicly as "the banquet of the twelve gods." The episode has been judged without exception as the first manifest and certain sign of the political connection between Octavian and Apollo. Suetonius provides the only information about it, and his account includes an anonymous, but popular, epigram probably composed shortly after the notorious occasion.

Cena quoque eius secretior in fabulis fuit, quae volgo δωδεκάθεος vocabatur; in qua deorum dearumque habitu discubuisse convivas et

---

19. Suet. *Aug.* 15; Dio 48.14.4; Sen. *de Clem.* 1.11.1.

20. For discussion of the political significance of this action, see Weinstock, *Divus Julius*, 398–99.

21. Taylor, *Divinity of the Roman Emperor*, 118–21; see esp. 119: "We need not suppose that Octavian was really claiming to be identified with Apollo. But it is easy to identify a man with his protecting god."

ipsum pro Apolline ornatum non Antoni modo epistulae singulorum nomina amarissime enumerantis exprobrant, sed et sine auctore notissimi versus:

Cum primum istorum conduxit mensa choragum,
   sexque deos vidit Mallia sexque deas,
impia dum Phoebi Caesar mendacia ludit,
   dum nova divorum cenat adulteria:
omnia se a terris tunc numina declinarunt,
   fugit et auratos Iuppiter ipse thronos.

Auxit cenae rumorem summa tunc in civitate penuria ac fames, adclamatumque est postridie: Omne frumentum deos comedisse et Caesarem esse plane Apollinem, sed Tortorem, quo cognomine is deus quadam in parte urbis colebatur. (*Aug.* 70)

[There was also his banquet, a private affair, which became public gossip and was commonly called "The Banquet of the Twelve Gods." The guests reclined in the attire of the gods and goddesses, and Octavian himself dressed up as Apollo. Not only Antony in his letters, who maliciously listed the names of the individuals present, reproached him, but also the following well-known anonymous verses:

As soon as the feast of those scoundrels hired a director,
   and Mallia beheld the six gods and six goddesses,
while Caesar played the impious, fallacious role of Phoebus
   and while he dined on new adulteries of the gods,
all the divinities withdrew themselves from the earth,
   and Jupiter himself fled from his golden throne.

The scandal of the banquet was aggravated because of the harsh times and famine in the city, and on the following day there was the cry that the gods had eaten all the grain and that Caesar was surely Apollo, but Apollo the Torturer, a name under which the god was worshiped in a certain part of the city.]

The exact date and occasion for the banquet are not known, but Taylor suggested the period shortly after the peace of Brundisium in 40.[22] This seems likely, since the report of famine and hunger in the city indicates a

---

22. Taylor, *Divinity of the Roman Emperor*, 119.

time when Sextus Pompey held control of the seas and had seriously inter-rupted the shipments of grain from Sicily. In general agreement with this opinion, Kenneth Scott attempted to identify the banquet more specifically with the festivities in honor of the marriage of Octavian and Livia, which occurred sometime in late December of 39 or early January of 38.[23] Scott believed that the curious reference to the feasting on *nova divorum . . . adulteria* in the epigram alluded to the scandalous ceremony and notoriety of the betrothal of Octavian and Livia, where Tiberius Claudius, the recently divorced husband of the new bride, formally gave away his former wife and even participated in the nuptial revelry, although Livia was at that time six months pregnant.

The odd circumstances of the marriage undoubtedly aroused gossip at the time, which was later revived by Antony when the sanctimonious Octavian reproached him for his desertion of his wife, Octavia (Octavian's sister), and his affair with the Egyptian queen. The suggestion of *adulteria* in the epi-gram would seem to imply a date before Octavian and Livia were actually married. Their presence together at a banquet, even a private one, if Livia were still married to Tiberius and visibly pregnant with his child at the time, would have given greater cause for criticism and scandal. We might also question whether the reception for Octavian's marriage, however lavish and grand, would involve the masquerade of guests as Olympian gods and god-desses.

Despite the uncertainties concerning the date and circumstances of the banquet (for example, no one seems able to explain the meaning of "Mallia" in the epigram), the episode should not affect the assessment of Octavian and his political machinations during this period. Several factors tend to suggest its insignificance in the matter of the political "Apollonism" of the adopted son of Caesar. Above all, we should keep in mind that this banquet was a private affair, as the words of Suetonius (*cena . . . secretior*) clearly reveal. Octavian and his guests certainly had not intended their grand affair to be a matter of public knowledge or personal rebuke. Octavian, presumably the host of the party, was not using the festive occasion to make any public declarations, whether of political or religious import. Furthermore, Octa-vian was not alone in this masquerade party, but presumably eleven guests also played their selected roles to complete the circle of the twelve Olym-pians. If Octavian played the role of Apollo, one may wonder if someone had the honor of being a Jupiter or Juno. It should be remembered that Suetonius reports that Antony "maliciously" included in his letter the names

---

23. K. Scott, "The Political Propaganda of 44–30 B.C.," *MAAR* 11 (1933): 30–31.

of all the guests on this occasion. We do not know the identities of the others who participated in the irreverent costume party and merriment, but we hear of no other guest accused of divine aspirations at this time.

The phrase *impia . . . Phoebi . . . mendacia* in the epigram might suggest a "charge of impiety," perhaps in reply to similar accusations directed by Octavian against Antony for his impersonation of Dionysus throughout the East.[24] The general tone of the verses supports this interpretation. But it is not likely that such "impious" actions of Octavian would have caused any notice or provoked the outrage of the public if the city had not been suffering the severe pains of a famine, which many in Rome may have attributed to Octavian and his hostile relations with Sextus Pompey. Arrogance and cruel indifference to the miseries of his fellow citizens aroused the anger of the urban population against Octavian, and his lavish private banquet at a time of such public distress was much more disturbing to the citizens of Rome than the fact that he and his friends had dressed up as the twelve divinities of Mount Olympus. The context of the passage in Suetonius' narrative suggests its meaning and importance to the Roman biographer. The episode of the banquet is introduced as one of the selected examples of the *variorum de-decorum infamiam* of Octavian's youth (*Aug.* 68). It is significant that there is no mention of another attempt by Octavian to claim a special association with the god. Suetonius continues his narrative with similar charges of arrogance and cruelty directed against Octavian, owing to the young trium-vir's willingness to proscribe individuals because of his own special fondness for Corinthian vases. "*Pater argentarius, ego Corinthiarius*" was written on one of his statues during the period of the proscriptions.[25] The irate and hungry mob did not refrain from addressing the new authority in Rome as Apollo after initial news of the banquet spread but not without adding the mocking epithet "Tortor" to his title.

Conclusions on Octavian's motivation and the episode's initial signifi-cance seem uncertain and speculative. It may be asserted with more assur-ance that the "Apollo" episode in the early years of Octavian's climb to power was a relatively minor affair that Octavian had certainly not intended as an overt or public declaration of his devotion or special relationship to the god, and that he must have later regretted the incident's unexpected conse-quences. His private display may have provoked some initial resentment among the city's unfortunate, but the incident did not acquire political consequence until his enemies later made use of it to substantiate the allega-

---

24. Scott, "Political Propaganda of 44–30 B.C.," 32.
25. Suet. *Aug.* 70.2.

tions of a young upstart's arrogance. While we need not challenge the story's authenticity, Octavian's masquerade at an expensive dinner party does not substantiate the claim that the triumvir had already taken serious political steps in Rome to promote his association with Apollo in the public eye.

Watchword at Philippi

The report in the ancient sources that the god's name was given as a watchword before the battle at Philippi might also seem to document the opinion of an early public association between Octavian and Apollo. The story survives that Brutus predicted his own defeat and death on the battlefield by a fateful exclamation of a Homeric verse at his birthday celebration in Athens shortly before the decisive confrontation at Philippi.[26]

> ἀλλά με μοῖρ' ὀλοὴ καὶ Λητοῦς ἔκτανεν υἱός.
>
> (*Iliad* 16.849)

[But destructive fate and the son of Leto have slain me.]

Later, the name of Apollo was given as watchword at Philippi and proved the recitation of the Homeric verse prophetic. Valerius Maximus (1.5.7) attributes the watchword to the side of Octavian and Antony, and most modern scholars agree.[27] But Plutarch, who also reports the story, confirms that some historians recorded that Brutus, not the triumvirs, chose the name of Apollo as the watchword for the second battle at Philippi.[28] The detail of his account and his reference to sources, although unnamed, seem to support Plutarch's version. The error of Valerius is easy to explain. The defeat of the Republican party at Philippi and the later and well-known association of Apollo with Augustus at Actium perhaps contributed to the belief that Apollo supported the cause of Octavian in his earlier battles. Because of his own avowed regard and bias for the family of the Caesars, Valerius may have simply refused to accept the association of Apollo with the man whom he

---

26. Val. Max. 1.5.7; Plut. *Brut.* 24.4–7; Appian *BC* 4.134.

27. Taylor, *Divinity of the Roman Emperor*, 118–19; Weinstock, *Divus Julius*, 15; and J. Moles, "Fate, Apollo, and M. Junius Brutus," *AJP* 104 (1983): 249–56. A. Gosling, "Octavian, Brutus and Apollo: A Note on Opportunist Propaganda," *AJP* 107 (1986): 586–89, however, contends that it was only after Philippi that Octavian took over the association with Apollo previously heralded by Brutus.

28. Plutarch does not offer any names. Asinius Pollio, Messala, and Livy all included praise of Brutus in their works (Tac. *Ann.* 4.34). Plutarch may also have derived information from the *Memoirs* of Brutus, written by Bibulus (Plut. *Brut.* 13).

earlier charged with parricide.[29] Numismatic evidence, however, strongly suggests that the Liberators, the party of Brutus and Cassius, and not the Caesarians, Antony or Octavian, were more closely associated with the god at this time.

The coinage of the Liberators has surprisingly attracted sparse attention from both numismatists and historians. The most notable exception is the remarkable issue of Brutus with the depiction of the pileus between two daggers.[30] With its striking legend of EID(ibus) MAR(tiis), it is one of the very few coins to merit any notice in the ancient sources.[31] When the followers of Brutus and Cassius fled from Rome after the sudden coalition between the former rivals for Caesar's legacy, they began to issue coinage in various mints throughout the East. The figure of Libertas, crowned with a diadem and veiled, broadcasted the claims of their propaganda.[32] The reverse types of these issues displayed the traditional symbols of the god Apollo, such as the tripod, laurel branch, and lyre. This fact and the occurrence of Apollo himself on other issues have led some scholars to presume a close affinity between Libertas and Apollo.[33] The connection between the two is obscure, if such a connection indeed existed at this time. More certain is the prominence of Apollo and his emblems on the coinage, a prominence indicating that the god had been clearly identified with the cause of Brutus at this time.

The coinage of the triumvirs offers an interesting comparison. The four moneyers of 42 B.C.E. issued a large series of aurei and denarii that displayed portraits of the three new rulers in Rome, exalted by an array of divine figures.[34] Of these deities, Venus and Mars are the most prominent.[35] Apollo appears on only two different issues (Crawford, *RRC* 494/22 and 23, aureus and denarius of the same issue, and 494/34). Apollo's twin sister, Diana, and

---

29. For such an opinion of Brutus by Valerius Maximus, cf. his prior remark before the report of the Homeric verse: *M. etiam Bruti dignus admisso parricidio eventus omine designatus est . . .* (1.5.7).

30. Crawford, *RRC* 508/3.

31. Dio 47.25.3.

32. Crawford, *RRC* 498 and 499, aurei of Cassius with obverse portrait of Libertas. Reverse is tripod with cauldron, decorated with two laurel branches.

33. Crawford, *RRC*, vol. 2, p. 741 n. 6. The passages of Servius and Macrobius, cited by Crawford (both late and unreliable), comment on the relationship between Apollo and Liber, not Libertas. Cf. M.L. Clarke, *The Noblest Roman: Marcus Brutus and His Reputation* (Ithaca, 1981), 142 n. 15, who also questions Crawford's assertion of a link between Apollo and Libertas at this time.

34. For the most comprehensive study of this series, see Buttrey, *Triumviral Portrait Gold of the Quattuorviri Monetales of 42 B.C.*

35. Crawford, *RRC* 494/6, 34, 42, and 43 (Venus), and Crawford, *RRC* 494/7, 8, 9, 16, 17, and 18 (Mars).

Venus are featured on the reverse types. Octavian's name is not present on either issue. More significant for their political associations and claims are issues that link the triumvirs with deities or symbols representing victory, good fortune, and concord. The figure of Hercules appears on an issue of Antony, the Vestal Aemilia on an issue of Lepidus; Venus and Aeneas are the only divine personages associated on the coinage of Octavian at this time. Only one issue honors Apollo on the coinage of Caesar's son (and even this identification is uncertain) until the appearance of Apollo Actius on an issue from Rome first minted as late as 16 B.C.E.[36] Though the numismatic evidence is not conclusive (and demands closer inspection), it tends to support the report in Plutarch that Brutus and the Liberators adopted Apollo as their protecting deity. Octavian's much later affiliation with Apollo would thus explain the passage in Valerius Maximus and the inclination of modern scholars to cite this incident as evidence of an early relationship.

Apollo and Atia

Suetonius (*Aug.* 94.4) records the tale of the seduction of Octavian's mother by a snake in the temple of Apollo. Late in the night, Atia entered the temple to perform some solemn service to the god and later fell asleep along with the other women who accompanied her. As Atia slept, the god, in the guise of a snake, came up beside her and impregnated her. When she awoke and purified herself the next morning, strange marks, resembling the very colors of the snake, immediately appeared on her body and could not be removed. Ten months later, a child was born, and Apollo was judged the father. The Roman biographer claims to have found the story in an obscure work, the *Theologumena*, by Asclepias of Mendes, about whom virtually no information is known. Asclepias may have been a contemporary of Augustus, and if this is so, it is surprising that no other contemporary alludes to the tale. Suetonius does not indicate a date or explanation for the story's origin. Dio Cassius (45.1.2) reports a similar tale of a supernatural birth that is perhaps suggestive of a common source. The Greek historian, however, places the story in his narrative of Caesar's deliberations to choose Atia's son as his successor. If Dio's report contains any truth, the stories of Octavian's birth may have been started by Julius Caesar to promote his future heir, and an upstart Octavian may have later allowed them to circulate to enhance his new position in Rome after Caesar's death.

---

36. *RIC²* 272. The obverse offers no legend and depicts a youthful male figure with locks of hair along his neck and a laurel wreath. The reverse portrays a veiled man who drives a team of oxen, perhaps representative of Octavian's role in the foundation of colonies. See my discussion in chap. 1: "The Coinage of the Victor."

Stefan Weinstock, who briefly examined the nature of the relationship between Apollo and the dictator Caesar in his comprehensive and stimulating analysis of the cult of the deified Julius, concluded that Atia's story was the "divine legitimation" of Octavian's political succession, and he credited this initiative of Julius for the later popularity of Apollo in the Augustan Age.[37] His conclusions are based not on Dio's authority, which he rightly questions, but on two epigrams of Domitius Marsus, an Augustan poet perhaps patronized by Maecenas and later admired by Martial. The epigrams are found together in the *Epigrammata Bobiensia*, preceded by a brief identification of their author and subject.[38]

Domitii Marsi de Atia matre Augusti:
Ante omnes alias felix tamen hoc ego dicor,
    sive hominem peperi femina sive deum.

(Epigr. Bob. 39)

[By Domitius Marsus about Atia, the mother of Augustus:
And so I am called fortunate above all women,
    whether I, a mortal woman, gave birth to a man or god.]

Hic Atiae cinis est, genetrix hic Caesaris, hospes,
    condita; Romani sic voluere patres.

(Epigr. Bob. 40)

[Here the ashes of Atia, here the mother of Caesar, stranger,
    is buried; thus the Roman fathers decreed.]

The date of the two epigrams remains the decisive factor. Atia died in the second half of 43 B.C.E., and Dio (47.17.6) reports that she was honored with a public funeral. Weinstock supposed that the funerary epigram to Atia (*Epigr. Bob.* 40) belonged to the period of mourning shortly after her death, and that the curious epigrammatic couplet that alludes directly to the divinity of Octavian (*Epigr. Bob.* 39) might be even earlier. Such an early date for either epigram by Domitius Marsus, however, is improbable. First, the claim of Atia's divine insemination would be striking if voiced during Octavian's still precarious political position in the early 40s. The young Caesar's sup-

---

37. Weinstock, *Divus Julius*, 14–15.

38. For text and commentary on the epigrams, see Courtney, *FLP*, 304–5, and D. Fogazza, ed., *Domiti Marsi Testimonia et Fragmenta* (Rome, 1981), 25–28, 44, who provides a useful bibliography on the epigrams (pp. 12–13).

port and reputation at this time derived from his adoptive and deified father, not from his mother or her surreptitious lover. Second, what little we know of Domitius Marsus' poetic career (Ovid *Pont.* 4.16.5 includes him in a list of contemporary poets, though he is deceased) suggests a period after the political ascendancy of Augustus, when the divinity of the princeps was a familiar theme of the poets, exploited as a novel expression of adulation or an empty and vainglorious boast.[39] It is also likely that the epigrams may have been part of a longer poem or a thematic collection.[40]

In any case, the origin of the stories that associated Apollo with the birth of Augustus should not be restricted to an early period and certainly should not be confined to Caesar's dictatorship. The immediate aftermath of Actium is a more attractive possibility. At this time the victor first received extravagant praise from the poets, and stories may have circulated in Rome about his extended stay in Alexandria and his celebrated visit to the tomb of the famous Macedonian conqueror.[41] The legends surrounding the birth of Alexander and the nocturnal visit provide an impetus for the similar tale of Atia and the snake. The story of a divine parent may also have developed in the final years of the Augustan Principate, when deification seemed imminent and only awaited the death of the aged princeps. In any case, Apollo replaced Zeus Ammon in the role of the divine father. The substitution of Apollo for Zeus testifies to the relationship between Augustus and the god, but it should not compel us to locate the origins of these claims as far back as the dictatorship of Caesar or even the period of the Second Triumvirate.

Apollo and the Poets

Contemporary poetry might seem to be the most reliable source of documentation for an early relationship between Apollo and Octavian. At least one scholar has voiced the bold opinion that Caesar's son at this time "was . . . letting the poets under his patronage term him the son of Apollo, the god of rational wisdom and beneficence to men."[42] Yet if one excludes

---

39. For discussion of Domitius Marsus' life, see Fogazza, *Domiti Marsi Testimonia et Fragmenta*, 15–17. On the varied approaches taken by poets on the topic of Augustus' divine nature and metamorphosis, see P. White, *Promised Verse: Poets in the Society of Augustan Rome*. Cambridge, Mass., 1993, 169–82.

40. Courtney, *FLP*, 304–5, is inclined to believe that *Epigr. Bob.* 39 is only a couplet of a longer composition and that both epigrams are literary exercises or showpieces rather than political documents of propaganda.

41. See my discussion in chap. 1: "Monuments in the East: Victory Cities and Actian Games."

42. Huzar, *Mark Antony: A Biography*, 193–94, 297 n. 17. As evidence of this extraordinary praise of the poets, she cites only Vergil's first eclogue (verses 7 and 41–43), where the *iuvenis*, not named by the poet, is called a *deus*.

for the moment the later role and importance of Apollo in the victory at Actium, any explicit connection between Octavian and the god is conspicuously absent. When the Augustan poets allude to the divinity or posthumous deification of Octavian, they do not mention any connection with Apollo.

In the opening of the *Georgics*, recited to the victorious Octavian on his return to Italy after Actium, Vergil wonders how he may invoke the son of Caesar (lines 24–42). His place among the gods is assured, but not his office. The poet does not attempt to liken the mortal to Apollo or to any figure of the divine council. Nor does he compare his exploits to any of the illustrious heroes whose services on earth for humankind earned them recognition in heaven. Pollux, Hercules, Bacchus, or Quirinus are among those gods whom Horace later offers to Octavian as examples.[43] For the poet of the *Georgics*, the youth would undoubtedly join the company of the immortals, but not as the son of Apollo. Later, in the inaugural verses of the *Georgics'* third book, Vergil offers to erect a temple for Octavian, a temple of song and praise to honor the conqueror of Trojan descent (lines 16–39). The extraordinary passage indicates a late date for the collection of four books, since Vergil alludes to the naval victory at Actium and the conquest of Egypt.[44]

atque hic undantem bello magnumque fluentem
Nilum ac navali surgentis aere columnas

(*Geor.* 3.28–29)

[And here too billowing with war and flowing greatly
the Nile and the columns rising with brazen prows]

Again we might expect to find here some allusion to the youth's special relationship with Apollo, especially when Vergil begins the book with an invocation of rustic deities that includes an allusive Callimachean reference to the god by the phrase *pastor ab Amphryso* in line 2. The only divinity of the poet's temple, however, will be Octavian.

in medio mihi Caesar erit templumque tenebit.

(line 16)

[I will have Caesar in the middle and he will possess the temple.]

---

43. Hor. *Odes* 3.3.9–18, 3.14.1–4, and 3.25.1–6.
44. For the date of the poem and commentary on the passage, see R.F. Thomas, ed., *Virgil, Georgics*, 2 vols. (Cambridge, 1988), 2:36–49.

While Vergil sings of the exploits and future honors of Octavian, his friend and fellow poet is silent. Before the publication of his three books of *Odes* in 23, Horace avoids lavish praise and often direct mention of Octavian. The *Satires* only allude to his powerful position in Rome and perhaps his success at Actium.[45] Among the *Epodes*, the ninth, central piece of the collection captures our immediate attention. The epode, so it has been assumed, celebrates the naval battle at Actium. I offer a close reading of the epode in chapter 3, but it may be noted at this point that the earliest extant poetical document on the battle avoids any suggestion of divine participation in the struggle. There is no recognition of Apollo and his role in the battle found in Horace's epode.

In the aftermath of Actium, when political stability and lasting peace were still only hopes and dreams of a better future, Horace composed the second ode of his first book. The ode begins with a despairing complaint and a dire forecast of doom. The horrors of the past civil wars still haunt the present generation in Rome. The poet implores the gods to bring help because of the ruinous state of affairs. A panoply of divine figures follows in the entreaties—Vesta, Jupiter, Apollo (with no particular attention or prominence), Venus, and Mars—before Horace chooses the son of Maia, who, so he reveals to his audience, has already appeared on earth in the guise of a *iuvenis*, Octavian. The choice of Mercury in the ode is puzzling and much disputed.[46] More significant for our purposes is the decision by a contemporary poet to identify Octavian with a deity other than Apollo. It is suggestive

45. Hor. *Sat.* 1.3.4–5, 2.1.10–20, 2.5.62–64, 2.6.55–56. While one might rightly object that the genre of satire is not suited to encomia, Horace does allude to Octavian's military exploits (*Caesaris invicti res*, 2.1.11; *Parthis horrendus* and *tellure marique magnus*, 2.5.62–64) and lineage (*demissum genus Aenea*, 2.5.63) in two passages from his second book. The consequences of Actium are clear, but it should be observed that Horace fails to mention any relationship with Apollo.

46. The choice of Mercury need not imply any special importance to this god on the part of Octavian. It cannot serve as the evidence of any worship of Octavian as Mercury at this time, as some have argued. For general discussion of the problems concerning the interpretation of this ode, see K. Scott, "Mercur-Augustus und Horaz *c.* I 2," *Hermes* 63 (1928): 15–33; J. Elmore, "Horace and Octavian (*Car.* I.2)," *CP* 31 (1931): 258–63; K. Barwick, "Horaz Carm. 1, 2 und Vergil," *Philologus* 90 (1935): 257–76; E. Fraenkel, *Horace* (Oxford, 1957), 242–51; S. Commager, "Horace, *Carmina* I, 2," *AJP* 80 (1959): 37–55, and *The Odes of Horace: A Critical Study* (New Haven, 1962), 175–94; L.A. MacKay, "Horace, Augustus, and *Ode*, I, 2," *AJP* 83 (1962): 168–77; G. Williams, *Tradition and Originality in Roman Poetry* (Oxford, 1968), 88–97; R.G.M. Nisbet and M. Hubbard, *A Commentary on Horace: Odes, Book 1* (Oxford, 1970), ad loc.; F. Cairns, "Horace, *Odes* 1.2," *Eranos* 69 (1971): 68–88; T. Gesztelyi, "Mercury and Augustus: Horace, Odes I 2, Some Contributions to the Problem of Their Identification," *AClass* 9 (1973): 77–81; P.A. Miller, "Horace, Mercury, and Augustus, or the Poetic Ego of *Odes* 1–3," *AJP* 112 (1991): 365–88; and White, *Promised Verse*, 177–82.

that Horace passed over a connection between Apollo and Octavian without any comment or indirect allusion and explicitly linked the young man with the son of Maia.

While explicit remarks on the divine connection between Octavian and Apollo are lacking in the contemporary poetry (and even in passages where the poets proclaim or allude to the divinity or future deification of Octavian), some still wish to see obscure allusions to this relationship in Vergil's *Eclogues*. Both ancient and modern commentators have long assumed that several vague remarks in Vergil's collection of bucolic poetry may be interpreted as subtle allusions to the poet's great esteem for the young Octavian. Although Vergil does not refrain from the explicit mention of contemporaries and friends throughout his early poetry (most notably, Asinius Pollio and Cornelius Gallus), it is curious that Octavian, whose name does not appear in any of the *Eclogues*, but who receives extraordinary praise in the *Georgics* and in the *Aeneid*, is so often assumed to be the recipient of the poet's attention without any specific or direct testimony in the text.[47]

Eclogue 1 is a notorious crux for scholars who seek to disclaim any suggestion of divine worship of Octavian in Italy at this early time. The unnamed helper of Tityrus, who is called a *deus* by the grateful herdsman in the first eclogue (lines 7, 18, and 42–43), is believed by many scholars to be the young Octavian. Even though the poem functions well without the subtle disguise of a real-life contemporary figure, few seek to dispute the allusion. The role of Octavian has been viewed as critical to the unity of the poem, "a successful integration of the imaginary and the real, of the fiction of bucolic-rustic existence and historical-political reality."[48] It is precisely the youth of this *deus* (*hic illum iuvenem vidi*, line 42) that seems to suggest, if not to demand, an allusion to Octavian. It is pertinent to this inquiry to question the nature and political significance of this *deus* of Vergil

---

47. G.W. Bowersock, "A Date in the *Eighth Eclogue*," HSCP 75 (1971): 73–80, first proposed a later date for the composition of the *Eclogues* when he argued that the unnamed addressee of the eighth eclogue, who is praised for his Illyrian triumph, is not Pollio but Octavian. If this identification is accepted, the poem (and the collection of *Eclogues*) must be dated to 35 B.C.E. or later. For contrary views of Bowersock's dating of the *Eclogues* and a detailed discussion of the subsequent scholarship, see D. Mankin, "The Addressee of Virgil's Eighth Eclogue: A Reconsideration," *Hermes* 116 (1988): 63–76, and J. Farrell, "Asinius Pollio in Vergil *Eclogue* 8," CP 86 (1991): 204–11, who argues more persuasively that the traditional identification of Vergil's addressee in the eclogue should be accepted.

48. Cf. E.A. Fredricksmeyer, "Octavian and the Unity of Virgil's First Eclogue," *Hermes* 94 (1966): 210, who concludes that the eclogue offers a mixture of praise and condemnation of Octavian. Fredricksmeyer argues that the poet is critical of Octavian's involvement in the confiscation of land but at the same time grateful for the youth's almost divine intervention and hopeful for the future.

and to ask whether a young Octavian, especially one who might be associating himself with Apollo at this time, lurks behind this poetic picture.

In the story of the pastoral poem, Tityrus reveals to his friend, Meliboeus, that he has found a benefactor in Rome who has recently secured for him his ancestral plot. In the eyes of the humble herdsman, this man will always be a god.

> namque erit ille mihi semper deus
>
> (line 7)

[for that one to me will always be a god]

The personal pronoun *mihi* is emphatic and telling. Tityrus does not speak the view of the other citizens in Rome; and later in the eclogue, he does not say that all altars, but only his own (*nostra*, line 43), will burn each month in the youth's honor. Even in the poetic setting, the worship of this god by Tityrus is thus only a private expression of gratitude by a herdsman, not a manifestation of public worship.[49] In the Vergilian landscape of *Eclogue* 1, Tityrus represents a grateful herdsman who offers his humble offerings and thanksgivings to his personal benefactor and saviour.[50] Whether or not Octavian is understood as the *iuvenis* who rescues the estate of Tityrus, the eclogue is not evidence for public recognition of Octavian's divinity or even for his worship in Italian cities, and it certainly does not testify to the youth's association with Apollo.

---

49. Some persist in seeing behind the poet's words evidence for the divine worship of Octavian or at least for the beginnings of a Hellenistic ruler cult in Italy. For this view, see W. Clausen, "On the Date of the *First Eclogue*," *HSCP* 76 (1972): 201–5. Appian (*BC* 5.132) records that statues of Octavian were placed in temples throughout the cities of Italy after the outcome at Naulochus in 36. This extraordinary honor reflects the deeply felt gratitude and initiative of individual cities much more than any encouragement or direct supervision by Octavian. It is well known that in later years when his position was more secure, Augustus was especially wary of such adulations. In Rome, when Agrippa sought to place a statue of Augustus in the newly built Pantheon (25 B.C.E.) the princeps refused. Agrippa instead placed a statue of the deified Julius in the temple and put statues of Octavian and himself in the anteroom. Augustus later boasts (*RG* 24.2) that he removed about eighty silver statues of himself from the city, and that from the money he received from them, he dedicated golden offerings in the Temple of Apollo. See the sensible remarks by White, *Promised Verse*, 171–73, who concludes that the *iuvenis* as *deus* is not "a revelation which Tityrus' interlocutor or anyone else is expected to embrace."

50. For similar sentiments and expressions, cf. Lucretius' opinion of Epicurus—*deus ille fuit, deus, inclute Memmi* (*de Rer. Nat.* 5.8)—and Cicero's adulation of P. Lentulus as *parens, deus, salus nostrae vitae, fortunae, memoriae, nominis* (*Red. Pop.* 11) and of Plato as *deus ille noster* (*Att.* 4.16.3).

The messianic fourth eclogue proclaims the birth of a child and the coming of a new Golden Age. After the initial pronouncement that the cycle of ages is about to begin anew and that the Age of Saturn will return, delivered in the solemn tone of an oracular declaration, the reader learns that Apollo is the present ruler.

. . . tuus iam regnat Apollo

(line 10)

[. . . now rules your Apollo]

The ancient scholiasts identified the poet's declaration of the reign of Apollo as foretelling the Augustan Principate and associated the god with its founder.

TUUS IAM REGNAT APOLLO et tangit Augustum, cui
simulacrum factum est cum Apollinis cunctis insignibus.
(Serv. *Comm. in Verg. Buc.* 4.10)

[TUUS IAM REGNAT APOLLO also alludes to Augustus,
whose statue was made with all the features of Apollo.]

quidam hoc loco [line 10] Octaviam sororem Augusti
significari adfirmant ipsumque Augustum Apollinem.
(Serv. *auc. Comm. in Verg. Buc.* 4.10)

[Some claim in this passage that there is an allusion to Octavia,
the sister of Augustus, and also to Augustus himself as Apollo.]

Modern scholars have often followed this interpretation and have accepted the allusion to Octavian. Ernst Bickel has maintained that the remark offers the young triumvir a double honor: Octavian will act as regent while the child comes of age (his own child, of course), and he is identified with Apollo, the god of the *ultima aetas* before the advent of the Golden Age.[51] Others have shared this opinion with equal conviction, though with less critical scrutiny.[52] The text requires closer examination.

---

51. E. Bickel, "Politische Sibylleneklogen," *RhM* 97 (1954): 210.

52. R. Hanslik, "Nachlese zu Vergils Eclogen 1 und 9," *WS* 68 (1955): 18–19, who cites the passage in Suetonius (*Aug.* 70) as evidence of Octavian's adoption of Apollo, accepts the allusion to Octavian and also explains the *deus* of the first *Eclogue* as a reference to Octavian

The eclogue begins in the manner and tone of an oracle. The poet's words are so convincing that some scholars believed them to be a close reproduction, not just a poetic imitation, of an actual Sibylline prophecy.[53] In its opening verses, Vergil speaks of a cyclic order of ages in the world, a conception he may have derived from a conflation of various current beliefs: the Hesiodic account of the four races of metals; the ancient Etruscan or Italic tradition of the ten ages of the gods; and the Eastern apocalyptic tales, whose growing influence had already penetrated Rome at this time. It would be a complicated and futile attempt to separate and identify the individual, often contradictory threads of the distinct religious and literary traditions that Vergil had chosen to borrow and adapt. The poet tells us all we need to know. The most important section of the poem for our purposes begins in line 4.

> Ultima Cumaei venit iam carminis aetas;
> magnus ab integro saeclorum nascitur ordo.
> iam redit et Virgo, redeunt Saturnia regna,
> iam nova progenies caelo demittitur alto.
> tu modo nascenti puero, quo ferrea primum
> desinet ac toto surget gens aurea mundo,
> casta fave Lucina: tuus iam regnat Apollo.
> teque adeo decus hoc aevi, te consule, inibit,
> Pollio, et incipient magni procedere menses.
>
> (*Ecl.* 4.4–12)

> [The final age of the Cumaean song now has come;
> the great order of the centuries is born anew.
> Now returns the Virgin, returns the reign of Saturn,
> now a new generation is sent down from lofty heaven.
> Only may you, on the newborn child under whom the iron race
> first will cease and a golden race rise throughout the world,
> look with kindness, chaste Lucina: now rules your Apollo.
> And under your consulship this glorious age will commence,
> Pollio, and the mighty months will begin to march forward.]

"durch Epiphanie gegenwärtige Gott Apoll." I. Scott Ryberg, "Vergil's Golden Age," *TAPA* 89 (1958): 116 n. 15, remarks that verse 10 is a "probable allusion to Octavian." Taylor, *Divinity of the Roman Emperor*, 119 n. 37, includes the interpretation of the scholiasts in a footnote in her discussion of the relationship between Octavian and Apollo, but she does not comment on its importance or veracity.

53. The most notable and persuasive proponent of this view is E. Norden, *Die Geburt des Kindes. Geschichte einer religiösen Idee*, 2d ed. (Leipzig, 1931).

The poet's opening statement sets the mood for the eclogue. The last age of the Sibylline prophecies has already begun. When the age began and when precisely it will end cannot be ascertained. Servius reports that the *haruspex* Vulcanius interpreted the comet that appeared at the funeral games of Julius Caesar as the heavenly sign that the tenth *saeculum* had begun.[54] Whether this story is true or gained popular acceptance at this time is not known. In any case, Vergil was not bound to comply with this belief, and the appearance of this story during a period marked by Caesar's assassination and by repeated civil strife may suggest that similar prophecies of both impending disaster and divine salvation had already begun to circulate in Rome. The fourth eclogue is perhaps a faithful and telling reflection of the contemporary feelings of uncertainty, wavering between extreme despair and optimism, about the immediate political future. The only fixed date for the poem is found in the direct address to Asinius Pollio and the reference to his consulship in 40 B.C.E. in lines 11–12.

In the eclogue's opening verses, Vergil explains that the cyclic repetition of the grand order of the ages is at hand. The present tense of *nascitur* and the three verbs that follow suggests that the new age is just beginning. The Virgin, whether or not she is Justice (perhaps borrowed from Hesiod's *Theogony*), is now returning (*redit*), and with her the *regna* of Saturn returns (*redeunt*). This is not the last age of the cycle, but it is most certainly the beginning of the new order, the much desired hope of the poet. The *nova progenies*, the new generation of this age, is already on its way to earth, sent down from the sky. But this propitious circumstance seems not yet to have occurred, although it must be imminent. Most conspicuous among this future progeny will be the *puer* whose birth will signal the end of the iron age, another name for the troubled present. Servius interpreted the phrase *tuus iam regnat Apollo* to mean that Apollo was the chief deity of the final part of the cycle before the Golden Age had begun.

> TUUS IAM REGNAT APOLLO ultimum saeculum ostendit,
> quod Sibylla Solis esse memoravit.
>
> (*Comm. in Verg. Buc.* 4.10)

> [TUUS IAM REGNAT APOLLO refers to the last age,
> which the Sibyl said was the Age of the Sun.]

The ancient commentator also quotes Nigidius Figulus, Pythagorean scholar and friend of Cicero, who wrote in the fourth book of his theological work,

---

54. Serv. *auc. Comm. in Verg. Buc.* 9.46.

de Diis, of an age of Apollo called by the name *ecpyrosis* (Serv. *auc. Comm. in Verg. Buc.* 4.10). Evidently, some traditions had placed Apollo in the role of the Sun god as the last deity before the great conflagration and the renewal of the cycle of ages. Vergil seems to allude to this meaning and significance for the Age of Apollo. Furthermore, the god plays no direct role in the course of future events and receives no further mention in the remainder of the eclogue. The reign of Apollo signals an auspicious beginning and new age only because the god rules over what will be the final age before the upheaval. Subsequent generations of Vergilian readers may interpret the reference to Apollo as a prophecy of the Augustan Principate and its deified ruler, much like early Christians later interpreted the birth of the *puer* as the Second Coming of the Messiah. In the turbulent decade following Caesar's assassination, Roman readers must surely have failed to detect the intricate and mysterious workings of history and God, so clear and certain to posterity. If Vergil had actually intended an indirect honor to the youthful triumvir, it is difficult to perceive its purpose. To assume any greater importance for Apollo in the eclogue, as do those scholars who attempt to make the god the presiding regent, divine patron, or father of the newborn child, distorts the content and tone of the oracular message.

To sum up, the early poetry of Horace and Vergil offers scant evidence to maintain the claim that Octavian was promoting a special bond with Apollo in the years before and immediately after Actium. The absence of prose accounts is unfortunate; no comments survive from the historians, either from the eloquent Augustan Livy or from the more severe Antonian Asinius Pollio, to make any assessment of such an association. Later Greek historians, such as Appian and Dio Cassius, are silent. Most unfortunate is the loss of the *Memoirs* of Augustus. But of the surviving literary evidence, it is important to observe that the later official and autobiographical record of the Augustan achievement, the *Res Gestae*, whose final composition belongs near the end of the Principate, at a time when the ruler's close connection with Apollo seems well established, does not offer any public recognition of a special relationship with the god. Surprisingly, there is not even any prominence bestowed on his splendid temple on the Palatine. When the chronicler of deeds makes reference to his new and lavish building for the god, it is without significance, buried in a lengthy list of temples erected in Rome by Augustus (*RG* 19). He adds only that he adorned Apollo's sanctuary on the Palatine with golden offerings (*RG* 24), and that he obtained the money for such dedications from melting down eighty silver statues of himself that had been set up throughout the city. The passage attests to the humility and devout piety of the man who dedicated a temple to Apollo much more than it proclaims a political assimilation or identification with the god.

Sometime after the outcome at Philippi, Octavian dressed up as Apollo in the company of his friends and later received the reproach of his fellow triumvir and an epigrammatist. While this episode has convinced subsequent generations of ambitious intentions and divine claims, contemporaries are silent about a relationship between the son of Caesar and Apollo. Despite the suggestion that Octavian chose the god as his divine protector as early as 42 and adopted his name as a watchword before the battle at Philippi, it is more likely from the numismatic evidence that Apollo was closely associated with the cause of Brutus and the Liberators, not with the armies of Octavian. The stories of a miraculous conception and divine parentage that linked Octavian with Apollo did not originate in response to the schemes of Julius Caesar or Octavian's rivalries with Sextus Pompey and Antony but belong to the period after the victory at Actium or perhaps much later. Octavian's name and title, *Caesar divi filius*, displayed on coinage, official documents, and monuments throughout the decade of the Second Triumvirate, publicly announced his connection with another god. It was not the youthful favorite of Apollo who first acquired and later secured his formidable political position in Rome during the troubled years of the 30s, but rather the son of Caesar and the illustrious descendant of Trojan Aeneas.

The Temple of Apollo

When Octavian vowed a temple to Apollo in 36 B.C.E., the Julian gens already held a strong and well-established connection with the god from as early as the fifth century, when Cn. Julius, consul of 431, dedicated a temple of Apollo in the Campus Martius.[55] The evidence is sparse, but it seems that the family of the Caesars continued to exalt the connection with Apollo in the first century; the reverse of a denarius issue of L. Julius Caesar, consul of 90, depicts a portrait of Venus with a two-horse chariot of Cupids, below

---

55. How the bond between Apollo and the family of the Caesars originated is difficult to establish. Scholars often suggest the importance of Vediovis, a mysterious figure, frequently associated with Apollo and the Julian gens. On this subject, see the discussion by Weinstock, *Divus Julius*, 8–12. An inscription on an altar dating from the end of the second century B.C.E. (*ILS* 2988) confirms the connection between the family and Vediovis, but too much uncertainty surrounds the origins and character of this divine figure to confirm him as the required link between the family of the Caesars and Apollo.

which appears a lyre, presumably in allusion to Apollo.[56] It is thus somewhat surprising that Julius Caesar, despite his family ties with the god and despite his birth on the most important day of the Ludi Apollinares, the 13th of July, does not seem to have shown any public interest in Apollo.[57] His coinage, a temple, and an official cult affirm his association with Venus, the mother of Aeneas and the Julian family.

Octavian inherited a family connection with Apollo, but one that Julius Caesar publicly ignored in favor of Venus. Perhaps shortly before the "banquet of the twelve gods" and his masquerade of Apollo, Octavian may have first come into direct contact with the god and his cult in Rome when he was officially enrolled as a member of the *quindecimviri sacris faciundis*. As one of the four prestigious religious bodies, the quindecimvirate regulated foreign cults in the city and kept charge of the Sibylline books. Because of these duties, members were recognized as servants of the Greek god who was closely associated with the prophecies of the Sibyl. In honor of their public service, a bronze tripod stood in front of the homes of the fifteen members.

Numismatic evidence testifies to Octavian's early enrollment in the college of the quindecimvirs. Shortly before 36, Octavian issued a series of denarii that depicted the tripod and laurel wreath, symbols of the god Apollo.[58] Scholars have been quick to interpret these coins as an indication of Octavian's special devotion to the god, but the appearance of these divine emblems on Roman coinage more often denotes the honor of membership in this priestly college.[59] The coinage confirms Octavian's status as quindecimvir by 37, although he may have been enrolled as early as his arrival in Rome in 44.[60] Octavian had already been selected as pontifex as early as 47, on his sixteenth birthday, and augur sometime before 43.[61] His earliest coinage,

---

56. Crawford, *RRC* 320.

57. See the discussion by Gagé, *Apollon Romain*, 467–73, who discounts the political significance of the "apollinisme direct de César." Gagé is surely right that Caesar's intentions to emphasize the Sibylline prophecies and Trojan connection with his family were only indirectly associated with Apollo.

58. Crawford, *RRC* 537/2 and 538/2.

59. Cf. comments by Grueber, *BMCRR* I, 432 n. 3.

60. Cf. Taylor, *Divinity of the Roman Emperor*, 120, who has suggested that Octavian, undeniably the most junior partner of the newly established Triumvirate, sought to promote his position as quindecimvir to vie with Lepidus, who, since the death of Caesar, had been Pontifex Maximus, and with Antony, who was his senior among the augurs.

61. For collection of the ancient evidence, see study by M.W. Hoffman Lewis, *The Official Priests of Rome under the Julio-Claudians: A Study of the Nobility from 44 B.C. to 68 A.D.*, American Academy in Rome Papers and Monographs 16 (Rome, 1955), 28, no. 3 (pontifex), and 40, no. 14 (augur). The early date for Octavian's entry into the college of augurs that she suggests (43 rather than as late as 40) seems more likely, based on the numismatic evidence (Crawford, *RRC* 490/2).

which probably dates from late 43, follows the tradition of long titulatures where the minter inscribed the offices of consul (COS), pontifex (PONT), and augur (AUG or A/G) around the circumferences of the coins.[62] Unlike Antony, however, who from his earliest coinage minted after Philippi until his legionary issues in preparation for Actium continued to display either the legend AUGUR or the crooked staff (*lituus*) that symbolized the priestly office,[63] Octavian removed official recognition of his membership in these religious bodies from his coinage and later even abandoned the title of triumvir. The evidence suggests that shortly after his victory at Naulochus, Octavian began to prefer the title of imperator, adopted as a praenomen, and the audacious claim to divinity expressed by the phrase *Caesar divi filius*.

The Vow of the Temple and the House on the Palatine

Octavian vowed a temple to Apollo in 36. Ancient testimony has established the date, but the intentions of Octavian are more difficult to ascertain. Prevailing opinion links the vow of the temple directly with Octavian's victory over Sextus Pompey at Naulochus, and some have even claimed that Octavian conceived his vow during the naval battle.[64] Like the Temple of Mars Ultor built in the Augustan Forum, initially vowed by Octavian during the conflict at Philippi, but completed and dedicated nearly forty years later in August of 2 B.C.E., the Temple of Apollo on the Palatine has been judged an impressive monument and a symbol of "Augustan" victory and military glory, though the sanctuary was first conceived amid the politics of the Second Triumvirate.

---

62. Crawford, *RRC* 490/2 (legend PONT AUG), 493 (legend PONT AUG), 517/1–2 (legend PONT), 517/7–8 (legend PONT with *lituus*).

63. For coinage of Antony with the title of augur or its symbol of the crooked staff, see Crawford, *RRC* 488/1–2 (*lituus*), 489/1-4 (*lituus*), 492/1–2 (*lituus*), 493 (legend AUG), 496/2–3 (*lituus*), 516/1–2 (legend AUG), 516/3–5 (*lituus*), 517/1–8 (legend AUG, sometimes with *capis*), 520 (*lituus*), 521/1–2 (*lituus*), 522/1–4 (legend AUG, with *lituus* and *capis*), 531 (legend AUG), 533/1–3 (legend AUG); 536/1–4 (legend AUGUR), 539 (legend AUGUR), 541/1–2 (legend AUG); 542/1–2 (legend AUG), 544/1–39 (legend AUG), 545/1–2 (legend AUG). For a discussion on the symbolic meaning of the *lituus*, see J.R. Fears, "The Theology of Victory at Rome: Approaches and Problems," *ANRW* II.17.2 (Berlin and New York, 1981), 792–93 n. 261. Octavian's issues of 37 B.C.E. (Crawford, *RRC* 537/1 and 538/1) depicted the traditional objects associated with the priestly offices of pontifex and augur—the ladle (*simpulum*), the sprinkler (*aspergillum*), the one-handled cup (*capis*), and the crooked staff (*lituus*)—although without any titulature of office.

64. Zanker, *Power of Images*, 50. Cf. also E. Lefèvre, *Das Bild-Programm des Apollo-Tempels auf dem Palatin* (Konstanz, 1989), 11, who begins his speculative monograph on the temple's "programmatic" design and artwork with the assertion that Octavian vowed the temple for his victory over Sextus Pompey and cites the relevant passage in Velleius, which cannot confirm this claim.

The ancient evidence for Octavian's vow derives solely from the narratives of Velleius Paterculus and Dio Cassius.[65] The historians vary on the particular incidents leading up to the vow, but both place Octavian's promise of a temple after his victorious return to Rome and connect the temple with his intentions to enlarge his private residence on the Palatine, not with any prayer to the god before battle or with his later celebration of his victory over Sextus Pompey.[66] Velleius offers an indication of the circumstances and sequence of events that perhaps led to Octavian's vow.

> Victor deinde Caesar reversus in urbem contractas emptionibus complures domos per procuratores, quo laxior fieret ipsius, publicis se usibus destinare professus est, templumque Apollinis et circa porticus facturum promisit, quod ab eo singulari exstructum munificentia est. (2.81.3)

> [Thereupon Caesar returned in victory to the city and declared that the large number of houses he had purchased through agents for the purpose of enlarging his own residence would be set aside for public use, and he promised to erect a temple of Apollo, surrounded with porticos, which he built with extraordinary munificence.]

Dio (49.15.5) alludes to the same story but differs on the chronology of events. According to the Greek historian, when lightning struck the area on the Palatine hill where Octavian had recently acquired property for building his own residence, he consecrated the land to Apollo. Whether the act was a grand display of public piety or a manifestation of his superstitious nature (Suetonius tells us that Augustus always carried a sealskin to protect him from lightning), the popular assembly responded at once to the gesture and voted that his private residence should be erected at public expense and that the triumvir should be protected from insult by word and deed to the same degree as the tribunes.[67] It is curious that Velleius omits the story of Apollo's divine intervention by the bolt of lightning; he perhaps preferred to ignore

---

65. Vell. 2.81.3; Dio 49.15.5.

66. On the residence of Augustus on the Palatine, see G. Carettoni, *Das Haus des Augustus auf dem Palatin* (Mainz, 1983). Octavian's first dwelling in Rome, near the Forum (*iuxta Romanum Forum supra Scalas anularias*), was modest and formerly belonged to the orator and Neoteric poet C. Licinius Calvus. At some later time, but before 36, Octavian moved to the Palatine and the home of Q. Hortensius Hortalus (cos. 69 B.C.E.), a building conspicuous neither for its size nor elegance (Suet. *Aug.* 72.1).

67. This privilege of inviolability should not be confused with the later grant of tribunician power (*tribunicia potestas*). Dio relates that Octavian received the full power for life in 30 (51.19.6) and also in 23 (53.32.5). The earlier date seems to be in error; either Octavian was

this claim and to emphasize instead the generosity of Octavian's decision to set aside his own property for public use (*publicis usibus*). The apologist for the Caesars fails to add, however, that Octavian's private residence was actually paid for by public expense.

Whatever the circumstances may have been leading up to Octavian's vow of a temple to Apollo, neither Velleius nor Dio indicates that the promise fulfilled any vow taken at battle or that the victor sought to commemorate his military success at Naulochus by the erection of a temple. The victory over Sextus Pompey had been hailed by Octavian, publicly and prematurely, as the end of the civil wars. Octavian celebrated an *ovatio*, rode into the city in triumphal style, and erected a *columna rostrata* in the Forum that proclaimed the restoration of peace on land and sea. The crushing defeat of Sextus enabled Octavian to commence his plans for the temple to the god, but it seems that he took no overt political steps to associate it with his victory in a civil war. Placed beside his own residence and closely connected with it, the new temple was a public expression of Octavian's personal devotion to the god. Earlier incidents—in particular, the famous "banquet of the twelve gods"—may indicate the origins of the youth's association with the god, but these isolated actions should not be viewed as evidence that Octavian at this time sought to exalt a close connection with Apollo to bolster his political position or transform his public image in Rome.

Sosius and the Temple of Apollo

During the years between Naulochus and Actium, while Octavian was engaged with the expansion of his own home and the construction of the Temple of Apollo (and, also at this time, of the Curia Julia; the Temple of Divus Julius; the shrine to Minerva, known as the Chalcidicum; and perhaps even the Temple of Mars Ultor), a long list of nobles, often triumphators, bestowed their private resources and bequeathed family names to new and refurbished temples, theaters, libraries, and other commemorative monuments. T. Statilius Taurus, triumphator of 34 B.C.E., erected a stone amphitheater in the Campus Martius and dedicated it four years later.[68] L. Marcius Philippus, who celebrated a triumph in 33, rebuilt the older Temple of Hercules Musarum and surrounded it with a lavish portico.[69] On the Aven-

---

offered this power at this time and declined it or he accepted it and surrendered it in his formal gesture of 27. More significantly, Augustus records on official documents the acceptance of this power in 23 and dates the years of his rule by his tenure of tribunician power from this year.

68. The *Fasti Triumphales Barberiniani* record his triumph; for the theater, see Suet. *Aug.* 29.5, Tac. *Ann.* 3.72, and Dio 51.23.1.

69. The *Fasti Triumphales Barberiniani* record his triumph in Spain in 33. Restoration of the temple probably belongs to this year. See Ovid *Fasti* 6.801–12; Suet. *Aug.* 29.5; Tac. *Ann.* 3.72.

tine hill, L. Cornificius, consul of 35, who celebrated a triumph *ex Africa* two years later, began restoration of the Temple of Diana.[70] In the Roman Forum, Paullus Aemilius Lepidus completed the reconstruction of the Basilica Aemilia, begun as early as 55.[71] And Asinius Pollio repaired the Atrium Libertatis and established in it the first public library in Rome.[72] During this often overlooked, but critical, period of fragile tranquillity and renewed prosperity between civil wars, Gaius Sosius, triumphator in 34 and consul two years later, may have restored the Temple of Apollo originally dedicated by the Julian family in the Campus Martius.[73]

---

70. Suet. *Aug.* 29.5.

71. For the refurbishment of the Basilica Aemilia (formerly called Aemilia et Fulvia), first undertaken in 55 B.C.E. by the aedile L. Aemilius Paullus, brother of the triumvir Lepidus, see Cic. *Att.* 4.16.14; Plut. *Caes.* 29; Appian *BC* 2.26. His son, Paullus Aemilius Lepidus, completed the project in 34 (Dio 49.42.2).

72. Suet. *Aug.* 29.5; Isid. *Orig.* 6.5. For ancient references to the Greek and Latin libraries established by Asinius Pollio in the Atrium Libertatis, which seems to have displayed portrait busts of authors and various museum works of art, see Ovid *Tr.* 3.1.71–72; Pliny *NH* 7.115, 35.10, 36.23, 36.24, 36.25, 36.33, 36.34.

73. It had once been claimed that Sosius erected a new temple, but archaeologists have not discovered any evidence of such a sanctuary, and it seems likely that Sosius chose to glorify his name through the refurbishment of the temple, originally dedicated by a member of the Julian family. Pliny twice (*NH* 13.53 and 36.28) refers to a temple as "Apollo Sosianus." Arguments for a later restoration in the Augustan Principate are not compelling. In a series of related discussions, Eugenio La Rocca has examined the temple's architectural remains and has argued that the restoration by Sosius represents his political allegiance to Augustus and that the mythological symbolism of its artistic decoration celebrates the victory over Antony and Cleopatra. See La Rocca, *Amazzonomachia. Le sculture frontonali del tempio d'Apollo Sosiano* (Rome, 1985); "Le sculture frontonali del tempio di Apollo Sosiano a Roma," in *Archaische und klassische griechische Plastik. Akten des internationalen Kolloquiums vom 22.–25. April 1985 in Athen*, vol. 2, *Klassische griechische Plastik*, ed. H. Kyrieleis (Mainz, 1986), 51–58; "Der Apollo-Sosianus-Tempel," in *Kaiser Augustus*, 121–36; and "Die Giebelskulpturen des Apollo-Sosianus-Tempels in Rom," *Gymnasium* 95 (1988): 129–40. Much of this subtle argument, later repeated by Zanker, *Power of Images*, 66–70, 84, derives from La Rocca's interpretation of the temple's richly decorated pediment, where sculptural fragments reconstruct a scene of an Amazonomacly. The claim by La Rocca that the pediment may have originally adorned an early fifth-century Temple of Apollo Daphnephoros in Eretria is attractive and plausible, but the interpretation that Augustan Rome (here represented by the architectural efforts of a former partisan of Antony and defeated naval commander at Actium) reshaped the political symbolism of classical Athens and the struggle between the Greeks and Persians into a complex and confused allusion to Octavian's war against Cleopatra is difficult to understand. First, we are forced to believe that the missing figures of the Amazon queen and Hercules (and/or Theseus) would invoke in the mind of the individual spectator the Egyptian queen and Octavian, respectively. That Augustus was later identified with the god Hercules (as Antony had also been identified) does not add any support or importance to this view. The prominence of Athena in this sculptural group is more problematic. What role does she play in Rome's political drama? Second, the appearance of snakes wrapped around the legs of a tripod on a capital from one of the temple's columns does not require a hidden allusion ("das Symbol ägyptischer Königmacht," as La Rocca, "Der Apollo-Sosianus-Tempel," 128, explains it), if we

Sosius, who later served as Antony's admiral during the disastrous naval campaign at Actium, was the triumvir's intimate friend and loyal partisan. This association between the two men has led some scholars to interpret Sosius' restoration of the Temple of Apollo as evidence that the political scheme of Octavian to promote a close relationship with Apollo and his decision to build a new temple to the god received stubborn opposition from Antony and his supporters."[74] The argument is not convincing; it presupposes a political atmosphere in Rome during the contentious period of the Second Triumvirate where the major rivals for power and their sometimes inconstant adherents not only endeavored to gain public recognition of the

---

consider for a moment that the temple had originally been dedicated to Apollo Medicus. Third, the triumphal procession depicted on the broken remains of an elaborately decorated frieze block need not represent the triple triumph of 29 as La Rocca and Zanker argue from the fact that the two seated figures of the *trophaion* wear trousers, an attire more characteristic of northern barbarians (as we are told, the triumphator had included Gauls and Germans in his Illyrian triumph). But in such clever reconstructions of political symbolism and propaganda, it seems to have been forgotten by the modern viewers that the foreign enemy had been interpreted on the temple's pediment as Egyptian, the immoral embodiment of the "East." The scene, even if the frieze belongs to the temple and not to an adjacent portico or structure, is probably not intended to depict a historical event or triumph (the manner of representation of the bound figures on opposite sides of the *trophaion* resembles the type familiar on many Roman coins), and it would be more prudent to avoid any specific identifications or allusions.

That the official date of the temple's dedication falls on the birthday of Augustus (*Fasti Arvalium, CIL* I², p. 330) is a more compelling reason to consider that the restoration belongs to a later age than the Second Triumvirate. But the day may have been changed after the restoration by Sosius. P. Gros, *Aurea Templa. Recherches sur l'architecture religieuse de Rome à l'époque d'Auguste*, BEFAR 231 (Paris, 1976), 33, who has compiled a list of the Augustan temples whose *dies natales* are known to have been altered to a day of greater personal significance to Augustus, reveals that such changes were not so unusual and that all the temples in the area of the Circus Flaminius (Temples of Jupiter Stator, Mars, Neptune, Juno Regina, and Felicitas) share the same date of dedication. Sosius, whom Octavian pardoned after Actium, may have retained his status in the Augustan Principate (a C. Sosius appears among the rolls of the quindecimvirs for the Ludi Saeculares, though it could be a son or other relative). Whatever the cause that saved the life of Sosius (Velleius contends that it was due to the *fides* of L. Arruntius and the *clementia* of Octavian, Vell. 2.86.2), it probably enabled him to maintain his priestly office, although perhaps only the honor of the name, without any distinction. Sosius may have suffered a fate similar to Lepidus, once the third member of the powerful Triumvirate. Despite the disgrace and isolation of a virtual internal exile after his failed attempt at rebellion in 36 B.C.E., Lepidus retained the solemn office of Pontifex Maximus until his death twenty-four years later.

74. Gagé, *Apollon Romain*, 496, characterized the work of Sosius as the "parade délibérée contre le projet d'Octave." Shipley, "Chronology of the Building Operations in Rome," 27 n. 3, anticipates this view: "At this time there was going on in Rome a good deal of 'jockeying for position' between the friends of Octavian and the agents of Antony. The fact that Octavian was building a new temple of Apollo on the Palatine was sufficient reason for an Antonian to endeavor to offset any religious advantage which might thus accrue to Octavian, by rebuilding the old temple with its four hundred years of religious tradition behind it."

special favor of individual gods but also competed to obtain exclusive rights over their worship. That Romans sought to acquire tangible political rewards from the building or refurbishment of solemn temples cannot be denied. Yet in the tradition of the Republic, the rewards of these architectural efforts, whatever their nature, fell directly on the individual and his family, not on a political faction and its leader.

Like Octavian, Sosius may have come into closer contact with Apollo through his membership in the quindecimvirs, and this religious office may have played a part in his decision to honor the god with the restoration of his temple in the Campus Martius. Sometime before 33, Sosius issued a series of coins from Zacynthus, an island west of the Peloponnesus (under the indirect control of Antony), which represent a tripod on one reverse and a portrait of Apollo on the obverse.[75] It has been suggested that the coins refer either to the restoration of the Apollo temple in Rome or to Sosius' role as quindecimvir.[76] Both interpretations assume too much importance for events in Rome and ignore the long-established traditions of the island community reflected on earlier coinage. The cult of Apollo held a prominent position in Zacynthus, and the coinage of Sosius probably reflects only this local interest in the god. Since it is known that the tripod and other emblems of Apollo were standard types on the coinage of Zacynthus from, at least, the fifth century, it becomes difficult to accept that Sosius intended the issues to convey a new significance for the old types or to allude to his building activities or religious post in Rome. As long as recognition of the new authority was given (several issues of Sosius depict also the portraits of Antony with the title of imperator), it seems that locals were free to continue traditional representations and fixed types. Another issue of Sosius displays

---

75. The date of the coins is difficult to determine. One issue records Sosius as simply quaestor (Q) a later issue as imperator (IMP) with a representation of a trophy, undoubtedly in reference to his victory in Syria when he captured Jerusalem in 37, for which he celebrated a triumph three years later. These issues probably date shortly before or after the date of the triumph. Another issue depicts a tripod on the reverse and a portrait of Apollo on the obverse, with the legend CO(n)S(ul) DESIG(natus). Since Sosius became consul in 32, the previous year is generally given as the date of issue. Yet Appian (*BC* 5.73) reports that Sosius had been chosen to be consul as early as 39 according to the informal arrangement by the triumvirs and Sextus Pompey at Puteoli. Furthermore, Appian names Sosius and Domitius Ahenobarbus as the consuls chosen in the deliberations of 36. On the coinage, see Sydenham, *CRR* 1271–74; P. Gardner, *A Catalogue of the Greek Coins in the British Museum: Peloponnesus*, revised and edited by R. Stuart Poole (London, 1975), 102, nos. 84–87; *RPC* 1.1:263, nos. 1290–93; M. Grant, *From Imperium to Auctoritas*, 41; Shipley, "Chronology of the Building Operations in Rome," 26.

76. For the former view, see Shipley, "Chronology of the Building Operations in Rome," 25–28. For the latter, see Lewis, *Official Priests of Rome under the Julio-Claudians*, 49, no. 12.

the trident and dolphin, common symbols for an island nation, which do not seem to be designed in specific reference to the Roman authority or the new administrator.

Though the temples of Sosius and Octavian may have been contemporary endeavors, it is not necessary to assume that the building projects were competitive or confrontational. The decisions to refurbish and build a temple of Apollo perhaps originated from shared duties as quindecimvirs and a mutual interest in the god of prophecy. The restoration of the Temple of Apollo by Sosius was neither directed against Octavian nor encouraged by Antony. From the elder Pliny, we know that the temple's adornment included works by the most renowned artisans of the Greek world: paintings by Aristides of Thebes, a contemporary of Apelles (35.99); a marble group of the Niobids by either Scopas or Praxiteles (36.28); statues of Apollo (two are attested), Latona, Diana, and the nine Muses by Philiscus of Rhodes (36.34); a statue of Apollo Citharoedus by Timarchides (36.35); and a statue of Apollo carved in cedar wood from Seleucia (13.53). As its name survives by Pliny, the older Temple of Apollo stood as the glorious achievement of Sosius alone.

The Dedication of the Temple

Octavian dedicated his new temple on the ninth day of October in 28. The significance of this date is difficult to assess. Gagé observed that the date of the temple's dedication does not fall on the anniversary of the naval battle (September 2) or on any other day publicly associated with the victory over Antony (such as the capture of Alexandria and the suicide of the Roman general on August 1) but rather falls on a day previously consecrated to an obscure triad of deities, Genius Publicus, Fausta Felicitas, and Venus Victrix on the Capitoline.[77] That the consecration to these deities still remained on two Augustan calendars beside the notice of the dedication of the Temple of Apollo Palatine may suggest that the triad continued to deserve respect during the Augustan Principate.[78] Gagé attributed the origin of the shrine or cult of the three deities to the time of Sulla, a likely possibility because of the appearance of the name Fausta, and concluded that Octavian had sought to transfer a triumphal context to the Palatine temple. The association of victory with each of these three deities, known from the Republican period, is

---

77. Gagé, *Apollon Romain*, 524–26.

78. Recognition of the three deities appears in the *Fasti Arvalium*—GENIO PUBLIC(o) FAU-STAE FELICITATI, VENER(i) VICTR(ici) IN CAPITOL(io)—and in the *Fasti Amiternini*—GENIO PUBLICI(o) [sic] FAUSTAE FELICITAT(is), V(eneris) V(ictricis) IN CAPIT(olio): *CIL* I², pp. 214, 245, and 331.

certain,[79] but it could be argued that almost all Roman deities, especially those fashioned from abstract concepts, held some affiliation with the good fortune and success of military endeavors. Given the uncertainty about this triad of divinities (whether they were associated in one shrine on the Capitoline hill is disputed), it seems a speculative effort to seek particular motivations behind Octavian's decision. It is more likely that no specific association with any of these three divinities was intended. What is more significant, however, is that Octavian did not choose a day that would have fostered a public and conspicuous association with the naval battle at Actium. It could easily be imagined that the completion and formal dedication of the temple (October 9) could have been arranged or hurried to coincide with the anniversary of Actium on the second day of September. The following day commemorated Naulochus, Octavian's earlier victory over Sextus Pompey, presenting what would seem a double incentive for the dedicatory ceremonies sometime in early September. Though Octavian could have chosen to associate his new sanctuary to Apollo with the celebrated anniversaries of his victories in civil war at Actium and Naulochus, both enrolled in the official state calendar and honored with annual vows of thanksgiving, he declined.

Various athletic competitions, gladiatorial fights, and dramatic performances regularly accompanied the formal dedication of Roman temples. At the consecration for the Temple of Divus Julius in 29, Dio (51.22.4) records that there were "contests of all kinds." The sons of Rome's oldest and most distinguished families performed the equestrian show known as the Lusus Troiae, while their fathers competed in chariot races of two- and four-horse teams. One senator fought in a gladiatorial combat; and for the entertainment of the crowd, wild beasts and tame animals were slain in vast numbers. In the following year, the formal dedication of the Temple of Apollo on the Palatine featured similar events: Circensian games restricted to fathers and sons of aristocratic families, an athletic contest staged in a wooden stadium built especially for the occasion in the Campus Martius, and a gladiatorial fight between captive prisoners. The celebration was extended for several days and continued without interruption or postponement even when Octa-

---

79. For discussion of the complicated origins of the Genius Publicus or Genius Populi Romani, dating from at least the first quarter of the last century B.C.E., see Weinstock, *Divus Julius*, 205–6. L. Licinius Lucullus (*cos.* 151 B.C.E.) built the first temple to Felicitas sometime after 145. For evidence of the ancient sources, cf. Weinstock, *Divus Julius*, 113–14, esp. n. 6. For the importance of Venus Victrix to Sulla, Pompey, and Caesar, see also Weinstock, *Divus Julius*, 83–87.

vian fell ill. It was left to his friend and fellow consul Marcus Agrippa to take over the required duties of the ailing leader of state.

Modern scholars have associated these games in 28 with those that Augustus records in the *Res Gestae*.[80]

Vota p[ro valetudine mea susc]ipi per consules et sacerdotes quinto quoque anno senatus decrevit. Ex iis votis saepe fecerunt vivo me ludos aliquotiens sacerdotum quattuor amplissima collegia, aliquotiens consules. (*RG* 9.1)

[The Senate decreed that every fourth year the consuls and priests should undertake vows on behalf of my health. In fulfillment of these vows, games were often celebrated during my lifetime, sometimes by the four most sacred colleges of priests, sometimes by the consuls.]

As I have already mentioned in my discussion of the Actian games in Nicopolis, it has been claimed that a close connection existed between these athletic contests in Rome and the Ludi Actiaci of Nicopolis, and that the games accompanying the dedication of the Temple of Apollo on the Palatine took their lead from the ceremonies associated with the foundation of Nicopolis and the first celebration of the Augustan Actian games.[81] Even an official title, *ludi Actiaci votivi pro valetudine Caesaris*, has been bestowed on the games in Rome.[82] Since these games have been cited, almost without exception, as evidence for the public association of the Palatine temple with the glory of Actium, the subject demands closer attention.

Dio (51.19.2) records the honor of a quinquennial festival among those distinctions that were voted for the victor as soon as the initial news of the Actian victory reached Rome. Here the Greek historian does not specify the

80. Most notably Taylor, *Divinity of the Roman Emperor*, 155, and Gagé, *Apollon Romain*, 512–13. To associate these games with those mentioned by Augustus in the *Res Gestae* is a plausible assumption, but it cannot be proved. The testimony of the princeps, however, is significant in another respect. We learn that games accompanied vows made on behalf of the *valetudine* (or *salute*) of Augustus. While the vows were held every four years, games were not established as a regular part of this solemn occasion. They might often (*saepe*) accompany the vows, but they apparently were neglected in some years. The games were thus not a fixed institution or occurrence. Most importantly, Augustus makes no connection between the vows or the games and his victory at Actium.

81. Gagé, "Actiaca," 92–97, and *Apollon Romain*, 512–13; Weinstock, *Divus Julius*, 315 n. 9, who remarks that there was "of course, some connection" between the games of 28 in Rome and those held at Nicopolis and in cities in the East.

82. For this title, see R. Rieks, "Sebasta und Aktia," 107–8, esp. n. 3.

name or character of the festival. There is no mention of "Actian" games; Dio simply relates that the festival was to be cyclical in its celebration and in honor of Octavian. However common in the Hellenistic East, such recurring festivals were unprecedented in Rome at this time. Julius Caesar, if Dio can be trusted, may have received this honor in 44, but the games were probably never celebrated.[83] Romans had received similar honors in the East, but such adulation, usually bestowed on local gods and heroes, had not previously been transferred to Rome.[84] The honor that was awarded to Julius, even if not carried out, may have served as a precedent by which his adopted son, victorious at Actium, would be exalted. In any case, Dio does not mention the celebration of these games during his narrative of the ceremonies of Octavian's triple triumph in 29.

When Dio later records the performance of games during the dedication of Apollo's temple in 28 (53.1.3–4), he identifies these games as the quinquennial festival that had earlier been voted among the honors for the victor at Actium. He also explains at this point that the recurring festival was celebrated occasionally[85] and supervised by one of the four major priesthoods in Rome in a rotating succession. As I have described above, the special occasion included Circensian games, athletic contests, and a gladiatorial combat. It is apparent from Dio's detailed description of these forms of public urban entertainment that they were distinctly Roman, not Greek, and certainly not games that imitated the model of the Actia in Nicopolis or the four traditional Panhellenic festivals. Furthermore, when Dio (54.19.7–8) reports that the festival was held again in 16 (there is no record of celebrations in 24 and 20 or in any other year during the Augustan Principate), it occurred in a period of extreme unrest, fear, and uncertainty in the city.

On the very night following Augustus' departure to Gaul (vicious rumors had circulated about the reasons for the princeps' travel), the Temple of Iuventus was destroyed by a fire. More ominous portents followed: a ravenous wolf rushed into the Forum and killed several people; colonies of ants were seen swarming together; and a torchlike flame shot across the evening sky, pointing toward the north, where military disturbances had recently occurred. Because of these foreboding signs, public prayers were

---

83. Dio 44.6.2. Appian (*BC* 2.106) seems to refer to the same festival when he mentions that the priests and priestesses were to perform public prayers on Caesar's behalf every four years. Appian, however, places the honor in 45 B.C.E., and it may be that the games were a later addition to the vows.

84. Weinstock, *Divus Julius*, 315, lists the sources for the Roman generals who had received such honors during the Republic.

85. The meaning of μέχρι του is unclear. The manuscripts Vaticanus Graecus 144 (V) and Marcianus 195 (M) read μέχρις οὗ.

offered for the quick and safe return of Augustus. Dio relates that the quindecimvirs represented Agrippa, who also was absent from the city, and celebrated on his behalf the quinquennial festival of Augustus, the festival of his "sovereignty" (τὴν πενταετηρίδα τῆς ἀρχῆς αὐτοῦ) as the historian describes it. There is no mention here that the event commemorated the Actian victory or marked the fifteenth anniversary of the battle as some scholars have speculated. Dio's account supports the evidence of the *Res Gestae*, where Augustus proudly records the senatorial honor of vows, offered every fourth year (*quinto quoque anno*) on behalf of his welfare (*pro valetudine*), and the frequent (*saepe*), though not regular, celebration of games with these vows. Apollo's association with these vows, if performed at his newly dedicated temple, should not be surprising. His role as a god of healing and protector of health was well known and publicly recognized in Rome; vows had once been undertaken on behalf of the welfare of the Roman people at the dedication of the god's temple on the Campus Martius in the fifth century (*pro valetudine populi vota*). The Apollo of the Palatine sanctuary may have assumed similar duties, now on behalf of the man who rescued his people from the perils and devastation of civil war. The athletic games often joined with these vows raised the new leader in Rome ever closer to a position once reserved only for the gods. The memory of Actium would have played no public role on this occasion.

The Art of the Temple

In magnificence and beauty, the Augustan temple had no rival.[86] A shining facade of white Luna marble, entrance doors with intricately decorated panels of ivory reliefs, and a renowned collection of works from the masters of Classical Greek sculpture embellished the new structure. Situated at the center of an elaborate architectural complex on the Palatine hill, the temple adjoined (or perhaps was encircled by) long passageways of colonnaded porticoes that displayed an impressive row of statues alluding to the bloody tale of the fifty daughters of Danaus and the fifty sons of Aegyptus. Within the colonnades or leading out from them, Augustus built a public library, divided into two sections for works of Greek and Latin literature, large enough for recitals by authors, and decorated with a gallery of portraits of literary artists. Although no visible remains of the ornate complex have survived the ravages of fire and time and only few and scattered fragments have been unearthed from the recent excavations on the Palatine, one may judge, if only from the descriptions of contemporary poets and from the

---

86. For such claims, see especially Joseph. *Bell. Iud.* 2.80–81 and Vell. 2.81.3.

praise of subsequent generations, that the Augustan Temple of Apollo richly deserved its honorific title of *nobilissima*.[87]

Though little survives of the temple, scholars have not been deterred from finding an official message of Augustan politics and ideology in the architectural space and decorative art that defined the god's sanctuary. In his informative and useful monograph on the temple's artwork, Eckard Lefèvre concluded that the programmatic display of art in the grandiose edifice and its surroundings had undoubtedly a "panegyrical purpose."[88] Interpretations of the expression and meaning of this panegyrical purpose vary. In the statues of the murderous Danaids, Erika Simon found allusions to Rome's war against Cleopatra and Egypt.[89] Showing that the ancient tale of the daughters of Danaus striking a blow against the sons of Aegyptus might represent the historical conflict between Hellas and Persia, Simon suggests that Romans would appropriate the potent symbolism of the action and understand Cleopatra and the "Egyptian danger" in a new context.[90] From the setting of the mythic tale in Egypt and the name Aegyptus, brother of Danaus, Barbara Kellum emphasized instead the "Egyptian" connection in the choice of the sculptural group. Contrary to Simon's interpretation of the symbolism of ethnic conflict in this representation, Kellum imagined "Cleopatra surrogates" in the figures of the Danaids who commit an impious crime.[91] Paul Zanker also judged the impressive statuary group of the

---

87. Ascon. *tog. cand.* 80–81. For various descriptive details from the Augustan poets, see Prop. *Elegies* 2.31, 4.6; Hor. *Odes* 1.31; Ovid *Tr.* 3.11.59–64.

88. Lefèvre, *Das Bild-Programm des Apollo-Tempels auf dem Palatin*, 23.

89. E. Simon, *Augustus. Kunst und Leben in Rom um die Zeitenwende* (Munich, 1986), 19–24.

90. Simon, *Augustus*, 23–24, implausibly suggests that the Augustan Danaid statuary group also alludes to the popular myth of Amymone, a Danaid, and Neptune, and that this association with Neptune (the god, of course, is not part of the sculptural group) recalls the victory at Actium. Simon cites as evidence the fact that Vergil includes the god in his narration of the naval battle (*Aen.* 8.699) even though he plays no prominent role in the fighting and is also joined by Venus, Minerva, and later Apollo. Simon is more persuasive when she suggests that the Danaids in the temple's complex may have been depicted by the sculptor in the act of carrying their wedding trousseau, not water jugs, as most versions of the myth record and as most modern critics have assumed. At least this suggestion seems likely if we accept that the bronze Danaids found in the Villa dei Papiri at Herculaneum are replicas of those that once adorned the *area Apollinis Palatini* in Rome.

91. B. Kellum, "Sculptural Programs and Propaganda in Augustan Rome: The Temple of Apollo on the Palatine and the Forum of Augustus" (Ph.D. diss., Harvard University, 1982) and "Sculptural Programs and Propaganda in Augustan Rome: The Temple of Apollo on the Palatine," in *Age of Augustus*, 169–76. Kellum attempts to relate the sculptural group with Vergil's *Aeneid* and the *balteus* of Pallas, which the poet says was decorated with this horrific scene of impiety (*impressumque nefas: una sub nocte iugali/caesa manus iuvenum foede thalamique cruenti*, 10.497–98), but Kellum fails to explain how Cleopatra, apart from her

Danaids as reminders of the recent past, but as painful reminders prompting "thoughts of guilt and expiation" and "misdeeds of civil war" in the minds of Roman viewers.[92]

Scholars have applied similar interpretations of political allegory to the known artwork of the temple's facade. The ivory panels on the doors of the temple depicted scenes of Apollo as the slayer of the Niobids and the victor over the Galatians (Gauls) in Delphi. The vengeance that the children of Latona inflict on the innocent children of the haughty daughter of Tantalus is claimed to recall the role of Octavian as avenger of his father. The remains of a terra-cotta plaque in a heavy, archaic style offer the struggle between Apollo and Hercules for control of the tripod in Delphi. The mythic scene of ancient ritual is said to be an allusion to the historical conflict between Octavian and Antony in which the political rivals espoused the respective gods as their divine patrons and supporters.[93] Finally, another broken scene depicts the naked hero Perseus in the act of offering to Athena the snake-tressed head of Medusa. The horrid *gorgoneion*, so it is argued, is a symbol of Cleopatra and Horace's *fatale monstrum*.[94]

However imaginative, fascinating, and eloquently argued, modern interpretations of political messages, indirectly transmitted by the temple's artwork through allegorical readings, subtle allusions, or hidden metaphors are impressionistic exercises derived from presumptions of a pervasive propaganda.[95] No official cult titles, no dedicatory inscriptions link the Augustan

---

connection with Egypt and the Ptolemies (Kellum reminds us that the Danaids, like the rulers of Egypt, traced their origins back to Greece) is guilty of impious murder and fratricide in her war against Rome.

92. Zanker, *Power of Images*, 85–89, and "Der Apollontempel auf dem Palatin," 31–32. Zanker contends that a statue of "Apollo of Actium" stood in the surrounding complex of the Palatine Temple near the statues of the Danaids. He associates the statue with the depiction of the god on the denarius issue of Antistius Vetus, *RIC*[2] 365–66. The identification of this figure is dubious. For the difficulties of interpreting this coin type, see my discussion in the epilogue.

93. For an interpretation of this terra-cotta plaque and similar fragments found in the area of the temple, see M.J. Strazzulla, *Il principato di Apollo. Mito e propaganda nelle lastre "Campania" dal tempio di Apollo Palatino* (Rome, 1990). Strazzulla's approach to the artwork is more balanced and cautious, interpreting the iconography as multifaceted and complex and in terms of Roman culture, religion, and society (not only political propaganda).

94. For a detailed examination of the "Medusa" plaque, see Strazzulla, *Il principato di Apollo*, 34–49, whose informative discussion reveals how often this image of the Gorgon appeared in Greek, Hellenistic, and Roman art. Because of her suicide and association with the asp, it is thus all the more surprising that Cleopatra in the role of Medusa is not part of the hostile propaganda and vituperation against the Egyptian queen that survive in the ancient literature.

95. In this regard, see K. Galinsky, "Venus, Polysemy, and the Ara Pacis Augustae," *AJA* 96 (1992): 457–75, and his cogent arguments for the "intentional polysemy" and "multivalency" of the Augustan Ara Pacis. Galinsky sensibly argues for a "middle ground between the mono-

Temple of Apollo on the Palatine with the god of Actium or the naval battle; no archaeological remains testify explicitly to such a public connection; finally, no historical evidence records any direct, political steps taken by Octavian to embellish the memory of Actium at the dedication of his temple. The murderous Danaids, the vengeful slaying of Niobe's children, and the divine struggle over the Delphic tripod require neither artful sophistication nor Augustan allusions to explain their inclusion in the artwork of a temple of Apollo. The sanctuary honored the god and the myths associated with the god. The choice of the artwork (how much we can or should attribute to the direct and personal intervention of Augustus has not been seriously addressed by art historians) probably reflects private taste and contemporary aesthetics. From literary testimony, we know that the Palatine sanctuary exhibited an array of sculptural pieces of famous Greek artisans of the later Classical period: an Apollo by Scopas of Paros; a Diana by Timotheus; a Latona by Cephisodotus, son of Praxiteles; and a bronze statuary group of four cattle by Myron.[96] Must we seek a political purpose or statement in the eclectic collection of masterpieces of sculpture so characteristic of Roman aristocrats and later emperors? Furthermore, it seems unlikely that the proud triumphator and conqueror would intentionally seek to portray or even to recognize the agony and suffering of civil war anywhere in Rome, least of all in his new temple to Apollo. And it is also difficult to understand why he would wish to acknowledge the divine claim of Antony by raising his rival's stature and dignity to that of Hercules, whose attempt to steal the oracle was only prevented by the intervention of Jupiter and his thunderbolt. It must not be ignored that the temple was initially vowed in 36. We can only speculate about the schedule and progress of building the temple, but it is reasonable to assume that from the expanse of the sanctuary's area, the

---

lithic, Symean view of the Augustan dispensation . . . and the notion that any subjective interpretation that we can cleverly construct today must be 1) subversive and 2) also have been on the minds of a Roman audience at the time" (p. 475). But Galinsky is more dogmatic and less persuasive when he later attempts to apply the same interpretative strategies and theories of reception to literary texts, notably to Vergil's *Aeneid*: "It is like reading the *Aeneid*. At the same time, it is not a matter of purely subjective and impressionistic understandings, which would lead to misinterpretation, but the variety of evocations operates within the framework of a clearly established overall meaning" (p. 471). The chief difficulty in Galinsky's reading of the *Aeneid* is what constitutes the "clearly established overall meaning" in this multilayered and and richly variegated text, with its subtle literary allusions, political tensions, and moral ambiguities. For many readers, this meaning is neither clear nor established.

96. Cf. Pliny *NH* 36.25, 36.32, 36.24, respectively. In an interesting aside, Pliny (34.58) mentions that a famous bronze Apollo of Myron, seized by Antony from the city of Ephesus, was not placed in the new temple in Rome but restored to the citizens of Ephesus in obedience to a warning given in a dream. Augustus alludes to this action in his *Res Gestae* 24.

intricate design of the grandiose complex, and the fine exterior and interior adornment, many decisions regarding the commission of the architect and artisans and the acquisition of famous works of sculpture must have been formulated long before the decisive confrontation at Actium. If one prefers to find contemporary political allusions in the artwork of the new temple and its surrounding complex, it would be more prudent to explore the political climate of the late 30s, the critical period of years following Naulochus when the son of the divine Julius consolidated his political authority and virtually assumed a supreme position in Italy.

The Temple and the Poets

Horace's *Odes* 1.31 announces the dedication of the god's temple on the Palatine and offers a humble prayer by the poet.[97]

Quid dedicatum poscit Apollinem
vates? quid orat de patera novum
    fundens liquorem? non opimae
        Sardiniae segetes feracis,
non aestuosae grata Calabriae
armenta, non aurum aut ebur Indicum,
    non rura, quae Liris quieta
        mordet aqua taciturnus amnis.
premant Calenam falce quibus dedit
fortuna vitem, dives ut aureis
    mercator exsiccet culillis
        vina Syra reparata merce,
dis carus ipsis, quippe ter et quater
anno revisens aequor Atlanticum
    inpune. me pascunt olivae,
        me cichorea levesque malvae.
frui paratis et valido mihi,
Latoe, dones et precor integra
    cum mente nec turpem senectam
        degere nec cithara carentem.

[What does the poet seek from Apollo on the
dedication of his shrine? What does he pray for,

---

97. I have followed the Teubner text of F. Klinger, 3d ed. (1959).

while he pours the new libation from the bowl?
    Not the rich crops of fertile Sardinia,
not the pleasant herds of sweltering Calabria,
not gold, not the ivory of India,
    not the fields that the silent stream
        of Liris harries with its still water.
Let those to whom it has been granted by Fortune
prune the Calenian vine, so that the wealthy
    merchant may drain from golden cups
        the wine paid by his Syrian wares,
dear to the very gods, since three and four times
each year he revisits the ocean of Atlas
    unscathed. For me, olives suffice,
        for me, endives and light mallows.
Grant, I pray, that I may enjoy what I have gained,
son of Latona, in good health and with mind
    unimpaired, and that I may pass an old age
        neither shameful nor without the lyre.]

The public occasion of the official ceremony in October of 28 afforded Horace an opportunity to express a personal prayer to the god. The poetic technique of beginning with an event familiar and fresh in the minds of his readers and of transferring its importance to a more immediate context and in more intimate terms is a favorite practice of this lyric poet.[98] In *Odes* 1.31, Horace does not allude to any special relationship between the god of the new temple and the recent events at Actium. If its illustrious builder had intended the sanctuary to be a victory monument, the public redemption of civil war, or even a declaration of his devotion and special relationship with the god, we do not learn it from Horace. The poet is not interested in such political concerns but prefers instead to use the occasion to make a prayer for his own welfare to a deity concerned with a poet. The noun *vates* is the postponed subject of the ode's opening question and emphatically begins the second verse. The contemporary ambiguity of the word (seer/poet) adumbrates the special bond between the poet and the god. Horace is not seeking riches, land, or precious stones; the poet will be content with what Fortune has already bestowed on him, humble surroundings, ample food, and a sound mind. The ode ends with the prayer that the poet's old age may never

---

98. Hor. *Odes* 3.14 is a fine example of this technique. Here the poet begins with the public celebration of the victorious return of Augustus from Spain and ends with the call to his servant for unguents, garlands, and wine for a private and humble offering to the gods.

be without song (*cithara canentem*). The god of the lyre, not Apollo Actius, is Horace's vision of the Augustan deity.

Propertius provides the fullest and most detailed description of the artistic works exhibited in Apollo's temple. The short piece invites an interesting comparison with the lyric poet's composition.[99]

> Quaeris, cur veniam tibi tardior? aurea Phoebi
>   porticus a magno Caesare aperta fuit.
> tota erat in speciem Poenis digesta columnis,
>   inter quas Danai femina turba senis.
> hic equidem Phoebus visus mihi pulchrior ipso
>   marmoreus tacita carmen hiare lyra;
> atque aram circum steterant armenta Myronis,
>   quattuor artificis, vivida signa, boves.
> tum medium claro surgebat marmore templum,
>   et patria Phoebo carius Ortygia:
> in quo Solis erat supra fastigia currus,
>   et valvae, Libyci nobile dentis opus,
> altera deiectos Parnasi vertice Gallos,
>   altera maerebat funera Tantalidos.
> deinde inter matrem deus ipse interque sororem
>   Pythius in longa carmina veste sonat.
>
>   (2.31.1–16)

[You ask why I come late to you? The golden portico
  of Apollo has been opened by mighty Caesar.
All of it has been laid out for view with Punic columns,
  between which stand the female throng of old Danaus.
The god's statue seemed more beautiful than Phoebus himself,
  carved in marble, uttering his song with a silent lyre.
And around the altar stood the herd of Myron,
  four oxen of the artisan, living statues.

Then in the middle the temple rose up in shining marble,
  even dearer to Phoebus than his ancestral Ortygia:

---

99. The text may be corrupt. I have followed the Oxford Classical Text (1960) of E.A. Barber with two substitutions. I have chosen to read *tota* instead of *tantam* in line 3 and *Phoebus* instead of *Phoebo* in line 5. In the best manuscript tradition, there is no break between this poem and the one that follows, which has been generally identified as a separate elegy (2.32). For discussion of the textual problems, see L. Richardson, jr, ed. *Propertius, Elegies I– IV* (Norman, Okla., 1977), 301–2.

And on the roof stood the chariot of the Sun,
   and the doors, the noble work of Libyan ivory,
the one mourned the Gauls hurled down from Parnassus' crest,
   the other, the deaths of Tantalus' daughter.
Then between his mother and his sister the god himself,
   the Pythian god, clad in a long robe, plays his song.]

Unlike Horace, the elegist offers no private prayer or solemn address to the god. Apollo's new temple has detained him; the dedication ceremonies are the excuse for his late arrival to his girlfriend. Propertius reviews the temple's artwork: the statuary group of the Danaids, the female throng and old man amid the array of Punic columns; the statue of Phoebus Apollo, a rival to the god's beauty; the herd of Myron around the altar, lifelike statues of the artist; and the chariot of the Sun standing on the temple's roof. On the ivory panels of the temple's doors, visitors beheld scenes of the punishment against Niobe and the subjugation of the Gauls at Delphi. The representations on the twin panels did not impress on Propertius any allusion to Octavian's celebrated vengeance against the assassins of Julius Caesar or glorification of the god's role. In the mind of the elegist, the temple doors evoke a mournful lesson of punishment and death. The Gauls have been repulsed and thrown down (*deiectos*) from the crest of Parnassus. Niobe has been punished by the deaths (*funera*) of her children. The powerful metaphor of *maerebat* highlights the elegist's emotions and sympathies. One door mourns the defeat of the Gauls, the other the death of the descendants of Tantalus, another victim of a god's punishment, however deserving. Apollo's role as defender and avenger has given way to the plight of his victims. Propertius abruptly cuts off the scene with the statue of the Pythian god, placed between those of his beloved sister and mother, as if in the act of singing his *carmina*.

The Apollo who secures Augustan victory in the naval battle against Antony and the Egyptian queen is nowhere to be found in the two poetic documents that derive their inspiration from the official dedication ceremonies of the temple. The god in his acknowledged role as Apollo Actius makes his first appearance in extant Latin literature almost ten years after the temple's dedication, in the eighth book of Vergil's *Aeneid* (8.704–5). Here, in the well-known *ecphrasis* of the hero's shield, Apollo looks down from above and with his bow secures the victory for Augustus at Actium. The passage concludes with the victor, triumphant in Rome, seated at the shining threshold of the god's temple as the long array of conquered peoples march by. A few years after the publication of the *Aeneid*, Propertius offers an aetiological hymn in praise of the god of the Palatine temple (*Elegy* 4.6). In the unusual elegy, the poet includes a narrative of the battle at Actium, whose outcome is decided by the intervention of the god. These passages might seem to confirm without any further doubt a public association between the temple on the Palatine and the victory at Actium. Modern scholars have often referred to the appearance of Apollo Actius in these two poems to support prevailing assumptions on the public perception of Apollo's temple in Rome and the officially directed propaganda on the naval battle. Refutations of such confident assertions and prevalent opinion require some preliminary remarks before proceeding to a detailed analysis of the individual poems. At this transitional point from historical inquiry to literary criticism, it seems prudent to review the examinations of the previous sections before offering a new approach toward the most famous of the "Actian" poetic documents: Horace, *Epode* 9, Vergil, *Aeneid* 8.671–728, and Propertius, *Elegy* 4.6.

To be sure, the historical evidence is not conclusive, but a reassessment of the modern opinion on the Actian victory and its role in the public ideology of the Augustan Principate seems in order. The all-too-familiar roll call of "Actian" monuments has been overly exaggerated and often misunderstood. In the immediate aftermath of his defeat of Antony and Cleopatra, Octavian does not seem to have taken any extraordinary steps to exalt the fame of his naval victory. The anniversary of the battle (September 2) was enrolled in the official calendars with solemn rituals, but similar honors had earlier been awarded for the victory at Naulochus (September 3) and, more importantly, were later added for the defeat of Antony and Cleopatra at Alexandria (August 1). Actium merited a triumph, but the triple triumph ceremonies were not a glorification of the naval battle. When the master of ceremonies placed the event in the middle of three consecutive days of celebration, the treasures of Egypt and the effigy of the queen with the asps in her arm upstaged the naval beaks of Actium. The Actian triumph was designed to be just one part of a much larger and more impressive accomplishment, conquest in the East and the establishment of peace on land and sea. Earlier in the same year (29), the Senate had voted the formal closure of the temple doors of Janus, a symbolic act that proclaimed the cessation of all wars throughout the Roman world. Following the three days of triumphal ceremonies, Octavian publicly acknowledged his debt and devotion to his father and formally dedicated the buildings named in his honor, the Curia Julia and the Temple of Divus Julius. Naval beaks decorated the podium of the temple, and a statue of Victory from Tarentum, decked with the spoils of Egypt, was placed in the Senate chamber.

Among the list of honors and decrees bestowed on Octavian, the Senate voted an arch to be erected in Rome (and Brundisium) to greet the returning victor. Though an arch had been voted following Octavian's victory over Sextus Pompey in 36, few scholars attach much credence to the claims of an earlier monument. The remains of a single arch situated between the Temple of Castor and Pollux and the Temple of Divus Julius have been associated with the memorial for the Actian victor. A lost inscription, judged to be the formal dedication of the arch, though the identification is not certain, celebrated the restoration of order in the state (*res publica conservata*), not the naval victory at Actium. The modern title of the arch as "Actian" is thus misleading, if not erroneous. Within a decade of its erection, the arch of a single span (if indeed it had ever been built) was replaced with a larger and more elaborate triple structure that glorified the return of the Roman standards and the victory over Parthia. Octavian's coinage in the aftermath of victory also displays no public recognition of Actium. The large series of coins, identified by the legends CAESAR DIVI F and IMP CAESAR, may, in fact, belong to the period before Actium and may have commemorated Octavian's earlier naval success at Naulochus. The issues probably continued in the years leading up to the campaign and battle at Actium, but the victory does not seem to have produced immediate or significant changes on the coinage. The legends AEGYPTO CAPTA and ASIA RECEPTA from issues that can be more firmly dated to the period of celebration beginning in 29 echoed the proud claims of the triumphal celebration in Rome.

The most famous and enduring monuments of Actium—the city founded by the victor on the site of the battle and the games held in honor of Apollo Actius—must be judged in the background of Octavian's reorganization and administration in this region. The foundation of Nicopolis addressed a serious and local concern; the city proved to be a successful synoecism of the neighboring communities and towns that had suffered from frequent invasions and Roman wars. In Alexandria, near the site of his victory over Antony, Octavian built a second Nicopolis. Motivations to emulate the deeds of Alexander, whose tomb Octavian visited and whose image he wore on his signet ring at this time, may have prompted him to build the cities in honor of his victory. These actions of Octavian were not directed toward Italy; instead, they delivered a forceful and clear message to the inhabitants of the Greek East, and perhaps even to the Parthian foes, that they must now deal with the new conqueror in the area and representative of Roman might and authority. The Actian games at Nicopolis were not the innovation of the Roman victor. Though Octavian raised the games to an "isolympic" status, local games to the god had already existed. In later years, the prestige of the Augustan Actia and the fierce rivalry for foreign athletes in local competitions prompted a large number of cities throughout the Greek East to establish their own Actian games. In Rome, Greek games awaited the artistic ambitions and philhellenism of the last of the Julio-Claudian emperors.[100] The quinquennial festival that had accompanied the formal dedication of Octavian's temple to Apollo in Rome was not an imitation of the Actian model. The temple to Apollo was vowed in 36 and dedicated eight years later on the ninth day of October. The date of the dedication has no known connection with the naval battle and at least indicates that Octavian took no public steps at this time to associate his temple with the god who secured his victory at Actium.

Presumptions of poetic intentions to celebrate Actium and to broadcast an Augustan propaganda must be set aside. The nature of the relationship that existed between Augustus and the poets is complex, varied, and unclear.[101] Extremes of opinion too often shape modern discussion. The poets are either advocates and veritable spokesmen for the Augustan regime (loyal adherents or reluctant admirers like Horace and Vergil) or uncompromising detractors and defiant figures of opposition (like Propertius, Tibullus, and especially Ovid). Such characterizations may contain some truths and insights into the political feelings of the poets, but more likely they are not merely inaccurate but, more importantly, inadequate. Common to all these assumptions and opinions is the persistent notion that the words of the poets

---

100. Nero's enthusiasm for Greek games is well documented—and much disparaged by ancient authors. In 59 C.E., shortly after the death of his mother, Nero instituted the Juvenalia to celebrate the shaving of his first beard. In the following year, he established the Neronia in Rome, a quinquennial festival of music, athletic competitions, and chariot racing, repeated five years later in 65. In honor of the birth of his daughter, Nero celebrated games, as Tacitus informs us, inspired by the Actian model (*certamen ad exemplar Actiacae religionis decretum*, *Ann*. 15.23). These were the only "Actian" games ever celebrated in Rome.

101. White, *Promised Verse*, 95–208, is required reading on this subject. In a systematic and sober assessment of the ancient evidence, White rejects the extreme view that Augustus dictated literary pursuits and even the more accepted view that the princeps orchestrated a conscious "policy of literary management" (p. 123). In his intent and actions, Augustus maintained the traditional attitude of the Roman aristocracy toward literature. Augustus welcomed praise from the poets; he did not demand it and rarely sought it. For a sensible discussion of the dangers in searching for political slogans and ideology in Augustan poetry, see J. Griffin, "Augustus and the Poets," 189–218. The contemplative meditations by W.R. Johnson, "The Emotions of Patriotism: Propertius 4.6," *CSCA* 6 (1973): 171–80, on the failure of both versions of what we have fashioned the "Augustan myth" are still provocative and pertinent.

are the individual threads to weave together a clear and coherent pattern of "Augustan" ideology and official policy. The intentions behind such efforts cannot be faulted or denied, but this modern endeavor in literary embroidery involves too many presuppositions and difficulties. The "glorification" of Actium is a case in point. The Vergilian description of the naval battle and triple triumph on the centerpiece of the shield of Trojan Aeneas (*Aeneid* 8.671–728) is almost uniformly deemed the "Augustan" representation and official propaganda of the Actian victory, the "salutary myth which enhanced the sentiment of Roman nationalism to a formidable and even grotesque intensity."[102] However one views the *ecphrasis* of the hero's shield (and I do not think it one of the few moments of pure brightness in an otherwise dark epic), it must be admitted that the poet creates a powerful, arresting image of epic conflict. Dolphins sweep the seas with their tails, and Roman gods oppose barbaric deities. Antony marshals his forces into battle, the ironic victor of the East; his foreign consort shakes her *sistrum* and fails to discern the twin serpents who lurk behind her. Cleopatra is the tragic *regina*, with echoes of Dido, the Carthaginian queen whose love affair also threatened the destiny of Rome. Cultures, values, and ideologies clash; the struggle is defined in geographic terms, East versus West. One civilization gives way to the might and fortune of the other, a scene that closely prefigures the final book of the epic, where Juno demands that the homeland of Aeneas must perish forever and yield to the emergence of Rome.

> sit Latium, sint Albani per saecula reges,
> sit Romana potens Itala virtute propago:
> occidit, occideritque sinas cum nomine Troia.
>
> (*Aen.* 12.826–28)

[Let Latium be, let Alban kings rule throughout the centuries,
Let Roman stock be powerful in Italian virtue:
Troy has fallen, fallen let her be and in name as well.]

Is this a poet's transmission, the skillful manipulation of "Augustan" propaganda? I think not. What Augustus actually felt about Actium, and, more importantly, what he did to make those feelings a part of his public image in Rome, we simply do not know. His own account in his lost *Memoirs* cannot be reconstructed with assurance. In his official chronicle of deeds (*RG* 25.2–3), Augustus assumes a somewhat defensive attitude toward the Actian

---

102. Syme, *Roman Revolution*, 440.

campaign. He proudly lists the roll call of provinces who swore allegiance to his words and records the number of those senators, consuls, and priests who fought on his side. But he offers surprisingly no judgment on the meaning of the victory and its momentous consequences. Of his public actions, passed down to us from coinage, inscriptions, and monuments, little survives to support the view that he sought to revive the memory of his achievement at Actium, at least not directly, and certainly not initially. This is perhaps what is most critical and significant. A public attitude toward the naval battle surely must have changed in the forty-five years Augustus ruled Rome after his defeat of Antony. And the attitude of the poets must also not have remained constant or uniform throughout these years; this attitude perhaps influenced or reshaped the way even Augustus sought to glorify the outcome at Actium.

On his triumphant return to Rome in 29, the victor at Actium downplayed his success in civil war. The propaganda to distort a struggle for supreme power in Rome into a foreign campaign and war against Egypt and a queen is not the propaganda to reconcile former foes and to establish a new government. And Augustus was never the dupe of his own propaganda. Throughout the critical decade of the 20s, in the aftermath of the Actian victory, the princeps turned to the consolidation of his position in Rome and the restoration of traditional government. Former political enemies (and even those who fought on the wrong side) were recruited to serve in the new settlement of power. Some, of course, declined, but more accepted the rewards of elected offices, provincial administration, and foreign campaigns. Exaltation of Actium would stir only resentment and bitter memories of civil conflict, however successful the nationalistic fervor and slander might have been in rousing widespread support and gaining victory. Once established in a more secure political position after the events of January 27, the ruler in Rome, with a new, more imposing name, sought to extol his public image in Rome by military feats abroad: the campaign in Spain (27–24), which finally completed Roman pacification of the province; and the extended excursion in the East (22–19), which resulted in diplomatic negotiations with the Parthians that were acclaimed as a military victory and publicly awarded a triumph, ostentatiously declined by Augustus. Here the princeps successfully acted the role of the Roman general shaped by Republican virtues and models.[103] These subjects of martial prowess captured the attention and

---

103. Cf. the sobering comments by E.S. Gruen, "Augustus and the Ideology of War and Peace," in *Age of Augustus*, 51–72, esp. 54–55, on the militarism of Augustus in Republican tradition and the emphasis on war, not peace, in official ideology and documents.

imagination of the poets much more than the fame of Actium. Contrary to modern opinion, the naval battle is not a common and conspicuous subject of praise among the Augustan poets, though they were quick to recognize the new status of the victor and to applaud the consequences of battle, both as an end to the recurring cycle of civil strife and as an opportunity for conquest in the East. Whatever significance Augustus attached to Actium in his political ideology and public image, it cannot be found in the poems of Horace, Vergil, and Propertius. Or at least it should not be rashly interpreted to have been the impetus for the poetic compositions. Far from any perfunctory or purely propagandistic response of uncomplicated eulogy, Actium provoked mixed emotions from the poets. Reactions fluctuated from initial joy and relief to anxiety and fear, from painful anguish over the past to hopeful dreams of the future, from pointed ridicule to uneasy silence. It is the aim and challenge of the subsequent chapters to explore these emotions in an effort to evaluate the contemporary response toward Actium within the immediate and individual context of each poem—and without presumptions of political intent or grand purpose.

Chapter Three

Posteri Negabitis: Horace and Actium

A poem that succeeds in attracting attention from readers and literary critics only as a historical document of contemporary propaganda, battle strategy, and the political "conversion" of its author is not a successful poem.[1] Such is the unfortunate lot of Horace's *Epode* 9. The interpretation of the poem has varied widely among scholars. Long-standing and sharply divided controversy surrounds the exact occasion and setting of the epode.[2] On one matter, however, there is a firm consensus. The epode has been seen, almost without exception, as an immediate and exuberant expression of patriotic feeling by the poet, uncomplicated and unequivocal in its praise of the victorious side and reticent about the painful reality of the campaign as civil war. The comments cited below are representative of the modern opinion.

> The ninth Epode also celebrates Cleopatra's defeat, though her death had not yet occurred. It seems to have been written either during or immediately after the battle of Actium. . . . Whatever the internal difficulties as to the exact *mise-en-scène*, the Epode does not complicate its emotional demands as the Ode (I.37) does. The victory is unequivocally a Roman one, while Cleopatra is presented with a mixture of hostility and disgust.[3]

> *Epode 9,* written in Rome at the announcement of the first news of the battle, is unique in the whole body of Horace's work: a true "war poem," in the somewhat pejorative sense that the expression has taken on today—a liberation of elemental sentiments, denigrating the vanquished and exalting all those who had been on the right side. . . .[4]

---

1. S. Commager, "Horace, *Carmina* 1.37," *Phoenix* 12 (1958): 47, once voiced the same complaint about critical reception of the Cleopatra Ode (*Odes* 1.37). For my comments on this ode, see n. 44.

2. For bibliography on the epode, see A. Setaioli, "Gli 'Epodi' di Orazio nella critica dal 1937 al 1972," *ANRW* II.31.3 (Berlin and New York, 1981), 1716–32, and, most recently, A. Cavarzere, ed. *Orazio, il libro degli Epodi* (Venice, 1992), 172.

3. Commager, "Horace, *Carmina* 1.37," 52.

4. J. Perret, *Horace*, trans. B. Humez (New York, 1964), 89; originally published as *Horace* (Paris, 1959).

The glorification of Octavian looks beyond the archaic lyric poet [i.e., Alcaeus]. This feature of the poem recalls the greatest of the Greek lyric poets, Pindar: a victory celebration, the supreme deity as the center of everything, and the victor himself are a Pindaric ensemble par excellence.[5]

Epode 9, if not an essay in panegyric along such lines [i.e., in the tradition of poets who accompany military leaders to hymn their successes], is nevertheless the clearly foreseen outcome of Horace's Actium-trip—that is, a piece of calculated propaganda, which claims authority for its version of events by the fact of the poet's autopsy.[6]

The nature of the past scholarly discussion regarding the interpretation of the Horatian epode is twofold. It derives not so much from how Horace reacts to the momentous event of recent history, its immediate and profound consequences, but from when and where the poet composed his epode. This stubborn preoccupation with biographical matters of composition is due chiefly to two problematic passages in the epode. The first involves the brief and pointed description of what seems to be (or substitutes for) the battle at Actium in lines 17–20. It has often been speculated that the type of information, namely, the desertion of the Galatian cavalry and the movement of the enemy ships, is too precise and perhaps too technical for a poet in Rome to relate; it suits better an eyewitness of the historic event. Hence arises the inclination of ancient historians to account for the specificity of the poet's words and meaning. W.W. Tarn supposed some form of "despatch" had been sent immediately after the encounter at Actium from Octavian to Maecenas in Rome and through Maecenas to Horace, his good friend and poet. Through his careful reconstruction of the poet's four-verse "despatch," Tarn attempted to confirm his view of the tactics, maneuvers, and outcome of the famous naval battle. Tarn confidently exclaimed, "That is how it happened that, for once, somebody [i.e., Horace] told the truth about Actium."[7]

The second and fiercely disputed difficulty is the phrase *fluentem nauseam* at the conclusion of the epode. The mention of *nausea* led Franz Bücheler to conjecture as long ago as 1878 that the word should imply real

5. E. Kraggerud, *Horaz und Actium. Studien zu den politischen Epoden*, Symbolae Osloenses Supplementum 26 (Oslo, 1984), 118 (author's translation).

6. L. Watson, "*Epode 9*, or the Art of Falsehood," in *Homo Viator: Classical Essays for John Bramble*, ed. M. Whitby et al. (Bristol and Oak Park, Ill., 1987), 122.

7. W.W. Tarn, "The Battle of Actium," *JRS* 21 (1931): 176.

seasickness and that it testifies that Horace was present at Actium and indeed aboard ship during the decisive naval battle.[8] Bücheler's interpretation of the phrase gave cause to Tarn and other critics to read the poem as if it were an actual news bulletin of the events at Actium to the citizens in Rome. Nonetheless, whether scholarship placed the poet aboard the ships of Octavian at Actium or in the more peaceful and tranquil environs of Rome, the outcome was the same: Horace was more journalist than poet.

Erik Wistrand's lengthy monograph on the historical background to the epode sought a final resolution to the vexing question of the poet's involvement in the naval battle. Wistrand, who soberly examined the ancient sources to support or deny the possibility of military travel by the poet, concluded that there was no "reliable external evidence" to determine either view; in short, "we have nothing to go by but the poem itself."[9] Wistrand's is a sound approach to reading any Horatian ode, but his conclusions reveal that he belies his own critical postulate when he allows unsubstantiated assumptions to prejudice his interpretation.

> The epode was written before the battle of Actium but after the initial successes won by Octavian's navy and cavalry, viz. in the last days of August, 31 B.C. It was written in the theatre of war, perhaps in Octavian's camp on the hill of Mikalitzi, Horace having followed his friend Maecenas into war in accordance with the same conception of the duties of friendship that made Maecenas take the field with Octavian. The poem reflects the tense impatient atmosphere reigning among the adherents of Octavian just before the battle whose issue was to decide their fate and Rome's.[10]

A host of literary critics and scholars united in their opposition to Wistrand and his predecessors, but not without their own assumptions and biases about the purpose of the epode. Eduard Fraenkel understood the poem's fictive scene as a private banquet among friends in the tradition of the Greek lyric poets Archilochus and Alcaeus. There is much reason to agree with this interpretation, but unfortunately Fraenkel allotted more space to a refutation of the conjecture by Bücheler concerning the meaning

---

8. F. Bücheler, "*Coniectanea,*" in *Index scholarum quae summis auspiciis regis augustissimi Guilelmi Imperatoris Germaniae*, ed. F. Bücheler, 3–26 (Bonn, 1878–79); reprinted in *Kleine Schriften* (Leipzig and Berlin, 1927), 2:311–33.

9. E. Wistrand, *Horace's Ninth Epode and Its Historical Background*, Studia Graeca et Latina Gothoburgensia 8 (Göteborg, 1958), 19.

10. Wistrand, *Horace's Ninth Epode*, 35.

of *fluentem nauseam* than to his own analysis of the theme, structure, and tone of the poem's narrative. As for the matter of the epode's composition, Fraenkel shared the view that the intense, emotional character of the poem's speaker suggested that *Epode* 9 was an immediate and uncomplicated response to the news of Octavian's victory.

> There exist in ancient literature very few, if any, poems in which the emotions at the height of a great historical crisis are expressed with such vigour and directness. There can be little doubt that Horace conceived the idea of this epode on the spur of the moment, before the military and political consequences of the battle of Actium could fully unfold. He then left the poem as he had written it.[11]

The curious shifts of mood and action throughout the course of the thirty-eight verses of the epode seem to confuse and complicate, if not to deny, the prevalent interpretation that the poem is a celebration of Caesar's victory. If the poet had intended simply to praise the recent success, why does he look back to the victory over Sextus Pompey, why does he express disgust at Roman service to a woman and her band of withered eunuchs, and why does he desire to forget his anxiety and fear about the affairs of Caesar by the demand for the same wine (Caecuban) that in the opening of the epode was to be reserved for the victory celebration in the home of Maecenas? That the defeated Antony had not been captured and had escaped from Actium with the fleet and treasure of his foreign wife still intact may have given any supporter of Octavian cause to worry, and this may help to explain, in part, the anxious fear that somberly concludes the poem. But this alone will not suffice to account for the "miserable complaint," the phrase by which L.P. Wilkinson characterized the opening sixteen verses of the epode.[12] The epode has long been viewed by past scholarship as a spontaneous outburst of feeling by the poet. Horace's motivation and intentions in writing the epode have not been a matter of serious inquiry or dispute. The epode has been read simply as a celebration of the recent Actian victory. Horace's presumed enthusiasm for Octavian's exploit at Actium has been judged to

---

11. E. Fraenkel, *Horace* (Oxford, 1957), 75.

12. L.P. Wilkinson, "Horace, *Epode* IX," *CR* 47 (1933): 2–6, was troubled by the "miserable complaint" of the first sixteen lines in contrast to the last twelve, which he thought seemed to be "unmistakably a paean of triumph." In an effort to find some reason for this disparity of tone, Wilkinson proposed the thesis that "the poem was written 'in tranquillity,' presumably at Rome not long after the battle, but that it is a dramatic presentation of the supposed feelings, the changing moods, of a participant on the Caesarian side during those days at sea off Actium" (p. 4).

outweigh his talents as a poet. What follows is an effort to rectify the imbalance of the modern critical reception toward the epode and to reconsider Horace's text through a close reading and analysis of its poetic discourse.

Initial Joy of Victory and the *mixtum carmen*

Quando repostum Caecubum ad festas dapes
   victore laetus Caesare
tecum sub alta—sic Iovi gratum—domo,
   beate Maecenas, bibam
sonante mixtum tibiis carmen lyra,
   hac Dorium, illis barbarum,

                              (lines 1–6)

[When will I drink the Caecuban set aside for festive banquets,
   happy in Caesar's victory,
under the high roof of your home (so may it please Jupiter),
   with you, my fortunate Maecenas,
with the lyre offering a mixed song with the pipe,
   the one in Dorian, the other in foreign measure,]

Horace commences the epode with an address to his friend and patron, Maecenas. In form, his is a question that expresses both anticipation and joy. The poet wants to know when the two will drink the choice Caecuban wine, reserved for special festive occasions. The cause of this hoped-for celebration is at once made clear; it will be in honor of Octavian's victory in battle. The second verse establishes the mood of festive joy, and the emphatic adjective *laetus*, neatly balanced by the two ablatives that refer to the name and honor of Octavian, might suggest that the poet is about to undertake a song of joy and of victory celebration. The celebration will take place in the palatial residence of Maecenas on the Esquiline (*alta . . . domo*), and music will accompany the select vintage. The setting of the banquet is not surprising, but the intruding exclamation *sic Iovi gratum* raises some questions.

Wistrand understood the parenthetical phrase as part of an "ancient pattern" going back to a Greek model, perhaps to Archilochus. He explains it thus:

There is a critical situation with misgivings as to the future, caused by disappointing delay of final victory; there is an assurance of Jove's benevolence; after an account of the war-situation, comprising both disgusting and, especially, hopeful features, there follows an invitation to have a carouse to forget all qualms for the outcome of the war and the welfare of Caesar.[13]

Gordon Williams criticized Wistrand's interpretation of the phrase for his "strong whiff of *interpolatio Christiana,*"[14] but some have surprisingly attached even greater importance to the role of Horace as *vates* who is interpreting the will of Jupiter. The phrase has been seen to anticipate and resemble the proclamations by Horace in the later *Odes* where the rule of Octavian on earth is paralleled to that of Jupiter in heaven (cf. *Odes* 1.12.51–60).[15] Others have proceeded further and more boldly in their interpretations. Egil Kraggerud's monograph is comprehensive in its approach and scope, provocative in its conclusions. Kraggerud interprets *Epodes* 1, 7, 9, and 16 as a carefully orchestrated and preconceived group by the poet, designed to convey his changing sentiment and attitude toward different phases in Rome's latest example of civil strife, culminating in the victory at Actium. In such a collection, *Epode 9* is to be regarded as the poet's final word on the great conflict and as the proclamation of his conversion and loyalty to Octavian. Kraggerud concludes that Horace is no longer simply the *comes Maecenatis* by the end of the *Epodes* but instead has become the *vates Caesaris.*[16] Thus, he contends that the mention of Jupiter anticipates the outcry of *io triumphe* later in the epode, and that the "Jove" in line 3 should be understood as Jupiter Optimus Maximus in his role as the presiding deity in the celebration of a triumph. The lofty home is not that of Maecenas but the Temple of Jupiter on the Capitoline hill. The poet's anticipated celebration is not the private symposium of friends but the public ceremony of a Roman triumph. Before one accepts the brief parenthetical remark as the poet's statement of intention to celebrate Octavian as triumphator or as god incarnate, closer examination of the text seems in order.

First, nothing in the first six verses suggests any formal or public celebration of Caesar's victory. From the mention of the stored away Caecuban, of the *domus* (immediately following a direct address to Maecenas by *tecum*),

---

13. Wistrand, *Horace's Ninth Epode*, 23.

14. G. Williams, *Tradition and Originality in Roman Poetry* (Oxford, 1968), 216. Williams' own view of the phrase is uncertain. He interprets the sense of the opening question to be that "a great victory has been won: when shall we celebrate?" For Williams, the question serves as the "equivalent of a polite order by the poet to commence the celebration which he indicates."

15. For example, see C. Bartels, "Die neunte Epode des Horaz als sympotisches Gedicht," *Hermes* 101 (1973): 288.

16. Kraggerud, *Horaz und Actium*, 119.

and of the music of the pipes and lyre, a private and intimate form of celebration seems more likely. Second, it is not certain that the phrase is intended to refer directly to the victory of Caesar or, far less, to any "divine approval" of Caesar's rule. D.R. Shackleton Bailey understood the phrase to imply some form of earnest prayer that such a welcome occasion of festivity might soon occur, and with no manuscript authority, he sought to emend the text to read *si* instead of *sic*.[17] The parallels he cites from Terence, Ovid, and Persius demonstrate clearly that such requests or hopes may be prefaced by an appeal to the gods to ensure their approval or to testify to their omnipotence in a particular matter (*si placet dis, faveant modo numina,* and *Iove dextro*).[18] But the emendation is unnecessary. The *sic* clause may also express a wish for the god's approval. The supplied verb of the clause is dependent on the opening sentence's main verb, *bibam,* which is in the future tense; it is a declaration of the poet's ardent hope that the god will approve and will take part in the celebration of Octavian's victory at the home of Maecenas. Whether we assume the subjunctive *sit* or the future *erit,* both refer to the hoped-for or anticipated occasion of Jupiter's participation in the festivities of Caesar's victory. It seems difficult to believe that this parenthetical inclusion would suggest to any reader of the poem at this point Jupiter's role in the solemn ceremony of a triumph. The god's approval of the festivities is as much a part of the banquet's setting as the wine and music (cf. the call to the Pompeius in *Odes* 2.7.17 to offer a banquet to Jove in gratitude for his return from exile: *ergo obligatam redde Iovi dapem*). The long separation between *alta* and *domo* that results from the intervention of this phrase draws special attention to the home of the poet's patron and its lofty and sumptuous heights (cf. Horace's allusion at *Odes* 3.29.10 to Maecenas' residence: *molem propinquam nubibus arduis*). The phrase *sic Iovi gratum* is thus not so much Horace's prayer or assurance of the god's role in Caesar's victory as much as his wish or confident expectation that he will celebrate this fortunate event with Maecenas.

Following the mention of the choice of wine and the locale of the banquet, Horace devotes two carefully balanced lines to an extended description of the *mixtum carmen* of the pipes and lyre that will accompany the festivities.

---

17. D.R. Shackleton Bailey, *Profile of Horace* (London, 1982), 80.

18. The list, of course, could be expanded. For example, Terence uses the same phrase, *si dis placet,* in *Ad.* 476. S.G. Ashmore's note in *The Comedies of Terence,* 2d ed. (Oxford, 1908), ad loc., is instructive for the passage in Horace: "a formula used only of past or present, never of future events, and employed chiefly when mention is made of matters of an astonishing or unexpected nature." Neither condition of this formula is applicable to the phrase in the epode. The verb in the opening question is in the future tense (*bibam*), and the celebration (or the victory) is certainly not of "an astonishing or unexpected nature," at least not to Horace.

The verses have been judged as nothing more than a decorative poetic addition to the symposiastic scene. The specification of the two modes, *Dorium* and *barbarum*, might suggest otherwise. From earliest tradition and practice, the deep and severe tones of the lyre in the Dorian mode of music were associated with war and battle; the lighter and sweeter sounds of flutes and pipes in the Phrygian mode were more suited to festive celebration and unfettered revelry.[19] Yet the difference lay not so much in the particular instruments (since, for example, the *tibiae* could play in either the Dorian or the Phrygian mode) but in the style of music and, more precisely, the type of scale. In the simplest terms, the Dorian mode was heavy and more somber; the Phrygian, delicate and more cheerful. While the music of different instruments, in the accompaniment of singers, could be mingled into a harmonious unison, the two modes could not be played simultaneously. That the playing of the two opposed modes should somehow alternate for the same occasion is most unusual, and E.C. Wickham long ago noted the difficulties that would arise if the poet's words in lines 5–6 were forced into a literal meaning.[20]

The problem is not with the phrase *mixtum carmen*. Horace uses it later in the opening ode of his fourth book: *lyraeque et Berecyntiae / delectabere tibiae / mixtis carminibus non sine fistula* (*Odes* 4.1.22–24).[21] In the epode, Horace is more specific. The *mixtum carmen* will be not only the combination of different instruments that can play in any mode but the interchange between the two discordant modes or scales, *hac Dorium, illis barbarum*. The lyre and the pipes will be playing out of harmony and in different scales. Wickham suggested that the occasion demanded both the martial tone suitable to the subject of war and the festive tone used to celebrate victory. This might seem the simplest solution, but I suggest that Horace intended something more: the contrast between these two scales

---

19. For discussions of the Dorian and Phrygian modes, see Plut. *de Mus.* 1136d–f and 1143. Plato (*Rep.* 398c–399d) excludes all styles of music from his ideal state except for the Dorian and Phrygian modes; for these, the philosopher says, "best imitate the tunes of men's successes and failures, their prudent sobriety and courageous action." Cf. remarks by J.C. Orelli, ed., *Q. Horatius Flaccus*, revised by J.G. Baiter and W. Hirschfelder, 2 vols., 4th ed. (Berlin, 1886), vol. 1, ad loc., and T.E. Page, A. Palmer, and A.S. Wilkins, eds., *Q. Horati Flacci Opera* (London, 1910; reprinted 1922), ad loc.

20. E.C. Wickham, ed., *Quinti Horatii Flacci Opera Omnia: The Works of Horace*, 2 vols., 3d ed. (Oxford, 1896), vol. 1, ad loc.

21. Unfortunately, there are problems with the text; some editors prefer *lyra* and *tibia* in the ablative. In either case, the occurrence of the phrase *mixtis carminibus* probably refers only to mixture of the different instruments or, less likely, to the mixture of instruments with the voices of singers. The appearance of the Berecyntian pipes testifies to the festive occasion and the adoption of the Phrygian mode.

both anticipates and corresponds to the shifts of tone in the course of the epode, shifts in tone that will not be fully realized until the final call for wine at the poem's conclusion. The emphatic adjective *barbarum*, a poetic substitute for *Phrygium*, concludes its line and brings to a close the long introductory question of the first six verses. The resonance inherent in the word serves as a fitting transition to Horace's reflection on the past conflict with Sextus Pompey and his description of the Actian campaign and victory.

The *Neptunius dux* and the Recollection of Naulochus

ut nuper, actus cum freto Neptunius
    dux fugit ustis navibus,
minatus urbi vincla, quae detraxerat
    servis amicus perfidis?

(lines 7–10)

[just as before when Neptune's admiral was driven from the sea
    and fled with his ships in flames,
having threatened the city with chains that he had removed
    from the faithless slaves, acting as their friend?]

It is from the anticipated joy and festivities of Octavian's victory that Horace looks back to an earlier occasion when the poet celebrated with Maecenas the defeat of Sextus Pompey and his band of supporters at Naulochus. For some critics of the epode, this reflection on the earlier naval battle (five years before Actium) makes Horace more propagandist than poet.

> Horace is not simply following a literary course here; he has chosen this poetic technique because it is apt for his main propaganda purpose—to disguise as far as possible the civil element of the Actian war, and indeed of the war with Pompeius, and to represent the first as a war against slaves and the second as a war against foreigners.[22]

---

22. F. Cairns, "Horace, *Epode* 9: Some New Interpretations," *ICS* 8.1 (1983): 83. This is essentially the view argued most recently by Watson, "*Epode* 9, or the Art of Falsehood," who seeks to demonstrate how the epode is "in its conception, quite as propagandist as Virgil's and Propertius' account of Actium" and how this characteristic of the epode depends "not on inventing 'facts,' but, more insidiously, in *slanting* [Watson's italics] the presentation of these facts in such a way as to evoke the desired response in the audience" (pp. 120–21). Like Kraggerud, *Horaz und Actium* and R.G.M. Nisbet, "Horace's *Epodes* and History," in *Poetry and Politics*, 1–18, Watson views Horace as an eyewitness to the battle, the poet taken on the military campaign so that he might "hymn the successes" of Octavian.

Octavian's war with Sextus was civil war, the struggle between Caesar and Pompey fought by their sons and a second generation. No contemporary propaganda could successfully obscure this reality. The victor boasted to his fellow citizens that the defeat of Sextus at last brought an end to the internal discord and bitter conflict in Rome. The character and reputation of his opponent and his supporters were especially vulnerable to Octavian's propagandizing attack. In the war of words, Sextus became not the distinguished son of Pompey the Great or the favorite of Neptune, god of the sea, as he proclaimed himself, but a pirate, an outlaw, and a traitor. His followers were runaway slaves and disgruntled veterans. Years later, in the *Res Gestae*, the victor would characterize the struggle in such a manner. The illustrious family name of his opponent and his Roman identity are conspicuously absent.

Mare pacavi a praedonibus. Eo bello servorum qui fugerant a dominis suis et arma contra rem publicam ceperant triginta fere millia capta dominis ad supplicium sumendum tradidi. (*RG* 25.1)

[I brought peace to the sea by removing the pirates. In that war, I captured nearly thirty thousand slaves who had fled from their masters and taken up arms against the state, and I handed them over to their masters for punishment.]

Horace derides Sextus by the invidious phrases *Neptunius dux* and *servis amicus perfidis*. Sextus' claim to divinity must have been well known to Horace's audience, and Horace pointedly ridicules the claim by emphasizing the fact that this beloved of Neptune was himself defeated at sea and forced to flee with his ships in flames. But the boasts of Sextus were dangerous as well as bold. The son of Pompey threatened the city with the chains he had taken from the faithless slaves of Roman masters. It would seem from such rhetoric that the poet was already a strong and loyal supporter of Octavian in the war with Sextus. But denigration of one side in Roman civil war does not necessarily imply wholehearted support for the other. I suggest instead that final judgment concerning the poet's "propaganda purpose" and the point of this reflection on the recent past should be withheld until his description of the Actian campaign, where we might realize more fully the nature and dimensions of the comparison between the two naval victories.

The Actian Campaign and Battle

Romanus, eheu,—posteri negabitis—
  emancipatus feminae
fert vallum et arma miles et spadonibus
  servire rugosis potest,
interque signa turpe militaria
  sol aspicit conopium.

ad hunc frementes verterunt bis mille equos
  Galli, canentes Caesarem,
hostiliumque navium portu latent
  puppes sinistrorsum citae.

(lines 11–20)

[The Roman, alas—future generations, you will deny it—
  enslaved in bondage to a woman,
carries stakes and weapons, and he—the Roman soldier—
  suffers to serve her withered eunuchs.
And amid the military standards—the shame—
  the sun looks on the foreign canopy.

At this sight, turning their two thousand snorting steeds,
  the Gauls chant Caesar's name.
The ships of the enemy lurk in the harbor,
  their swift prows turned to the left.]

An exclamation of indignation and sorrow introduces Horace's reader to Actium—the campaign and victory. It is a powerful and provocative introduction. The scene shifts suddenly from past recollection to present reality. The connection is made by the forceful *Romanus*. The adjective at last finds a subject only after the emotional interjection, parenthetical imperative, participial phrase, verb, and double object. The delayed appearance of *miles* compels the reader to return to *Romanus* and to reflect on the serious implications of the poet's declaration on the Actian campaign. Horace has no simple "propaganda purpose" in mind, as Cairns has described it.[23] Far

---

23. Cairns, "Horace, *Epode* 9," excludes any mention of this passage from his interpretation of the epode.

from hiding the true nature of the conflict and disguising the struggle as simply a war against Egypt, Horace openly laments Roman complicity with the enemy. At the same time, his ominous foretelling of posterity's denial of this complicity only emphasizes his own painfully true recognition of the dimension of civil discord in this "foreign" campaign. The *femina* of line 12 is Cleopatra, queen of Egypt, and the *rugosi spadones* are her effeminate followers—both characterizations of the enemy fitting Octavian's prewar propaganda. But the shameful subservience of the *Romanus miles* to a woman and her wrinkled crew of eunuchs is the emphatic point of the outburst.

The ignominious condition of the "Roman soldier" receives a long and emotional description. Kraggerud explains the force of the phrase *emancipatus feminae* in line 12 by understanding Cleopatra as the explicit "buyer" of the soldier/slave and Antony as the unmentioned "seller."[24] The verb *emancipare* strictly means "to free from someone's *mancipium*" with the dative, but it acquires the additional meaning "to transfer from one *mancipium* to another" or simply "to sell."[25] Kraggerud has argued that Antony alone is implied by the phrase *Romanus miles* and that the singular noun bestows some feeling of pardon and amnesty to the nineteen legions of Roman soldiers who chose to take sides against Octavian and later surrendered. The poet's act of generosity should seem surprising to any reader of the *Epodes*; Horace was not so generous to his compatriots in *Epodes* 7 and 16, nor was he at all reticent about the recurrence of civil war in Rome.

> Quo, quo scelesti ruitis? aut cur dexteris
>   aptantur enses conditi?
> parumne campis atque Neptuno super
>   fusum est Latini sanguinis?
>
>   (*Epode* 7.1–4)

> [Where, where are you rushing, criminals? Or why do your hands
>   take up the swords, once sheathed?
> On the fields and over the sea of Neptune has
>   too little Latin blood been poured?]

> Altera iam teritur bellis civilibus aetas,
>   suis et ipsa Roma viribus ruit;
>
>   (*Epode* 16. 1–2)

---

24. Kraggerud, *Horaz und Actium*, 84 (author's translation).
25. Wickham, *Works of Horace*, vol. 1, ad loc.

[Already a second generation is exhausted by civil wars,
    and from her own strength Rome herself collapses;]

For Horace, the blood of Remus is *sacer* to the descendants of Romulus
(*Epode* 7.19–20). Later poems in his collected three books of *Odes* also
testify to his strong feelings on civil war, Roman guilt, and the punishment
of the gods (*Odes* 1.2, 1.14, 1.21.13–16, 1.35.29–40, 2.1, and 3.6).

Rather than assume that Horace seeks to spare the soldiers of Antony
from the guilt of civil war, we must consider what the poet's purpose would
be in calling Antony the *Romanus miles*. Here *miles* must be the decisive
word. If Antony alone is implied, the noun is surely a scornful addition and
disparagement of Antony's role in the war. Octavian's opponent would thus
be ridiculed as not only the slave to a woman (*emancipatus feminae*) but her
foot soldier as well (*fert vallum et arma miles*). Octavian's propaganda surely
said as much, and the Roman Senate confirmed this view when it officially
declared Cleopatra *hostis* without any reference to Antony.[26] But Horace
does not deny Antony the leading role in the war; he refers directly to the
nature of the conflict as civil war (*Romanus* cannot mean otherwise), and,
more importantly, he later addresses Antony as the *hostis* who abandons his
crimson military cloak, the emblem of his command, and flees south on his
uncertain course (lines 27–32). Finally, the emphatic force of *Romanus* in
the opening of the verse, the passion in the exclamation *eheu*[27] immediately
following the adjective, and the boldness in the address to future generations, *posteri negabitis*, would seem to suggest that something more than
one man's treachery and servile complicity with a woman and her band of
eunuchs disturbs Horace; it is the reality and horror of civil war.

The phrases *emancipatus feminae* (line 12) and *servire . . . potest* (line 14)
recall and draw a comparison with the *servis perfidis* who were freed by
Sextus Pompey and who once threatened the welfare and freedom of the city.
In the present conflict, the treachery is more incredible, and the situation is
more precarious because the enemy is supported by Rome's own strength,
her own soldiers. In Horace's Actian conflict, the Roman soldier exchanges
roles with the Egyptian slaves. The *Romanus miles* serves the *rugosis spadonibus*.[28] The phrase *servire . . . potest*, which describes the action of the

---

26. On the implications of the political decision to declare Cleopatra only as the *hostis* of
Rome, see M. Reinhold, "Declaration of War against Cleopatra," 97–103.

27. For the emotional intensity of the interjection, cf. *Odes* 3.2.9, where the *adulta virgo*
sighs when she beholds from the walls of the city her betrothed in deadly combat.

28. Augustus is said to have claimed as much in his *Memoirs: et Augustus in commemora-
tione vitae suae refert Antonium iussisse ut legiones suae apud Cleopatram excubarent et eius
nutu et iussu parerent* (Serv. *Comm. in Verg. Aen.* 8.696).

miles, is almost a verbal oxymoron. In the following two verses, the sun shines on the foreign pavilion amid the Roman standards. The appearance of the *signa* testifies to the complicity and participation of Roman soldiers in the battle. The military standards, the proud symbol of austere Roman glory, are the ironic antithesis to the shamefully sybaritic gauze of the Egyptians. The jarring insertion of *turpe* between *signa* and *militaria* and the emphatic postponement of *conopium* until the end of the verse accentuate the perversion of this vivid scene and at the same time reveal the speaker's disgust. The scene closes with the penetrating rays of the sun exposing the shameful and obscured truth of the Actian campaign.[29]

From the servile condition and shame of the *Romanus miles*, Horace turns to the actions of the foreign enemy. The brief battle description Horace chooses to relate seems closer to preliminary maneuvers than to actual fighting. Here historians have sought to discover the strategy of Antony and its failed outcome. Textual problems and obscurity of meaning have frustrated such attempts. The reading of the first two words at the beginning of line 17 is not certain. But whether one chooses the phrases *ad hunc* (of the best manuscript authority), *ad hoc, adhuc,* or *at huc*, the identification of the *Galli* is clear. These are the Galatians, ruled over by Amyntas, an ally of Antony who deserted to Octavian shortly before the confrontation.[30] Scholars are puzzled about why Horace chose to single out this one example of desertion to the side of Octavian. The ancient scholiast understood an implicit contrast between the foreigners who sided with Octavian and the Romans who served eunuchs.

> quorum mentio ideo facta est ut Romanos qui sub praepositis spadonibus aequo animo militarent magis oneraret per comparationem Gallorum qui hoc dedignati ad Caesarem se contulerunt. (Porphyrion *Comm. in* Hor. Epod.)

---

29. By the choice of the verb (*aspicit*), Horace perhaps calls to mind the attribute of the Sun, well known and familiar in ancient literature, as the observer of all human activity (cf. Ovid *Meta.* 2.32: *Sol oculis . . . quibus aspicit omnia*). The omniscient god is often the witness of human and divine acts of foul murder or rape, such as the abduction of Persephone and the feasting of Thyestes on his own children and in historical times, the assassination of Julius Caesar (Verg. *Geo.* 1.463–65; Tib. 2.5.75–76; Ovid *Meta.* 15.785–86; Pliny *NH* 2.98; Plut. *Caes.* 69.5; Dio 45.17.5).

30. Plut. *Ant.* 63.3. Plutarch seems to be in error when he includes Deiotarus as one of the defectors. Dio (48.33.5, 49.32.3) relates that Deiotarus died in Galatia in 40 B.C.E. and that Antony later gave the rule of Galatia, Lycaonia, and portions of Pamphylia to Amyntas, although he had only been the secretary of Deiotarus.

[And thus their mention is made so that the Romans who served of their own accord under the eunuchs who had been placed over them would suffer in comparison with the Gauls who scorned this and transferred their allegiance to Caesar.]

The contrast is bold and effective, but there is also a bitter irony in the fact that the much celebrated foe of Julius sided with Octavian and the Caesarian party while the Roman soldier served a foreign queen.[31]

The meaning of the following two lines, which concern the movement and disposition of the enemy's fleet, is more difficult to assess. Special attention and close scrutiny have fallen on the curious phrase *sinistrorsum citae*. Efforts at explanation have not been very successful. Scholars seek to interpret the lines as an allusion to the enemy's defeat and flight back into the Ambracian Gulf. The most recent attempts range from Cairns' literary suggestion that *sinistrorsum* is an example of Horace's erudition and a literal translation of a Homeric phrase to Pelling's historical argument that it referred to Antony's right wing backing water to port when his ships attempted to retreat from Agrippa's successful flanking maneuver.[32] Neither interpretation is fully satisfactory. What has often been overlooked by scholars is the meaning of the earlier phrase *portu latent*. In fact, Pelling begins his argument with the brusque dismissal "there is no problem in *portu latent*." He concludes from the brief phrase that the "fleet has withdrawn, and is skulking in harbour instead of fighting." This view presupposes a naval engagement or at least an initial formation, which Horace prefers not to mention. I suggest instead that the two lines actually refer to the activity of the ships before the battle. Antony's fleet is "skulking in harbour" because it is reluctant to engage, or it at least initially refused to engage. This much the ancient sources confirm. Plutarch (*Ant.* 65.4) refers

---

31. The suggestion by Cairns, "Horace, *Epode 9*," 82, that Horace was trying to be precise in his ethnography by specifying the Galatians as *Galli* rather than as *Galatae* or *Gallograeci* (not poetic choices in any case) or that he was "demonstrating *doctrina* of the type generally affected by Hellenistic and Augustan poets" is dubious. In books 33–35, Livy regularly calls the Galatians *Galli* and only adopts the term *Gallograeci* where some confusion might arise with their relations in Europe. Cf. Livy's explanation of this relationship (38.17.9).

32. Cf. Cairns, "Horace, *Epode 9*," 90, and C.B.R. Pelling, "*Puppes sinistrorsum citae*," *CQ* 80, n.s. 36 (1986): 177–81, respectively. That Horace's phrase refers to "backing water to port" is not new, but Pelling explains this odd type of movement by the fact that the large, heavy ships of Antony on the right wing, once caught off from the center, could not expect to make it safely back to harbor and were dependent on their catapults to protect them. The "suspended fire-pots," which Pelling claims "were hung forward, ahead of the bows," would become ineffective if they turned in flight.

to Octavian's uneasy feelings when he surveyed his line of battle and saw that the enemy ships remained still in the narrows, with "the appearance of riding at anchor." Dio (50.31.4–6) also mentions that Antony's ships had refused to engage (or even withdraw) when Octavian's ships first advanced. Surprised at the enemy's reaction, Octavian ordered his sailors to rest their oars and wait. Finally, when Octavian attempted to form a crescent ring and surround the enemy, Antony's ships reluctantly joined battle. Horace may be referring to this initial phase of the battle, but we should be especially cautious to presuppose his interest in or knowledge of historical facts or detail.[33] More likely, the poet wants his brief and pointed description of the enemy ships to correspond in manner and tone to his previous couplet on the surrender of the Galatian cavalry. The connective *que* and the parallel structure of the verses suggest that this correspondence is Horace's intention. Horace has emphasized the desertion of the enemy on both land and sea (*terra marique victus hostis*, line 27). The poet is thus not attempting to narrate individual phases of the Actian battle or to provide a "running commentary" of its outcome;[34] instead he has focused on what must be seen as the preliminaries to the fight, in which the disgrace of Roman soldiers who carried arms in service to a woman and her band of eunuchs caused even former foes to shift allegiance and hostile ships to remain in harbor with their prows turned aside. From such an inglorious exposition of the conflict's nature and outcome, the poet turns suddenly to the martial virtues of the "victorious" general and the address to Triumphus.

The Cry of Triumph and the *nec parem ducem*

> io Triumphe, tu moraris aureos
>   currus et intactas boves?
> io Triumphe, nec Iugurthino parem
>   bello reportasti ducem
> neque Africanum, cui super Carthaginem
>   virtus sepulcrum condidit.

(lines 21–26)

---

33. It is interesting to observe that Plutarch and Dio differ about which side began the naval engagement. Plutarch (*Ant.* 65.4) records that only at the sixth hour and when a wind was rising from the sea did Antony's soldiers become impatient and move their left wing in motion. Dio (50.31.5) relates that Octavian was more impulsive and gave the signal for both his wings to advance and encircle the enemy. Antony, fearing the flanking movement, advanced with trepidation and as best as his heavy ships could maneuver in the water.

34. Nisbet, "Horace's *Epodes* and History," 16. Nisbet prefers to imagine Horace actually at the scene of battle and argues that *nausea* refers to the "sufferings on shipboard rather than the excesses of the celebration itself."

[Hail Triumphus! Do you hold back the golden
   chariots and unyoked oxen?
Hail Triumphus! You have not brought back
   a general like the one in Jugurtha's war
and not Africanus, whose valor built him
   a tomb over Carthage.]

When the poet raises the ritual cry of *Io Triumphe*, the startled reader must
realize that the battle at Actium is already won. The preliminaries to war—
the refusals or reluctance to engage (lines 17–20)—must substitute for any
description of battle. The absence is striking and disturbing for those
scholars who seek documented information from the "poet's despatch to
Rome." The poet instead asks the god Triumphus why he delays the golden
chariots and sacrificial animals, symbols of the splendor and solemnity of
the Roman triumph. This emotional and twice-repeated appeal to the Triumph god has been interpreted, almost without exception, as both a reflection of Horace's anxious and ardent desire to begin the festivities and an
opportunity to praise the military exploits of the victor of Actium. This is
perhaps why Wilkinson concludes that Horace was "swept off his feet" with
enthusiasm and impatience when he composed the epode.[35] And Kraggerud
understood the appearance of the verb *moraris* to imply "not concern" but
"impatience."[36] For it was only a question of time before Rome would
witness the glorious triumphal procession along the Sacra Via.

The key word is *moraris*. From such interpretations, the address to Triumphus has lost its force as an interrogative, and the verb has lost its
meaning. It has become instead almost a poetic or rhetorical alternative to
an imperative, calling on the god himself to start the celebration.[37] But the
difference between the two, I suggest, is a matter not of style but of meaning.
The poet forces us to ask what would be the cause for any delay. Since the
victory was won, Octavian's return to the city might seem to be the only
impediment to an actual celebration of a triumph. But the tone and content
of the preceding verses do not proclaim any cause to celebrate a triumph.
The characterization of the present campaign, where all roles are reversed,
where the *Romanus miles* serves the *femina* and her band of wrinkled men,
and where only foreign allies hitherto associated with the enemy are inspired
to cry the praise of Caesar, prepares us to expect something much different

---

35. Such is the characterization of the poet's feelings in the epode by Wilkinson, "Horace,
Epode IX," 68.
36. Kraggerud, *Horaz und Actium*, 103.
37. Williams, *Tradition and Originality in Roman Poetry*, 218.

from a frenetic outcry of joy. After such a description of the battle, Horace's appeal to the Triumph god must surprise our expectations.

From a long and distinguished list of triumphs from Rome's glorious past, Horace selects two for his comparison. The selection has a specific purpose. Instead of looking back to the recent past, to the multiple and grand triumphs of Pompey or Julius Caesar—the standards that Octavian would strive to surpass with his own triple triumph ceremony—Horace turns to the victories of Gaius Marius and Scipio Africanus. The connection between the three triumphators is the homeland of their vanquished opponents, the continent of Africa. To make this point of the comparison more explicit, the poet directs his reader's attention to the identity of the defeated adversaries. Marius was the Roman general who finally overcame the cunning and elusive Numidian king to whom Horace refers not by the Roman name of the glorious victor but by the identity of the foreign adversary, distinguished by the suggestive phrase *Iugurthino . . . bello.* Though Scipio receives his illustrious title in line 25,[38] the famous cognomen Africanus underscores the source of his virtue and serves to accentuate the common link between the victors. The enemy here is Carthage and, more particularly, Rome's most feared and dangerous foe, Hannibal, although he is not named. The comparison ends abruptly, and Horace shifts attention to the defeated enemy, now called simply the *hostis.*

The Defeat and Flight of the *hostis*

terra marique victus hostis punico
  lugubre mutavit sagum.

---

38. Two points here. First, some editors have chosen to read *Africano* to make the phrase parallel to *Iugurthino bello.* The symmetrical construction is not necessary. Second, Horace does not distinguish clearly between the two men who shared the cognomen of Africanus. Scipio Africanus (the Elder), victor over Hannibal at Zama, celebrated his triumph in 201 B.C.E. Scipio Aemilianus, the grandson of the former by adoption, razed Carthage to the ground in 146 and returned to Rome the next year to celebrate a lavish triumph. Whether it is the elder Scipio, the victor over Hannibal, or the younger Scipio, the destroyer of Carthage, or even some conflation of the two men from the same family, the point of the comparison varies little. The elder Scipio, however, seems preferable for two reasons: his defeat of Hannibal (to parallel Jugurtha and the nameless enemy of Octavian) and the mention of *sepulcrum.* The scholiast of Horace reports a somewhat dubious story on the removal of the bones of Scipio from the Vatican Hill to a tomb in Ostia: *Devicta enim Carthagine virtute Scipionis Africani, cum Afri adversum Romanos denuo rebellarent, consulto oraculo responsum est, ut sepulcrum Scipioni fieret, quod Carthaginem respiceret; tunc levati cineres eius sunt de pyramide in Vaticano constituta et humati in sepulcro eius in portu Carthaginem respiciente* (Pseud-Acron *Comm. in Hor. Epod.* 9.25). Cf. Livy 38.53.8, 38.56.3, 45.38.7; Sen. *Ep.* 86.1; and Strabo *Geo.* 5.4.4, who attest to the fact that the illustrious vanquisher of Hannibal died at Liternum and that his tomb was also there. Livy (38.56.3) admits that there were other stories.

aut ille centum nobilem Cretam urbibus,
   ventis iturus non suis,
exercitatas aut petit Syrtis Noto,
   aut fertur incerto mari.

                    (lines 27–32)

[On land and sea the enemy is conquered and
   exchanges his crimson garb for a cloak of mourning.
Either he seeks Crete, famed for her hundred cities,
   in flight with winds not in his favor,
or he seeks the Syrtes, harassed by the South wind,
   or he is adrift on the uncertain sea.]

The mention of the enemy's *lugubre sagum* in line 28 is a curious detail. Yet apart from Francis Cairns' fanciful interpretation of the unnamed *hostis* as Hannibal and of the passage itself (lines 29–32) as an extension of the comparison with Scipio,[39] the phrase has received little attention from scholars. The choice and manner of description give cause to reconsider the purpose and sentiment of the passage. Why does Horace describe the defeat by the exchange of cloaks? More important, why does he describe it in a fashion that focuses on the plight of the defeated and unexpectedly evokes some measure of pity and sympathy for the unnamed Antony?

The *sagum* was the traditional cloak of all Romans in the time of war, while the toga was the sign of peace. The phrase *saga sumere* was conventional and was often used to imply a state of preparation for battle.[40] Yet neither *punicum sagum* nor *lugubre sagum* was a familiar term. In fact, both are the inventions of the poet. We are led then to ask what his intention is by each description. The first adjective, *punico*, is a variant of the more common form *puniceo*. As the preceding two verses alluded to the defeat of Carthage, a wordplay on the adjective *Punicus*, for Punic or Carthaginian, is not unlikely. It serves as a link between the two vanquished foes. To describe Antony, the choice of the color probably refers to the purple cloak of the Roman military commander. And yet it is the exchange of cloaks, from the purple *sagum* to one of mourning, that Horace uses as a dramatic representation of the defeated enemy.

Lugubre is a powerful word. Its emphasis comes from its initial position in line 28, the juxtaposition of the two objects of exchange, and, above all,

39. Cairns, "Horace, *Epode* 9," 83.
40. Examples are common in Cicero: *Phil.* 5.12.31, 6.1.2, 8.11.32, 14.1.2. The phrases *ad saga ire* (Cic. *Phil.* 14.1.1) and *esse saga* (Cic. *Phil.* 8.11.13) also occur.

the emotions it characteristically evokes. The adjective often connotes mourning and lamentations. The neuter plural of the adjective (*lugubria*) is a familiar term used to indicate the garments of mourning. The adjective, however, is not common in Horace, who uses it sparingly, only three times in the collection of *Odes*; and it is reserved for poignant and sorrowful occasions. In the first book (*Odes* 1.24.2), the adjective is used to describe a funereal dirge, the song (*lugubris cantus*) to lament the recent death of Quintilius, dear friend of both Horace and Vergil. In one of the Roman Odes (*Odes* 3.3.61), it occurs in connection with the grievous omen (*alite lugubri*) that would allow Troy to rise again from the ashes of its destruction. But in the eloquent and plaintive ode to Asinius Pollio in the opening of the second book of *Odes*, the poet applies the word to *bellum* (*quae flumina lugubris / ignara belli*). It occurs near the end of the ode (line 33), where an extended series of rhetorical questions forms a powerful climax to the poet's anticipation of reading Pollio's intended history. The cause of his emotional outcry is the painful recollection of the past war between Caesar and Pompey. The horrors of civil war still haunt the poet.

The dramatic scene of the enemy's exchange of cloaks reveals that there is no uncertainty concerning the outcome of victory, at least according to the poet. The traditional phrase *terra marique victus* confirms the complete success. The enemy's only recourse is to abandon his role as soldier and flee. But at the same time that Horace has shown Octavian to be the victor, he describes the situation of the defeated foe to elicit sympathy or, at least, greater interest in the reader for the fate of Antony. This does not mean, and should not imply, that Horace espouses the cause of Antony or wavers in his support of Octavian. Nonetheless, however firm Horace's loyalty, civil war allows the poet no occasion to exult over the vanquished. The defeated party receives no condemnation. The poet's words are conspicuously free of abuse and scorn at this moment. We do not find here the emotional exclamation of horror and shame expressed earlier in the epode. Antony's condition is more pitiful than disgraceful.

Antony's wanderings on sea testify to his helpless and sorrowful plight. The thrice repeated *aut* clauses introduce speculation on his location and emphasize the fact that his ultimate destination is not only uncertain but beyond his control. The powerful forces of nature refuse to comply with his commands. If he wishes to flee to the island of Crete, famed for its hundred cities, the winds are not favorable (*ventis . . . non suis*). If he seeks instead Africa, he finds that the Syrtes are harassed by the South wind (*exercitatas . . . Noto*) and deny access. Finally, the choice of the passive verb *fertur* aptly describes his powerless, indecisive course. From the specification of the locale, first Crete and then the coast of northern Africa, it would seem that the flight of Antony is directed south, perhaps back to Egypt, the home of Cleopatra. His course, however, is blocked at every turn. Horace does not declare the goal of the enemy's flight. He leaves it in doubt. The scene concludes abruptly, with the location and fate of the enemy as unsure as the *incerto mari.*

Final Anxiety, Fear, and the *fluens nausea*

capaciores adfer huc, puer, scyphos
    et Chia vina aut Lesbia:
vel quod fluentem nauseam coerceat
    metire nobis Caecubum.
curam metumque Caesaris rerum iuvat
    dulci Lyaeo solvere.

(lines 33–38)

[Bring here, young lad, larger cups,
    and the Chian and Lesbian wines,
or what might check my seasick stomach,
    measure out the Caecuban.
Our anxiety and fear for Caesar's affairs it delights
    to release with sweet Lyaeus.]

The epode ends as it began, with a call for wine. And yet this is not the sort of invitation to which Horace introduced his reader in the opening of the epode. The earlier outcry of shame and disbelief that the *Romanus miles* served the nameless *femina* and her effeminate crew has cast a gloom of painful truth over the character and meaning of Actium. The reality of civil war lurks behind the specious claim of victory over a foreign foe. Immediately following the speculation on the flight of the defeated, but still not captured, Roman enemy, Horace demands larger cups and more wine to help him forget what he describes as his *curam metumque Caesaris rerum.* The conclusion of the epode seems both abrupt and disturbing to many readers. The poet leaves us with an uneasy feeling of uncertainty and worry about the immediate future and the consequences of the victory. This is not what one might expect from a song of victory jubilation or what Kraggerud has called a *praeludium triumphale.*[41] Most puzzling to modern critics is the

---

41. Kraggerud, *Horaz und Actium*, 111.

final request for the Caecuban wine because of its paramedicinal capability to check Horace's *fluens nausea*. The call for this wine looks back to the opening verse of the epode, but its demand now is to relieve an aching stomach. The question of the poet's *nausea* has vexed scholarship since Bücheler's conjecture in the nineteenth century. That the phrase *fluentem nauseam* evoked in the contemporary reader an allusion to seasickness, occurring as it does in a poem that refers to the successful outcomes of two naval battles (Naulochus and Actium), is not unlikely. The original meaning of the word and the subject of the poem may indicate that Horace intended by the phrase a clever wordplay on its etymology. I would not dispute this possibility, but it adds little to our understanding of the poem's setting or mood. The phrase certainly does not mean that Horace is seasick or, far less, that the scene of his banquet has somehow shifted to the troubled waters of the Ambracian Gulf. The speaker of the poem has begun to drink, and his call for larger cups, more wine, and a mixture of different wines, the sweet Greek vintage and the more robust Italian Caecuban, suggests that some heavy drinking lies ahead. The relative clause to explain his desire for Caecuban (or, as some would argue, a special variety of the Caecuban, distinct from the type mentioned in the epode's opening) does not mean that the poet has already become ill, but that he anticipates this possibility and wishes to avoid the unpleasant consequences of his drinking.

The epode closes with the verb *solvere*. The meaning of the emphatic and final word is reinforced by the etymological connection in *Lyaeo*. Lyaeus is the Greek epithet for Bacchus, the god of wine, who "loosens" and "releases" the cares of men. As Horace declares here and on other occasions,[42] it sometimes "delights" (*iuvat*) to forget bitter woes in the sweetness of wine. This final expression of anxiety and fear (*curam metumque Caesaris rerum*) contrasts with the initial suggestion of joy and hope at Octavian's victory (*victore laetus Caesare*). The call for wine at the end of the epode is surely not the celebration in the home of Maecenas.[43] The Caecuban wine now serves a much different purpose: to check the poet's *nausea* and to help him forget. The narrative of the epode displays an intense and mixed emotional reaction to the campaign at Actium. The poem is thus not an accurate,

---

42. Horace often declares the merits of wine, perhaps nowhere more delightfully and effectively than in his famous "Ode to the Wine Jar" (*Odes* 3.21, see especially verses 13–30). For a similar sentiment, see also Horace's words in *Epist.* 1.5.16–18. The cheerful qualities of wine (*dulcis*, *Epod.* 9.38, and *iocosum*, *Odes* 3.21.15) contrast sharply with the troubles it seeks to cure (*curas* and *mentibus anxiis*, *Odes* 3.21.15, 17; *sollicitis animis onus*, *Epist.* 1.5.18; and *curam metumque*, *Epod.* 9.37).

43. Nisbet, "Horace's *Epodes* and History," 17, ignores the explicit purpose of the wine expressed by the poet and misses the point when he interprets Lyaeus to imply that "the Caecuban, the token of victory, is bringing liberation from foreign bondage."

detailed or "running" commentary on the historical campaign and battle. Nor is it to be understood as a "piece of calculated propaganda" for the victor and as a jubilant paean of glorious triumph. Rather it is a poet's personal and complex response to a critical and still confused situation. The first news of victory in the Ambracian Gulf brought an abrupt end to the once real and serious threat of war in Italy. The joy Horace feels because of Octavian's victory is sincere and deeply felt (*victore laetus Caesare*), but this initial emotion later gives way to pain and distress (*eheu*) when he reflects on the nature of the struggle where the *Romanus miles* serves beside withered eunuchs of a woman and where the shameful Egyptian canopy covers the proud standards of Roman military might. The conflict is civil war, and however much support Horace gave to Octavian's cause, these sympathies did not lead the poet to deny this painful reality.

The central section of the poem (lines 17–20) is a description of Actium. But the events of the decisive naval battle surprisingly receive no attention in Horace's epode; instead the poet focuses on the desertion of the enemy on both land and sea, where the Gauls, the once recalcitrant foe of Julius Caesar, now shout the name of his son, and where the enemy's ships turn prows and lurk in port. Horace almost seems to prefer that the battle was never waged, that the enemy either defected or refused to engage on both land and sea (lines 17–20). The lyric poet refrains from any detailed description or narrative of action. If we seek underlying motives for Horace's distortion of historical facts or avoidance of particulars, they might be found better in his concerns and fears of renewed Roman civil war than in his unrestrained patriotic fervor and propagandistic gestures. Horace's *Epode* 9 is thus not the singular exception of political panegyric in the collection of *Epodes* but rather represents the culmination of a difficult period of anxiety and trepidation where the acclaim of Octavian's victory fails to eclipse the shameful reality and tragedy of civil war. The sentiments of disquiet and despair, so forcefully expressed in *Epodes* 7 and 16, have not been dispelled. The success at Actium promises a final resolution to the conflict of war and a triumphant occasion for celebration, but it is only a promise; the poet is hopeful but neither confident nor calm. Subsequent events at Alexandria, the suicides of the Roman *dux* and the Egyptian queen, will at last allay his apprehension about the future and offer a more fitting cause for public ritual and festivity.

Future generations, Horace impassionately predicts in *Epode* 9, will deny the reality of Actium (*posteri negabitis*, line 11). Horace's subsequent poetry confirms his own fearful predictions. Apart from the brief allusion to the flames and ships of the Actian battle in *Odes* 1.37,[44] a conspicuous silence falls on Actium in the four books of Horace's *Odes*. No individual poem exalts the military success of Octavian in civil war, and no passage refers

---

44. I have refrained from a detailed analysis of Horace's *Odes* 1.37, the so-called Cleopatra Ode. The ode celebrates the defiant suicide of the Egyptian queen, not her defeat at Actium. Literary critics have long recognized the ode's artistic merits and called into question any simple propagandistic aim of the literary piece. What W.H. Alexander, "*Nunc Tempus Erat*: Horace, *Odes* I, 37, 4," *CJ* 39 (1944): 233, had once scorned as "an almost perfect example of bad taste in the field of applied patriotism" is now read as a "kind of manifesto of the Horatian imagination," as Steele Commager, "Horace, *Carmina* 1.37," 55, eloquently described it. Commager's perceptive discussion highlighted the tight dichotomy in the ode's structure, mood, and content. His article on the ode marked a significant turning point in the modern appreciation of the poem. From the tension of the antithetical structure and tone, Commager recognized a "double moral commitment" in the poet, where Actium became in the course of the ode "as much a moral as well as military watershed" (p. 51). Commager summed up the arresting contrast from the clamorous opening declaration of public exultation and victory to the less strident, more private, and indeed introspective note of triumph at its end. The recurrent images and motifs of drinking and freedom throughout the ode, the striking effects in the choice and placement of key words (chief among these is the phrase *fatale monstrum*, line 21), and the subtle nuances and ambiguity of these words contribute to shaping a gradual and subtle transition from the initial feelings of contempt and fear to the final and more profound display of the poet's sympathy and admiration for the defeated foe. Through the exaggerated emphasis on Octavian's keen pursuit of the queen and the epic comparison, Horace makes the contrast between victorious and vanquished, conqueror and conquered, all the more striking and surprising in the ode's final scene when the queen eludes the triumphator's chains. With the concluding word *triumpho*, Horace's reader reflects not on the victor, his glorious conquest and the solemn and public ceremony of his lavish triumph, but on the queen, her defiance and escape. Actium, the consequences and celebration of this victory, fail to impress the poet at the end of the ode. His interest lies rather in the private and internal victory won by the defeated queen, the woman who finally takes control of her own life paradoxically by ending it. In the last act, the *non humilis mulier* becomes the ode's real triumphator. Like the slave who stands behind the successful conqueror, Horace reminds Octavian that he is only mortal.

For a somewhat different interpretation of the meaning of the final stanza, see G. Davis, *Polyhymnia: The Rhetoric of Horatian Lyric Discourse* (Berkeley and Los Angeles, 1991), 239–42. Following closely on the encomiastic techniques and principles of Pindaric odes, Davis revives the traditional reading, once articulated by Wickham, that the noble suicide of the queen at the end of the ode merely serves "to promote Octavian" and that her death functions "to remind lesser mortals of the non-discriminatory nature of *mors* (even queens and tyrants must die)." There is much to commend in this reading, but I would add to this group of foreign potentates Roman conquerors as well. For, much like his Greek models (Alcaeus as well as Pindar), Horace subtly reminds his *laudandus* of the omnipotence and vagaries of Fortune, the goddess who can change haughty triumphs to mournful funeral processions (*o diva . . . praesens . . . superbos vertere funeribus triumphos*, *Odes* 1.35.1–4). And if poets like Horace and Vergil began at this early time to speak of the immortality of Caesar's son, it was precisely because his mortality (and the Roman state) was in such a precarious situation. Much like the epode on Actium, the ode exhibits a complexity of emotions and shifting parallels. From their formal openings in a celebratory and joyous mood, both poems conclude with a somber and critical reflection on the meaning and nature of the victory. To be sure, Horace praises the Roman victor—and admonishes him.

directly to the naval battle or Actian victory.[45] The Augustan achievement in foreign affairs—the planned or expected campaigns in Britain, Germany, and the East—demands Horace's attention when the poet extols the military glory of the *princeps*. The conquest of foreign lands and vengeance against the Parthians will bestow immortality on Augustus (*praesens divus habebitur / Augustus, Odes* 3.5.2–3). Though fears of renewed civil conflict still haunt the poet in the *Odes*,[46] Horace prefers to pass over, without either comment or criticism, Octavian's political career before Actium and his association in Roman civil war.

Odes 1.2 perhaps best represents Horace's attitude toward the new ruler in Rome in the aftermath of the victory at Actium. Distinguished by its prominent position as the second poem of the collection of three books, the ode begins with a despairing complaint about the violent storm sent by Jupiter to punish the Romans for the crime of civil strife. The tone here is reminiscent of the emotional appeals of *Epodes* 7 and 16. The ode, however, offers a promising solution beyond fanciful flight toward the Isles of the Blessed. Horace calls on various gods to end the upheaval on earth: Apollo

---

45. Critics are inclined to interpret the description of Gigantomachy in the fourth Roman Ode as an allegory that associates Jupiter's victory over the Giants with Octavian's victory over Antony and Cleopatra (lines 42–80). Cf. L.A. MacKay, "Horace, *Odes*, III.4: Date and Interpretation," *CR* 46 (1932): 243–45; L.P. Wilkinson, *Horace and His Lyric Poetry*, 2d ed. (Cambridge, 1951), 69–72; S. Commager, *Odes of Horace*, 194–202; R.A. Hornsby, "Horace on Art and Politics (*Ode 3.4*)," *CJ* 58 (1962): 97–104; A.H.F. Thornton, "Horace's Ode to Calliope (III, 4)," *AUMLA* 23 (1965): 96–102; A.J. Dunston, "Horace—Odes III.4 and the 'Virtues' of Augustus," *AUMLA* 31 (1969): 9–19; M.S. Santirocco, *Unity and Design in Horace's Odes* (Chapel Hill, 1986), 120–21 n. 30. For a discussion of the Gigantomachic theme in Vergil and Horace, see P. Hardie, *Virgil's Aeneid: Cosmos and Imperium* (Oxford, 1986), passim. In the "Ode to Calliope," Horace adapts the familiar myth of the Gigantomachy to equate Augustan rule with the Olympian order of the universe (cf. also *Odes* 1.12.49–52 and 3.1.5–8). Though few readers might fail to recognize the political implications of the myth, Horace refrains from explicit past associations. When the victory of the Olympians is assured and won, the poet turns suddenly from the glory of the victorious to the mournful condition of the vanquished. Mother Earth grieves for her overthrown brood and laments their defeat (lines 73–75). The ode concludes abruptly with the eternal confinement of Pirithous, the lover (*amatorem trecentae / Pirithoum cohibent catenae*, lines 79–80). An identification with Antony cannot be excluded. As Commager, *Odes of Horace*, 201–2, once cautioned, the fallen *monstra* of Gaia should not be limited to only the partisans of Antony. Octavian (and later Augustus) had many enemies or treacherous friends. The defeated Giants may represent all Romans who fought in the wars from Mutina to Actium. The prominence of Apollo in the Olympian battle (lines 60–64) is significant ("tactful nationalism," as Commager characterizes it, p. 200), but Horace ignores any contemporary political associations and instead refers to the god by traditional epithets (*Delius* and *Patareus*) and geographic locales (the dewy waters of Castalia and the thickets of Lycia).

46. Cf. *Odes* 1.2.1–24, 1.14 (if the allegory of the ship is political); 1.21.13–16, 1.35.33–40, 2.1.17–40, and 3.6.

as the god of prophecy (*Apollo augur*, line 32); smiling Venus, whom Mirth and Cupid flutter about (*Erycina ridens*, line 33); and Mars, sated too long with his play of war (*heu nimis longo satiate ludo*, line 37). The savior, however, is the youthful Octavian, whom Horace fashions as the winged *filius Maiae*. Whatever political or personal motivations prompted the poet to make this association,[47] Octavian's public image at this time is unambiguous: *patiens vocari / Caesaris ultor* (lines 42–43). The phrase faithfully reflects the emphasis that Octavian had placed in his role as his father's avenger. The formal dedications of the Temple of Divus Julius and the new Senate chamber named in honor of his father, the Curia Julia, followed the triumphal celebrations of 29 B.C.E. The ode concludes with a prayer and an admonition. Horace asks Mercury/Octavian to return to heaven late after an extended stay among the people of Quirinus and not to depart too soon, despite their wrongs (*nostris vitiis*, line 47). He exhorts the youthful god to love great triumphs (*magnos . . . triumphos*) and the titles of Father and Leader (*Pater atque Princeps*) and to lead a campaign against the unavenged Parthians (*Medos . . . inultos*). The admonitory tone of the ode's final stanza presupposes the military outcome at Actium and the political consequences in Rome, but the poet eschews praise of the naval battle and victory. Unlike *Epode 9*, where joyful enthusiasm in Octavian's victory gives way to reflection and despair, *Odes* 1.2 concludes with the hope and promise of deliverance from woes by the godlike intervention of Octavian. Actium belongs to the shameful and bloodstained past, which Horace prefers to ignore.

In his first book of *Epistles*, Horace recalls the Augustan victory at Actium for the last time. *Epistles* 1.18 is addressed to Lollius, perhaps the son of the consul of 21 B.C.E.[48] Horace offers advice on friendship and the proper relationship with powerful patrons. The context of the epistle implies the offer of some important position by Augustus, but the situation is left

---

47. For bibliography on this subject, see n. 46 in chap. 2. In the opening of *Sat.* 2.6, Horace extends his gratitude to Mercury (*Maia nate*, line 5) for the gift of his country estate. If the satirist intends Octavian by this acknowledgment to the son of Maia, the triumvir's association with the god may not be political (there is little evidence to suggest that the association had political consequences); rather it may have been personally motivated by the poet, who recognized the character of the youthful son of Jupiter in the *filius divi*. Cf. *Odes.* 1.10, a prayer Horace offers to the *facundus nepos Atlantis*.

48. On the identity of this Lollius, see Fraenkel, *Horace*, 315 n. 2, who argues against the traditional association of Lollius (Lollius Maximus in *Epist*. 1.2) with an unknown son of Marcus Lollius, the consul of 21. R. Syme, *The Augustan Aristocracy* (Oxford, 1986), 396, also doubts the identification and points out that the name is rather common. For a sound discussion of the central theme of friendship in Horace's epistle, see R.S. Kilpatrick, *The Poetry of Friendship: Horace, Epistles I* (Edmonton, Alberta, 1986), 49–55 and 167 (for bibliography on previous scholarship).

unclear and deliberately vague. In the epistle's opening, Horace reminds his literary friend of their close association and intimacy (*si bene te novi*). The phrase *liberrime Lolli* at the end of the initial verse introduces Lollius to Horace's reader; the epithet establishes from the start Lollius' assertive and spirited character and sets the tone for the recommendations that follow. While Horace is confident that Lollius will not assume the role of a parasite (*scurrantis speciem*) when he professes his friendship, he discloses his concern for another failing, contrary in nature to the obsequious behavior of the *scurra*, a fault nearly more grievous (*vitium prope maius*, line 5). This opposite vice is the coarse behavior (*asperitas*) Horace brands unsophisticated, inappropriate, and offensive (*agrestis et inconcinna gravisque*, line 6). More serious is the fact that this *asperitas* aspires to the noble claims of independence and virtue.

> dum vult libertas dici mera veraque virtus
>
> (line 8)

[while it seeks to be called pure freedom and true virtue]

Horace responds that virtue is neither of these harsh extremes but rather the Aristotelian doctrine of the mean (*medium vitiorum et utrimque reductum*, line 9).

Examples of the excessive behavior to avoid illustrate his point. The exemplum of Amphion, who gave way to his brother's feelings and abandoned his lyre, argues that one should yield to the gentle commands of a powerful friend (*tu cede potentis amici / lenibus imperiis*, lines 44–45). Horace later encourages Lollius to share in his patron's pursuits of hunting, a solemn sport for Roman men, and to set aside the melancholy of his churlish Muse. Lollius' robust health and distinguished military career under Augustus supports the recommendation. As a youth, Lollius served the princeps in his military campaign in Spain. At this point Horace enjoins Lollius not to withdraw or be absent from his patron's pursuits without an excuse (*ac ne te retrahas et inexcusabilis absis*, line 58). Though Horace avows that Lollius cares to do nothing beyond the bounds of decorum and propriety, he reminds his friend of his amusement on his father's estate.

> quamvis nil extra numerum fecisse modumque
> curas, interdum nugaris rure paterno;
> partitur lintris exercitus; Actia pugna
> te duce per pueros hostili more refertur,

adversarius est frater, lacus Hadria, donec
alterutrum velox Victoria fronde coronet.

(lines 59–64)

[Although you seek to do nothing improper or immoderate,
sometimes you play a game on your father's estate;
The army shares the boats; an Actian battle is acted out
in warlike fashion by your slaves, with you, the leader.
The enemy is your brother, the Adriatic is the lake,
until swift Victory crowns either of you with a laurel.]

From the confident presumption that Lollius is anxious to please Augustus, editors and commentators are inclined to point out the allusion to "Actian" games in Rome and the fondness of Roman emperors for *naumachiae*. The immediate context of the passage and the character of Lollius (*liberrimus*) should suggest something much different than a playful imitation of public celebrations. From what little is known about the quinquennial festival in Rome (and I have argued earlier that the festival was not a celebration of Actium), we can be sure that the athletic competitions did not include a dramatic staging of the famed naval battle. Horace's vivid description of Lollius' amusement demands closer scrutiny. The setting for this staged naval battle is the youth's ancestral estate on the Adriatic coast. Each side is apportioned boats, and slaves (*pueros*) act out the roles of the participants of the famous battle. Lollius is *dux*, perhaps a pointed allusion to Octavian's public claim that was later voiced in the *Res Gestae* (*me belli quo vici ad Actium ducem depoposcit*, 25.2). The enemy, however, is emphatically revealed as Lollius' brother (*adversarius est frater*, line 63). Lollius' game is a war between brothers. Unlike Actium, the victor in this battle is neither fixed nor certain; the nimble goddess of victory may honor either antagonist (*alterutrum*). The youth's nautical sport mocks the harsh reality of Actium as the final conflict in Roman civil wars. Or at least this is the implication of Horace's verses. While Lollius may have meant no serious offense by his "occasional simple pastime"[49] (*nil extra numerum fecisse modumque*, line 59), others may not be so sure. Horace counsels Lollius that his patron must have confidence that he shares his views and concerns. Only then will he approve and favor his game.

---

49. Fraenkel, *Horace*, 318, observes only innocent fun and friendly competition in Lollius' amusement: "a few delightful sentences of the sea-battle of Actium which he [i.e., Lollius], his brother, and the boys of the neighbourhood used to perform on a lake or pond of the paternal *villa*."

consentire suis studiis qui crediderit te,
fautor utroque tuum laudabit pollice ludum.

(lines 65–66)

[When he will believe that you favor his pursuits,
he will support and praise your game with either thumb.]

Horace is concerned about his friend. His intemperance, independent spirit, and rigid severity (*deme supercilio nubem*, line 94) bode trouble. Lollius is an energetic and rash young man whose outspoken nature and lack of restraint threaten his future relationship with a *potens amicus*. Even more than ten years after the victory over Antony and Cleopatra, when Augustus took down the Roman standards from the temples of the Parthians (*sub duce qui templis Parthorum signa refigit*, line 56), Actium could still evoke discomfort; the topic required proper respect and discretion. Horace preferred tactful silence. An Augustan victory in civil conflict must have seemed a horrible and painful oxymoron to the Roman lyric poet. Horace never addressed in his poetry the former role of the princeps in civil war. Actium was not an exception. A more exalted and glorious treatment of the decisive battle awaited the grandeur of Vergil's epic verse.

Before an assessment of the Vergilian myth of Actium and its public reception, the early elegies of Propertius require critical evaluation. The initial hostility of the Umbrian poet toward Caesar's heir, his victories in civil war, and an emergent political regime is readily acknowledged by modern scholars, and the elegist's shrill discourse and bleak images of Actium serve to articulate deeply felt emotions and an unabashedly biased judgment on the achievements of Augustus. But more than an independent expression of political opposition or capricious irreverence, the theme of Actium constitutes an important and integral component of Propertius' artful meditations on love, poetry, and death in his second and third books of elegies. Chapter 4 seeks to analyze the Propertian conception of the Actian victory and his powerfully arresting representations of the naval battle through the vivid imagery of a watery grave, the fitting and ignoble climax of Roman civic strife.

Chapter Four

Bellaque resque tui memorarem Caesaris:
Propertius and the Memorials of Actium

"Caesar's affairs . . . for a background":
The Propertian *recusatio* and Actium

Thus much the fates have allotted me, and if, Maecenas,
I were able to lead heroes into armour, I would not,
Neither would I warble of Titans, nor of Ossa,
                              spiked onto Olympus,
Nor of causeways over Pelion,
Nor of Thebes in its ancient respectability,
    nor of Homer's reputation in Pergamus,
Nor of Xerxes' two-barreled kingdom, nor of
    Remus and his royal family,
Nor of dignified Carthaginian characters,
Nor of Welsh mines and the profit Marus had out
    of them.
I should remember Caesar's affairs . . .
                    for a background,
        (Ezra Pound, *Homage to Sextus Propertius* (1917), 5.2)[1]

"I should remember Caesar's affairs . . . for a background." Thus Pound
translates, or rather I should say, thus Pound censors, excises, and deletes the
the Propertian catalog of Octavian's military achievements in the elegist's
introductory poem of his second book. The serious classicist may be somewhat distressed at the violent extraction of the text,[2] but Pound's free adaptation of the elegist's verses contributes much more than it seems to take

---

1. E. Pound, *Personae: The Collected Poems of Ezra Pound* (New York, 1926), 217–18.
For a history of the translation's original publication and its critical reception, see the assess-
ment of Pound's attitude toward the Roman elegist by J.P. Sullivan, *Ezra Pound and Sextus
Propertius: A Study in Creative Translation* (Austin, Tex., 1964; London, 1965).
    2. One critic of the *Homage* had written in a review, "If Mr. Pound were a professor of
Latin, there would be nothing left for him but suicide." For this and other gems of criticism on
Pound's *Homage to Sextus Propertius*, see Sullivan, *Ezra Pound and Sextus Propertius*, 1–16.

away. The calculated omission by punctuation (. . .) is not without its subtle effects on Pound's reader. In the empty space between three dots, Pound deftly repudiates the once impressive claims of martial prowess and glory due Rome's second Caesar and, more to the point for the modern literary critic, scoffs at any notion of our interpreting the elegist's eloquent exposition as an expression of serious praise and sincere flattery. The clever, deliberate, and absolute rejection of the historical particulars, that elaborate and elongated list of names and places assembled to exemplify the *bellaque resque . . . tui Caesaris* ("Caesar's affairs," as Pound brusquely discards them), reveals, more boldly and clearly than any literal or freestyle translation could ever accomplish, Pound's own predisposition and individual bias toward understanding the political attitude of the Augustan elegist.

More Pound than Propertius, the classicist might quickly retort. But for Pound, as for many modern readers of the Roman elegiac poet, the stylized and lengthy catalog of battle names, conquered cities, and triumphal parades in lines 27–34 of *Elegy* 2.1 is an unimpressive, unconvincing display of political panegyric and military accomplishment. The grand refusal by the elegist to sing the praises of Caesar in epic verse seems to many of us today to resonate in flat and hollow notes. In objective literary terms (as objective as poetics can ever be), the passage fails or seems to fail in two important respects. The bombastic assemblage of epic-sounding panegyric, squeezed between verses that celebrate the beauty of Cynthia and the poet's steadfast devotion to this woman, does not achieve with resounding success its avowed and much assumed task in the poem, that is, the exaltation of Octavian. This much Pound detected, and in a style distinctive and much his own, he transferred the Roman poet's apparent lack of success in this passage to a triad of periods and an amusing, although meaningful, suppression.

But the Propertian verses seem to fail in another, more serious and dissatisfying way. If the verses are understood as part of a weak or insincere demonstration of the adulation of the new leader in Rome (or, as some critics may interject, a consciously ineffective one), the protracted digression, nonetheless, does not really offer a substantial contribution or serious complication to the thematic development and message of what must be seen as the programmatic piece of Propertius' second collection of elegies. Actium and the consequences of this victory provoked an almost immediate response and manifest recognition of the changed circumstances in Rome among the poets in the circle of Maecenas.[3] Any such recognition of these

---

3. An important distinction should be made at this point. While the consequences of the Actian victory are reflected in the contemporary poetry, this reflection of the change does not

changes, however, changes that were both dramatic and significant in the political leadership and structure in Rome, does not necessitate or imply a change in the elegist's political attitude. The poet, who concluded his *Mono-biblos* with the poignant recollection of the Perusian graves (*Perusina . . . sepulchra*, 1.22.3) and the horrors of Roman discord to identify his native Umbria (*Romana . . . discordia*, 1.22.5), seems an unlikely candidate to launch his second book of elegies with fulsome praise of the recent victor in civil war. The roll call of battles from Octavian's past reverberates in the elegist's opening poem from his second book; the *Actia rostra* climax the parade of spoils in the Propertian *recusatio*. The elegist returns to the theme of Actium in *Elegies* 2.15, 2.16, and in the concluding poem of the book, 2.34. In the first section of this chapter, I consider how we should evaluate the content and tone of the elegist's attitude toward Actium in the immediate years after the historic event.

The Propertian *recusatio* defies the customary, conventional, and compli-mentary. In his revisionist study of the Roman elegist, J.P. Sullivan described the *recusatio* in Propertius as representing "a whole new genre, that simul-taneously displays his poetic abilities, rejects Augustan pressures, and de-fines the true nature of his art."[4] If I may expand on this view, I suggest that the *recusatio* of *Elegy* 2.1 discloses to the reader of the *Monobiblos*, already well forewarned and prepared, even more certain signs of the individual poetic genius and independent political spirit of Propertius. In the opening of his second book, the poet manifestly declares the source of his literary inheritance, inspiration, and goals and, at the same time, boldly prepares us for his stubborn refusal to comply with the slogans and claims of the new political regime in Rome and its powerful leader.

The Propertian *recusatio* and Actium (*Elegy* 2.1)

Elegy 2.1 begins with a surprising revelation from the poet. No mythologi-cal power, no Olympian deity, neither the Muse, Calliope, nor even Apollo himself, should be credited with the inspiration of his verse. The elegist's *ingenium* comes from a woman, *ipsa puella*. Propertius boasts that his wres-tling with Cynthia will be the theme of a long Homeric epic and that whatever she has said or done will be the material of the greatest history.

---

involve and should not imply the specific recognition or, much less, the glorification of the decisive naval battle itself. Cf. the *recusatio* in the programmatic piece of Horace's second book of *Satires* (2.1.10–20) and the passages in Vergil's *Georgics* (1.24–42, 1.503–14, 3.16–48, 4.560–62) where there are clear signs of the changed status of Octavian following his victory at Actium, but where there is no direct reference to the battle.

4. J.P. Sullivan, *Propertius: A Critical Introduction* (Cambridge, 1976), 124.

seu nuda erepto mecum luctatur amictu,
   tum vero longas condimus Iliadas.
seu quidquid fecit sive est quodcumque locuta,
   maxima de nihilo nascitur historia.

(lines 13–16)

[or she wrestles naked with me, her dress torn off,
   then I truly compose long Iliads.
Whatever she has done or whatever she has said,
   the greatest chronicle is born from nothing.]

The words *Iliadas* and *historia*, both nouns emphatically ending their respective verses, bring subtly to the surface a subject and style usually far removed from the interest of Latin love elegy, namely, the glorification of heroes and battles in epic verse and historical prose. From the mention of *historia* the poet changes direction and proclaims more directly his *recusatio*.

quod mihi si tantum, Maecenas, fata dedissent,
   ut possem heroas ducere in arma manus,

(lines 17–18)

[But if only, Maecenas, the fates had granted to me
   that I could lead a hero's hands to arms,]

"But if only, Maecenas, the fates had granted to me," exclaims the elegist to his patron, the subject of his verse would be not Cynthia but heroes in arms. The reader is suspicious, and rightly so. Six ornate verses follow that elaborate on the intentions of the elegist before he turns to the affairs of Caesar (lines 19–24). Propertius begins with the struggle of the Titans and concludes with the accomplishments of Marius. Imbedded between these two are the stories of Thebes and Troy, the power of Xerxes to build a canal, the kingdom of Remus, and the arrogance of Carthage. By an impressive and convincing array of citations, editors of this passage have demonstrated that these stories from myth and history constituted the conventional themes of Greek and Latin epic. While the themes that Propertius rejects for his epic are perhaps conventional, in the sense that his audience was well familiar with the events and personages, the pointed emphasis that identifies and shapes the subject matter cannot but have its effects on the reader. Before we even hear the name of Caesar, the tone and character of the Propertian epic has been well established and defined.

non ego Titanas canerem, non Ossan Olympo
   impositam, ut caeli Pelion esset iter,
nec veteres Thebas, nec Pergama, nomen Homeri

(lines 19–21)

[I would not sing of Titans, not Olympus with Ossa
   piled on so that Pelion might be a path to heaven,
not ancient Thebes, not Pergamum, Homer's name]

The order of epic themes proceeds from Greek mythology through Roman history. The Titanomachy, the struggle of the Titans against the rule of the Olympians, a familiar theme of epic verse and allegory, begins the list. The Titans threatened to place mountains one on the other, Ossa on Olympus, with Pelion as the crown. The intentions of the earthborn monsters were not so much to redecorate the architecture of the heavenly firmament as to replace its current administration. From the nondescript mention of Thebes and Pergamum, the glory of Homer, the elegist moves down almost seven hundred years in Greek history to Xerxes and his failed endeavor to conquer Greece.

Xerxis et imperio bina coisse vada

(line 22)

[not Xerxes' command that the two seas unite]

The brevity of the Propertian verses manipulates the reader's viewpoint of the chosen theme. The phrase *bina coisse vada* defines the Persian king's imperium and points out his bold aspirations, and monumental failure. The king's efforts to defy the laws of nature, to make armies march on sea and ships sail through mountains, were famous examples of excessive pride and humbling defeat.[5] The imperium of Xerxes resembles the struggle of the Titans and their failed quest to build a path to the heavens. The focus on the

---

5. Modern editors agree on the accomplishment of the Persian king that the elegist has in mind: Xerxes' digging of a canal (about a mile and a half) across the isthmus of Mount Athos in preparation for his invasion of Greece. That the phrase *bina coisse vada* refers specifically to the canal at Mt. Athos may be right, but there is also strong reason to suppose that the contemporary reader thought of the famed crossing of the Hellespont as well. A long list of passages from orators and poets demonstrates how the two deeds of Xerxes were frequently paired in antiquity as exemplary models of an excessive arrogance and ambition to defy the laws of nature: Lys. 2.29; Isoc. *Pan.* 89; Cic. *Fin.* 2.112; Lucr. *de Rer. Nat.* 3.1029–33; *Culex* 31–34; Sen. *Suas.* 2.3, 5.7; Juv. 10.173–78; Lucian *Rhet. Pr.* 18. See the collection of evidence by J.E.B. Mayor, ed., *Thirteen Satires of Juvenal*, 2 vols. (London and New York, 1888), 2:127–30.

Titans and Xerxes establishes a background for the Propertian epic that lacks any conventional treatment of heroes in battle and the rewards of victory. Neither the Olympian victors nor the Greeks captured the interest of the elegist. He has preferred instead to highlight the defeated and their unsuccessful ambitions.

Remus, Carthage, and Marius shift the reader to Roman themes.

> regnave prima Remi aut animos Carthaginis altae,
>   Cimbrorumque minas et bene facta Mari:
>
> (lines 23–24)

[not the first rule of Remus or the pride of lofty Carthage,
    not the threats of the Cimbri and the deeds of Marius:]

In a bold and rather astonishing synecdoche of sorts, the rule of Remus (and not of Romulus and Remus) proclaims the foundation of Rome. The phrase *regnave prima Remi* has generally been interpreted to be an indirect or somewhat casual reference to the legendary origins of the city. Editors explain that the name of Remus is used *metri gratia*.[6] It is a common, but unconvincing, explanation that seeks to alleviate the unease that the name of Remus creates in this setting. The false attribution of the first kingship to Remus evokes the famous story of the struggle of power between the twin brothers to found a new city; it also hints at this struggle's bloody outcome. Romulus, not Remus, became Rome's first king, an honor the elegist prefers to confer on Remus. The cause of this mistaken or misleading conferment is not haphazard; the name of Remus continues the theme of the defeated and betokens Roman civil war.[7] Whatever the subject or theme of the Propertian epic, its tone is decidedly negative and unheroic.

---

6. That the genitive *Romuli* is metrically impossible here is no explanation. Propertius employs some form of the name or its adjectival equivalent in eight passages: 2.6.20; 3.11.52; 4.1.32; 4.4.26, 79; 4.6.43; 4.10.5, 14. Surely the poet could devise a verse with the name of Romulus (or of both twins) if he so desired.

7. Horace's verdict is clear on the murder of Remus and its profound consequences on Rome (*Epod.* 7.17–20). The guilt of this past crime still haunts the present generation. Cf. also Verg. *Geo.* 2.533. In his third book of *Elegies*, Propertius also refers directly to the murder of Remus (3.9.49–50). In the epic poem that the elegist promises to his insistent patron, a passage most similar to the sentiment of the *recusatio* in *Elegy* 2.1, Propertius begins with the story of early Rome and how the walls were made firm by the slain figure of Remus (*celsaque Romanis decerpta palatia in tauris / ordiar et caeso moenia firma Remo*). The juxtaposition of the two dissimilar images, the cattle chomping grass on the lofty Palatine hill and the walls made secure by the slaughter of Remus, is unsettling. The idyllic innocence of early Rome (a favorite conceit of contemporary Augustan poets) is tainted with the crime of fraternal murder. Remus has become the sacrificial victim that establishes the walls of Rome.

The arrogance of Carthage (*animos Carthaginis*) and the threats of the Cimbri (*Cimbrorumque minas*) also call to mind those who once boasted of greatness, threatened much, and ultimately were defeated. The epithet *altae*, by which Propertius distinguishes Rome's most formidable enemy, raises the stature of the city, which, like Thebes and Troy, was probably celebrated in epic verse more for its defeat and utter destruction than for its former greatness. The emphatic finale to the list, the *bene facta* of Marius, a relation by marriage to Julius Caesar, might seem to offer an exception and a compliment. The mention of the Cimbri in the first half of the verse may imply that the *bene facta* of Marius refers to his celebrated role in the war against the German tribes—or perhaps to his more famous victory over the Numidian king Jugurtha.[8] The noun, however, is an odd choice to describe military glory. We should keep in mind that the list of epic themes rejected by the elegist focused much more on defeat than success: the scheme of the Titans to overthrow the Olympians; the names of Thebes and Troy, cities of similar fates, both captured and destroyed; Xerxes' failed expedition against the Greeks; the first "kingship" of Remus; the arrogance of lofty Carthage; and the threats of the Cimbri. The benefactions, the meritorious deeds of Marius, complete this list. The vagueness of the word and the long political career of Marius allow doubt about the elegist's intended reference.[9] This ambiguity is fitting and perhaps deliberate. Marius was a figure of mixed reputation. Livy's judgment is indicative of how subsequent generations judged Marius.

adeo quam rem publicam armatus servavit eam primo togatus omni genere fraudis, postremo armis hostiliter evertit. (*Per.* 80)

[And thus the state that he saved by his arms, first in peace by every kind of deceit and later in war, he violently overturned.]

---

8. But cf. here the sentiment of Propertius 3.5.15–16, where the victor Marius will sit beside the captive Jugurtha in the underworld and share the same fate.

9. Commentators often remark that Propertius alludes to Cicero's poetic treatment of Marius. A fragment of thirteen verses survives in Cicero *Div.* 1.106, but little is known about the poem. On modern conjectures on its subject, length, and date, see Courtney, *FLP*, 174–78; T.F. Carney, "Cicero's Picture of Marius," *WS* 73 (1960): 83–122; L. Alfonsi, "Properzio II, 1, 23–24 e il *Marius* di Cicerone," *SIFC* 19 (1943): 147–53; and P. Ferrarino, "La data del *Marius* Ciceroniano," *RhM* 88 (1939): 147–64. It is likely, however, that the Ciceronian treatment of Marius was favorable. For the most part, Cicero praises the man who also claimed the Volscian town of Arpinum as his place of birth (*Cat.* 4.21, *sit aeterna gloria Marius, qui bis Italiam obsidione et metu servitutis liberavit*; *Cat.* 3.24; *Pis.* 43; *Red. Pop.* 9; *Rab. perd.* 29; and *Sest.* 37); later, however, Cicero deems him *omnium perfidiosissimus* (*ND* 3.80).

His military campaigns preserved Rome; and yet his consulships (especially his last shared with Cinna) attacked and almost destroyed the Republic. To which *bene facta* of Marius does Propertius refer? The elegist gives no answer, but the ambiguous tone and pointed emphasis of the previously listed themes of epic praise might evoke memories of Marius' sordid career in civil war.

From the undefined *bene facta* of Marius, Propertius turns to record the more certain *bellaque resque . . . Caesaris*. In recent years, literary critics, more sensitive to Propertian nuance, ambiguity, and subversion, have detected in the poet's catalog of Caesarian military prowess indications of subtle undercutting and calculated rebuke. W.A. Camps had already suggested that the topics listed in lines 25–34 "might well have painful associations for Octavian, as well as for Propertius himself."[10] Camps concluded, however, that the somewhat awkward choice of topics in the list lacks serious attention or importance.

> But it would be rash to see much significance in this. The list of wars waged is historical . . . and it is a list of wars about which the poet will *not* be writing, as the context shows.[11]

That the list of wars is historical is indeed very much to the point. These battles were part of a recent and, as Camps himself characterized it, painful part of Roman history, civil war. By way of an instructive contrast, when Horace praises the new ruler in Rome and his accomplishments, it is not Philippi or Perusia (the sentiment of *Epodes* 7 and 16 still pervades and is felt in the *Odes*), the tainted victories from Octavian's early and disputed rise to power, and it is surely not Naulochus and Actium for which the poet celebrates the victor.[12] As I have argued earlier, Horace's *Epode 9* offers something much different than a jubilant paean to the Actian victory, and the famous Cleopatra Ode (*Odes* 1.37), although it begins with a resounding note of celebration, concludes more soberly with the focus on the woman who strangely earns the poet's respect and a private triumph in the midst of the public ceremonies. Instead, the anticipated deeds of glory in the East, most particularly, the defeat of the Parthians, earn Octavian the poet's esteem and a place among the gods.[13]

---

10. W.A. Camps, ed. *Propertius: Elegies, Book II* (Cambridge, 1967), 69.

11. Camps, *Propertius*, 69.

12. See the discussion on the choice of topics in the Propertian *recusatio* by S. Commager, *A Prolegomenon to Propertius*, Lectures in Memory of Louise Taft Semple, University of Cincinnati 3 (Norman, Okla., 1974), 50–54.

13. Cf. the character and tone of Horace's praise of Augustus in his first three books of

The Propertian catalog of the *bellaque resque . . . tui Caesaris* begins with
only a name, nondescript and unadorned: Mutina.

nam quotiens Mutinam aut civilia busta Philippos

(line 27)

[for how often [I would sing of] Mutina or the Roman graves at
    Philippi]

The elegist at first offers no detail, no indication of how he wants his reader
to perceive the victory from Octavian's early career in Rome. But Propertius
soon discloses his sentiment and personal bias. Placed in the same verse, the
battle at Mutina is linked closely with the outcome at Philippi. For observers
both ancient and modern, Philippi most often marks the end of the Roman
Republic. Although Augustus later asserted that the campaign was a just
war against the murderers of his father (*RG* 2), few contemporaries probably shared this opinion. The Propertian treatment of Philippi is both brief
and damning. An adjective (*civilia*) defines the battle as civil war, and a noun
(*busta*) conveys its dire consequences. The sudden and terse insertion of the
apposition is startling. Octavian's military success is a graveyard of Roman
citizenry. If Propertius had left us uncertain about the direction of his epic by
the emptiness of Mutina's name, the characterization of Philippi brings the
theme of civil war into a sharper focus. An allusion to the naval battle at
Naulochus, the victory over Sextus Pompeius, succeeds the dead at Philippi.

aut canerem Siculae classica bella fugae

(line 28)

[or the naval battle and flight from Sicily]

The circumlocutory manner that Propertius chooses to refer to this occasion
is curious, and the grammar is somewhat unusual.[14] While the phrase has

---

Odes: 1.2.49–52, 1.12.49–57, 1.21.13–16, 1.35.29–40, 2.9.17–24, 3.4.29–36, 3.6.13–16,
3.14.1–4.

14. The genitive *fugae* is difficult to understand. Richardson, *Propertius, Elegies I–IV*, 213,
suggested that *fugae* refers to the "refugees themselves," and that by this Richardson means
"Sextus Pompey's command of the remnants of the Pompeian armies and his work in rescuing
fugitives from the proscriptions under the triumvirs in 43–42." This meaning of *fuga*, however,
is not likely. No example of this noun in the singular can be cited that refers to the participants
in a flight, and even the use of the plural in this context is rare. G.P. Goold, ed. and trans.,
Propertius, Elegies, Loeb Classical Library 18 (Cambridge, Mass., 1990), 119, translates
Siculae fugae as "the rout off Sicily." This is implied by the verse, but I suggest that the phrase

not the force or suggestive resonance of the *civilia busta* of Philippi, the emphasis once again is on an occasion of defeat, a defeat in Italy. The war with Sextus and Octavian's ultimate victory at Naulochus are reduced to just one episode, an enemy's flight from Sicily. This phrase alone defines the substance and meaning of the naval wars, the *classica bella* of Octavian.

The destruction of a city of Etruscan origins follows—and disrupts the chronological order.

eversosque focos antiquae gentis Etruscae

(line 29)

[or the overturned hearths of the ancient race of Etruria]

Overturned hearths (*eversos focos*) identify the victory at Perusia. The poignant emphasis on the hearths invites the reader to recall the most bitter moments of this incident from the winter of 41/40: the difficult siege of the city, its subsequent destruction by fire, and the stories that its leading citizens were slaughtered before an altar of Divus Julius.[15] Here it should be kept in mind that the noun *focus* does not simply mean "fireplace."[16] A *focus* was the most sacred place in the Roman home, employed for sacrifices and humble offerings, the place where images of the household gods would be kept. From its common appearance and coupling with the word *domus*, the hearth should be seen as the symbol of the Roman home and family.[17] The language, sentiment, and content of the verse evoke a vivid image of destruction and sacrilege. There is no proud or glorious Roman victory here. But this is not all. The full impact of the verse's sentiment and message comes at its end. When the verse concludes, the hearths are revealed to the reader and much more emotionally to the special addressee of this passage as

---

Siculae fugae should also call to mind what the noun most often signifies in a military context, a defeat and enemy's flight from battle—in this case, the flight of Sextus after his defeat at Naulochus. It should also be noted that the official condemnation of Sextus and his party as a band of fugitives and pirates (cf. *RG* 25.1) is absent from this verse. It seems perverse to make *fuga* reflect this view.

15. For details of the Perusine episode, see Appian *BC* 5.32–49. For the story of the erection of an altar dedicated to Divus Julius on which three hundred Roman senators and knights were slaughtered, see Suet. *Aug.* 15 and Dio 48.14.4; cf. Sen. *de Clem.* 1.11.1; *nempe post Perusinas aras et proscriptiones.*

16. Cf. the translation of H.P. Stahl, *Propertius, "Love" and "War": Individual and State under Augustus* (Berkeley and Los Angeles, 1985), 165: "fireplaces used to be sacrosanct."

17. As a metaphor for the home, often coupled with *domus*, see Ter. *Eun.* 815, Cic. *Rosc. Am.* 8.23, and Hor. *Epist.* 1.14.2. In the same elegy, Propertius employs the phrase *patriis . . . focis* (line 62) to refer to the home of King Minos of Crete.

belonging to the ancient Etruscan race (*antiquae gentis Etruscae*). Maecenas' boastful claim of ancestry is well known. Horace twice praises his royal descent by the illustrious titles *atavis edite regibus* (*Odes* 1.1.1) and *Tyrrhena regum progenies* (*Odes* 3.29.1); and in his third book of elegies, Propertius also addresses his patron as the *eques Etrusco de sanguine regum* (*Elegy* 3.9.1). Maecenas could not have failed to miss the point.

For more than one scholar today[18] the Perusine episode marks the exception to the elegist's catalog, the one ripple of discontent in an otherwise untroubled sea of adulation. The present discussion has attempted to refute this narrow view of the passage. The preface to the *bellaque resque . . . Caesaris* is more than ornamental; it hints at the elegist's bias against the conventional subjects of epic. The selection of themes—the emphasis on the *imperium* of Xerxes and the *regna prima* of Remus—should belie the expectations of any reader who longs to hear the traditional stories of battles and kings. There is perhaps some cause for surprise and second thoughts, but not yet any serious discomfort, in these themes, safely removed in mythology or the distant past. The list of Octavian's military triumphs, however, is more immediate and unsettling. Mutina is only a name; Philippi is commemorated by the tombstones of slain citizens (*civilia busta*). The emotional force of this potently compressed phrase hits the Roman reader hard. An allusion to the victory at Naulochus follows—naval battles (*classica bella*), distinguished and identified by the encompassing phrase *Siculae . . . fugae*. Again an outcome of defeat signals Octavian's victory. The grim scene of the overturned hearths of Perusia finally brings to the fore the recollection of civil war and establishes the background for the entrance of Actium.

---

18. The various interpretations of this verse by past scholarship merit some comment. R. Reitzenstein, "Properz-Studien," *Hermes* 31 (1896): 186, understood the reference to this event as the poet's palinode to *Elegy* 22 of the Monobiblos. H.D. Meyer, *Die Aussenpolitik des Augustus und die augusteische Dichtung* (Cologne, 1961), 69 n. 3, called it "einen Hinweis auf die erstaunliche Naivität des Properz." K. Galinsky, "The Triumph Theme in the Augustan Elegy," *WS* 82 (1969): 82, who explored the motif of the Roman triumph in Latin love elegy, described the series of battles leading up to the climax of the great Actian triumph in Propertius 2.1.17–34 as "rather malapropos." Much more astonishing, however, is the reticence of Stahl, whose penetrating and insightful examination of *Elegy* 1.22 and its significance to the *Monobiblos* has recently advanced Propertian scholarship to a new level of clarity and understanding. Stahl rightly questions the effect of line 29 on the contemporary reader, mindful of the poet's concluding message in the *Monobiblos* and, most particularly, on Maecenas; yet he concludes that "nothing is said openly, of course, and all the victories Octavian would like to hear about are mentioned." Cf. the views of the Propertian *recusatio* by Commager, *Prolegomenon to Propertius*; W.R. Nethercut, "Propertius 3.11," *TAPA* 102 (1971): 413, esp. n. 4.; and M.C.J. Putnam, "Propertius 1.22: A Poet's Self-Definition," *QUCC* 23 (1976): 121–23.

> et Ptolemaeei litora capta Phari,
> aut canerem Aegyptum et Nilum, cum attractus in urbem
>   septem captivis debilis ibat aquis,
> aut regum auratis circumdata colla catenis,
>   Actiaque in Sacra currere rostra Via.

(lines 30–34)

> [and Ptolemaic Pharos, its shores captured,
> or I would sing of Egypt and when the Nile was dragged into the city
>   and paraded by, enfeebled with its seven captive waters,
> or the necks of kings surrounded by golden chains,
>   and the Actian prows racing down the Sacra Via.]

The *Actia rostra* climax the pageantry of the triumphal shows that the elegist deploys before his reader in lines 30–34. The marvels of Egypt bedazzle his audience; and for a brief moment, one can almost forget the tombstones of the Roman dead and the destruction of Italy. The captured shores of Ptolemaic Pharos, the Nile dragged with its seven streams into the city, and the royal prisoners in gilded chains distract attention from the more painful reality of civil war. As I argued earlier, the victor arranged the order of the triumphal ceremonies to obscure the fact that he had achieved victory in civil war.[19] The Actian triumph was celebrated on the middle day, squeezed between the Illyrian and Egyptian triumphs. The triumphal parade on the final day that celebrated the conquest of Egypt was the most magnificent, the climax of the three-day affair. The vast riches and treasures removed from Egypt decorated Rome's temples, monuments, and streets. And whatever could not be removed and carried across the Mediterranean, representations and pictures depicted: the famed lighthouse at Pharos, the Nile, and even the dead queen lying on her royal couch with a serpent coiled about her arm. The poetic version of the triumphal processions that concludes Propertius' mock sally into epic presumably reflects the atmosphere of this occasion and offers us a glimpse of the glitter and spectacle that few Romans must have missed at that time. A closer examination of the five verses also reveals how the poet is no less a skilled manipulator of his audience's emotions than the triumphal organizer of the whole affair.

Propertius begins with the shores of Pharos. It was on this island jutting out from the Egyptian capital that there once stood the famed lighthouse of

---

19. See the discussion in chap. 1: "The Triple Triumph Ceremony."

Ptolemy Philadelphus, the veritable symbol of Alexandrian ingenuity and power. The epithet to distinguish the royal lineage of Egypt's ruling house (*et Ptolemaeei*, line 30) follows closely on *Etruscae*, an adjective that emphatically closes the preceding verse. But the succession of the two genitive names should not be understood as some accident of the elegist's verse. The weaker connective *et* links the two distinguished lineages in a most uncomfortable proximity. The more disjunctive *aut* would seem preferable, and at least one editor has suggested the emendation since the conjunction introduces the changes of scene in lines 27, 28, 31, and 36. Nothing prepares the reader for the sudden shift from the overturned *focos* of Perusia to the captive *litora* of Pharos. The capture of the lighthouse island succeeds the destruction of hearths in an uneasy smoothness. It is only with the mention of the Nile in the following verse that it becomes clear that we are actually in the midst of Octavian's triple triumph ceremonies. The Nile is dragged into the city with its seven captive streams, weak and submissive. The enemy, the unnamed kings, pass before us, their necks burdened by the dubious adornment and honor of gilded chains. Traditionally the royal prisoners were the last, the most prized in the long parade of spoils before the chariot of the triumphator. If the anxious reader expects the procession to come to an end at this point or to hear about the trappings of the victor's decorated car, he is sorely disappointed. The elegist abruptly concludes the ceremonial parade with the beaks of Antony's ships captured at Actium racing down the Sacra Via.

The dramatic postponement of Actium and its triumph until the denouement of this epic catalog of Octavian's wars irrevocably shatters the fragile illusion that the victorious general endeavored to create by his carefully orchestrated arrangement of triumphs. The alteration of Octavian's staged order of events leaves Actium, not the spoils of Egypt, foremost in the reader's mind as the triumphal pageantry comes to its end. Whatever distance Octavian may have sought to make between his early career in civil war and his later victories at Actium and Alexandria, the elegist refused to make the appropriate distinctions. The conquest of Egypt and the Actian battle immediately follow the devastation of Perusia. Propertius fashions Actium as the culmination of a succession of civil conflicts beginning with Mutina. The catalog of Octavian's triumphal displays introduces his reader to the theme of Actium and associates the most recent victory with defeat, destruction, and death; it is an introduction that should not be forgotten when the elegist invokes the memories of Actium in his second book again.

The Actian Sea and Roman Bones (*Elegy* 2.15)

Elegy 2.15 begins with a succession of emotional outbursts that expresses the poet's overwhelming joy as he recounts the experience of his lovemaking during the past night.[20] The pure and uncomplicated emotions of the morning after gradually give way in the course of the poem to serious reflection on the subjects of life and death and the true meaning of immortality. Actium, imbedded in these reflections, is the poignant example of what would never happen if all men would desire to lead the elegist's style of life.

> qualem si cuncti cuperent decurrere vitam
>   et pressi multo membra iacere mero,
> non ferrum crudele neque esset bellica navis,
>   nec nostra Actiacum verteret ossa mare,
> nec totiens propriis circum oppugnata triumphis
>   lassa foret crinis solvere Roma suos.
>
> (lines 41–46)

> [if everyone desired to lead such a life like mine
>   and to lie down overcome by many draughts of wine,
> there would be no cruel sword and no ship of war,
>   nor would the Actian sea toss our bones,
> nor would Rome, so often besieged by triumphs over
>   herself, exhausted in grief, throw down her hair.]

It is important here to understand fully the implications of this passage and to determine what precisely the victory at Actium means to the elegist. The introductory phrases *ferrum crudele* and *bellica navis*, generic in nature, prepare the reader for the poet's denunciation of war and for his dislike of

---

20. Cf. the discussion of *Elegy* 2.15 in Stahl, *Propertius, "Love" and "War,"* 215–33. My differences with Stahl's compelling interpretation of the poem are minimal and arise from his suggestion that Propertius "occasionally dresses his rejection of the Zeitgeist in the garb of Antony as he was pictured in official propaganda" (p. 228). The elegist's condemnation of the battle at Actium as a tragic occasion of civil war (*nostra . . . ossa*) and Roman misery (*lassa . . . crinis solvere Roma suos*), however much it is critical of the boasts of Augustus, does not allude to, or much less redeem, the reputation of Antony. Propertius contends that if all men (*cuncti*, line 41, presumably includes Antony) pursued his style of life, there would be no warfare and thus no Actium. However one may seek to assess the appearance of Antony in 2.16, the memory of Augustus' foe plays no role in the elegist's view of Actium expressed in 2.15.

21. For an illuminating discussion of the rejection of war in an early elegy of Propertius (1.6), see Stahl, *Propertius, "Love" and "War,"* 91–98. The development of this theme reaches its most elaborate and serious expression in the first five poems of the elegist's third book. Cf. also the exploration of this theme in Tibullus 1.1 and 1.10.

the socially esteemed life of the soldier. It is a conventional theme in elegiac verse, already familiar to the reader of Propertius.[21] What is not conventional and profoundly different is the role of Actium in this passage. For the elegist, the Actian episode implies not only the hardships of war and the abandonment of peaceful pursuits, but civil strife and Roman dead (*nostra . . . ossa*).

The dead at Actium were Roman. The elegist's emphasis on the physical remains of those who were killed in battle or perished at sea is shocking,[22] and the personal adjective conveys the message in no uncertain terms that the cruel sword and the naval ship belong to civil war. The elegist expands this view and proceeds to link the grievous outcome in the Actian sea with Rome, its triumphs, and its recent experience of civil war. The striking phrase *propriis . . . triumphis* is unparalleled. The meaning of the adjective *propriis* cannot become clear until the reader comes to the subject, *Roma*, postponed until almost the very end of the verse. Here the elegist's intentions are brought into sharper focus when he subverts the traditional perception and meaning of the Roman triumph and its glory. His language is powerful, and the imagery of the scene is particularly vivid. The tone is mournful and anguished. The enemy of Rome was no foreign foe but Rome itself (*propriis*). Victory did not achieve an end to war but rather turned out to be an actual assault on Rome (*oppugnata*). And finally, far from any resounding note of jubilant celebration, the occasion became the scene of mournful lamentations, resembling a funeral train much more than a triumphal procession (*crinis solvere . . . suos*). The weariness (*lassa*) of Rome, besieged so often (*totiens*) by such triumphs, puts the Actian victory firmly in the background of civil wars. It was not an isolated occasion. The dead in the Actian waters may thus be seen as representative of all Romans who died in the recent civil wars.

Propertius exclaims in despair and perhaps anger that his style of life, his drinking (*pocula nostra*) never offended any god.

> haec certe merito poterunt laudare minores:
> laeserunt nullos pocula nostra deos.
>
> (lines 47–48)

> [This at least posterity will rightly be able to praise in me:
> my cups offended none of the gods.]

---

22. Dio (50.34–35) informs us of the horrible deaths inflicted on Antony's men that resulted from Octavian's decision to attack the ships with fire.

The implication is that Actium, the final battle in Roman civil war, had offended the gods (*laeserunt* seems the emphatic point of verse 48, not *pocula*, which some editors unnecessarily seek to emend). The scene of the waters tossing the bones of the Romans who died at Actium leads the elegist to cry out to his beloved not to forsake the enjoyment of life while they live. The concluding imagery of the poem pictures a scene where the petals fall from the withered garlands around the elegist's head and float scattered about in his winecups.

> tu modo, dum lucet, fructum ne desere vitae!
>   omnia si dederis oscula, pauca dabis.
> ac veluti folia arentis liquere corollas,
>   quae passim calathis strata natare vides,
> sic nobis, qui nunc magnum spiramus amantes,
>   forsitan includet crastina fata dies.

(lines 49–54)

> [Only may you not, while it is light, abandon the joy of life!
>   if you give me all your kisses, you will give too few.
> And just as the petals fall from withered crowns
>   that you see scattered about, afloat in the cups,
> so for us, who now breathe deeply in love,
>   perhaps tomorrow's day will bring us death.]

The fallen petals floating in the cups represent the brevity and fragility of human existence; and in an eerie resemblance, the vivid image of swirling shapes recalls the arresting scene of Roman bones tossed about in the Actian sea. The dead are like the dried wreaths, lifeless symbols of an earlier and happier time. It is a powerful finale to one of the most profound and poignant reflections by the elegist on the intensity and immortality of love.

The Actian Sea Again (*Elegy* 2.16)

Propertius returns to the scene of the Actian waters in the poem that immediately follows *Elegy* 2.15, and the poet's sentiment about Actium is much the same. In the opening verses of *Elegy* 2.16, Propertius complains that a praetor has returned from Illyria with riches to entice Cynthia. Greed conquers past affection, and the wealthy suitor claims the rewards of his conquest. Angry, confused, but still hopelessly in love, the elegist appeals to Cynthia to abandon her infatuation with the man whom he disparagingly calls *barbarus*. Warning her of the extreme dangers of accepting gifts by calling up the horrible fates of Eriphyle and Creusa (lines 29–30), the elegist turns suddenly to reproach himself. So many days have gone by since he cared to attend the theater and the Campus, since he took even any pleasure in food. The helplessness of his situation forces him to exclaim at the shame of his love affair (*at pudeat certe, pudeat!*). At this point the elegist reacts to this denunciation by the assertion that base love (*turpis amor*) is usually deaf. For proof of this popular claim, he posits the example of Antony and the dead at Actium.

> cerne ducem, modo qui fremitu complevit inani
>   Actia damnatis aequora militibus:
> hunc infamis amor versis dare terga carinis
>   iussit et extremo quaerere in orbe fugam.
> Caesaris haec virtus et gloria Caesaris haec est:
>   illa, qua vicit, condidit arma manu.

(lines 37–42)

> [Look at the leader who recently, amid the helpless cries, filled
>   the Actian waters with the soldiers he condemned:
> a disgraceful love bid him to give flight with his ships
>   and seek escape to the ends of the world.
> This is Caesar's exploit, and this is Caesar's glory:
>   by the hand with which he conquered, he buried his arms.]

This is the crucial passage that becomes one of Jasper Griffin's "swallows that make a summer" in his provocative interpretation that the elegist associates himself with Antony both politically and personally.[23] Hans-Peter Stahl, who follows Griffin's lead, interprets the passage to imply that "Propertius indicates an at least partial identification of himself with Antony."[24] This leads Stahl to make equations between the elegist and Antony in *Elegy* 2.15 and 2.34, where an association with the triumvir is absent. This claim of a personal identification with Antony by Propertius requires reassessment and modification. Not only does it falsely attribute some relationship

---

23. J. Griffin, "Propertius and Antony," *JRS* 67 (1977): 18. Griffin sets forth his claim in the preface of his discussion: "Propertius' presentation of himself in poetry as a lover—romantic, reckless and obsessed—is closely related to the figure in history of Mark Antony" (p. 17). My objections to Griffin's view have been anticipated by R.F. Thomas, "Turning Back the Clock," review of *Latin Poets and Roman Life*," by J. Griffin, *CP* 83 (1988): 59–61, who charges Griffin with "anachronism" and with "forcing the evidence, against its will, to fit his general thesis."

24. Stahl, *Propertius, "Love" and "War,"* 229.

between the lover of Cleopatra and the poet, some expression of sympathy or support for the vanquished rival of Augustus, but this assumed identification with the cause of Antony also implies a politically partisan attitude toward Actium that fails to understand and denies the full meaning and sentiment of the elegist's words. The notorious love affair of Antony with the Egyptian queen is not, as Stahl contends, "the model that explains Propertius' case." This *infamis amor* is rather the cause that led the general to condemn his own soldiers to death in the Actian waters. This is not "Propertius' case" but the ultimate and most tragic example of the powerful and injurious consequences of *amor*. The narrative frame and context of the elegist's declaration support this view.

Shame and deafness introduce the example of Antony.

> at pudeat certe, pudeat!—nisi forte, quod aiunt,
>   turpis amor surdis auribus esse solet.
>
> (lines 35–36)

> [But the shame, surely the shame!—unless perhaps, as they say,
>   a disgraceful love tends to have deaf ears.]

Antony's *infamis amor* (line 39) looks back to *turpis amor* (line 36). And the phrase *fremitu . . . inani* serves as the implicit connection with *surdis* in line 36. The *dux* was deaf to his own men, unable to hear and respond to their cries. Antony thus shares the plight of the *amator*. But this is not the evidence to confirm political affiliation or personal sympathy for the defeated Augustan foe. The consequences of Antony's deafness are serious and deadly. Propertius seeks to illustrate by his example the extreme and destructive consequences of passion, the helplessness of the lover's situation. It becomes rather difficult to find here any identification with Antony once we realize fully that the phrase *fremitu . . . inani* implies the death throes and drowning of those soldiers who sided with the Roman *dux*. The hapless fate of these men (*damnatis . . . militibus*) merits the poet's attention and sympathy. The pointed sentiment of *Elegy* 2.15 (*Actiacum . . . mare*, line 44) is recalled by the same image of the Actian waters swirling with Roman dead (*Actia . . . aequora*, 2.16.38). Once again Actium is portrayed as a tragic scene of civil war and loss of life. While the *infamis amor* may explain, it cannot redeem Antony's role at Actium. And the poet's concluding compliment to Octavian (lines 41–42) is a most unusual manner in which to praise a Roman victor in battle. The *virtus* and *gloria* come not from his courage in fighting or from military success over the enemy but from the pardon that the victor bestowed on the vanquished.[25] The glory of Actium in the judgment of the elegist is found in the fact that Octavian *set down*, not *took up*, arms. Neither the victor nor the vanquished comes off well as an admirable or noble figure in the Propertian scene at Actium.

Vergil and Actium (*Elegy* 2.34)

Looking back to his opening programmatic piece, Propertius returns to the theme of Actium in the closing poem of this collection of elegies.

> me iuvet hesternis positum languere corollis,
>   quem tetigit iactu certus ad ossa deus;
> Actia Vergilium custodis litora Phoebi,
>   Caesaris et fortis dicere posse ratis,
> qui nunc Aeneae Troiani suscitat arma
>   iactaque Lavinis moenia litoribus.
> cedite Romani scriptores, cedite Grai!
>   nescio quid maius nascitur Iliade.
>
> (lines 59-66)

> [Let it delight me to lie down in ease amid yesterday's crowns,
>   for the god whose aim is unerring has pricked me to the bone.
> Let Vergil be able to sing of the Actian shores that Phoebus
>   guards and Caesar's brave ships of war,
> he who now is lifting up the arms of Trojan Aeneas
>   and the city walls founded on Lavinian shores.
> Give way, Roman writers, give way, Greeks!
>   something is on the way greater than the Iliad.]

Elegy 2.34 is a complex and confused poem, which some scholars prefer to divide into two independent pieces.[26] Propertius urges his friend, Lynceus, to abandon his former literary pursuits, notably, philosophy, tragedy, and epic, and to imitate instead the poetry of the Alexandrian poets Philetas and Callimachus. The intent of the elegist to introduce Vergil into his argument is twofold. Vergil's current plan to compose an epic poem is the very antithesis of everything that Propertius holds dear, although his earlier poetry, the *Eclogues* and *Georgics*, can be the model that Lynceus may follow.

---

25. Syme, *Roman Revolution*, 299–300, does not allow us to forget about those whom the victor at Actium failed to spare despite the official boast of *clementia* (*RG* 3).

26. For a cogent discussion of the poem's unity, see Stahl, *Propertius, "Love" and "War*," 172–88, with bibliography of earlier interpretations.

It should be observed here that, while Propertius introduces Vergil as the poet who could sing (*dicere posse*) of the Actian shores and Caesar's brave ships, he identifies him most definitely as the author of the still unfinished *Aeneid* (the *qui* clause beginning line 63).[27] In sharp contrast to his own desires to lie amid the garlands of yesterday, Propertius attributes to Vergil the capability and power (*posse*) to sing of the mighty theme of Actium. This declaration alone cannot confirm the notion that Propertius actually supposed that Vergil was intending to celebrate Actium either in the *Aeneid* or in another epic poem.[28] But it does confirm that Propertius links Actium and epic in an elegant and inextricable nexus of associations. The reference to the Actian shores and the Caesarian ships seriously affects the way the reader is to assess and judge Vergil's inchoate literary endeavor. The introductory juxtaposition of *Actia* and *Vergilium* is effective and manipulates our opinion of the epic poet's ambitions.

The sentiment that pervades the recollection of Actium in *Elegy* 2.15 and 2.16 has already prejudiced the Propertian reader against the merits of this theme. Actium's associations with epic verse look back to the opening poem of the elegist's second book. The *posse* in line 62 contrasts with the inability of the elegist in his *recusatio* of *Elegy* 2.1.

> quod mihi si tantum, Maecenas, fata dedissent,
> ut possem heroas ducere in arma manus
>
> (lines 17–18)

---

27. It is likely that Propertius knew of the poem's opening. For discussion of what the elegist knew of the *Aeneid*, see H. Tränkle, "Properz über Vergils Aeneis," *MusHelv* 28 (1971): 60–63, and Stahl, *Propertius, "Love" and "War,"* 350–52 n. 19. Stahl argues that Propertius was under the false impression that the epic on Aeneas was composed for only one reason: "to please the man whose final step to unrestricted power (in his own understanding) was his victory at Actium." I wonder if the elegist misunderstood Vergil's intentions or perversely misrepresented the epic in progress. Though critics are inclined to believe that Propertius already knew of Vergil's *ecphrasis* of the hero's shield (8.626–728), it is not necessary to suppose his intimate knowledge of the passage to explain his characterization of the *Aeneid* as a panegyric to Augustus and his victory at Actium. Propertius had previously associated Actium with epic in his *recusatio* of 2.1; there, Actium was the culmination of Roman civil war, the theme of his epic to Augustus, if he ever pursued such intentions (2.1.34). In his efforts to establish his own identity and to define his poetic inspirations, Propertius makes Vergil and his epic ambitions (whatever Propertius actually thought or knew of them) the antithesis of his own literary and moral convictions, what Stahl aptly calls the poet's *definitio sui per negationem* (p. 103).

28. See Quinn, *Virgil's Aeneid*, 47, who boldly asserted that "everyone in Rome interested in literature knew that Vergil had spent ten years writing a poem to celebrate the victory at Actium"; and Richardson, *Propertius, Elegies I–IV*, 315, who believed that Vergil had intended to compose an *epyllion* to celebrate Actium.

[But if only, Maecenas, the fates had granted to me
    that I could be able to lead a hero's hands to arms,]

This declaration launched a catalog of epic themes that led to the *bellaque
resque . . . Caesaris*, which culminated in the Actian *rostra* in triumphal
display.

Actiaque in Sacra currere rostra Via

(line 34)

[and the Actian prows racing down the Sacra Via]

Vergil is thus the poet who could sing (*dicere posse*) of Octavian's wars and
deeds. Like Horace, who commends Agrippa and his military prowess to the
epic talents of Varius in his *recusatio* of *Odes* 1.6, Propertius, looking back
to his own *recusatio* in 2.1, proclaims Vergil the more fitting epic poet and
panegyrist. It seems unlikely that Propertius intends a sincere compliment to
the aspiring epic poet;[29] the subsequent praise of Vergil's earlier works—in
particular, the love interests in the *Eclogues*—extending for ten verses, implies a sharp contrast with his new endeavor—and a subtle rebuke.

➵✖✦

Unlike the record of Octavian's battles that Pound omits from his bombastic
delivery of the Propertian *recusatio*, the elegist's bow to Vergil's *Aeneid*
inspired the talents of the modern poet. The extravagant language and
mocking tone of the translation of *Elegy* 2.34 can leave little doubt about
how Pound viewed the elegist's disaffection with Vergil and the theme of his
incipient epic poem.

Upon the Actian marshes Vergil is Phoebus' chief of police,
    He can tabulate Caesar's great ships.
He thrills to Ilian arms,
    He shakes the Trojan weapons of Aeneas,
And casts stores on Lavinian beaches.
Make way, ye Roman authors,
                    clear the streets, O ye Greeks,

---

29. In a penetrating and generally convincing analysis of the elegy, Stahl refuted the prevailing opinion that understood the verses as simply a gesture of praise to Vergil's *Aeneid*. Sullivan,
Propertius, 124, had previously doubted the complimentary nature of the reference to Vergil.

For a much larger Iliad is in the course of construction
(and to Imperial order)
Clear the streets, O ye Greeks!

(Ezra Pound, *Homage to Sextus Propertius*, 12)

Pound demeans and ridicules the Vergilian ambition in the Homeric art. He exaggerates, distorts, and far exceeds the original tone and intent of the Propertian verses. The Roman elegist is more subtle and restrained in his censure of his fellow poet. He neither disparages Vergil nor his poetry.[30] Though the wearied shepherd-poet rests from his pipes, he is still praised.

quamvis ille sua lassus requiescat avena,
    laudatur facilis inter Hamadryadas.

(2.34.75–76)

[Though he is weary and rests his pipes,
    he wins praise among the favoring Hamadryads.]

And his song of Hesiodic precepts for crops and vineyards invites comparison with the lyre of the Cynthian god.

tale facis carmen docta testudine quale
    Cynthius impositis temperat articulis.

(2.34.79–80)

[You make a song with your skilled lyre such as
    the Cynthian god deftly plays with his fingers.]

Vergil's new Iliadic endeavor, however, is not suited to either Propertius or his verse. For the elegist, epic poetry meant gods and kings, ambitious campaigns and grandiose failures, troops, ships, and war. The theme of Actium offered all this and more. Above all, Octavian's victory in the Ambracian Gulf meant waters swirling with bones and the mournful triumphs of Rome over its own citizens. In the aftermath of Actium, when the victor was seeking to base his political regime more on the promise of a glorious future than on his record in the ignominious past, Propertius stubbornly

---

30. Here I disagree with Stahl, *Propertius, "Love" and "War,"* 181–84, who argues that Propertius mocks "Vergil's bucolic idea of love" and regards it as "too superficial." That apples can buy (*mercaris*) love is not a sneer at Vergil's naive conception of love but an allusion to a popular motif of bucolic poetry already established in Theocritus.

refused to look ahead. The painful memories of civil war and Roman dead kept blocking his view.

The Elegist's Defense: Rome's Fear of Cleopatra and the Shame of Civil War

In the opening verses of *Elegy* 3.11 Propertius asks why his reader is surprised and has accused him of shameful cowardice because he cannot break free from the chains of his female master.

> Quid mirare, meam si versat femina vitam
>   et trahit addictum sub sua iura virum,
> criminaque ignavi capitis mihi turpia fingis,
>   quod nequeam fracto rumpere vincla iugo?

(lines 1–4)

> [Why are you surprised if a woman rules my life and
>   drags off a man in bondage under her authority?
> Why fashion shameful charges of cowardice against me
>   because I cannot break the shackles of slavery?]

These introductory questions reflect a conventional theme of Latin love elegy, the sexual domination of the poet by his mistress, where the socially constructed and defined roles of the sexes are reversed. A woman (*femina*) governs the life of a man (*virum*); she is creditor and master, and he is bondservant and slave (*addictum sub sua iura*). The imagery is part of the common stock of tropes and metaphors of the poet-lover as indebted servant and slave of his mistress. The elegist, however, boldly offers no denial of the charges incurred from his inferior status. He prefers instead to put forward an extended list of female *exempla*, mythological and historical, to demonstrate to his faultfinding reader the power that women have exerted over men. Chief among these female subjugators is the infamous Egyptian queen, Cleopatra, the indisputable proof that even Rome, the mighty conqueror and ruler of the world, once trembled at the threats of a woman.

Propertius proceeds to develop his case by an imposing array of examples, and he seems to carry it off to a most logical, though somewhat ridiculous, conclusion: if the elegist is guilty of the charges leveled against him, so are all Romans, who once feared the Egyptian queen and almost submitted to her will and control, and who were only liberated by the almost divine intervention of Caesar Augustus. The clever demonstration of this quasi-legal defense may seem on first view to be only the amusing and innocent fun of the poet-lover. Understood on such terms, the Propertian elegy becomes an impressive, imaginative display of rhetorical virtuosity and ridiculous exuberance. Nonetheless, the veiled and the not-so-veiled allusions to the atrocities of civil war, the recurrent accusations against Rome of shameful and timorous conduct, and the final call to the sailor of the Ionian Sea to remember Caesar's achievement at Actium should indicate that something more is at issue than troubled love affairs and female domination.

This long, often obscure, and difficult poem is the textual critic's nightmare, and interpretations of the elegy and its intended purpose have varied widely. Logical connections of individual sections fail to seem self-evident, and emendations have multiplied in a desperate search to find coherence and meaning in the thematic structure and development of the poem. The predominant role of Cleopatra in the second half of the elegy intrigues us; her characterization confounds us. The chief cause of controversy and dispute is the excessive attention—often negative, caustic, and overtly propagandistic in its tone—that Propertius focuses on the Egyptian queen, a defeated enemy who had been dead for almost ten years when this elegy probably first circulated. When the elegist instructs his reader to learn to fear (*disce timere*) from his own experience (*exemplo . . . meo*, the possessive adjective placed emphatically at the end of the verse, line 8), we are quite unprepared for sixty-four verses of extended exempla, none of which relates in any straightforward manner or by any explicit parallels to the poet's own love affair. Cynthia, his beloved and the *ingenium* of his poetry, is absent from the elegy; the reader does not even learn the name of the elegist's mistress. After the opening words of protest, written in a conventional style, the subject of the poet's domination by a woman disappears suddenly and completely from the elegy, replaced by an unusually long tirade against the Egyptian queen and a recurring charge against Rome for the shame incurred by the fear of this woman. The elegy concludes with an allusion to Actium, a demand to the nameless sailor to remember Caesar throughout the Ionian Sea.

> Leucadius versas acies memorabit Apollo:
> tantum operis belli sustulit una dies.
> at tu, sive petes portus seu, navita, linques,
> Caesaris in toto sis memor Ionio.
>
> (lines 69–72)

> [Leucadian Apollo will recall the enemy lines turned in flight:
> one day removed such a vast assembly of war.

But you, sailor, whether you seek port or leave,
  remember Caesar over all the Ionian Sea.]

Owing in large part to the inordinate attention focused on Cleopatra throughout most of the poem and to the abrupt and surprising conclusion, most modern commentators have viewed the Propertian elegy as a panegyric to Augustus and his Actian victory. W.A. Camps defined the elegy simply; in his view, *Elegy* 3.11 is a "patriotic" poem.

> Despite the poet's refusal in Elegy ix to attempt "patriotic" poetry, this elegy is a "patriotic" poem, for which the love-theme does no more than furnish what is frankly a peg.[31]

L. Richardson, jr suggested that the elegy might have been composed for an official occasion, perhaps the first anniversary celebration of the *ludi quinquennales* in 24 B.C.E., the festival that Richardson has assumed commemorated Actium.[32] The elegist, Richardson adds, "makes no apology for either his vituperation of the Egyptian queen or his adulation of the victorious Caesar." But if this "patriotic" interpretation is adopted, it must also be admitted that the elegist has abandoned the attitude toward Actium expressed so forcefully and audaciously in his second book. There the Propertian verdict on Actium was bold, impassioned, and unambiguous. Octavian's naval victory over Antony and the Egyptian queen was won in civil war. The question before us is whether the elegist's attitude toward Actium has substantially changed in the years between the publication of his second and third books. The two collections of elegies act as bookends for a decade of immense and significant political change in Rome with the ever increasingly firm establishment of Augustan rule. Conquest in the East and the vengeance of a Parthian victory were no longer empty political slogans and a poet's fancy. In this section, I argue that while the poet's approach to the subject of Actium differs in this artful and clever tirade against the queen, his attitude is much the same: Propertius could not view Actium without the painful associations of past civil war, and the monumental victory could never become an occasion of proud or glorious triumph.

The elegy's initial question makes it clear that the poet's subservience to a woman should not be a matter of surprise or censure for his reader. The

---

31. Camps, *Propertius: Elegies, Book III*, 104.

32. Richardson, *Propertius, Elegies I–IV*, 359. Goold, *Propertius, Elegies*, 295 n. *a*, repeated the claim by Richardson. See my discussion in chap. 2: "The Temple of Apollo"; there I argue that the quinquennial games in Rome did not celebrate the memory of Actium.

elegist does not deny the charge of an *ignavi capitis* but considers the accusation to be unfair. To prove his point, he first offers the examples of the sailor and the soldier.[33]

> venturam melius praesagit navita mortem,
>   vulneribus didicit miles habere metum.

(lines 5–6)

> [The sailor foresees better his coming death,
>   from his wounds the soldier has learned to fear.]

What seems so odd here is the use of conventional figures of courage to demonstrate what is a priori the opposite emotion, fear. But in the elegist's view, fear is not necessarily a sign of moral weakness, a cause for reproach, or even the absence of courage. Fearing or yielding to what (or who) is superior is not cowardice but prudence. From his own experience of storms at sea, the sailor can foresee better the threat of death, and from his battle scars and wounds, the visible reminders of his escapes from battle, the soldier remembers his close encounters with death. Both men have learned to have fear (*didicit . . . habere metum*), and rightly so. Implicit in these examples is the presumption that no one could censure such men as these for experiencing fear, since they choose to face such fear again and again, each time the one sails out to sea and the other marches into battle. Once confident that he has convinced his censorious reader that the emotion of fear in itself is not reproachable, Propertius proceeds to a more difficult supposition for any Roman, namely, that the fear of women should not be seen as a sign of cowardice for a man.

> Colchis flagrantis adamantina sub iuga tauros
>   egit et armigera proelia sevit humo,
> custodisque feros clausit serpentis hiatus,
>   iret ut Aesonias aurea lana domos.
> ausa ferox ab equo quondam oppugnare sagittis
>   Maeotis Danaum Penthesilea ratis;
> aurea cui postquam nudavit cassida frontem,
>   vicit victorem candida forma virum.

---

33. Some editors have wished to change the phrase *venturam . . . mortem* to *ventorum . . . motum* (or *morem*). For discussion of proposed emendations, see P. Fedeli, ed., *Sesto Properzio. Il libro terzo delle elegie* (Bari, 1985), 362. The various emendations, however, do not seriously alter the sense of the passage.

Omphale in tantum formae processit honorem,
  Lydia Gygaeo tincta puella lacu,
ut, qui pacato statuisset in orbe columnas,
  tam dura traheret mollia pensa manu.
Persarum statuit Babylona Semiramis urbem,
  ut solidum cocto tolleret aggere opus,
et duo in adversum mitti per moenia currus
  nec possent tacto stringere ab axe latus.
duxit et Euphraten medium, quam condidit, arcis,
  iussit et imperio subdere Bactra caput.
nam quid ego heroas, quid raptem in crimina divos?
  Iuppiter infamat seque suamque domum.

(lines 9–28)

[The Colchian woman led the fiery bulls under adamantine yokes
  and sowed battles in the warrior-bearing soil,
and she closed the savage jaws of the guardian serpent
  so that the golden fleece might come to the home of Aeson.
Fierce Penthesilea from Lake Maeotis once dared from horseback
  to oppose the ships of the Greeks with her arrows;
And after the golden helmet laid bare her face,
  her shining beauty conquered the conquering man.
Omphale came into such renown for her beauty,
  the Lydian girl who bathed in the lake of Gyges,
that he, who had set up the pillars in the world he pacified,
  pulled soft burdens of wool with his hands so rough.
Semiramis founded Babylon, the city of the Persians,
  such that she erected a work strengthened by a wall of brick,
and two chariots, sent against each other on the city ramparts,
  could not graze their sides by the touch of their axles.
She even led the Euphrates through the midst of the citadel she built
  and ordered Bactra to submit its head to her rule.
But why should I bring into accusation heroes and gods?
  Jupiter shames himself and his own house.]

The descriptions of Medea, Penthesilea, Omphale, and Semiramis offer a
glorified account of feminine *res gestae*. In the elegist's accounts of the
myths, women usurp the labors and claim the honors and rewards generally
attributed to men. The deeds of Medea, and her deeds alone, are responsible
for bringing the golden fleece to Greece. *She* drove (*egit*) the bulls, sowed

(*sevit*) battles in the soil, and closed (*clausit*) the savage jaws of the snake. Jason, the hero who accomplished the arduous tasks, looms vaguely in the background, identified only by his family's name *Aesonias* in line 12. Penthesilea, the Amazon queen, appears as the conqueror of Achilles in the narrative of the elegist. Female beauty (*candida forma*) overcomes the Greek hero when her face, laid bare (*nudavit*), transforms the victor into the vanquished, the male lover who succumbs to passion. The achievement of the Lydian queen Omphale is even more remarkable. Unlike Medea and Penthesilea, Omphale receives no accolades for martial prowess and daring. Through the force of the poet's verses, a girl (*puella*) conquers the hero who pacified the world (*pacato . . . orbe*), and the man is the slave (*traheret . . . pensa*) of his female conqueror. Finally, when Semiramis is introduced as the founder of a city (*Persarum . . . Babylona . . . urbem*) in line 21, her achievement is Herculean (the verb *statuit* recalls the task of the god who set up columns at Gibralter, *statuisset*, line 19). The solid walls of Babylon, built of baked brick and large enough for two chariots to pass along without grazing one another, attest to the woman's admirable civic accomplishments. The Euphrates and Bactra (epic-sounding names familiar to any Roman reader in the 20s)[34] have submitted to her rule. Even the most stubborn male critic might yield to the elegist's convincing figures of female ferocity and intimidation. With the mention of Jupiter, the omnipotent father and ruler of the gods, who disgraced himself and his family by his relations with women (lines 27–28), Propertius abruptly cuts off his mythology instruction and turns to the lessons of Roman history.

> quid, modo quae nostris opprobria vexerit armis,
>   et famulos inter femina trita suos?
> coniugii obsceni pretium Romana poposcit
>   moenia et addictos in sua regna Patres.

(lines 29–32)

> [What of her who recently brought disrepute to our arms,
>   the woman, serviced to exhaustion by her own slaves,
> who demanded as the price of her foul marriage the Roman
>   walls and the Fathers as captive subjects to her rule.]

To some recent critics, Propertius seems to change his earlier tactics and startles his reader by throwing up an episode from Rome's recent past, the

---

34. For Bactra as an enemy of Rome in Augustan poetry, see Hor. *Odes* 3.29.28 and Verg. *Aen.* 8.688; for the Euphrates as a symbol of the Parthian empire, see Verg. *Geo.* 1.509, 4.561; *Aen.* 8.726; and Prop. 2.10.13, 4.6.84.

war against Antony and Cleopatra.[35] But the phrases *raptem in crimina* and *infamat seque suamque domum* in the preceding verse serve as an effective transition and indicate clearly that the elegist has not forgotten the earlier accusations of shame that his reader brought on him. Propertius introduced his list of female exempla with a stated purpose for his reader, *disce timere.* The characterization of the prior four women from the domain of Greek myths and oriental legend demonstrated this power of women; and the description of Cleopatra, however startling and different in style, continues the poet's prevailing point of view. If the tone of the verses that describe Cleopatra seems more negative and perhaps derisive, and if this woman, unlike the prior examples, seems to be censured more than admired, the cause must be seen as part of the elegist's avowed line of defense and his declared intention to instruct his reader why he should fear women. By his example of the Egyptian queen, the elegist reminds his Roman reader of the fear that a woman once provoked in the city. The truth of the historical situation, however, is plain and indisputable; Cleopatra threatened much but accomplished very little. This fact, potentially damaging to his argument, does not impede the elegist, because he is nonetheless able to exploit successfully for his own rhetorical advantage and poetic strategies the exaggerated claims of what has been deemed an "official" propaganda. Cleopatra was declared the enemy in Rome, and the elegist could employ this deceit to prove his point.

Like Medea and the other female exempla, Cleopatra is the focus of the reader's attention. Recognition of Antony's role in the struggle, however veiled, does not contribute to the elegist's argument. Propertius prefers instead to exaggerate the magnitude of the queen's threats and the danger that she, not Antony, posed to Rome. This calculated decision should not be seen merely, if at all, as an adherence to official propaganda or a suppression of the truth. Antony is absent not because Propertius followed the Augustan lies and distortions about the Actian campaign or, much less, believed them but because the Roman general's participation fails to support the elegist's argument. Propertius seeks to exalt his female warrior. A male partner or even subordinate only weakens his point. Cleopatra demonstrates her superiority over men or at least her intimidating gestures toward men not by the servile submission of Antony but by the fearful reaction of Rome.

---

35. This introduction of the Egyptian queen has indicated to some critics that the elegist has abandoned the line of defense that he earlier assumed in the poem and changed his moral viewpoint toward the situation. Stahl, *Propertius, "Love" and "War,"* 237, is especially troubled by this sudden about-face, as he understands it, and argues for a latent and subversive meaning in the poet's verses beneath the facade of official eulogy. My disagreements with this view are set forth in my interpretation of this section.

The tone, however, becomes abusive. Such phrases as *famulos inter femina trita suos, coniugii obsceni*, and, above all, *meretrix regina* (line 39) imply severe censure of Cleopatra. But the scorn that the elegist casts on the Egyptian queen should not be read in isolation. Focus on the queen obscures the fact that the brunt of the elegist's sharpened attacks falls more heavily on Rome. The public enemy of Rome is a woman (*femina*). The assertion of her sex is not a disgrace to Cleopatra. But the fact of her femininity has brought *opprobria* to male Roman arms (*nostris . . . armis*). As the dowry of her foul marriage (*coniugii obsceni*), the insatiable bride demanded the walls and city of Rome (*Romana . . . moenia*) and the enslavement of those men distinguished by the title *patres*. The union was not *obscenum* to Cleopatra. This is the Roman viewpoint, and male discomfort. The phrase *addictos . . . Patres* calls to mind the opening *addictum . . . virum*, but now not only the poet but the very representatives of Roman (and male) authority and power could suffer from the bondage of a woman. Even the dignity of royal stature that was customarily lavished on defeated enemies of Rome, more to enhance the glory of the victor than to honor the vanquished, is denied the queen. Her rule is represented by two cities that were famous for deceit, treachery, and bloody ruin to Rome: Alexandria and Memphis (lines 33–34). When Cleopatra is called a queen, she is the ruler of incestuous Canopus and a whore (*scilicet incesti meretrix regina Canopi*, line 39), the one mark of disrepute branded on the family of the Ptolemies, who claimed descent from the illustrious Macedonian kings (*una Philippeo sanguine adusta nota*, line 40).[36]

In the course of this avalanche of abuse, intended to expose Rome's shame for fearing this woman, the elegist makes a slight detour from his chosen task and prolongs his digression on Memphis to offer comment on the shameful murder of Pompey. It is precisely this artistic technique of the poet, the ornate, obscure, and seemingly superfluous, that is so characteristic of Propertian elegy and so often misunderstood. The intrusion, it must be confessed, distracts the reader from the elegist's initial premise. By the end of this digression, the reader is left somewhat perplexed, unsure what Propertius is up to.

noxia Alexandria, dolis aptissima tellus,
    et totiens nostro Memphi cruenta malo,

---

36. For a fascinating and important discussion of the conflicting images of Cleopatra in Ptolemaic Egypt and Augustan Rome, see M. Wyke, "Augustan Cleopatras: Female Power and Poetic Authority," in *Roman Poetry and Propaganda in the Age of Augustus*, ed. A. Powell (Bristol, 1992), 98–140.

tris ubi Pompeio detraxit harena triumphos!
   tollet nulla dies hanc tibi, Roma, notam.
issent Phlegraeo melius tibi funera campo,
   vel tua si socero colla daturus eras.

(lines 33–38)

[Guilty Alexandria, the land most fit for treachery,
   and Memphis, so often bloody at our destruction,
where the sand robbed Pompey of his three triumphs!
   No day will remove this mark of shame from you, Rome.
Better your death would have been on the Phlegrean fields
   or if you had to give your neck to your father-in-law.]

Hans-Peter Stahl has recently argued that the reader who looks beneath the surface of these verses will find Julius Caesar and his notorious liaison with Cleopatra in Egypt and in Rome.[37] No contemporary reader would be unaware of that love affair, and no one would certainly fail to recognize Caesar as the unnamed father-in-law in line 38. But mention of Pompey and, more particularly, of his ignoble death in Egypt seems a rather roundabout way of calling attention to Cleopatra's hold over Caesar. I suggest instead that the apostrophes to Alexandria and Memphis continue the abuse that the poet has already inflicted on the Egyptian queen, and, more importantly, that they lead into the central theme and message of the elegy, Rome's fear of a woman and the shame incurred from such a fear.

In lines 33–34, the poet apostrophizes the two cities of Egypt, Alexandria and Memphis. He brands the first guilty (*noxia*) and treacherous (*dolis aptissima*) and the second stained with blood (*cruenta*), so often to the ruin of Rome (*nostro . . . malo*). The crime of Egypt, the land that is represented by these cities, is revealed to be the heinous murder of Pompey. In his flight from defeat at Pharsalus, Pompey arrived in Egypt only to be murdered.[38] His body was beheaded, stripped of its Roman garb, and cast ignobly into the surging waves. The glory of his three triumphs (*tris . . . triumphos*) did not at all avail the Roman general in the sands of Egypt. No day will remove this shame, as the poet interjects in line 36. But we must consider who suffers shame in the view of the elegist. Propertius unexpectedly changes the addressee (the surprising revelation *tibi, Roma, notam* ends the pentameter) and shifts the focus of attention (and blame) to Rome and the disgrace

---

37. Stahl, *Propertius, "Love" and "War,"* 240–46.
38. For the story of Pompey's death, see Plut. *Pomp.* 80.1–4.

incurred by Pompey's murder. The stain (*notam*) belongs not to Egypt, guilty, treacherous, and bloodstained, but to Rome. Egypt's crime is Rome's shame. By the direct apostrophe, Rome's disgrace is explicit, but there is an implicit underlying cause. Egypt may have committed Pompey's murder, but the reader is invited to reflect further on the responsibility of this crime.

Propertius now turns to address Pompey directly in lines 37–38 (*tibi* and *daturus eras*) and exclaims that it would have been far better for him to die in battle if indeed he had to offer his neck to his own father-in-law. While there is some dispute over the meaning and specific references implied in these verses, most editors agree that an allusion to Pharsalus must be found in one of the two verses.[39] The *socero* in line 38 refers, of course, to Julius Caesar. But this is not Caesar the lover of Cleopatra, as Stahl would like us to imagine. This is rather Caesar the kinsmen of Pompey and his victor. The true cause of Pompey's death in Egypt is civil war. The Roman would never have fled to this country if it were not for the war with his fellow citizen and his defeat at Pharsalus. This is the *nota* that Propertius brands on Rome, not Egypt. The change of addressee (the third in this long digression) is subtle and calculated for its effect. From the guilt and deceit of Alexandria, from the blood of Memphis, so often ruinous to Rome (a sentiment that echoes the outburst *nec totiens propriis circum oppugnata triumphis* in *Elegy* 2.15.45), Propertius shifts to reproach Rome for the shameful murder of Pompey and, finally, to speak to the victim himself by calling inordinate attention to his ignoble fate (lines 37–38). The protracted digression on Memphis and Pompey's murder is thus not a wandering lapse of purpose or a bombastic show of nationalistic fervor; the passage hits hard at the central message of the elegist, Roman complicity and guilt in civil war.

The confrontation between Egypt and Rome immediately follows in lines 39–46. Propertius' swollen display of hyperbolic rhetoric and vaunting claims reflect (and perhaps to some extent parody and ridicule) Octavian's

---

39. Here I disagree with those editors who wish to see in the phrase *Phlegraeo campo* a reference to Pompey's sickness in Naples in 50 B.C.E. For the evidence that the phrase can refer to Thessaly and is thus an allusion to Pharsalus, see E. Paratore, *L'elegia III, 11 e gli atteggiamenti politici di Properzio* (Palmero, 1936), 48–52. The site was famous in antiquity for the Gigantomachy, and poets varied in locating this cosmic conflict in the volcanic area around Naples or in the Thessalian plains. Thus, there is ambiguity concerning the location of the *Campi Phlegraei*. The passages much quoted in support of the location in Naples and the allusion to Pompey's illness (Cic. *Tusc.* 1.86; Vell. 2.48.2; Juv. 10.283; Plut. *Pomp.* 57; Appian *BC* 2.28) only confirm the already well-established fact of Pompey's close encounter with death in Naples. The following verse in Propertius' elegy, *vel tua si socero colla daturus eras* (38), does not refer to Pompey's defeat at Pharsalus in a figurative sense but can, and should, be read in a literal one; it refers to the offer of Pompey's head to Julius Caesar by the agents of Ptolemy XIII (cf. Plut. *Pomp.* 80.1–4).

propaganda against the queen. The elegy's central argument, however, quickly builds to a logical and inevitable climax.

> scilicet incesti meretrix regina Canopi,
>   una Philippeo sanguine adusta nota,
> ausa Iovi nostro latrantem opponere Anubim,
>   et Tiberim Nili cogere ferre minas,
> Romanamque tubam crepitanti pellere sistro,
>   baridos et contis rostra Liburna sequi,
> foedaque Tarpeio conopia tendere saxo,
>   iura dare et statuas inter et arma Mari!
>
> (lines 39–46)

> [To be sure, the prostitute queen of incestuous Canopus,
>   the one mark of shame branded on the blood of Philip,
> dared to oppose barking Anubis against our Jupiter,
>   to force the Tiber to bear the threats of the Nile,
> to drown out the Roman trumpet with her rattling sistrum,
>   to pursue Liburnian beaked prows with the poles of her skiff,
> to extend the shameful canopies over the Tarpeian rock,
>   and to give laws amid the statues and arms of Marius!]

Like Penthesilea against the Greek ships, the queen had the audacity to wage war against Rome (*ausa* begins lines 13 and 41). She opposed deities, barking Anubis against Roman Jove; she engaged rivers in battle, the Tiber against the Nile; she sought to drown out the Roman military trumpet with the rattling *sistrum*; she pursued the mighty Liburnian prows with the poles of the Nile barges; and finally she dared to extend her disgraceful canopy over the Tarpeian rock and to administer laws amid the trophies and statues of Marius. Everything the elegist declares here was probably part of the jingoistic propaganda of Octavian before Actium, but everything is now manipulated to prove how a woman has intimidated Rome and threatened its security and freedom. The crescendo that Propertius builds in this confrontation between Rome and Egypt (exemplified by the clash of national symbols, gods, rivers, military instruments, ships, seats of power, and finally rulers) reaches its dramatic peak in lines 47–50. The elegist concludes with a rhetorical question, asking what advantage it served Rome to expel the Etruscan king, who was branded with the name *Superbus*, if a woman (*mulier*) was to be endured.

quid nunc Tarquinii fractas iuvat esse securis,
  nomine quem simili vita superba notat,
si mulier patienda fuit? cape, Roma, triumphum
  et longum Augusto salva precare diem!

(lines 47–50)

[What good is it now to have broken the axes of Tarquin,
  whose proud life branded him with a similar name,
if a woman was to be endured? Take, Rome, your triumph,
  and, saved, pray for a long life for Augustus.]

The rhetoric of Propertius has reached its logical conclusion. If the credulous reader accepts now (as perhaps contemporaries did then) the stories of the Egyptian queen's imperious threats, and if the reader acknowledges the danger that Cleopatra, not Antony and the fellow citizens who supported him (all carefully omitted from the elegist's argument), posed to Rome's security, Propertius has won his case. Rome was afraid, and afraid of a woman. Propertius can now address Rome directly: "Claim—seize—your triumph [*cape*, not *cane*, as some editors feel the necessity to emend], Rome, and, saved from this woman [*salva*], pray for a long life for Augustus." On one level, these verses might seem to praise the victor of Actium and to express deep gratitude for his service to Rome at such a dire moment of peril. Unlike the heroes of Greek mythology (Jason, Achilles, and Hercules), the Roman conquered the daring female warrior. The immediately preceding passage, however, has defined the struggle in explicit terms: the Egyptian queen has challenged the authority of Rome. The alternatives are sharply delineated: Rome's freedom or the rule of a woman (*mulier patienda fuit*), a tyranny worse than the hated reign of Tarquinius Superbus. With lines 49–50 understood in relation to the prior characterization of Rome's confrontation with the queen, the meaning of the triumph is clear; it is not a triumph over a foreign nation or one over a formidable enemy but a triumph over a woman (*mulier*).[40]

---

40. Stahl, *Propertius, "Love" and "War,"* 240–46, understood a subtle and sinister undercutting of the Augustan achievement by the hidden reference that the victor had accomplished nothing else than rescue Rome from the mistress of Julius. But the allusion to Caesar in this passage is forced. The six verses (41–46) that exemplify and intensify the confrontation between Rome and Egypt refer to Octavian's war against Antony and Cleopatra, not to the illicit affair between Caesar and the queen. Her bold threat to dispense justice on the citadel of Roman power, the Capitoline hill, does not look back to her notorious stay in the *horti Caesaris* but was a central part of Octavian's propaganda against Antony (Hor. *Odes* 1.37.6–10; Man. 1.914–18; Ovid *Meta.* 15.827; Lucan 10.63; Dio 50.5.4).

The words *fugisti tamen,* beginning line 51, mark off a new section and conclude the story of Cleopatra. Thus far, it has been Propertius' aim to demonstrate Rome's fear of Cleopatra in the past. But the mention of Augustus' triumph allows the reader, still skeptical of the poet's rather audacious claim, to retort that Rome, nonetheless, put an end to the woman's threats, defeated her decisively in battle, and forced her to commit suicide. The resounding proof, of course, is the triple triumph ceremonies of 29, a glorious affair even the poet witnessed.

> fugisti tamen in timidi vaga flumina Nili:
>   accepere tuae Romula vincla manus.
> bracchia spectavi sacris admorsa colubris,
>   et trahere occultum membra soporis iter.
>
> (lines 51–54)

[But you fled into the wandering streams of the timid Nile:
  your hands received the Romulean chains.
I saw your arms bitten by the sacred asps
  and your limbs take in the hidden journey of slumber.]

Something strange and surprising has happened in these verses. This is no longer the *meretrix regina,* the *femina* who sleeps with her slaves, the one *nota* of a distinguished ancestry. This portrait of the woman in flight resembles more the soft dove and hunted hare from Horace's ode or Vergil's *regina* on the shield of Aeneas, who is pale with signs of her approaching death as she seeks the comforting embrace of a grieving Nile.[41] At this point in the elegy, Propertius suddenly seems more restrained, indeed more detached, in his treatment of the queen. The *tamen* in line 51 perhaps is a clue to the change in tone.[42] The reader may detect here an emphasis on the body of the woman (the poet moves from her hands to her arms to her limbs), an emphasis that exposes a more human side of the scorned enemy. The immediacy of the drama surrounding her defeat, capture, and death is felt in the suddenly direct apostrophe to the woman, the first and only address to

---

41. Paratore, *L'elegia III, 11,* 75, who recognized the different treatment of the queen here ("è una bella descrizione") compared it unfavorably to Horace's *Odes* 1.37. But the intentions of the two poets in each passage could not be more different. Unlike the lyric poet, Propertius is attempting not to exalt the queen's final days and suicide but to expose, by a change in emphasis and point of view, the vulnerability of the enemy (a woman) and the hypocrisy of the official story.

42. Cf. W.R. Nethercut, "Propertius 3.11," *TAPA* 102 (1971): 428–29, and his discussion of *tamen.*

Cleopatra in the poem. "You fled [*fugisti*]," the poet exclaims, "to the wandering streams of the timid Nile: your hands [*tuae . . . manus*] received the Romulean chains [perhaps a pointed reminder of the name Augustus declined to accept because of the Roman founder's murder of his brother Remus]." Immediately from hands (*manus*, at the end of its line), Propertius turns to her arms (*bracchia*), bitten by snakes that have acquired an aura of reverence (*sacris . . . colubris*). Finally, the poison of these sacred creatures becomes in the words of the poet a sleep that comes on its victim unseen and surreptitiously (*occultum . . . soporis iter*).[43] The sentiment here might be called more Vergilian than Propertian, and the reader must be a little puzzled by or, more likely, somewhat wary of the staged melodrama. For, before the poet allows his reader to be carried off in any deep swell of emotion and sympathy for the queen, a tongue, drunken with continual wine, speaks and abruptly brings us back to the matter at hand, Rome's fear.

> "Non hoc, Roma, fui[44] tanto tibi cive verenda!"
>   dixit et assiduo lingua sepulta mero.
>
> (lines 55–56)

> ["With such a citizen, Rome, you should not have feared me."
> Thus spoke the tongue buried in wine without end.]

The phrase *non . . . fui . . . verenda* explains to the startled reader that Rome's fear of the woman was undeserved, a fact that even the drunken tongue of the queen (or elegist) realized. The poignancy of the prior verses turns out to be a deceit, intended to display the other side of the queen, equally fallacious as the image of the audacious whore and equally a figment

---

43. I understand *membra* as the subject of *trahere*. Richardson's attempt to find the sense of "overpower" in the verb is not compelling. H.E. Butler and E.A. Barber, eds., *The Elegies of Propertius* (Oxford, 1933; reprinted Hildesheim, 1969), 291, offer a good translation: "Her limbs drink in the slumbrous poison's secret advance."

44. Another textual problem. The manuscript tradition reads *fuit* in line 55, but some editors prefer *fui*. Fedeli, *Properzio. Il libro terzo delle elegie*, 386–87, offers an extended discussion on past opinions and his own arguments to maintain the manuscript tradition. The reason voiced most often to read *fuit* (with the tongue understood as that of the elegist) concerns the Propertian proclivity of drinking. This passion cannot be denied, but it plays no importance in this elegy. The drunkenness of the queen, however, was notorious (Hor. *Odes* 1.37.14 and Plut. *Ant.* 29.1). Whatever reading is preferred, to whomever one attributes the statement of the drunken tongue, the tone and overall effect of the words are much the same. The fear of the queen was undeserved. The compliment extended to Augustus by the phrase *tanto cive* in line 55 seems somewhat less flattering if it is understood to be spoken by the drunken tongue of the woman whom he defeated.

of the propaganda of the victor. Despite all her threats, Rome had no need to fear this woman. The enemy fled, was captured, and took her own life. The victory over Cleopatra by Caesar Augustus (*tanto . . . cive*) attests to this truth. This the poet concedes, and through an intoxicated tongue, he openly taunts Rome with this truth. The bluntness of this fact is brought into sharper focus.

> septem urbs alta iugis, toto quae praesidet orbi,
>   femineas timuit territa Marte minas.[45]
>
> > (lines 57–58)

> [The lofty city of seven hills, ruler of the whole world,
>   frightened by war, cowered at a woman's threats.]

Despite the seven hills and the Roman conquest of the world (a phrase recalling the characterization of Hercules in line 19: *qui pacato statuisset in orbe columnas*), Rome was afraid of the threats of a woman. The pleonasm of the consecutive words *timuit territa* is not awkward, as one scholar has suggested in frustration,[46] but reinforces the pointed message of the verse. Despite the feminine sex, foreign birth, and dissolute ways of the enemy, despite the mighty power that the city held over all the world, and despite its almost divine savior, Rome was frightened.

In most modern editions of the elegy, lines 59–68 constitute a confused muddle of missing and transposed verses. Abstaining from any exercise in textual reconstruction or excision, I prefer instead to sum up the more pertinent and less controversial points.[47] The elegist offers a motley group of exempla where the daring feats of Marcus Curtius, Publius Decius, Horatius Cocles, and Marcus Valerius Corvus testify not only to the courage shown by legendary heroes but to the important role that the gods played in Rome's

---

45. Line 58 is omitted by the codex Neapolitanus (and by Goold, *Propertius, Elegies*, who followed Richmond's earlier censure), but it is probably authentic, though perhaps corrupted. I have retained the manuscript reading of *femineas* (Korsch corrected the text to *femineo*).

46. Following Marklund's earlier suggestion, Richardson, *Propertius, Elegies I–IV*, 367, is inclined to alter the text from *territa* to *edita*.

47. Both Nethercut, "Propertius 3.11," 429–36, and Stahl, *Propertius, "Love" and "War,"* 246, endeavor to understand the sequence of verses as offered by the best manuscript tradition. Nethercut, who reviews the various conjectures of changes to the text, attempts to find logical connections in the transmitted order. His explanation of the transition of thought and meaning in lines 59–60 and 67–68 is especially dubious. Most textual critics despair, and the majority of editions, E.A. Barber—editor of the Oxford Propertius (Oxford, 1960)—and Fedeli, *Properzio. Il libro terzo delle elegie*, prefer to transpose lines 67–68 to come before 59.

past. This seems to be the link between the heroes, since the suggestion of divine intervention on behalf of Rome is explained in the concluding couplet, where past and present are juxtaposed.

> haec di condiderant, haec di quoque moenia servant:
> vix timeat salvo Caesare Roma Iovem.
>
> (lines 65–66)

[These walls the gods had founded, these walls the gods also keep safe: scarcely should Rome, while Caesar is alive, fear Jupiter.]

The elegist may again be seeking to exalt the connection between Romulus and Augustus, if the phrase *di condiderant* alludes to Romulus and his foundation of the Roman walls and if *di . . . servant* refers to Augustus and his victory over Cleopatra.[48] But he follows with an extraordinary and exaggerated claim: as long as Caesar is alive and well (*salvo Caesare*), Rome has nothing to fear, not even Jupiter (surprisingly, *Iovem* closes the verses, with emphasis).[49] The father and ruler of the gods may be seen here as the ultimate example of what men should fear, but there is something rather odd in the sentiment and logic when the verse that proclaims emphatically by its repetitive strain that the gods established and preserve Rome from peril (gods who are deified mortals) is immediately followed by the suggestion that Rome should hardly fear the supreme ruler of all gods. The couplet seems a sarcastic finale to the central theme of this section, Rome's fear. The achievement of Caesar delivered the city, the ruler of the world, from the threats of a woman. By this point, Propertius has won his case; the higher the poet exalts Caesar and his victory over Cleopatra, the greater the danger the reader is forced to confess that this woman posed to Rome and the greater the fear that she provoked.

From these memorials of Roman history and divine intervention, Propertius turns to recall the achievement at Actium. In what Richardson has called a "characteristic epigrammatic envoi," the poet bids the sailor to be mindful of Caesar Augustus as he sails throughout the Ionian Sea (lines 69–72, quoted earlier in this section).[50] Some have wished to see here an echo of the

---

48. For the allusion to Romulus, see M. Hubbard, "*Propertiana*," *CQ* 18 (1968): 318.

49. Editorial reactions vary: Camps, *Propertius: Elegies, Book III*, 110, refrains from comment; Richardson, *Propertius, Elegies I–IV*, 368, labels the outburst "this curious near blasphemy"; and Fedeli, *Properzio. Il libro terzo delle elegie*, 393–94, can find comfort in the modifying element of *vix*.

50. Richardson, *Propertius, Elegies I–IV*, 368; Fedeli, *Properzio. Il libro terzo delle elegie*, 395.

opening section where the poet adopts the exemplum of the sailor (line 5).[51] If it is an echo, it is rather faint, and its significance to Actium is difficult to understand. More important, however, is the recurring sentiment conveyed by *memor* in the final line, *memorabit* (line 69), *cognomen* (line 64), *testatur* (line 63), and *monumenta* (line 61 and perhaps line 59). Apollo Leucadius will commemorate the *versas acies* of Actium (line 69). The reader can perhaps follow the thematic connection and the implicit conclusion with more confidence. The battle at Actium is thus the achievement of Caesar Augustus that will stand beside the deeds and *monumenta* of past Roman heroes. But this is not the only message in the final command by the poet to recall Actium.

Military defeat (*versas acies*) introduces Actium. This is what Apollo Leucadius will commemorate. The poet defines more fully the character of this memorial. The precise meaning of the phrase *tantum operis belli* that begins line 70, however, is not certain. Editors have most often suggested that the phrase alludes to Antony's mighty array of forces.[52] More curious in its choice of emphasis, however, is the phrase *sustulit una dies*. While it is true that the naval clash occurred during the span of one day, there is hardly anything extraordinary in this accomplishment. Most great battles are fought in a day. Actium, in fact, started late and lasted well beyond the afternoon (cf. Plut. *Ant.* 68.1). Octavian himself remained at sea throughout the night; only the rays of the morning sun convinced him that he had achieved a complete victory. The poet, I suggest, aims at something else. The phrase to describe the battle at Actium closely recalls the words that expressed the poet's earlier outburst over the murder of Pompey in Egypt.

tollet nulla dies hanc, tibi, Roma, notam.

(line 36)

[no day will remove this mark of shame from you, Rome.]

The repetition of subject and verb links the two verses. Here it should be remembered that Propertius rebuked Rome, not Egypt, for the disgrace of Pompey's murder. The underlying cause had been civil war. When the reader

---

51. Cf. Nethercut, "Propertius 3.11," 442–43; Stahl, *Propertius, "Love" and "War,"* 246–47.

52. Cf. Butler and Barber, *Elegies of Propertius*, 293; Richardson, *Propertius, Elegies I–IV*, 368; and Fedeli, *Properzio. Il libro terzo delle elegie*, 394. Camps, *Propertius: Elegies, Book III*, 112, is unsure and speculates whether the phrase might mean *tantam molem*. Others have changed the text; Housman conjectured *tanti operis bellum*.

looks back to the earlier verse and recalls its caustic tone and bitter sentiment, the *una dies* that characterizes Actium may be seen in a different
perspective. The achievement of Actium has not removed the *nota* that was
branded on Rome long ago in the past civil war. Prompted to recall the
digression on Pompey's murder in Egypt at the very moment the poet ostensibly praises the glory of Augustus, the reader is invited to view the memorial of Actium in the background of Roman civil war.

The epithet of Leucadius for Apollo requires some explication. Critics
offer various reasons: Propertius actually refers to the Temple of Apollo
Actius (the choice of Leucadius must be due to either geographical confusion or literary indifference);[53] Apollo Leucadius and his temple were associated at some later time with the commemoration of Octavian's victory at
Actium (yet no ancient evidence testifies to this claim);[54] or, as most editors
are inclined to point out, the site of Apollo's temple on the headland of the
island of Leucas provided an excellent view of the enemy's flight (as if
Apollo's temple at Actium, which Octavian enlarged after his victory and
honored with exalted athletic games, did not overlook the site of battle).[55]
None of these explanations is fully satisfactory or compelling. The same
queries confront scholars who wonder why Vergil's aetiological allusion to
Nicopolis and the Actian games (*Aen.* 3.274–80) also excludes the god's
proper epithet. I suspect that the elegist, much like the epic poet, chose the
epithet Leucadius for its literary, and political, associations. In ancient literature and legend, the island was often associated with horrific deaths, chiefly
suicides or human sacrifices.[56] Sappho's leap from Leucas had a well-
established tradition, even before Ovid's poem in the lyricist's voice (*Her.*
15).[57] One ancient source explains that those who hurled themselves in
desperation from the heights of the island desired to find their parents or
longed in vain to satisfy a mutual love;[58] another source tells us that sailors
(or convicted criminals) were chosen on the island as sacrificial victims and
dedicated to the local god.[59] Further testimony is found in Ovid's *Fasti*,

---

53. See D.R. Shackleton Bailey, *Propertiana* (Cambridge, 1956), 175 n. 1.

54. Richardson, *Propertius, Elegies I–IV*, 368.

55. Butler and Barber, *Elegies of Propertius*, 293; Camps, *Propertius: Elegies, Book III*,
112; Fedeli, *Properzio. Il libro terzo delle elegie*, 394; and Nethercut, "Propertius 3.11," 435.

56. For an informative discussion on the legend and literary tradition of Leucas, see M.
Paschalis, "Virgil's Actium-Nicopolis," in *Nicopolis I*, 60–62.

57. For a collection of the ancient testimony on Sappho, see H. Dörrie, *P. Ovidius Naso.
Der Brief der Sappho an Phaon*, Zetemata 58 (Munich, 1975), 231–56.

58. Serv. *auc. Comm. in Verg. Buc.* 8.59.

59. Serv. *Comm. in Verg. Aen.* 3.275. Strabo (*Geo.* 10.2.9), who confirms the tradition of
the island's practices of human sacrifice, records an archaic rite of throwing convicted criminals
from Leucate's rocky crags in a solemn offering to Apollo Leucadius.

where he describes the Roman custom of tossing straw effigies of men into the Tiber, a ritual that formerly, before the arrival of Hercules to Italy, was a grim human sacrifice performed, as the poet describes it, in the Leucadian manner (*tristia Leucadio sacra peracta modo, Fast.* 5.630). The multiple associations of the island's gloomy history and legends may thus also reverberate in the third book of the *Aeneid*, where the Trojans are made to land at the future site of the Augustan battle and offer their gratitude to Jove for their safe arrival. Here Vergil describes the towering peaks of the island (*Leucatae nimbosa cacumina montis,* line 274) and the god who is feared by sailors (*formidatus nautis,* line 275). Propertius surely could not have been indifferent to the island's popular and gruesome reputation when he exclaims that the Leucadian god will commemorate the *versas acies* of Actium. His reader will recall the earlier scene of Actium where the sea tossed the bones of Roman dead (*nec nostra Actiacum verteret ossa mare,* 2.15.44) and the waters were filled with the soldiers whom Antony's love affair had condemned to death (*Actia damnatis aequora militibus,* 2.16.38). The final address to the sailor "to remember Caesar" (*Caesaris . . . sis memor*) adumbrates the elegist's feelings toward Actium and its painful associations with civil war; the poem ends abruptly and forcefully, not with an empty gesture of praise addressed to a voyaging seaman or rich merchant, but with a compelling invitation to his reader to reflect more seriously on the victory at Actium and to remember the mournful outcome of battle and the ignominious memorial of Roman civic strife.[60]

Elegy 3.11 dates almost ten years after Octavian's naval victory at Actium and perhaps five years after the publication of the elegist's second book. This skillful display of poetic art, rhetorical finesse, and creative imagination reinterprets Rome's struggle against Cleopatra as an elegist's defense for his cowardly subservience to his girlfriend. The poet's love affair with Cynthia, however, is not the central theme of his elegy. Her name does not even appear in the poem. Propertius uses the historical exemplum of Rome's war with Cleopatra not simply to illustrate his own helpless situation but to turn the tables on his critical reader and to remind him of his own weakness and cowardice. Implicit in this comparison is the rebuke that Rome suffered for its own fear of Cleopatra. In the course of his argument, Propertius reveals

60. Here I suggest that the address to the sailor to remember Caesar is linked closely with the poet's earlier emphasis on memorials. Sailors traditionally mourn for those who have died at sea and pay their respect to those whom the sea has claimed without the proper rites of burial.

the shame that Rome incurs for its fear of a woman as something more real and serious. The shame is an indelible brand; it is civil war. At the end of this long elegy that focuses on Cleopatra, Propertius takes his reader back to the stain of Pompey's murder in Egypt and leaves him with a final demand to recall the victor at Actium and his accomplishment in the Ionian Sea. Propertius has not forgotten.

Much like Horace, Propertius fails to applaud the victory at Actium in any purely perfunctory or uncomplicated manner. The reality of civil war prohibits any political panegyric. The tone of the elegist may be more bitter and defiant, but the underlying sentiments of both poets are similar. The defeat of the Roman *dux* and the Egyptian queen is not Rome's glory. Augustus can boast of other accomplishments. The publication of Vergil's *Aeneid* closely succeeded the Propertian third book of elegies. While substantial sections of the epic poem must have circulated privately in literary circles as Propertius composed his second and third books, the impact of Vergil's epic poem is directly felt only in the elegist's fourth and final collection, where his sixth piece ostensibly offers a hymn to Apollo Palatinus. Modern critical opinion is quick to presume that an official occasion—Actian games in Rome—and the increasing pressures of the princeps are responsible for the apparent change in the elegist's attitude toward Actium. A more likely influence is Vergil, the poet of the *Aeneid*, who fashioned on the shield of his hero an epic narrative of civil war, and whose verses created a cultural myth of Actium. The nature of this Vergilian myth, its poetry and political repercussions, form the subject of the following chapter.

Chapter Five

"No, Virgil, No": The Battle of Actium on the Shield of Aeneas

No, Virgil, no:
Not even the first of the Romans can learn
His Roman history in the future tense,
Not even to serve your political turn:
Hindsight as foresight makes no sense.

How was your shield-making god to explain
Why his masterpiece, his grand panorama
Of scenes from the coming historical drama
Of an unborn nation, war after war,
All the birthdays needed to preordain
The Octavius the world was waiting for,
Should so abruptly, mysteriously stop,
What cause should he show why he didn't foresee
The future beyond 31 B.C. . . .

In these opening verses from Auden's "Secondary Epic,"[1] the twentieth century berates the greatest of the Roman poets. No, not even Vergil can make us believe the scenes of a glorious Roman future transposed to the decorative panels of the shield of Aeneas. What disturbed Auden about the nature of the Vergilian shield has disturbed many readers of the *Aeneid*. As the modern poet protested, Roman history did not "so abruptly, mysteriously stop" on that fateful day in September of 31 B.C.E. in the troubled waters of the Ambracian Gulf, or even two years later, in Rome, on those hot August days during the lavish spectacle and show of the Augustan triumphal ceremony. The might and authority of Rome would not always extend over the race of the Nomads and the arrow-bearing Geloni, from the double-horned Rhine to the indignant Araxes. Despite the prophecy of Jupiter, the imperium of Rome was not made without end. Auden scornfully disparaged

---

1. W.H. Auden, "Secondary Epic," in *Homage to Clio* (New York, 1955).

the images that he viewed on the shield as manifestations of extreme nationalism and Roman imperialism, branding the celebrated passage at the end of the eighth book of the *Aeneid* as the poet's "political turn."

Almost two centuries earlier, G.E. Lessing had also objected to what he reckoned as the patriotic pride of the Roman poet.

> The shield of Aeneas is therefore, in fact, an interpolation, intended solely to flatter the pride of the Romans; a foreign brook with which the poet seeks to give fresh movement to his stream. . . . Homer makes Vulcan devise decorations, because he is to make a shield worthy of a divine workman. Virgil seems to make him fashion the shield for the sake of the decorations, since he deems these of sufficient importance to deserve a special description long after the shield is finished.[2]

In his famous essay on originality and imitation of art, Lessing turned to consider Vergil's depiction of the shield only to find the means for an unflattering comparison between the two epic poets. For Lessing, the Homeric shield represented on its broad surface the beauty and marvel of the universe, the whole range of human experience and achievement. The tragedy of Achilles subsumed the universal dilemma of mortal man. In contrast, the Vergilian shield seemed static and frigid, a series of curiously selected scenes, empty of vitality, emotion, and universal appeal.[3] The Roman poet failed to copy the noble example set before him. Patriotic pride and political propaganda make poor craftsmen of poetry.

More recent critics of the *Aeneid* have prudently avoided subjective comparisons between Homer and Vergil and have refrained from censure of Roman patriotism and politics; instead, scholars have sought to analyze the shield of Aeneas on its own literary terms, on the basis of the themes and techniques that Vergil employs in the epic. The description of the hero's

---

2. G.E. Lessing, *Laocoon* (1776); trans. E. Frothingham (Boston, 1890), 116–17.

3. Cf. P. Hardie, *Virgil's Aeneid: Cosmos and Imperium* (Oxford, 1986), 336–46, on the criticism of the shield since Lessing and on the close relationship of the Vergilian shield to the Homeric model. In response to the recent efforts by scholars to emphasize the profound differences between the two epic shield descriptions, Hardie argues that the Shield of Achilles is the "central model" for the Shield of Aeneas, and that the Vergilian shield merges the cosmic setting with the history of Rome by an "ideological equation of *cosmos* and *imperium*." For a sober criticism of Hardie's interpretation, see the review by J. Griffin, *JRS* 78 (1988): 229–33. Griffin raises serious doubts about the meaning of the "Gigantomachic" echoes that, as Hardie contends, pervade Vergil's *Aeneid*. Neither a clear nor a consistent pattern emerges in the examples Hardie cites, and more often an arresting ambiguity and blurring of sharp contrasts shape the epic poet's characterization of the hero's struggles.

shield has been viewed as part of the poet's intentions to link the mythic past of Troy with the political reality of Augustan Rome. The shield complements the prophecy of Jupiter to Venus (1.257–96) and the pageant of Roman heroes in the underworld (6.756–886) in the content and tone of its message; it is the culmination of Vergil's efforts to link Caesar Augustus with the poem's hero, Trojan Aeneas.

> The Augustan reader of the book recognizes the meaningful continuity of Roman history in the parallels between the experiences of Aeneas and the events of Roman history, especially those of the Augustan Age: he sees in Aeneas the complementary figure to Augustus.[4]

Since the early 1960s, however, the *Aeneid* has been read as an ambiguous or, at times, profoundly pessimistic epic.[5] The so-called Harvard school of Vergilian criticism revolutionized the traditional view of the poem. Critics stressed the distinction between the poet's voices in the *Aeneid*, "a public voice of triumph, and a private voice of regret."[6] Throughout the epic, from Aeneas' tragic flight from Troy to his arrival in Latium, where he must wage a war against Turnus and the Italians, the bright image of glory and victory is marred by the harsh reality of individual tragedy and defeat. Vergil's *Aeneid* embraces and at the same time defies Homeric models, constructing a new type of hero, pious, dutiful, and deliberative. His final victory for the cause, the angry killing of Turnus, is also viewed in terms of a personal defeat. Individual studies on the poem's potent symbolism, recurring imagery, and allusive echoes have converged in interpretations of a dark and irrational Vergilian world.[7] But the heavy pendulum of literary interpretation ever swings. In response to such pessimistic readings of the *Aeneid*, critics have forcefully resurrected a positive and propagandistic message of the poem, particularly in search for philosophical justifications for the hero's

---

4. G. Binder, *Aeneas und Augustus. Interpretationen zum 8. Buch der Aeneis*, Beiträge zur klassischen Philologie 38 (Meisenheim am Glan, 1971), 152 (author's translation).

5. For an informative survey of the trends in Vergilian scholarship since the nineteenth century, see S.J. Harrison, "Some Views of the *Aeneid* in the Twentieth Century," in *Oxford Readings in Vergil's Aeneid*, ed. S.J. Harrison (Oxford and New York, 1990), 1–20. Cf. also W.R. Johnson, *Darkness Visible: A Study of Vergil's Aeneid* (Berkeley and Los Angeles, 1976), 1–22.

6. A. Parry, "The Two Voices of Virgil's *Aeneid*," *Arion* 2.4 (1963): 79.

7. W.R. Johnson's *Darkness Visible* emphasized the violence and cruelty of Juno's intervention in human affairs. His eloquent and sensitive discussion gives perhaps the fullest expression to the pessimistic view of the *Aeneid*.

anger and Turnus' mournful descent into the underworld in the last verses of the epic.[8]

Nonetheless, throughout these evolving critical perceptions of the *Aeneid*, its underlying messages and mixed sentiments, the judgment on the shield of Aeneas has surprisingly remained fixed; the passage is deemed as one of the few shining and untarnished moments of hope and glory, a detached and uncomplicated expression of the poet's patriotic pride and his optimism for the future. Those critics who are inclined toward the more somber and pessimistic interpretations of the poem refrain from extended analysis[9] or prefer to extract the whole passage from the context of the *Aeneid* and to view the poet's gesture to Augustus and his victory at Actium as a reluctant obligation, an expression of sincere jubilation, or a moment of delusion. To many readers, the *ecphrasis* of the hero's shield suggests what the *Aeneid* could have been if Vergil had composed a panegyric epic. The following quotations represent the accepted opinion of a generation of esteemed Vergilian scholars.[10]

The purpose of the *Aeneid* is clear enough. The poem commemorates a great victory, the battle of Actium, which came soon to symbolize the end of decades of bloody civil war. The victory itself is commemorated in a long showpiece in *Aeneid* 8. Among the scenes upon the wonderful shield of Aeneas is a stylized symbolic picture of the battle. At the formal core of its structure the *Aeneid* fulfills its purpose as a patriotic poem.[11]

Nevertheless, from the description of Augustus' return in triple triumph, with all races and nations in abject surrender at his feet, one

8. For this reactionary view, see especially K. Galinsky, "The Anger of Aeneas," *AJP* 109 (1988): 321–48, and H.P. Stahl, "The Death of Turnus: Augustan Vergil and the Political Rival," in *Between Republic and Empire*, 174–211.

9. Apart from the commentaries on the eighth book of the *Aeneid*, the most detailed discussions or individual studies on the shield's *ecphrasis* are by scholars who have emphasized the patriotic and uncomplicated tone of the passage; see especially C. Becker, "Der Schild des Aeneas," *WS* 77 (1964): 111–27; Binder, *Aeneas und Augustus*, 150–282; and Hardie, *Virgil's Aeneid*, 336–76, whose original and provocative work on the poet's incorporation of cosmological models in his conceptualization of Roman history and Augustan imperialism represented a new direction in Vergilian scholarship. For an imaginative realization of the illustrations and their placement on an actual shield, cf. D.A. West, "*Cernere erat*: The Shield of Aeneas," *PVS* 15 (1975–76): 1–7; reprinted in *Oxford Readings in Virgil's Aeneid*, 295–304.

10. Cf. Quinn, *Virgil's Aeneid*, 47, who concludes from Propertius' address to Vergil and his bold endeavor into epic (2.34.61–66) that all of Rome had been expecting a panegyrical epic on Actium: "Everyone in Rome interested in literature knew that Virgil had spent ten years writing a poem to celebrate the victory at Actium."

11. Quinn, *Virgil's Aeneid*, 22.

feels that Virgil too felt himself keenly admiring, at least for the moment, that peace gained through might which was the glory of the regime he felt called upon to eulogize and which forms so important a theme in *Aeneid* VIII.[12]

The shield is related pointedly to Aeneas' role in the epic, defining its positive aspects, ignoring any possible tragic factors.[13]

The focus of this chapter is the Vergilian treatment of the battle at Actium and the victor's triple triumph ceremony that closes the poet's *ecphrasis* of the shield. It is not my intention here to view the particulars of the poetic description of the Actian battle and the subsequent triumphal display as simply the evidence or reflection of an official propaganda toward these events. Such an isolation or concentration on specifics distorts the overall picture and often overlooks the nuances and subtleties of the poet's collocation of words, images, and ideas. Rather, my primary intent is to examine the Vergilian passage in the context of the epic, without the presumption of the poet's purpose or public obligation to the Augustan regime. The contribution of Vergil's *Aeneid* to the glorification of Actium and its victor should not be undervalued or denied. What should not be assumed with such assurance, however, is that Augustus actually sought or expected the attention bestowed on this final victory in civil war or that the epic poet intended his description of Actium to be read as a manifesto of Roman might and imperial glory. I argue that, however much we may search in vain for the expectations of contemporaries and strive to assess the literary objectives or success of the poet, the shield's *ecphrasis* at the end of the eighth book of Vergil's *Aeneid* served more to mold a new "Augustan" conception and ideology of the Actian victory than to endorse or transmit any prior propaganda of the battle.

A selection of vignettes from early Roman history precedes the description of Actium on the shield. The poet's curious assortment of scenes demands some explication. Editors once sought to find a central and unifying theme to the assembled array of past deeds of heroism, the means to establish a poet's criterion of selection. The opinions of W. Warde Fowler and

---

12. M.C.J. Putnam, *The Poetry of the Aeneid: Four Studies in Imaginative Unity and Design* (Cambridge, Mass., 1965; reprinted Ithaca, 1990), 150. Putnam's analysis of book 8 in his chapter "History's Dream" omits any discussion of the shield apart from a brief comment on the opening scene of the infants in the cave.

13. W.S. Anderson, *The Art of the Aeneid* (Englewood Cliffs, N.J., 1969; reprinted Bristol and Wauconda, Ill., 1989), 73–74.

Douglas L. Drew are representative of these earlier efforts—and of the inadequacies in this one-sided approach to interpreting the *ecphrasis*.

> Here in the eighth book we have a long list, not so much of triumphs, as of escapes from terrible perils both moral and material, ending with the Battle of Actium, the most wonderful escape of all, the escape from a broken empire and the threatened dominion of an Oriental queen in alliance with an unscrupulous Roman, the impersonation of self-seeking magnificence, of individual passion as against the wisdom and order of the State.[14]

> I suggest that these four groups of scenes correspond to the four virtues which were (*teste clupeo*) Augustus', viz., *virtus, clementia, iustitia, pietas*; and that Virgil has even kept to the inevitable order in which we find the virtues mentioned in connection with Augustus' shield.[15]

More recent commentators have been reluctant to recognize only one central theme mediating the shield's *ecphrasis*. Their reluctance is well founded; nonetheless, critics stress the positive "moral" aspects of the shield.[16] R.D. Williams viewed the initial scenes as the "presentation of Roman virtues, of *exempla* of the Roman character."[17] W. Clausen has argued for an "Augustan conception of Roman history" on the shield, where the poet's selection of scenes from early Rome represents "that era of pristine virtue extending from the infancy of Romulus to the sack of the city by the Gauls, the first great crisis of the Republic."[18] One can easily point out the individual acts of heroism on the shield: the descendants of Aeneas (*Aeneadae*), Horatius Cocles, and Cloelia holding off the Etruscans, who are supported by the king Porsenna (8.646–51); Manlius on the citadel, awakened by the sacred geese that warn of the attack of the Gauls (8.652–62). These scenes are stirring testimonials to the extraordinary daring and courage that so often can be read in the historical and literary accounts of early Rome. And yet other scenes do not fit into such strict characterizations. The dismemberment of Mettus (8.642–45) hardly seems to constitute an "escape from terrible peril," either moral or material; and the violent seizure of the Sabine

---

14. W. Warde Fowler, *Aeneas at the Site of Rome: Observations on the Eighth Book of the Aeneid*, 2d ed. (Oxford, 1918), 103–4.

15. D.L. Drew, *The Allegory of the Aeneid* (Oxford, 1927), 27–28.

16. Cf. G. Williams, *Technique and Ideas in the Aeneid* (New Haven, 1983), 154–55.

17. R.D. Williams, ed., *The Aeneid of Vergil*, 2 vols. (London, 1972–73), 2:265–66.

18. W. Clausen, *Virgil's Aeneid and the Tradition of Hellenistic Poetry*, Sather Classical Lectures 51 (Berkeley and Los Angeles, 1987), 80–81.

women (8.635–41), however one seeks to explain or justify the action, is not an admirable display of Roman *virtus*. Too often critics ignore these dramatic episodes entirely or look beyond these images and stress their positive consequences on Roman expansion and conquest.[19] Vergil, however, compels his reader to see not only the courage and glory of war but also its horror and tragedy.

The Vergilian shield is a much more complex and critical reflection on Rome, past and present, than any absolute expression of national pride or unrestrained eulogy of Augustan might and authority. A subtle tension pervades within and among the individual scenes, building from the narrative momentum and subjective emotion of each passage and resulting in what Viktor Pöschl once characterized as the basic truth of Vergilian art and the essence of the poem, "a sequence of moods, a series of changing sensations."[20] The shield of Aeneas culminates in Actium and Augustan triumph, a culmination that ultimately must be judged by this series of historical scenes viewed in rapid succession and with fluctuating emotions and conflicting passions.

Introduction to the Shield
illic res Italas Romanorumque triumphos
haud vatum ignarus venturique inscius aevi
fecerat ignipotens, illic genus omne futurae
stirpis ab Ascanio pugnataque in ordine bella.

(8.626–29)

[There the history of Italy and the triumphs of the Romans,
not ignorant of the prophets or unknowing of the coming age,
the lord of fire had fashioned, there all the generations of the
stock born from Ascanius and the wars fought in succession.]

Romulus and Remus
fecerat et viridi fetam Mavortis in antro
procubuisse lupam, geminos huic ubera circum
ludere pendentis pueros et lambere matrem

---

19. For example, Hardie, *Virgil's Aeneid*, 348, views the rape of the Sabine women as "an act vital for the perpetuation of the inhabitants of the new city" and considers the execution of Mettus "an implicit allusion to the consequent destruction of the city of Alba Longa by Rome."

20. V. Pöschl, *The Art of Vergil: Image and Symbol in the Aeneid*, trans. G. Seligson (Ann Arbor, Mich., 1962), 140; originally published as *Die Dichtkunst Virgils. Bild und Symbol in der Äneis* (Innsbruck-Vienna, 1950).

impavidos, illam tereti cervice reflexa
mulcere alternos et corpora fingere lingua.

(8.630–34)

[He had fashioned too, outstretched in the green cave of Mars,
the mother wolf, and the twins, hanging around her teats
as they played like boys and licked their mother
without fear; bending back her smooth neck, she
fondles one and the other and shapes their bodies with her tongue.]

Rape of the Sabine Women

nec procul hinc Romam et raptas sine more Sabinas
consessu caveae, magnis Circensibus actis,
addiderat, subitoque novum consurgere bellum
Romulidis Tatioque seni Curibusque severis.
post idem inter se posito certamine reges
armati Iovis ante aram paterasque tenentes
stabant et caesa iungebant foedera porca.

(8.635–41)

[Not far from here, he had added Rome and the Sabine women,
lawlessly carried off from the seated crowd during the time
of the great Circus games, and suddenly a new war surged,
the sons of Romulus against old Tatius and stern Cures.
Afterward, the same kings, the struggle set aside,
stand in arms before the altar of Jove, holding libation bowls,
and join together in treaties over the sacrifice of swine.]

Punishment of Mettus

haud procul inde citae Mettum in diversa quadrigae
distulerant (at tu dictis, Albane, maneres!),
raptabatque viri mendacis viscera Tullus
per silvam, et sparsi rorabant sanguine vepres.

(8.642–45)

[Not far from here four-horse chariots, sent in opposite sides,
had torn Mettus apart (Alban, you should have kept your word!),
and Tullus was dragging the fleshy insides of the deceitful man
through the woods, and the brambles dripped a bloody dew.]

Porsenna and the Aeneadae

nec non Tarquinium eiectum Porsenna iubebat
accipere ingentique urbem obsidione premebat;
Aeneadae in ferrum pro libertate ruebant.
illum indignanti similem similemque minanti
aspiceres, pontem auderet quia vellere Cocles
et fluvium vinclis innaret Cloelia ruptis.

(8.646–51)

[There, too, Porsenna commanded that the exiled Tarquin
be received and pressed the city with a mighty siege;
the sons of Aeneas rushed to the sword on behalf of liberty.
You would see one man indignant, another threatening,
because Cocles was daring to tear away the bridge
and Cloelia was swimming the river, her bonds broken.]

The Attack of the Gauls

in summo custos Tarpeiae Manlius arcis
stabat pro templo et Capitolia celsa tenebat,
Romuleoque recens horrebat regia culmo.
atque hic auratis volitans argenteus anser
porticibus Gallos in limine adesse canebat;
Galli per dumos aderant arcemque tenebant
defensi tenebris et dono noctis opacae.
aurea caesaries ollis atque aurea vestis,
virgatis lucent sagulis, tum lactea colla
auro innectuntur, duo quisque Alpina coruscant
gaesa manu, scutis protecti corpora longis.

hic exsultantis Salios nudosque Lupercos
lanigerosque apices et lapsa ancilia caelo
extuderat, castae ducebant sacra per urbem
pilentis matres in mollibus.

(8.652–66)

[On the top Manlius, guardian of the Tarpeian citadel,
stood before the temple and defended the lofty Capitol,
and the palace bristled, fresh with the thatch of Romulus.
And here in silver the goose, fluttering through the golden

colonnades, cried out that the Gauls were on the threshold.
The Gauls were amid the thickets, laying hold of the citadel,
defended by the shadows and gift of a gloomy night.
Golden is their hair, and golden their dress;
they glimmer with striped cloaks, and their milky necks
are entwined with gold; each one brandishes two Alpine
spears in his hand, his body protected with a long shield.

Here he had wrought the leaping Salii, the naked Luperci,
the woolen caps, and the shields fallen from heaven;
the chaste matrons led the sacred objects through the city,
riding in their cushioned carriages.]

Catiline and Cato
         hinc procul addit
Tartareas etiam sedes, alta ostia Ditis,
et scelerum poenas, et te, Catilina, minaci
pendentem scopulo Furiarumque ora trementem,
secretosque pios, his dantem iura Catonem.

(8.666–70)

        [At a distance from this he added
too the dwellings of Tartarus, the lofty portals of Dis,
and the punishments of the wicked, and you, Catiline, hanging
on a menacing crag and trembling at the faces of the Furies,
and far apart the pious, and giving laws to them, Cato.]

The first scene of the hero's shield depicts the infants Romulus and Remus. The she-wolf has recently given birth; she permits the twin boys to play
about her and to draw her milk without fear; with her smooth neck bent
back, she fondles the boys, first one, then the other, and she fashions their
bodies with her tongue. She is called by the poet a mother (*matrem*, line
632). The savage nature of the wolf has been tamed; man and beast are
reconciled in a manner evocative of the peace from the Saturnian Golden
Age or Evander's Latium. Critics have compared the passage to the opening
invocation to the mother of Aeneas in Lucretius' *de Rerum Natura* where the
goddess of Love seduces the savage spirit of Mars.[21] There are also possible

---

21. Cf. Putnam, *Poetry of the Aeneid*, 147–49, who observes an implicit allusion to Lucretius in this opening scene.

echoes of Ennius' treatment of early Rome (*lupus femina feta repente*, Vahlen *Ann.* 68).[22] The opening scene testifies to the important role Mars plays in the origins of Rome. The emphatic genitive *Mavortis* links the green cave with Mars, the father of the infant twins. But the focus of the poet's description is not on the birth of the twins or their paternal ancestry but on the "mothering" by the wolf and the innocent play of the boys, a scene vividly expressed in literal, figurative, and symbolic terms. Before a Vergilian reader might contemplate the implications of this striking image where the boys lick (*lambere*) the animal's teats and the wolf fashions (*fingere*) their bodies with her tongue, the poet shifts to Rome in line 630. The play of the boys yields to the actions of men. The mention of *Romam* serves as a chronological as well as geographical transition, an allusion to the foundation of the city where Romulus killed his brother in anger; nonetheless, the poet refrains from an explicit commentary. In the second scene on the shield, Romulus is the leader of his people, and the outcome of his seizure of the neighboring women is war.

The setting of the subsequent scene is Rome, but before we learn of the cavernous theater and the celebration of the Circensian games, the Sabine women have been carried off violently (*raptas*) and, as the poet adds, *sine more*. The outcome of the violence is at once made clear in line 637. It is war, sudden and new (*novum consurgere bellum*). Vergil's description of the nature of this struggle and of its participants is interesting in its detail and emphasis. The abductors receive the extraordinary name the sons of Romulus. Commentators speak here of "epic convention" and cite a list of examples to explain the usage:[23] the poet seeks to emphasize the ancestry of the Roman race, and the patronymic seems to include the whole community whose descent comes from one common ancestor. But no extant historical or literary tradition makes Tatius an aged man. The characterization of the two antagonists, the sons of Romulus and the *senex* Tatius, supported by the stern figures from Cures, calls attention to the peculiar nature of the war. It is in fact the most repugnant aspect of civil war, sons against fathers (or more precisely, here, sons against future fathers-in-law).[24]

Earlier, in book 6 of the *Aeneid*, where Aeneas views the long parade of future Roman heroes in the underworld, the phrase *nova bella* describes the impious struggle that the two sons of Brutus will wage against their father in

22. Serv. *Comm. in Verg. Aen.* 8.631: *sane totus hic locus Ennianus est.*

23. C.J. Fordyce, ed., *P. Vergili Maronis Aeneidos Libri VII–VIII* (Oxford, 1977), 172.

24. Cf. F. Cairns, *Virgil's Augustan Epic* (Cambridge, 1989), 96–98, who explores the *gener-socer* theme on the shield and in Anchises' address to Caesar and Pompey in the underworld (6.826–35).

their treacherous effort to restore the banished Tarquin. The claim of liberty is tainted by a father's murder of his sons.

> . . . natosque pater nova bella moventis
> ad poenam pulchra pro libertate vocabit.

(6.820–21)

> [. . . and the sons who stir up new wars, the father
> will call to punishment for the sake of fair liberty.]

The phrase *nova bella* conveys suggestions not only of a new outbreak of hostilities but of something strange and seditious, such as the conflict between a father and his sons. The adjective *novus* often implies an innovation, a strange phenomenon, whatever is different from before.[25] Like the war between the Romans and Sabines, the rebellion by the sons of Brutus is a shocking development. The defense of the newly formed and still fragile Republic by the man who is claimed as its founder is portrayed instead by the poet as a father's forced execution of his rebellious sons. On the shield, the seizure of the Sabine women is depicted as an act contrary to previous custom (*sine more*) and an impetus of a war (*novum . . . bellum*) waged between the sons of Romulus and the aged Tatius. The hostilities, however, conclude with the solemn rituals of peace and the conciliation of families.

In the third scene on the shield, the poet depicts the epilogue to the war against Alba Longa. Mettus Fufetius,[26] the dictator of Alba Longa, promised to help the third Roman king, Tullus Hostilius, in his war against neighboring Fidenae. Mettus, Livy declared, was a coward as well as a traitor (*Albano non plus animi erat quam fidei*, 1.27.5). Not daring to stand his ground in battle and not daring to desert openly, he withdrew his troops to safety at the last moment and exposed the flank of Roman troops. Tullus, however, did not retreat from battle; and in the end, the Romans were successful in their war against Fidenae. The Albans were rewarded with Roman citizenship—and the destruction of their city. Tullus, however, did not allow the crime of Mettus to go unpunished. He inflicted on the faithless coward an extreme and unparalleled punishment in Roman history, an ex-

25. Cf. the definitions (paragraphs 3, 9, and 10) in the *Oxford Latin Dictionary*, ed. P.G.W. Glare (Oxford, 1982), s.v. *novus*.

26. For discussion on the spelling of this name (Livy consistently uses the form "Mettius"), see P.T. Eden, ed., *A Commentary on Virgil: Aeneid VIII*, Mnemosyne Supplementum 35 (Leiden, 1975), 169. Cf. F. Ahl, *Metaformations: Soundplay and Wordplay in Ovid and Other Classical Poets* (Ithaca, 1985), 306–7, who suggests a syllabic play in the mutilation of Mettius' name and his dismemberment.

ample for posterity. Two teams of horses were tied to the arms and legs of Mettus. Driven in opposite directions, the animals tore apart the human body. Placed immediately and so abruptly after the establishment of solemn compacts of peace and alliance before the altar of Jove (8.639–41), this sudden intrusion of a barbaric execution of a man who breaks his faith is a startling surprise.

The violent and gruesome nature of this scene scarcely fits in with prevailing interpretations about the hero's shield and its supposedly celebratory and positive tone. Many critics ignore the scene or prefer to view the episode as a vague allusion to the destruction of the city of Alba Longa, even though the focus of the scene is the horrific punishment of a neighboring king and traitor, not Roman conquest or territorial expansion.[27] The bold declaration by Brooks Otis, "Everywhere [i.e., on the shield] violence is defeated, evil is punished, *religio* observed,"[28] also fails to convince here. The violence of the punishment even seems to exceed the enormity and evil of the crime. Comparison with the account of this historical incident in Livy indicates that this is not only modern sentiment. The contemporary Roman historian shares our horror and can find solace only in the fact that this monstrous deed was never repeated. In the long history of the Roman people, it was a horrible aberration. Romans could otherwise boast that more humane forms of punishment were inflicted on defeated enemies of all races.

> Avertere omnes ab tanta foeditate spectaculi oculos. Primum ultimumque illud supplicium apud Romanos exempli parum memoris legum humanarum fuit: in aliis gloriari licet nulli gentium mitiores placuisse poenas. (Livy 1.28.11)

> [Everyone averted their eyes from such a disgusting spectacle. For the first time and the last time, the Romans inflicted this type of punishment, so utterly disrespectful of the laws of humanity: except for this

---

27. Cf. Hardie, *Virgil's Aeneid*, 348, who concludes "the birth, preservation, and eventual unlimited expansion of Rome, not the history of Italy, form the real subject of the Shield." The scene is especially damaging to Drew's allegorical reading of the passage (*Allegory of the Aeneid*, 26–31) and the claim of an allusion to the golden *clupeus virtutis* of Caesar Augustus. Awarded to the recent victor of Actium in 27 B.C.E. (*RG* 34.2; *CIL* IX, 5811) the Augustan shield proclaimed the four virtues of *virtus*, *pietas*, *iustitia*, and *clementia*. According to Drew's interpretation, the scene of Mettus' punishment illustrated the virtue of *iustitia*. Even if one is inclined to accept that this savage act is an example of "grim and grisly Justice, righteously administered," as Drew characterized the scene, it seems very difficult to understand why the poet would include this episode of Roman history on a shield that at the same time extolled the virtue of *clementia*.

28. B. Otis, *Virgil: A Study in Civilized Poetry* (Oxford, 1963), 342.

one occasion, we may boast above any nation that we imposed more
civilized forms of punishment.]

The particulars of Vergil's description demand closer scrutiny. The phrase
haud procul introduces and sets off the scene. The name of Mettus in the
middle of verse 642 slows down the pace of the opening two dactyls. The
verb of the sentence, the verb that clarifies the action, is postponed to
the opening of the following verse. *Distulerat* informs us of the brutal punishment inflicted on Mettus. Quintilian (9.3.27) comments on the emotional
effect of this passage where Vergil combines the figures of apostrophe and
parenthesis. *At tu* is a startling interruption of the scene. The apostrophe to
Mettus is one of only two found on the shield. The other is also an example
of moral failure, Catiline in Tartarus. It may be useful to consider the poet's
apostrophe to Mettus more closely.

The vocative *Albane* is of special significance to the Vergilian reader. The
poet's attention to Mettus' race is not without effect or meaning. The Alban
race evokes a host of images and scenes in the *Aeneid*. Here we might think
of the long list of Alban kings that Vergil includes in the underworld scene in
book 6. We might also think of the Alban sow that Aeneas discovers on the
bank of the Tiber in the opening of the eighth book. And finally we cannot
forget the city that Ascanius is destined to found, Alba Longa, recalled in
several passages throughout the epic, but more immediately in the preface to
the shield's description, where we learn that the god of fire has fashioned
"the whole race of the future stock descended from Ascanius" (*genus omne
futurae / stirpis ab Ascanio*, 8.628–29). If Mettus is viewed in this historical
and epic context, the Alban king is not the faithless and foreign foe who
breaks the solemn compact of alliance; rather he is part of that future stock
descended from Ascanius and at the same time part of the wars (*pugnataque
in ordine bella*, line 629) that the Romans must wage in Italy to become one
race.

Maneres completes the verse and offers a discomforting feeling of structural balance and semantic contrast with the opening verb *distulerat*. The
verb *raptabat* in line 644 evokes an earlier scene in the epic, that of Achilles
dragging the lifeless body of Hector around the walls of Troy, mentioned first
in book 1 (*ter circum Iliacos raptaverat Hectora muros*, line 483), where
Aeneas gazes on the scenes from his tragic past depicted on the panels of the
Temple of Juno at Carthage. In the second book, the same verb is applied to
Hector when his shade appeared to Aeneas in his sleep, a mournful shade
still bearing the bloody marks on his disfigured body of the dragging by the
horses of Achilles (*raptatus bigis ut quondam, aterque cruento / pulvere*

perque pedes traiectus lora tumentis, lines 272–73). In the description of Mettus' dismemberment, the subject of the verse is postponed, and surprisingly the reader learns that it is Tullus who has usurped the role of Achilles in Latium and drags the dead body of his enemy. Not the four horses but Tullus scatters the fleshy insides (*viscera*) of Mettus throughout the woods. Furthermore, the appearance of *silvam* may not be simply a superfluous addition of description. Vergil perhaps alludes to Silvius, the posthumous son of Aeneas and Lavinia, whose name—Anchises tells his son in the underworld—is *Albanum*, and who, reared in the woods, will be a king and the father of kings, whose race will rule over Alba Longa.

> Silvius, Albanum nomen, tua postuma proles,
> quem tibi longaevo serum Lavinia coniunx
> educet silvis regem regumque parentem,
> unde genus Longa nostrum dominabitur Alba.
>
> (6.763–66)

> [Silvius, an Alban name, your posthumous son,
> whom late in your old age your wife Lavinia
> will rear in the woods, a king and the father of kings,
> from him our race will rule in Alba Longa.]

Reminded of the Alban king's descent from Silvius, the son of Aeneas, Vergil's reader must judge the crime of Mettus and his gruesome punishment with greater horror and revulsion.

The scene concludes with a perversion of nature; the bramble bushes are reddened and drip a bloody dew. The heavily spondaic line (four spondees in the opening four feet) conveys a slow and mournful tone to the story's finale. Again we might think back to the prior scene of the sacrifice of the slain sow that binds the two warring kings and establishes the peace. The treachery of Mettus breaks the peace. Mettus is a liar, but he is also a man; Vergil poignantly identifies the torn innards as *viri mendacis*. A sacrifice again closes a scene from early Rome, but this time the sacrifice is human.

Treachery and internal conflict again threaten the security of early Rome when the king of Clusium, Lars Porsenna,[29] assists the deposed Tarquin in his attempt to reclaim power in Rome (lines 646–51). The issue of the conflict here is clear and uncomplicated—*libertas*. The descendants of Ae-

---

29. Like Mettus, Porsenna is a Vergilian variation. Though Livy adopts the same spelling of the name, Servius explains that Vergil added the second "n" *metri causa*. See discussion of spelling by Eden, *A Commentary on Virgil*, 171.

neas rush into battle to defend their newly won freedom from tyranny. Individual heroics, both male and female, represent the struggle. Horatius Cocles holds back the invading army until the bridge can be cut down, and Cloelia escapes from her imprisonment and swims across the Tiber to safety. Throughout the selected scenes of early Rome on the shield, and especially in lines 630–66, the epic poet echoes elements from Livy's history.[30] Like Livy, Vergil conceives the invasion of the Etruscan king as part of Rome's struggle for freedom against the dangers of tyranny. In reality, Porsenna's assault on Rome (perhaps successful, as some ancient sources claim) documents the aggressive expansion at this time of the powerful Etruscan king, who took advantage of the internal strife in Rome. That Porsenna acted in the interest of the Tarquins is unlikely.[31]

The themes of this Vergilian vignette are oppression, defiance, and civic strife. The name of Tarquin and an allusion to the Etruscan king's banishment (*Tarquinium eiectum*) emphatically introduce the scene. But it is Porsenna who acts more like the tyrant when he gives orders (*iubebat*) to the Romans to take back their former ruler and oppresses the city with a mighty siege to enforce his haughty demands. For a second time (*Romulidis*, line 638), a patronymic title begins the verse and describes the citizenry of Rome. It has been observed that the name neatly balances *Romulidis* and serves at this point "to emphasise the nation's dual ancestry."[32] But more than a complement to the honor bestowed earlier on Romulus (line 638), the title *Aeneadae* holds a particular significance for the reader of Vergil's epic. The patronymic *Romulidis* alluded to the nature of the war between Romans and Sabines, a form of civil conflict where sons-in-law fought the fathers of their prospective brides. There the Romans were not actually "the sons of Romulus," as the poet chooses to call them; rather they were fighting to ensure that there would indeed be sons of Romulus. Without the seizure of women, the greatness of Rome would endure for only the present generation (*hominis aetatem duratura magnitudo erat*, Livy 1.9.1). The title "sons of Aeneas," however, evokes a different meaning in line 648. The fight for the descendants of Aeneas is for liberty (*pro libertate*), and the phrase, placed in the same position of the verse, recalls Anchises' words to which I referred

---

30. The omission of Mucius Scaevola, who plays a prominent role in Livy's account, perhaps can be explained as part of Vergil's attempt to balance the actions of Horatius Cocles and Cloelia. The complementary heroics of the pair are linked by their leaps into the Tiber in their efforts to escape the enemy.

31. R.M. Ogilvie, *A Commentary on Livy, Books 1–5* (Oxford, 1965), 255, examines the veracity of the episode and concludes that Porsenna probably captured the city, but not in alliance with his Etruscan neighbors and not in an effort to restore the Tarquin king.

32. K.W. Gransden, ed., *Virgil, Aeneid Book VIII* (Cambridge, 1976), 166.

earlier. On the shield, Vergil downplays the role of Brutus. Here the family of the Tarquins is driven out not by the consul but by the descendants of the epic's hero (*Aeneadae*), who rush into arms for the cause of liberty. This is the first and only direct reference to Aeneas in the shield's *ecphrasis*. That Vergil sought to extol the Trojan ancestry of the Romans is plausible enough, yet the patronymic may carry a stronger, more emotional and immediate address in the context of Rome's most recent fight against tyranny. Although all Romans might claim descent from Aeneas, the family of the Caesars usurped this honorific distinction. Vergil proclaims the illustrious descent of the Caesars from the Trojans in Jupiter's prophecy to Venus (*nascetur pulchra Troianus origine Caesar*, 1.286) and also in Anchises' address to his son in the underworld (*hic Caesar et omnis Iuli / progenies magnum caeli ventura sub axem*, 6.789–90). The phrase *Aeneadae* may thus allude to the association of the most famous descendant of Aeneas, Augustus Caesar, with the claims of *libertas* and civil war.[33]

The attack of the Gauls on the Tarpeian citadel (8.652–66) is the longest, most elaborate and confusing scene on the hero's shield before the centerpiece of Actium and Augustan triumph. The images shift quickly from Manlius on the citadel, to the goose in the porticos, to the Gauls in the thickets, to a solemn procession of archaic rituals in Rome. A clear and conspicuous emphasis falls on color and the metalwork of the shield. Gold and golden objects demand our attention. *Aurum* is found in noun or adjective form four times in a span of seven verses (*auratis . . . porticibus; aurea caesaries; aurea vestis; colla auro innectuntur*). The effect of the protracted description of the Gauls, of their physical features and military equipment, is unsettling. Tension builds as our eyes linger on the enemy, the danger to the city becomes more real and precarious, but the release from this suspenseful interlude (and, more importantly, Rome's deliverance and triumph) never comes. Instead, an epilogue is abruptly appended that seems loosely connected with the threat of the Gauls.[34]

---

33. Binder, *Aeneas und Augustus*, 182, interprets the phrase as a complimentary gesture to Augustus and cites the reference to *libertas* from the opening words of the *Res Gestae*: *annos undeviginti natus exercitum privato consilio et privata impensa comparavi, per quem rem publicam a dominatione factionis oppressam in libertatem vindicavi*.

34. P.T. Eden, "The Salii on the Shield of Aeneas: Aeneid 8.663–6," *RhM* 116 (1973): 78–83, argues that the Salii scene is linked closely with the immediately preceding scene of the attack of the Gauls. Eden interprets the description of the ancient rites as an allusion to Camillus, the victor over the Gauls, and as a substitution of a triumphal scene. Less convincing are his contentions that successful warfare (*triumphos-bella*) is the one unifying theme of the shield and that the nine scenes on the shield (excluding the Actium centerpiece) are arranged chiastically around the fifth scene, the siege of Porsenna.

Solutions vary to explain the emphasis on the craftsmanship and metals. An allusion has been seen to the ivory-decorated doors on the Temple of Apollo on the Palatine, which depict on one panel the repulse of the Gauls (Galatians) who attacked Delphi in 279 B.C.E. Philip Hardie has recently argued for this influence and has further suggested that the scene of the Gauls on the Capitol and, above all, the centerpiece of the hero's shield—the battle of Actium and triumph of Augustus—incorporate the political icon-ography and imagery of the Attalids of Pergamum, which Vergil exploits and adapts to his own conceptions of Roman imperialism.[35] According to Hardie, Vergil is indebted to the Hellenistic tradition in which the triumph of the city and its ruler is compared to the Gigantomachic struggle, the victory of the Olympian gods over Titans and Giants. The historical events of 390 and, especially, 31 are thus conceived by the poet as moral exemplars of the "divine assertion of cosmos over chaos." There is much to support this view. According to Livy's history of early Rome to which the Vergilian scene is much indebted (5.32–55), the attack of the Gauls constitutes a critical juncture in Roman history. This dramatic episode concludes his initial publication of five books *ab urbe condita.* Camillus, the victor over the Gauls, saves his city a second time when he argues against the migration to the recently captured city of Veii. The role of the gods is paramount in the deliverance of the city. Nonetheless, despite this recognition of the event's significance and its attention, both Augustans fail to interpret the episode as an occasion of Roman victory or as the righteous triumph over the forces of destruction and chaos, as Hardie seeks to argue. On the contrary, for histo-rian and poet alike, the assault of Rome by the Gallic enemy was rather a crisis of moral failure, punishment, and defeat; its phases are neglect of the gods, divine retribution, subjugation and capture, and, finally, deliverance. And although the gods fought on the side of the Romans and ensured their destiny to rule the world, it was the neglect of these same gods that brought them into such a precarious situation. The story of the Gauls' attack on the city is more a warning and fearful prediction than a proud assertion of supremacy or a joyous occasion of celebration. Livy's narrative and, espe-cially, the speech of Camillus confirm this view.

Quid haec tandem urbis nostrae clades nova? Num ante exorta est quam spreta vox caelo emissa de adventu Gallorum, quam gentium ius ab legatis nostris violatum, quam a nobis cum vindicari deberet eadem

---

35. See especially Hardie, *Virgil's Aeneid,* chap. 4, "Gigantomachy in the *Aeneid*: II," 120–56, and chap. 8, "The Shield of Aeneas: The Cosmic Icon," 336–76.

neglegentia deorum praetermissum? Igitur victi captique ac redempti tantum poenarum dis hominibusque dedimus ut terrarum orbi documento essemus. Adversae deinde res admonuerunt religionum. (Livy 5.51.7–8)

[What then of this recent disaster that has befallen our city? Did it happen before the voice from heaven that warned us about the coming of the Gauls was ignored, before the law of nations was violated by our envoys? We should have punished this wickedness, but we let it pass by that same neglect of the gods. And so we have been conquered and our freedom purchased so that we might be an example to the world of such punishments by gods and men. And so adversity reminded us of our religion.]

The Vergilian description of the Gauls' attack begins with Manlius, whom the poet calls the protector of the Tarpeian rock (*custos Tarpeiae . . . arcis*). The name is significant and intimates a story of treachery and cruel retribution familiar to the readers of Livy's history of early Rome (1.11.5–9). During the war with the Sabines, Tarpeia, the daughter of the Roman commander who guarded the citadel, was bribed by golden gifts (*pro aureis donis*) to admit the enemy into the strongly protected fortress. For Livy, the story serves as a moral lesson. Once inside, the enemy rewarded the girl with her death. As payment for her services, the foolish girl had demanded from the enemy what was on their left arms; she had expected to wear their golden bracelets, but she had received instead their shields, which crushed her defenseless body.

The gold of the Gauls is not simply a visual detail of the poet, the metal employed in the representation of the scene on the hero's divine shield. The emphasis on gold brings to mind the reputed avarice of the enemy, to which the speech of Camillus testifies (*caeci avaritia in pondere auri*, Livy 5.51.10); more particularly, it brings to mind the one-thousand-pound weight of gold that Rome agreed to pay the invading enemy for the city's deliverance (as Livy calls it with disdain, the *pretium populi gentibus mox imperaturi factum*, 5.48.8). *Indignitas* was added to the shameful deed when the Gauls weighed their payment on scales improperly and unfairly balanced to one side. The objections of the Roman tribune were met with the infamous words *vae victis*. The intervention of Camillus, however, rescued the Romans. The gold was not paid, and the Gauls were ordered to leave the city. Subsequent battles, one in the city and the other on the road to Gabii, bestowed the titles of father of his country and second founder of Rome on the victor. Unlike the scene of the battle of Actium, Vergil omits the triumphal conclusion of the episode. In fact, there is no depiction of victory or, indeed, of a victor in this extended passage. The description of religious ceremonies that follows in 8.663–66 perhaps alludes to Camillus and his solemn words on the sanctity of the ancient rituals in Rome and on the dire consequences when they are neglected, but the triumphator himself is nowhere to be found. Like Livy, Vergil confirms the role of the gods in the preservation of Rome. The scene on the shield, however, is not simply of "danger triumphantly averted" and "ceremonial celebration."[36] The final scene of the matrons riding through the city in their soft-cushioned carriages looks back to an earlier episode that also involves gold. After the capture of Veii, the Roman women received the honor of the *mollia pilenta* from a grateful Senate because of their generous sacrifice of their golden ornaments to discharge Camillus' vow of a tenth of the spoils to Apollo. The voluntary gesture offers a subtle and pointed contrast to the greed of the Gauls and the shameful bargaining of the Romans.

The solemn rituals shift abruptly to Tartarus and a scene of eternal punishments and rewards (8.666–70). The choice of the two figures who are seen, Catiline and Cato, is puzzling. The great generals of the late Republic—Marius, Sulla, Pompey, and Caesar—and their military triumphs, as well as the heroes of the wars against Carthage, Spain, and Greece, are passed over in silence. More surprising, however, is the poet's decision to include the realm of Tartarus on the hero's shield. Not merely a Homeric imitation or a physical description of the cosmos, the gloomy setting in the underworld affects our perception of the two characters. The one receives his punishment from the Furies; the other gives laws among the pious. Evil is punished, and virtue is rewarded. The contrasting situations would thus seem to fit neatly into the standard interpretations of the passage. But this somewhat narrow viewpoint ignores the emphasis and detail of the poet's words.

We hear first of Tartarus (the adjective *Tartareas* introduces us to the sudden and dramatic change in scene) and the lofty portals of Dis. The punishment of the wicked follows, and for the second time in these opening scenes, the poet focuses our attention on an individual by a second-person

---

36. Hardie is unconvincing when he argues that the attack of the Gauls concludes with an allusion to Roman victory and a triumphal celebration and corresponds closely to the final scene of Actium and the Augustan triple triumph (*Virgil's Aeneid*, 125). However one interprets the purpose of lines 663–66, it seems difficult to conceive the leaping Salii, naked Luperci, and chaste matrons as participants in the triumph of Camillus or in any way similar to the array of conquered nations and peoples who parade before Augustus.

apostrophe (the first apostrophe was to Mettus in line 643). Again, the poet's address, almost an appeal or warning, is directed to a figure of moral failure. The horrid fate of Catiline is revealed in the following verse. While the guilt of the failed conspirator is unambiguous and presumed, his appearance on the shield can only serve to remind the Vergilian reader of those forces of discord and civil conflict that so often haunted the recent past. The sudden emergence of Cato, however, makes this bitter memory of civil war more implicit and immediate. His name dramatically concludes line 670 and marks an astonishing finale to the scene in Tartarus. In any other context, the phrase *dantem iura Catonem* might seem to refer to the conservative senator Cato Censor rather than to his equally distinguished descendant Cato Uticensis. At least the name would be ambiguous.[37] Here, however, coupled with Catiline, this Cato must surely be the enemy of Julius Caesar who committed suicide rather than live under a tyrant. Vergil's praise of Cato is not unique in contemporary poetry (cf. *Catonis* / *nobile letum* in Horace *Odes* 1.12.35–36 and *praeter atrocem animum Catonis* in *Odes* 2.1.24). It would be simplistic and misleading, however, to see Cato's name as the bold manifestation of a poet's lingering Republican sentiment. The deliberate and striking contrast with Catiline, a fitting symbol of rebellion, extols the vanquished opponent of Caesar as an emblem of justice and authority. The emphatic addition of Cato, evoking in the minds of contemporary readers painful memories of civil conflict and defeat, concludes the fleeting and illusory glimpses of Roman history and leads directly to the centerpiece of the shield—the battle at Actium and the subsequent triumph by Caesar Augustus.

The scenes depicted on the hero's shield proceed in a swift and uneven movement. Vergil compels his reader to shift back and forth, up and down around the armor's edges before focusing on the dramatic centerpiece. The progression of historic events is chronological but eclectic and uneven. The focus of the shield of Aeneas is Italy (*res Italas* begins the poet's explanation of the shield's scenes in line 626); the themes are war and conquest in the story of Rome's expansion in the Italian peninsula and the incorporation of its neighboring peoples and former enemies. The Sabines, the Albans, the Etruscans, and even the invading Gauls of northern Italy are destined to be part of the Roman nation. That the battle at Actium would be the culmina-

---

37. Cf. D.C. Feeney's illuminating discussion on the ambiguity in the name *Scipiadas* in *Aen.* 6.843 in "History and Revelation in Vergil's Underworld," *PCPS* 32 (1986): 13–14. Feeney persuasively argues that the poet's pointed description in verses 842–43 offers multiple identifications and allusions to four generations of Scipiones.

tion of this poetic arrangement of fleeting images and historic personages must come as a startling development to any Vergilian reader; nothing in the preliminary scenes on the shield's periphery would signal to any Roman contemporary that Actium was the centerpiece of the hero's armor. Too often critics seek to explain how these initial scenes on the shield (8.630–70) correspond to the message of Augustan victory and triumph; it seems at least as reasonable, if not more prudent, to inquire how the confrontation at Actium relates to the encircling images of warfare, treachery, and civil conflict that visually and emotionally prepare the reader for the dramatic centerpiece.

The Battle of Actium
haec inter tumidi late maris ibat imago
aurea, sed fluctu spumabant caerula cano,
et circum argento clari delphines in orbem
aequora verrebant caudis aestumque secabant.
in medio classis aeratas, Actia bella,
cernere erat, totumque instructo Marte videres
fervere Leucaten auroque effulgere fluctus.
hinc Augustus agens Italos in proelia Caesar
cum patribus populoque, penatibus et magnis dis,
stans celsa in puppi, geminas cui tempora flammas
laeta vomunt patriumque aperitur vertice sidus.
parte alia ventis et dis Agrippa secundis
arduus agmen agens, cui, belli insigne superbum,
tempora navali fulgent rostrata corona.
hinc ope barbarica variisque Antonius armis,
victor ab Aurorae populis et litore rubro,
Aegyptum virisque Orientis et ultima secum
Bactra vehit, sequiturque—nefas—Aegyptia coniunx.
una omnes ruere ac totum spumare reductis
convulsum remis rostrisque tridentibus aequor.
alta petunt; pelago credas innare revulsas
Cycladas aut montis concurrere montibus altos,
tanta mole viri turritis puppibus instant.
stuppea flamma manu telisque volatile ferrum
spargitur, arva nova Neptunia caede rubescunt.
regina in mediis patrio vocat agmina sistro,
necdum etiam geminos a tergo respicit anguis.

omnigenumque deum monstra et latrator Anubis
contra Neptunum et Venerem contraque Minervam
tela tenent. saevit medio in certamine Mavors
caelatus ferro, tristesque ex aethere Dirae,
et scissa gaudens vadit Discordia palla,
quam cum sanguineo sequitur Bellona flagello.
Actius haec cernens arcum intendebat Apollo
desuper; omnis eo terrore Aegyptus et Indi,
omnis Arabs, omnes vertebant terga Sabaei.
ipsa videbatur ventis regina vocatis
vela dare et laxos iam iamque immittere funis.
illam inter caedes pallentem morte futura
fecerat ignipotens undis et Iapyge ferri,
contra autem magno maerentem corpore Nilum
pandentemque sinus et tota veste vocantem
caeruleum in gremium latebrosaque flumina victos.

(8.671–713)

[Amid these scenes, an image of the swollen sea surged far around,
fashioned in gold, but dark blue waves foamed with white billows,
and all around, dolphins, shining with silver, swept the seas
in a circle and cut the swell with their tails.
In the middle, the brazen ships, the battle at Actium,
were in view, and you would see all Leucate ablaze
with Mars in array, and the waves gleam with gold.
On one side, Caesar Augustus, leading the Italians into battle,
with the senators and people, with the Penates and great gods,
stands on the lofty stern, his brow in joy spews forth twin flames,
and the star of his father appears above his head.
Elsewhere, Agrippa, with the winds and gods in his favor,
towers above and leads the column of ships; his brow gleams,
beaked with a naval crown, the proud ornament of war.
On the other side, Antony with barbaric wealth and varied arms,
the victor from the peoples of the Dawn and Red Sea,
bringing with him Egypt and the strength of the Orient
and remote Bactra, and there follows—the shame!—his Egyptian wife.
All rush together, and the expanse of the sea is torn up
and foams from the pulling of oars and three-pronged beaks;
they seek the open sea; you would think the Cyclades, uprooted,

swam in the sea or mountains rushed against mountains on high;
   with such a massive force the men press against the turreted
   sterns.
From their hands, flaming tow and weapons of flying steel
are scattered; the fields of Neptune redden with fresh slaughter.
The queen, in the middle, calls the lines with her ancestral rattle,
not even yet does she see behind her the twin snakes.
Monstrous gods of every kind and barking Anubis
hold weapons against Neptune and Venus, against Minerva.
In the very middle of the battle rages Mars,
engraved in iron, and the grim Dirae from above,
and Discord advances, exultant in her torn garb,
and behind her Bellona follows with bloody whip.
Actian Apollo, watching the battle, bent back his bow
from above, and at this terror, all Egypt and India,
all Arabians, all Sabaeans turned their backs in flight.
The queen herself was seen calling the winds and
spreading sails and just now releasing the slackened ropes.
The god of fire had depicted her amid the slaughter,
pale with approaching death, carried by the waves and Iapyx.
And opposite her the Nile, his great body in mourning,
expanded his folds and with his whole raiment summoned
into his dark blue bosom and hidden streams the conquered.]

The Triple Triumph Ceremony

at Caesar, triplici invectus Romana triumpho
moenia, dis Italis votum immortale sacrabat,
maxima ter centum totam delubra per urbem.
laetitia ludisque viae plausuque fremebant;
omnibus in templis matrum chorus, omnibus arae;
ante aras terram caesi stravere iuvenci.
ipse sedens niveo candentis limine Phoebi
dona recognoscit populorum aptatque superbis
postibus; incedunt victae longo ordine gentes,
quam variae linguis, habitu tam vestis et armis.
hic Nomadum genus et discinctos Mulciber Afros,
hic Lelegas Carasque sagittiferosque Gelonos
finxerat; Euphrates ibat iam mollior undis,
extremique hominum Morini, Rhenusque bicornis,
indomitique Dahae, et pontem indignatus Araxes.

Talia per clipeum Volcani, dona parentis,
miratur rerumque ignarus imagine gaudet,
attollens umero famamque et fata nepotum.

(8.714–31)

[But Caesar in threefold triumph rode within the Roman walls
and consecrated his eternal vow to the Italian gods,
three hundred mighty shrines throughout the whole city.
The streets resounded with joy, games, and applause.
In every temple stood a chorus of mothers, in every temple, altars.
And before the altars, slaughtered bullocks strewed the ground.
He himself sat on the snowy threshold of shining Phoebus
and viewed the gifts of the nations and fitted them to the proud
doorposts; the conquered races passed in long array,
varied in languages as in their style of dress and arms.
Here the tribe of Nomads and ungirdled Africans,
here the Leleges and Carians and quivered Gelonians, Mulciber
had fashioned; the Euphrates went by, with waves already tamed;
the Morini, the most distant of men; the Rhine of two horns;
the unconquered Dahae; and the Araxes, indignant at its bridge.]

An image of the swollen sea introduces Actium in line 671. The adjective *tumidi* might at first suggest a storm or disturbance at sea (cf. the *tumida aequora* Neptune calms after the storm scene in book 1, line 142), but Vergil refrains from developing this initial suggestion. Instead, the reader learns that the image of the sea is golden. *Aurea* emphatically begins line 672. Dark blue waves foam with billows of white; dolphins, brilliant with silver, sweep the waters in a circle and cut through the swell with their fins. In this opening description of the marine setting, Vergil sets before us once again, as in the initial scene of the green cave with the twins and she-wolf of Mars, a brief glimpse of apparent calm, natural beauty, and innocent wonder. The poet's enthusiasm for the vibrant colors of the ocean, for the frolic of dolphins amid the foaming swirl, can only beguile us with its beauty, but such beauty beguiles us for the short span of four verses. Suddenly, in line 675, the image of playful sport gives way, and in the middle, we can perceive the brazen ships of war, the battle of Actium. *Actia bella* identifies the scene. The poet's subsequent words revoke the emotion and peace of the opening verses.

As critics remind us, there is much in the shield's description of the Actian conflict to suggest Vergil's intentions to link Aeneas with Augustus. The phrase "standing on the lofty stern" (*stans celsa in puppi*) recurs in book 10 (line 261) to describe Aeneas, who, from high above, beholds the camp of the Trojans on his return to battle. And there too flames surround the head of the Trojan hero, denoting the mark of divine favor, just as they appear on the head of Augustus. Tempted as we may be to make this connection between the two, and not only tempted but compelled by the verbal echoes here and in other passages to make this connection, nonetheless, we are also alerted to the strange irony of this future moment of proud Roman glory when Augustus leads into battle not the sons of Romulus and not the race of its Trojan founder but the Italians (*Italos*), the very people against whom Aeneas is about to wage his war in Latium. His is a war, as the poet reminds us more than once in the epic, that the Trojan hero enters with nothing but reluctance for what he knows to be its final senselessness and waste.

The *hinc* of line 678 is answered by another in line 685. The enemy of Augustus is named; he is Antony. This identification is a stunning revelation, stunning when perceived in the context of the almost total suppression of that name in the descriptions of Actium by contemporary poets. Among the Augustan poets, Horace nowhere mentions the name of Antony. In *Epode 9*, he is the unnamed *hostis*. He is passed over without even a suggestion of his presence in the famous Cleopatra Ode (1.37). And everywhere else in Horace, there is a hushed silence about Antony—and about Actium. Propertius refers to Antony, to his notorious love affair with the Egyptian queen, and to his ultimate fate in only two passages: by the epithet *dux* in 2.16.37–40, where he describes the waters at Actium filled with the futile groans of his condemned soldiers; and explicitly by Antony's *nomen* in 3.9.56, where he refers to his suicide at Alexandria. In *Elegy* 4.6, the poem whose action is the counterpart to this scene in Vergil, Propertius is strangely reticent and refrains from including Antony's involvement in the naval battle.

Antony is introduced into the Vergilian scene of battle by name; he is described, however, as an Eastern potentate and an enemy of Rome. He carries with him the opulence of the Orient and its varied strength. But in the beginning of line 686, the poet also calls Antony *victor*, an impressive and ironic epithet for a man who will soon be defeated in one of the most significant battles in Western civilization. He leads with him Egypt, the strength of the East, and the farthest land of Bactra. His Egyptian wife follows, the *nefas*, as the poet emphatically interjects—a perverse counterpart to the ally of Augustus, Marcus Agrippa. All Italy supports the just cause of Augustus. Antony is no longer Roman; instead, he is an Eastern king and lover. The Egyptian woman who follows is called his wife.

Historians and literary critics alike refer to this passage as the culmination of the official view on the Actian conflict in the propaganda terms of East versus West, the unmediated slander and deceit of a victorious regime. The confidence of the claim is surprising, since neither Horace nor Propertius interprets the battle as a mighty struggle between opposing civilizations or geographic areas. The enemies of Rome are a woman, Egypt, and a band of eunuchs. And though the evidence is fragmentary, this seems to be the force of Octavian's propaganda against Antony before the war.[38] I have already suggested the irony in the fact that the descendant of Trojan Aeneas is leading Aeneas' enemy (*Italos*) into battle. The description of Antony strangely corresponds in more than one respect to the situation of the hero in Italy. Both men are the objects of unfair and harsh ridicule because of their Eastern habits: Antony—by the propaganda of Augustus, and Aeneas, on several occasions throughout the epic—by Iarbas, the African king, in book 4 (4.215–18); by Remulus Numanus, the brother-in-law of Turnus, in book 9 (9.598–620); and finally in a savage attack by Turnus himself in the opening of book 12.

> . . . da sternere corpus
> loricamque manu valida lacerare revulsam
> semiviri Phrygis et foedare in pulvere crinis
> vibratos calido ferro murraque madentis.
>
> (12.97–100)

> [. . . grant to me to lay low his body
> and with a powerful blow to tear away and shatter the breastplate
> of this effeminate Phrygian and to defile his hair in the dust,
> curled by the hot iron and drenched with myrrh.]

The selected manner of Vergil's description of the Eastern forces of Antony offers the reader a pointed reference to an earlier scene in the epic. The phrase *ope barbarica* in 8.685, which introduces us to Antony before we even hear his Roman name, recalls the once proud grandeur of Troy and its fall. The adjective *barbaricus*, which Vergil reserves for only two occasions in the *Aeneid*, formerly described the doorposts of Priam's palace, doorposts proud with barbaric gold and spoils.

---

38. For Octavian's propaganda against Antony, see K. Scott, "Political Propaganda of 44–30 B.C.," and, more recently, P. Wallmann, *Triumviri Rei Publicae Constituendae. Untersuchungen zur politischen Propaganda im Zweiten Triumvirat (43–30 v. Chr.)* (Frankfurt, 1989), 249–350.

> barbarico postes auro spoliisque superbi
> procubuere
>
> (2.504–5)

> [doorposts, haughty in barbaric gold and spoils,
> fell down]

Vergil describes the doorposts as proud just before they fell forward in ruin (*procubuere*), hurled down by the flames of destruction.[39] A foreign and royal bride is destined for the Trojan hero in his new homeland. Amid the destruction of Troy, the shade of Creusa foretold to her husband that a kingdom and royal wife (*regia coniunx*, 2.783–84) awaited him in Hesperia. And in the sixth book of the epic, the Sibyl prophesied ominously how a foreign wife (*coniunx hospita*) and a foreign marriage (*externi thalami*) would once again be the cause of so much evil to the Trojans.

> causa mali tanti coniunx iterum hospita Teucris
> externique iterum thalami.
>
> (6.93–94)

> [the cause of such evil to the Trojans is again an alien bride
> and again a foreign marriage.]

Oddly, therefore, both antagonists in the battle of Actium, as they are depicted by the poet on the shield, seem to anticipate the single protagonist of the epic, Aeneas himself. Vergil denies us any straightforward and uncomplicated allegorical reading, any simple equation that matches Augustus with Aeneas. The complexity and overlapping of allusions confuse the claims of the opposing sides and mark an uneasy introduction into the scene of battle.

In 8.689–703, a fierce struggle ensues, cosmic in its dimensions, as if islands moved in conflict or as if tall mountains clashed. The fields of Neptune grow red with fresh slaughter. The metaphor is found in Ennius (*[pont]i caerula prata*, Vahlen *Ann.* 143) and Cicero (*Neptunia prata*, *Arat.* 129), but the imagery of color is uniquely Vergilian. The deep red color of blood stains the blue-black waters just as the bloody dew of Mettus dripped on the

---

39. It has been plausibly suggested that Vergil borrowed the phrase *ope barbarica* from Ennius. The phrase occurs not in Ennius' epic, the *Annales*, but in one of his tragedies, the *Andromacha*. Here too Ennius employs it to describe the splendor that was once of Troy (*O pater, o patria, o Priami domus / saeptum altisono cardine templum / vidi ego te adstante[m] ope barbarica / tectis caelatis laqueatis / auro eboro instructam regifice*, Vahlen *Scenica* 92–96).

bramble bushes. The *nova caede* (line 695) takes us back to the *novum bellum* between the sons of Romulus and the aged Sabine king and to the impious war of sons against a father in the assembled throng of Roman heroes in the underworld.

From the reddening of the Neptunian fields, we come to the figure of Cleopatra, who appears amid the battle lines, calling the host with her native *sistrum*. Cleopatra's active participation in the campaign and battle dominated subsequent Augustan propaganda. But Vergil does not insert into the midst of the Actian battle the brief glimpse of this woman only to serve as a medium of further abuse and scorn. The *Aegyptia coniunx* of Antony is now called *regina*, the queen. On hearing the mention of *regina*, we might think back to the first of the two queens of the *Aeneid*, the Carthaginian queen whose love affair with Aeneas threatened the promise and destiny of Rome, the tragic and lovely Dido. And we may think of the second *regina* of the epic, the wife of aged Latinus, whose maddened opposition to the marriage of her daughter to Aeneas, even now as we come to the end of the eighth book, threatens the welfare of her city and makes necessary the armor Aeneas requires. Like Dido and Amata, the Egyptian queen is also fated to die. Twin snakes lurk ominously and unseen behind her, foreshadowing her approaching death. It is a sudden and surprising shift in tone to the passage. Throughout the *Aeneid*, snakes represent the supernatural forces of evil and destruction, especially when they appear in pairs.[40] Twin snakes (*gemini anguis*) threaten the life of the infant Hercules earlier in book 8 (line 289). In book 7 (line 450), they project from the hair of the Fury Allecto, as she sounds her whip and hurls her torch at Turnus. And in the most dramatic and frightening appearance of these creatures in the *Aeneid*, twin serpents with huge coils and scaly backs emerge from the peaceful depths of the sea and make their way for the shores of Troy, bearing death to the priest Laocoön and his young sons (2.203–4). Here, on the shield, the twin snakes that forebode the death of the Egyptian queen are known only to the reader. Vergil has intensified the pathos of the moment by the subjective disclosure that the queen does not foresee her death; the queen does not yet look behind her to see the agents of her destruction (*necdum etiam . . . respicit*).

Gods of every strange and monstrous form wage war against the Olympian deities. Neptune, Venus, and Minerva oppose the barking Anubis. Philip Hardie explores in full the Gigantomachic aspects of the battle of Actium in the shield's *ecphrasis*.[41] Hardie's cosmic and cosmogonic inter-

---

40. For a discussion of the passages where twin snakes appear in the *Aeneid*, cf. Binder, *Aeneas und Augustus*, 241–42.

41. Hardie, *Virgil's Aeneid*, 336–76.

pretation of the passage supports the popular view that Vergil offers on the hero's shield a pure and uplifting vision of Roman imperialism and eternal dominion, the triumph of Western civilization over the barbaric East, the victory of order and reason over the forces of chaos and discord. And herein lies the cause of Auden's caustic wit and serious complaint in "Secondary Epic," whose opening verses introduced this chapter. The painful experience of two world wars had made the twentieth-century poet especially distrustful of the fraudulent and boastful claims of extreme nationalism, imperial power, and manifest destiny. The symbolic aspects of the poet's elevation of the war between Caesar's heir and Antony into a struggle of cosmic dimensions, and the profound implications of this symbolism, are obvious to readers of the *Aeneid*, whether ancient or modern. And yet such symbols are often disappointing and never quite as clear and one-dimensional in Vergil as some might expect them to be.

Much has been said, and much more inferred, by critics about the ideological and propagandistic dichotomies that underlie the opposing forces depicted on the hero's shield: "reasoned order" vs. "directionless irrationality."[42] Apollo represents reason and wisdom. Even Minerva in line 699 has been understood as the Athenian goddess of wisdom and prudence.[43] Mars, the Dirae, and Discordia represent the enemy forces of disorder and madness. The final victory of Augustus over Antony assures the universal order. However attractive this view may be, the poet's description of the fighting cannot support this idealized portrait; instead, it rejects the simplicity and neatness of such an interpretation. The gods that represent the senselessness, violence, and destruction of war are not allied with Antony and his Eastern throng; they are not the foreign enemies opposed to Augustus and the Italians; and they do not belong to one group or the other, to one political

---

42. The phrases come from David Quint's stimulating essay on the influence of the shield's *ecphrasis* upon modern European epic in *Epic and Empire: Politics and Generic Form from Virgil to Milton* (Princeton, 1993), 37. In the catalog that he has arranged for the binary oppositions underlying the poet's description of the Actian battle, Quint attributes the gods representing chaos (Mars, Dirae, and Discordia) to the forces of Antony and Cleopatra, even though Vergil places them directly in the midst of the two battle lines (*medio in certamine*, line 700), and though nothing in the poet's description of the god or the events of battle supports the view that Apollo serves as a symbol of cosmic order and rationality.

43. Hardie, *Virgil's Aeneid*, 99, is tempted to see the goddess Minerva as the "representative of reason and wisdom, fighting on the side of the legitimate champion of Rome." He implausibly suggests that the Pheidian statue of the goddess in the Parthenon, whose shield depicted reliefs of an Amazonomachy and Gigantomachy on its exterior and interior panels, respectively, influenced the poet's decision to include Minerva among the fighting Olympian participants. For such an interpretation, see R. Cohon, "Vergil and Pheidias: The Shield of Aeneas and of Athena Parthenos," *Vergilius* 37 (1991): 22–30.

faction or ideology. Mars, the grim Dirae, Discordia, and Bellona contend in the very middle of the Actian struggle (*medio in certamine*, line 700). The madness of war is not partisan; it does not choose sides, and it rejects the appropriate distinctions between ally and foe, Roman and barbarian. Instead, the fury engulfs both sides and all combatants. And as so often happens in the second half of the *Aeneid*, moral convictions and proud assertions of righteous causes ultimately give way and lose their validity in the course of fighting on the battlefield.

Apollo Actius enters suddenly into the scene of confrontation (line 704). The Egyptians, Indians, Arabs, and Sabaeans flee in terror at the sight. The enemy is defeated, and the Romans are victorious. This is the first appearance in extant Latin literature of Apollo Actius, the god who assures the victory at Actium. Horace ignores the role of the god in his treatment of the battle (*Epode* 9), and Propertius composed his aetiological hymn on the Temple of Palatine Apollo and the battle at Actium (*Elegy* 4.6) after the publication of the *Aeneid* and perhaps in direct response to the epic description of the battle on the Vergilian shield. His earlier poem (*Elegy* 3.11) alluded indirectly to the god's role in the battle in a closing address, but there Propertius called on Apollo Leucadius, not Apollo Actius. In Vergil's characterization of the Actian battle, the god plays a dramatic and crucial role, though this fact is neither surprising nor extraordinary in the context of an epic scene where the divine forces of each side have already been arrayed by the poet. Vergil attributes the victory to the intervention of the god and his archery, and later the triumphator sits on the threshold of the god's temple in Rome during the procession of conquered nations (*ipse sedens niveo candentis limine Phoebi*, line 720). The Augustan victory is divinely sanctioned and won. Apollo usurps the role of presiding deity over the naval battle and the triumphal celebrations.

The poet's emphasis on Apollo's role in the battle should not be understood (or need not be explained) as the reflection of an Augustan attitude toward the battle or as the ultimate expression of a contemporary political ideology. To be sure, at Nicopolis, near the site of the naval battle, the proud victor acknowledged his gratitude to Apollo by the enlargement of the god's temple and the exaltation of local games to an "Olympian" status. Yet the dedicatory inscription to Octavian's Actian "campsite memorial," the elaborate display of captured ships' prows, surprisingly excludes the role of Apollo in the battle and instead grants thanksgiving offerings to Neptune and Mars for the victory on land and sea. In Rome, the returning conqueror celebrated a triple triumph; and earlier in the same year, the Senate closed the doors of the Temple of Janus. There seems to be no prominence or attention bestowed on Apollo during these occasions. As I have argued previously, Octavian did not take any official or overt steps at this time to associate the Temple of Apollo on the Palatine with his victory at Actium. Neither Horace in his *Odes* nor Propertius in first three books of *Elegies* alludes to the Augustan temple's public connections with Actium before the epic poet. The Vergilian representation of battle, the victory of Roman might and morals over the allied peoples of the "barbaric" East, and the subsequent union and assimilation of these formerly hostile cultures, prefigured in the triumphal ceremonies described in lines 714–27, anticipate the resolution of the conflict between Aeneas, the *Troianus dux*, and Turnus, the leader of the Italians, at the end of the epic. The implications of the poet's decision to exalt the final episode of Roman civil war into a heroic struggle, divinely fought and won by the aid of Apollo, are serious, profound, and immediate. The political impact and literary influence of Vergil's Actian description will be explored more fully in the discussion of Propertius' *Elegy* 4.6, which scornfully mocks the new cultural and ideological attitudes toward the battle that become defined in the second decade of the Augustan Principate.

Amid the slaughter of battle (*inter caedes*, line 709), the queen appears, pale with the signs of her own approaching death. If Vergil sought to make us think back to Dido in the prior brief glimpse of the queen, calling the host with her native *sistrum*, he compels us to do so now. The phrase *pallida morte futura* occurs in the tragic scene in the fourth book where Dido is about to fall on the sword of her Dardanian lover (4.644). For the second time in the passage, the poet alludes to the future death of the Egyptian queen. Cleopatra's death is imminent, but the craftsman/god (*ignipotens*) allows us to see her only in flight. The final three verses in the treatment of the battle (lines 711–13) suddenly shift the scene to Egypt, to an image of the mighty Nile in grief. The river god is seen mourning with his great body, extending his folds, and calling with his whole robe. The object of this mournful embrace into his dark blue bosom and hidden streams is postponed. We are expecting through the three verses that it is the queen whom the Nile will receive into his folds. The verse concludes surprisingly and emphatically with *victos*. The plight of the Egyptian queen is extended to include all the conquered.

The shield's *ecphrasis* does not conclude with the poignant image of a grieving Nile and the flight of the queen. An emphatic *at* announces the change of scene. Immediately and abruptly we return to Augustus, to the Roman walls, and to a triple triumph. Dutiful and pious, the triumphator displays his gratitude to the Italian gods by the dedication of three hundred shrines. The streets roar with joy, games, and applause. Augustus himself sits on the snowy white throne of shining Phoebus and accepts the tribute of the conquered peoples. He affixes the spoils to his proud doorposts (*superbis / postibus*). The passage evokes the solemn occasion of the Roman triumph, but it also recalls the scene at Troy where the palace of Priam once boasted of such honor and splendor, and where the doorposts, proud in barbaric gold and spoils, fell down in ruin to the flames of the victorious Greeks (*barbarico postes auro spoliisque superbi / procubuere*, 2.504–5). In this climactic moment of Rome's greatest triumph, the proud destiny so often proclaimed to the hero of the epic, Vergil reminds his reader of the former glory of a tragic past and links Rome inextricably with the fate of Troy.[44] Some may be comforted with the image of *Troia redux*; others, like Horace, may fear the consequences.

> Troiae renascens alite lugubri
> fortuna tristi clade iterabitur
>   ducente victrices catervas
>   coniuge me Iovis et sorore.
> Ter si resurgat murus aeneus,
> auctore Phoebo, ter pereat meis
>   excisus Argivis, ter uxor
>   capta virum puerosque ploret.
>
> (Horace *Odes* 3.3.61–68)

> [Troy's fate, born again under mournful auspices,
> with grievous disaster will come again
>   when the conquering hosts will be led
>   by me, the wife and sister of Jove.
> If thrice its bronze walls should rise,
> by the will of Phoebus, thrice it would perish,
>   cut down by my Argives; thrice the wife,
>   a captive, would weep for her husband and sons.]

---

44. R.J. Rowland, Jr., "Foreshadowing in Vergil, *Aeneid*, VIII, 714–28," *Latomus* 27 (1968): 839–40, recognized the emphasis of *superbis* but doubted if the adjective conveyed any ambiguity or "odious implications." In his list of other examples of the word in the *Aeneid*, Rowland surprisingly omits the critical passage in book 2 (lines 504–5). Cf. D. Gillis, *Eros and Death in the Aeneid* (Rome, 1983), 139, who views *superbis* as an ominous word and interprets the final scene as a "subtle warning . . . to one who, like Aeneas, had disregarded mercy to those who had been humbled."

When the poet assembles the conquered, varied in tongue, manner of dress, and arms, they represent an impressive gathering of forces that have been subdued by the might of a conqueror. The long array serves as a powerful climax to the description of a shield that extolled the triumphs of the Romans (*Romanorumque triumphos*) and the wars fought in order (*pugnata in ordine bella*). The very names of the defeated strike our ears as exotic and distant. These are not the Egyptians, against whom the war was officially waged, or the Indians, Arabs, and Sabaeans, whom Vergil fancifully included in his depiction of the Actian battle; nor are they among those various conquered peoples whom Octavian collected in 29 to adorn his triple triumph ceremony to make it appear as a triumph over the East. Vergil has another purpose in mind by his selection of these peoples.

The list begins with the continent of Africa—the race of Nomads and the ungirdled Africans. The first by the origin of their name (*Nomades*, those who roam for pasture) and the second by their distinctive epithet (*discincti*, a term often applied to those without weapons)[45] betoken the simplicity and innocence of a pastoral life, free from war and its devastation. The implication of victory is clear: conquest means the loss of this lifestyle. The Lelegae and Carians, the ancient inhabitants from Asia Minor, often linked together, follow. The arrow-bearing Geloni extends the range of conquered nations to the farthest borders of Scythia. The long array concludes with the Morini from northern Europe, the Dahae from the East, and three rivers, the Euphrates, Rhine, and Araxes. The message of the final verse demands closer scrutiny.

Indomiti begins line 728, an adjective previously applied by the epic poet to the *agricolae* of Italy (7.521), rustics whom the madness of Allecto had spurred on to war against the invading Trojan foreigners. Now the word describes the Dahae, the distant people at the end of a long array of conquered tribes. The might of the Roman victors ignored the claims of their once proud title, *indomiti*. It has become an empty-sounding and ironic epithet. Again Vergil seeks to remind us of what has been lost as much as of what has been gained. The Araxes closes the scene of triumph. The waters of the Araxes, flowing north into the Caspian Sea, once marked the easternmost border of Armenia, the entrance into the kingdom of the Medes.[46]

---

45. In military language, the adjective refers to the absence of a sword belt and is coupled with *inermis*. Cf. Livy 35.11.7, Suet. *Aug.* 24.2, and Fron. *Str.* 4.1.43. Lewis and Short, *A Latin Dictionary* (Oxford, 1879), cites the Vergilian passage and gives the meaning of "voluptuous, effeminate."

46. *RE* 2.1 (1895): cols. 402–4 distinguishes four rivers by this name, all in the area of what was known to the Romans as Armenia. Herodotus (1.202.3) relates that the river he calls

Alexander the Great once built a bridge over this river on his march to sack Persepolis, the famed citadel of Darius. The ancient commentator appends the sequel that the river later reclaimed its rights and broke apart the bridge the Macedonian conqueror had imposed over its span, only to be tamed again by a stronger bridge built by Caesar Augustus.[47] The claim, not repeated by another ancient source, is especially dubious and bears all the traces of a learned invention created to explain the appearance of the Araxes in the Vergilian text. More likely, the Araxes should be seen as a symbol of the contemporary Parthian kingdom, Rome's feared enemy in the East; the bridge, placed over the waters of the Araxes, is suggestive of the future defeat of this much feared foe and alludes to the bold promise by Caesar Augustus to avenge the shameful defeat of Marcus Crassus, a promise later fulfilled by the terms of a negotiated peace rather than by the force of arms. The political significance of the poet's patriotic prophecy of Roman triumph in the East should not be ignored; but here I am more concerned with the river's indignation.

The final protest of the Araxes foreshadows the end of the epic. The verb *indignatus* links the triumphant display of Caesar Augustus and the farthest extent and glory of Roman imperialism with the ultimate victory of Trojan Aeneas and his fated destiny in Italy; it links them in a way that the reader of the *Aeneid* cannot anticipate and cannot fully comprehend as the hero puts on his shoulder the burden of the shield . This same word, *indignatus,* Vergil applies to the closing scenes where he describes the deaths of Camilla, the female warrior, and Turnus. In fact, Vergil employs the same verse for the deaths of the two enemies of Aeneas, the final verse of the *Aeneid.*

vitaque cum gemitu fugit indignata sub umbras.

(11.831, 12.952)

[and with a groan her [his] life fled indignant to the shades below.]

In book 11, Camilla, struck down by the spear, whose sound she does not even hear, falls from her horse, releases her armor, and protests her death with a groan. And in the last scene of the epic, Turnus begs for his life, but fury and madness drive in deeply the sword of Aeneas. The shade of Turnus,

---

the Araxes rises in the country of the Matieni and has forty mouths. In another passage (1.201), he reports the disputed claim that the river is even bigger than the Danube. The river's size and numerous branches probably account for the discrepancies among the ancients concerning its exact location in Armenia.

47. Serv. *auc. Comm. in Verg. Aen.* 8.728.

fleeing to the dark underworld with a mournful resentment, concludes the epic. And thus, here on the shield of Aeneas, this cosmic icon, this emblem of eternal dominion and imperial rule, this symbol of the fame and fates of the descendants of the Trojan hero, Vergil also directs our attention ever so subtly and evokes our sympathy to the indignation of a conquered river.

At the end of his "Secondary Epic," Auden's mocking tone becomes more serious.

> No, Virgil, no:
> Behind your verse so masterfully made
> We hear the weeping of a Muse betrayed.

Auden's charge of betrayal prejudges the Roman poet and his intentions in the *Aeneid* and convicts him of jingoistic patriotism and nineteenth-century nationalism. The final scene on the Vergilian shield, however, discloses a more complex image of Actium and Augustan triumph. Linking Actium with the past, Vergil places the battle as the culmination of a long series of wars and Roman triumphs. But the poet also complicates his reader's emotions as the displays of righteous pride and public jubilation fail to eclipse the episodes of cruel violence, irrational strife, and individual sorrow. The Vergilian concept of victory, not only on the hero's shield, but throughout his national epic, is more often perceived in terms of defeat. Public triumph and joy inevitably give way to private loss and suffering. The reality of civil war behind the Actian facade prefigures the conflict of the epic's final four books, the fierce struggle between Trojan Aeneas and Italian Turnus, the representative leaders of two races who are destined to be one. While the Roman poet gave eloquent and sincere expression to the promise and hope of a bright Augustan future, he could not forget the misery and loss inflicted in the still recent past.

Vergil concludes the eighth book with Aeneas' reaction to the scenes on the shield.

> Talia per clipeum Volcani, dona parentis,
> miratur rerumque ignarus imagine gaudet,
> attollens umero famamque et fata nepotum.
>
> (8.729–31)

[He marvels at such scenes on Vulcan's shield, the gift of his mother,
and though ignorant of the events, he rejoices in their pictures,
uplifting on his shoulder the fame and fortunes of his descendants.]

Aeneas marvels and rejoices at the images on the shield; he is also ignorant.
Placed in the center of the verse, the adjective *ignarus* is emphatic and
meaningful. The ignorance of the hero looks back to the poet's introduction
of the shield's description and offers a stark contrast to the divine crafts-
man's knowledge (*haud . . . ignarus*, 8.627). The hero of the *Aeneid* rejoices,
though he cannot fully comprehend the message of the shield's elaborate
artwork, which reveals the outcome of his much proclaimed destiny and the
grandeur that is due to Rome and Augustus.[48] The *ignarus* Aeneas inspects
the future of his race; Vergil's omniscient reader reviews his own past. The
difference in perspective perhaps reflects the complex attitude of the poet
toward his subject, a mixture of emotions and conflicting passions. Vergil
looked forward to the fulfillment of Aeneas' destiny, the final suppression of
the madness and violence of war.

> Furor impius intus
> saeva sedens super arma et centum vinctus aënis
> post tergum nodis fremet horridus ore cruento.
>
> (1.294–96)

> [within, impious Furor,
> sitting above the savage arms, bound with a hundred brazen knots
> behind his back, will roar horribly with his mouth dripping blood.]

But despite the hundred brazen chains and firm imprisonment, the impious
monster roars, and his mouth is still bloody. Even the establishment of peace
and Augustan rule cannot remove this memory and suppress this continuing
fear.

The epic poet profoundly shaped and defined anew the contemporary
perception of Actium. Like Horace and Propertius, Vergil recognized the
painful reality of Roman civil war (*Antonius* in line 685 is explicit recognition, even if he is described as a foreign king) and expressed feelings of
shame and disgust (*nefas* in line 688 derives from the shocking fact that the

---

48. See Johnson, *Darkness Visible*, 111–14, for an illuminating analysis of "the wonder, the
ignorance, and the joy"; cf. Hardie, *Virgil's Aeneid*, 369–76, who examines Aeneas' "Atlan-
tean" shouldering of the cosmic shield.

Roman married a foreign woman; *Aegyptia coniunx* immediately follows the exclamation and emphatically closes the line). The clash of brazen ships in the Actian sea is a powerful and symbolic climax to the early history of Rome, represented as a continuous succession of wars and the conflict of peoples in Italy. For Vergil, the battle at Actium is neither a national crusade against Egypt to thwart the regal ambitions of the dissolute and seductive queen, as hostile propaganda distorted Rome's enemy, nor a political struggle between former allies and their adherents for supreme power and authority in Rome, as every contemporary painfully realized. Vergil's Actium mixes elements of both truth and falsehood, history and legend, propaganda and pathos. The poet's almost mythic interpretation of the past results in a mighty clash of cultures, a Roman victory over barbarian foes, supported and achieved by the assistance of the Olympian gods. To the contemporary reader of the *Aeneid*, the victory can be seen not only as a spontaneous occasion of celebration but as the fulfillment of dreams, the final cessation of hostilities, and the embarkation of a new age. The god of archery, who looks favorably on Aeneas and the Trojan race, has secured the Augustan victory with his bow. It is the last act in the destiny of the epic's hero, the motivating impulse and theme of the *Aeneid*.

The symbolic framework of Vergil's *Aeneid* did not so much reflect a public image of Actium as it created or redefined the role of this victory in Augustan political culture. Vergil gave Augustus and his regime what Actium had previously lacked, not simply poetic expression and epic grandeur (what any composer of hackneyed verses might provide), but political interpretation, meaning, and import. Viewed from the perspective of more than a decade that witnessed an enduring, if at times fragile, political success, the Augustan victory entered the Roman public consciousness as a critical moment of a collective history and national culture, what Auden disparaged as the poet's "grand panorama" of history without end. To seek the political or private concerns that motivated the epic poet in his narrative discourse on the hero's shield is a vain and disconcerting effort. Individual readers, whether ancient or modern, make their own judgments on the message and meaning of the *Aeneid*. With his untimely death in September of 19 B.C.E., Vergil left behind a great poem and, with it, the impetus of something powerful, alluring, and unreal—a political myth of Augustus and Actium.

Chapter 6 considers how the recalcitrant elegist who previously had scorned the glory of the naval battle and its victor responded to the epic grandeur and exalted image of Actium. It is my view that Propertius 4.6, the literary hymn to Apollo Palatinus, can be more properly understood in the aftermath of the public reception and acclaim of the *Aeneid*. And placed in a political context more than fifteen years after the victory in the Ambracian Gulf, after the much celebrated return of the Roman standards from the Parthians and the revived boasts of conquest in the East, the solemn ceremonies of the Ludi Saeculares, and the formal adoptions of Gaius and Lucius Caesar, the elegist's final piece on Actium reflects a significant turning point in the development of a political conception of Augustan military success. Former triumphs and ignoble conflicts in civil war are recast in powerfully new ideological and symbolic terms, and memories of a not too distant past are reconstituted to affirm a more illustrious image of conqueror and ruler.

Chapter Six

Alexandrian Poetics and Roman Politics: Propertius 4.6

Is *Elegy* 4.6 serious political panegyric or deliberate and ironic parody? These extreme points of view have polarized modern attitudes toward the Propertian elegiac hymn that celebrates the naval battle at Actium. Any attempt today to assess the intentions of the elegist cannot proceed without at least some acknowledgment of the controversy of opinion that has turned the elegy into a veritable battleground of fierce scholarly contention. Interpretations of the poem have shifted back and forth during the past thirty years, with the most recent discussions seeking to reassert the traditional claim of unfeigning eulogy and a poet's conversion.[1] The critical opinion that prevailed until the end of the 1960s understood the poem as a serious and sincere expression of Augustan adulation. *Elegy* 4.6 was seen as the ultimate gesture, the ceremonious display of the poet's reluctant and late acceptance of the founder of the Augustan Principate. In an informative discussion of the influences of Callimachus on the Roman elegist, Hugh Pillinger also judged the political implications of the Propertian hymn to Augustus and his patron deity.

> And, in fact, in this hymn of praise to Augustus we have Propertius' most elaborate and enthusiastic endorsement of the imperial house and mission. . . . His poem then is as much a hymn to Apollo as a glorification of Augustus, or perhaps we should agree with the poet that it is a hymn to both at once, the glory of Augustus being prefigured in the brilliance of Apollo.[2] The consummate Alexandrian piece has thus become not only the manifest sign of the elegist's newly claimed poetic program in his fourth book but a bold and resolute affirmation of his evolving views on the victory at Actium and his allegiance to Augustan Rome.

---

1. For a review of the scholarship on this poem, see P.J. Connor, "The Actian Miracle: Propertius 4.6," *Ramus* 7 (1978): 1–3.

2. H.P. Pillinger, "Some Callimachean Influences on Propertius, Book 4," *HSCP* 73 (1969): 190 and 192, respectively.

The subsequent decade of the 1970s witnessed a succession of spirited attacks on this opinion as critics began to examine the composition and merits of the poem more closely. J.P. Sullivan had once been the lone voice of dissent when he first suggested in his comparative study of Ezra Pound and Propertius that the Augustan elegist was not serious in his eulogy of the victor at Actium.[3] Sullivan later expanded on his suggestion when he considered the Actian poem in the context of the elegist's fourth book. Again he questioned the motivations of the poet: "neither Propertius' heart nor talents are engaged in this poem"; "the whole thing reads like a parody of court poetry."[4] Other critics followed Sullivan's lead and cast further doubt on the elegist's sincerity,[5] but it was not until W.R. Johnson's provocative essay "The Emotions of Patriotism: Propertius 4.6" that a close analysis of the poem's structure and artifice supported the claims of parody and playfulness.[6] In a brilliant display of eloquence, Johnson rushed to the defense of the Propertian elegy that had once been castigated by Gordon Williams as "a thoroughly bad poem" and "one of the most ridiculous poems in the Latin language."[7] Johnson countered that the "ambitious mannerist" had not overextended himself and that he had not failed to comprehend the serious nature of his subject. Johnson observed with a critic's glee the poet's conscious and playful manipulation of the ambiguity in the contemporary understanding of the term *vates* and described in facetious terms the peculiar predicament of Propertius in the guise of the sacrificing priest.

> In any case, what we have so far is a very charming and dissipated master of great light verse who, having somehow got himself into a chasuble, cannot manage to distinguish between his chalice and his inkwell.[8]

For Johnson, the implications of the elegist's role-playing were clear and suggestive: Propertius refused to accept (not failed to recognize) the earnest-

---

3. Sullivan, *Ezra Pound and Sextus Propertius*, 63.

4. Sullivan, *Propertius*, 146 and 147, respectively.

5. Cf. J.P. Hallett, "Book IV, Propertius' recusatio to Augustus and Augustan Ideals" (Ph.D. diss., Harvard University, 1971), 107: "we can easily believe that 4.6 may be an intentional failure"; and F. Sweet, "Propertius and Political Panegyric," *Arethusa* 5 (1972): 174: "[Propertius'] solution to the moral problem of Actium is to treat the subject in a light Callimachean style."

6. W.R. Johnson, "The Emotions of Patriotism: Propertius 4.6," *CSCA* 6 (1973): 151–80.

7. G. Williams, *Tradition and Originality in Roman Poetry*, 51, and "Poetry in the Moral Climate of Augustan Rome," *JRS* 52 (1962): 43, respectively.

8. Johnson, "Emotions of Patriotism," 154.

ness and gravity of his chosen topic, namely, the glorification of Actium. The assault on the poem's serious and solemn pretensions achieved the pinnacle of rhetorical excellence and conviction.[9]

In more recent years, critical scholarship on *Elegy* 4.6 has begun to echo the traditional view before the controversy of motivations first emerged. Interpretations of the elegy have come full circle. R.J. Baker responded to objections that the Propertian elegiac hymn omits any credible or meaningful description of the battle at Actium and shapes Apollo's role into an exaggerated and silly intervention.[10] Baker argued forcefully that Propertius sought to celebrate the victorious outcome at Actium but not the actual battle. The distinction is subtle, but it highlights the fact that the narrative section of the poem fails to meet the reader's expectations of an epic confrontation. While it should not be too surprising that the action of the naval battle attracted sparse attention from the devotee of Philetas, the overall tone of the god's speech to Augustus is somewhat disquieting, if not unsettling. Rejecting any notion of ambiguity or unease, Francis Cairns viewed the Propertian elegy according to strict and narrow rules of generic composition and attempted to demonstrate how the thematic structure of the poem revealed a Roman "choric hymn," motivated and influenced by the encomiastic hymns of Pindar and Callimachus.[11] Emboldened by the restrictions of a rigid literary tradition and genre that he had imposed on the creative spirit of the Augustan elegy, Cairns sought to locate a specific and public occasion for the poem's composition; he speculated that a painting of the Actian battle in the Temple of Apollo Palatinus actually inspired the poet and served as a visual backdrop at the elegy's formal recital.[12] Finally, from a much different critical methodology and literary perspective, Hans-Peter Stahl

---

9. Connor, "Actian Miracle," agreed with much of Johnson's interpretation of the Propertian elegy but vigorously objected to the notion of any "high-spirited" fun and "parody" as the primary motivations behind the composition. Propertius, Connor argued, was not amused at the Actian victory but "took a dim and jaundiced view of the whole affair." The outcome in the Ambracian Gulf was too serious a matter for the elegist (and Augustus and his contemporaries) to ridicule. As Connor prefaced his analysis of the elegy (pp. 3–4): "The tone is often cramped and bitter . . . the total effect of the poem is so unsettling and unnerving . . . that the reader is forced to consider the whole question of Actium—and Augustus and the poets—in rather an earnest way and is compelled to view the whole procedure with despondency and alarm."

10. R.J. Baker, "*Caesaris in nomen* (Propertius IV, vi)," *RhM* 126 (1983): 153–74.

11. F. Cairns, "Propertius and the Battle of Actium (4.6)," in *Poetry and Politics*, 129–68.

12. Cairns, "Propertius and the Battle of Actium (4.6)," 154: "If the first (or imagined) performance of Propertius 4.6 was in the temple of Apollo Palatinus before a painting of the battle at Actium, this would shed further light on the declamatory emphasis of the central description, since the performance would have been accompanied by gestures pointing at the various features of the painting standing before the eyes of the chorus and audience."

reached a similar conclusion about the intentions of *Elegy* 4.6. In his comprehensive study of the elegist's literary career and ambitions, Stahl recognized and cogently argued that an inherent and pervasive tension motivates Propertius' first three books of *Elegies*, a tension between public expression and private sentiment, between surface content and hidden meaning, between eulogy and ridicule; his contention that the *Elegy* 4.6 means only what it says, that the Callimachean hymn is a solemn and unambiguous panegyric to Augustus, is all the more significant, damning, and disappointing to those who are reluctant to view this central piece from the Propertian fourth book as an example of the final concession to political pressures.

> The elegy leaves its reader with the impression that the New Propertius knows no loyalty other than to his Emperor and his country. There is no longer any visible split between façade and core, because all his speech is homogeneously patriotic.

> But parody, though easily enough suggesting itself to the reader of a later age, appears excluded both by the poem's homogeneously adulatory surface (no ambiguity, no irreverent twinkling of the author's eye is indicated) and by its close relation to the other protestation of loyalty given in 4.1A.[13]

In such a fiercely combated and sharply divided issue, it is difficult not to take sides. The choices seem straightforward. Either the elegist must be sincere and serious in what he says or he is not. Either *Elegy* 4.6 is the final acknowledgment of, and uneasy surrender to the demands of the political establishment to compose court poetry or, as Sullivan first understood the elegist's intentions, it is "the climax of Propertius' *recusatio*, the defiant proof of Propertius' inability to write the sort of poetry Horace and, latterly, Vergil wrote more successfully."[14] Both interpretations are extreme and unfairly make the elegy into a touchstone of the poet's political convictions and moral resolve. Shared by both critical viewpoints is the historical event by which almost all scholars have confidently assigned a fixed date of composition for the elegy. Modern commentators and critics have linked *Elegy* 4.6 with a formal celebration of "Actian" games before the Temple of Apollo

---

13. Stahl, *Propertius, "Love" and "War,"* 254 and 371 n. 2, respectively.

14. Sullivan, *Propertius,* 146.

15. Cf. G.A.B. Hertzberg, ed., *Sex. Aurelii Propertii elegiarum libri quattuor,* 3 vols. (Halle, 1843–45), 3:28, 458–59; J.P. Postgate, ed., *Select Elegies of Propertius,* 2d ed. (London, 1884; reprinted 1968), 207; P. Fedeli, ed., *Sesto Properzio. Elegie, libro IV* (Bari, 1965), 171; and Camps, *Propertius: Elegies, Book IV,* 104.

Palatinus in 16 B.C.E.[15] It is a common and unchallenged notion, and prior interpretations of the elegy all too often have followed immediately from and are closely dependent on this dubious claim of a public performance and an official request. I have already argued against the general view that Augustus established "Actian" games in Rome. The quinquennial festival, celebrated in 16 after Augustus had left the city, honored his sovereignty (τὴν πεντα-ετηρίδα τῆς ἀρχῆς αὐτοῦ, Dio 54.19.8), not his victory at Actium or the anniversary of the battle. Presumptions of a public celebration of cyclical games with the elegist's attendance misrepresent, if not deny, the poet's literary motivations and, at the same time, and perhaps with more serious consequences, ignore how the Propertian elegy belongs to a political and literary climate far removed from the uncertainty and anxiety that conclude Horace's *Epode* 9 and the passion of individual grief and the hopeful dreams that punctuate Vergil's *Aeneid*, especially the final scene on the shield of Aeneas.

Both the epode and the epic *ecphrasis* of the shield, the two poetic passages to which *Elegy* 4.6 is most often compared and by which it has been deemed a rhetorical travesty and forced imitation, reflect the same emotional conflict in the immediate aftermath of Actium. The *Aeneid* embodies the feelings and aspirations of an earlier generation, extending from the outbreak of the civil war between Julius Caesar and Pompey to the final establishment of peace by Augustus. Vergil's epic anticipates the Augustan conception of Rome, formalized and realized only in subsequent decades. The Propertian elegy is the product of a profoundly different and changing political scene where a political ideology gradually emerges, looking back toward reclaiming the past as much as staking out the future. With the return of Augustus from the East, the avowed triumph over the Parthians and the return of the captured military standards reiterated and at last fulfilled the earlier boasts of Roman conquest and universal peace; the joyous celebration of the Ludi Saeculares and Horace's solemn prayer to Apollo and Diana ushered in the beginning of a new era; and, finally, the formal adoption of Gaius and Lucius, the sons of Marcus Agrippa and Julia, represented the makings of an imperial dynasty and seemed at the time to secure a succession. Much like Horace's fourth book of *Odes*, composed near the end of the teens, Propertius' fourth book of *Elegies* articulates the sentiments of a Roman age of rebirth and redefinition.

Horace seems to accept the rewards of an imperial order and established peace with sincere and deeply felt praise for Rome and Augustus. The state and ruler have fused into an indivisible concept of authority and solemnity, much like the temples dedicated to the two deities in the Greek East. The poet's fearful concerns for a renewal of civil strife often struck a discordant note in his first three books of *Odes*, but his hopes for stability and order under the leadership of the *filius Maiae* have at last become confirmed by the successful establishment of the Principate.

> custode rerum Caesare non furor
> civilis aut vis exiget otium,
>   non ira, quae procudit ensis
>   et miseras inimicat urbis.
>
> <div align="right">(<i>Odes</i> 4.15.17–20)</div>

[With Caesar as the guardian of the state, not madness
of civil strife nor violence will drive out the peace,
    not the anger that forges the swords
        and brings to war the wretched cities.]

However we judge its sincerity and motivations, the Propertian elegy must be evaluated in the same political and literary context as Horace's final collection of *Odes*. The acclaimed poet laureate, however, did not link the god of the lyre with the victory at Actium, neither in the *Carmen Saeculare*, the public hymn to the twin children of Latona during the celebration of the Ludi Saeculares, nor in his final edition of *Odes*. Despite the new political order and public acclaim, Horace remained silent on Actium. For him, civil war could never be a moment of uncomplicated jubilation or the impetus of myth making. The humble poet might playfully recall (or imagine) his lost shield at Philippi (*Odes* 2.7.9–12 and *Epistles* 2.2.49–50), but the memory of Republican defeat is still pained when he responds to the expectations of Pollio's history on civil war (*Odes* 2.1). Horace remembers the triumviral past only to clarify and affirm the Augustan present. We are thus compelled to ask why Propertius, the elegist, who had previously associated Actium with sorrow, bitterness, and shame, would take up this theme of civil war to declare his newly found allegiance to Augustus (as it is claimed) and, what is equally important and difficult, why he would do so at this time, more than fifteen years after the naval battle.

❧❉❧

Propertius' *Elegy* 4.6 begins on an apparently solemn note. The polyptoton *sacra/sacris* at the opening and closure of the poem's inauguratory verse imparts a formal and ritualistic tone to what purports to be the proceedings of a sacrifice. The sacred rites demand the obligatory silence from the participants and the slaughter of a sacrificial victim.

Sacra facit vates: sint ora faventia sacris,
   et cadat ante meos icta iuvenca focos.

(lines 1–2)

[Sacred rites the poet performs: Let tongues be still for sacred rites;
   strike the heifer and let her fall before my hearth.]

The officiating spokesman of the ceremony is the *vates*, both priest and poet. Here, in the opening ten verses, Propertius plays with the contemporary ambiguity in this term as he exploits its religious and literary associations, shifting back and forth in his description of the ceremony to mingle the two aspects of the *vates* into an uneasy union.[16] It should first be admitted that the reader of the Propertian elegy does not, and cannot, know in the opening passage that he is about to hear a "mythic hymn" or that this hymn is "choric," as one scholar has sought to label the elegy.[17] The heavy, solemn tone of the initial verses must be unexpected from the elegist, however much we seek to identify the espousal of a new poetic program and the expressions of patriotic Roman fervor in the Propertian fourth book. The assumption of priestly garb and voice should be judged with some caution and circumspection. The avowal of inspiration from the poetry of Callimachus and Philetas in lines 3–4 do not affirm expectations of either a choric or mythic hymn, and far less demand a public occasion. The accumulation of the personal pronouns *meos* (line 2), *mihi* (line 5), and *me* (line 7) in the poem's initial verses need not refer to the assembled chorus or to the elegist in the distinguished role of *choregus*. The designation of the *focos* as *meos* in the second verse should indicate at once that the performance of this song is more private than public, more personal than official, more literary than literal. The allusive phrases *Philiteis corymbis* and *Cyrenaeas aquas* in the subsequent couplet establish more clearly to the reader the poet's literary intentions and define the peculiar nature of this sacrificial offering.

The Roman elegist sets out to rival the foremost representatives of the Alexandrian tradition, Philetas and Callimachus.

cera[18] Philiteis certet Romana corymbis,
   et Cyrenaeas urna ministret aquas.

---

16. See the discussion of the poem's style by Williams, *Tradition and Originality in Roman Poetry*, 52; cf. also Johnson, "Emotions of Patriotism," 153–54, and Connor, "Actian Miracle," 4.

17. Cairns, "Propertius and the Battle of Actium (4.6)," 139: "So, given that Propertius 4.6 is a mythic hymn, the reader would in the first place expect it to be choric."

18. I prefer to read *cera*, following the manuscript tradition, not the conjecture *serta*. Cf. D.R. Shackleton Bailey, *Propertiana*, 244–45.

costum molle date et blandi mihi turis honores,
    terque focum circa laneus orbis eat.
spargite me lymphis, carmenque recentibus aris
    tibia Mygdoniis libet eburna cadis.
ite procul fraudes, alio sint aere noxae.
    pura novum vati laurea mollit iter.

Musa, Palatini referemus Apollinis aedem:
    res est, Calliope, digna favore tuo.
Caesaris in nomen ducuntur carmina: Caesar
    dum canitur, quaeso, Iuppiter ipse vaces.

(lines 3–14)

[Let the Roman wax-tablet strive with the ivy crown of Philetas;
    let the pitcher supply the waters from Cyrene.
Give me soft unguents and the tribute of pleasing frankincense,
    thrice around the hearth let the woolen chaplet be wound.
Sprinkle me with libation waters; on altars of fresh turf
    let the ivory pipe pour forth its song from Mygonian jars.
Go far from here, deceits, let injuries be elsewhere.
    The pure laurel smoothes a new path for the priest.

Muse, we will sing of the Temple of Apollo Palatinus:
    the subject is worthy of your favor, Calliope.
In honor of Caesar's name, songs are given: while Caesar
    is sung, I beg, may even you, Jupiter, attend.]

The avowal of allegiance to Callimachus and Philetas is familiar to the elegist's readers. The programmatic pieces of the second and third book of elegies (2.1, 2.10, 2.34, 3.1, 3.3, and 3.9) testify to the homage Propertius previously paid to his cherished literary predecessors and models.

The introductory lines of *Elegy* 4.6, however, differ in several crucial and important respects. In his earlier declarations of grandiose endeavors, the elegist applied the artistic principles of Callimachus as the cause (or rather the excuse) for his inability to compose epic verse. Now the ivy wreaths of Philetas and the waters of Callimachus serve the ambitions of the elegist; the pure laurel softens a new path (*novum . . . iter*). In his third book of *Elegies*, Propertius imagined epic themes of Alban kings and battles as he relaxed under the soft shade of the Helicon. But Phoebus chided him with his ivory *plectrum* and showed him that the new track must be made in mossy ground (*nova muscoso semita facta solo est*, 3.3.26). At the end of the same elegy,

Calliope appears and sharply reminds the poet that the themes of his songs are garlanded lovers and outwitted husbands (3.3.39–52). In 4.6 Propertius actually invokes Calliope to introduce his song. The subject of his verses, the Temple of Apollo Palatinus, deserves the attention of the Muse of epic. In such a background, the subsequent narrative may thus be understood as an aetiological *carmen* on the foundation of the temple, perhaps in the style and tone of Callimachus' four books of *Aetia*.

Those scholars who have sought to identify and assess Propertius 4.6 as a "mythical hymn celebrating Apollo" seem to miss the point of its formal introduction. The elegist's song honors not Apollo, at least not ostensibly or singularly, but the founder of the Palatine temple. The theme of the elegist's song is the temple (*Palatini referemus Apollinis aedem*), and the subject of his praise is Augustus (*Caesaris in nomen ducuntur*). The polyptoton of Augustus' name (*Caesaris/Caesar*) and the solemn associations of this rhetorical device intimate that Augustus, not Apollo, is the divine recipient of the elegist's song. Even Jupiter should yield while Augustus is praised. The Propertian elegy, however it may be classified or judged according to the principles of genre, is not a formal hymn to Apollo, mythic or choric. The elegist imitates features of the literary hymns of Callimachus, but the differences are serious and profound. Throughout the elegy, the poet does not address the god in apostrophe, he makes no appeal for his presence, and he fails to request either his assistance or blessing. At the end of the extended epic narrative, ostensibly intended to explain the origins of the temple, the elegist abandons his chosen theme, and an assembly of poets begins further songs of praise to honor Augustus (lines 71–86). Apollo is absent from the rest of the poem, yielding to the inspirational service of the god Bacchus (*Bacche, soles Phoebo fertilis esse tuo*, line 76). The identification of the temple's name, *Palatini . . . Apollinis aedem*, is also significant. This, not the modern appellation of *Actius* or *Actiacus*, is found consistently in the ancient sources as the Augustan temple's epithet (official or otherwise).[19] The name *Palatinus* identifies the temple to the reader of the elegy.

---

19. For example, P.V. Hill, "The Temples and Statues of Apollo in Rome," *NumChron* 2, ser. 7 (1962): 129–35, consistently refers to the Palatine temple by the name of Apollo Actius. The elegist refers to the Palatine temple by the epithet of Navalis (*atque ubi Navali stant sacra Palatia Phoebo*, 4.1.3) in another poem of his fourth book. The title, more literary than official or public, is certainly an indication that Propertius at least, and at this time (contrast his attitude expressed in 2.31), intimates an association between the Augustan temple on the Palatine and the victory at Actium. Cf. Ovid *AA* 3.389 (*laurigero sacrata Palatio Phoebo*). Historical sources, without exception, refer to the Augustan temple by its epithet Palatinus (Aug. *RG* 19.1; Pliny *NH* 34.14, 36.13, 36.24, 36.25, 36.32, 37.11; Suet. *Aug.* 29.1, 31.1, 52; Joseph. *Bell. Iud.* 2.80–81; Dio 49.15.5, 53.1.3; Serv. *Comm. in Verg. Aen.* 8.720; Ascon. *tog. cand.* 80–81; *Fasti Arvalium* (*CIL* I², p. 214); *Fasti Amiternini* (*CIL* I², p. 245).

From the declaration of his intentions, the elegist proceeds at once to
describe an epic setting of battle in lofty-sounding verses.

> est Phoebi fugiens Athamana ad litora portus,
>   qua sinus Ioniae murmura condit aquae,
> Actia Iuleae pelagus monumenta carinae,
>   nautarum votis non operosa via.
> huc mundi coiere manus: stetit aequore moles
>   pinea . . .

(lines 15–20)

> [There is a port of Phoebus receding into Athamanian shores,
>   where a bay stills the sounds of the Ionian waters,
> the sea, the Actian monument of the Julian fleet,
>   for the prayers of sailors, not an arduous passage.
> Here the forces of the world collected: there stood on the sea
>   a mass of pine . . .]

From the very opening of the scene, Propertius makes clear the god's
connection with the battle that follows. The receding haven and surrounding
area belong to Phoebus. And in a manner that closely resembles the initial
scene of the Vergilian treatment of the battle, where bright dolphins sweep
the waters and cut the swirl with their tails (*Aen.* 8.671–74), the Propertian
description of the battle's locale also begins on a peaceful and tranquil
note.[20] The bay stills (*condit*) the waters of the Ionian Sea. The *pelagus* offers
a safe refuge in answer to the prayers of sailors in need. The elegist identifies
the *pelagus* as the Actian memorial of the Augustan fleet. The double apposition is puzzling, and the grammar is perverse. Textual critics offer co-
pious and varied emendations, both sober and fanciful, but the transcribed
verse may be sound or at least not quite as illogical or unintelligible as some
commentators have bemoaned. First, the elegist's choice of *pelagus* should
not unduly trouble the Propertian reader;[21] this body of water is not the
"open sea" but the *sinus*, the Ambracian Gulf. The epic-sounding word
brings to mind the elegist's previous characterizations of Actium and the

---

20. See Johnson's discussion ("Emotions of Patriotism," 157–60) on the poet's artifice in
these verses, in particular, his uses of alliteration and varied figures of speech.

21. Richardson, *Propertius, Elegies I–IV*, 449 is especially vexed by line 17. Richardson
argues that the manuscript tradition "cannot be forced into reasonable sense, despite the
willingness of editors to provide us with a translation." He asserts that *pelagus* must mean the
"open sea."

scene of the naval battle (*Actiacum mare* in 2.15.44 and *Actia aequora* in 2.16.38). Like *mare*, *pelagus* may refer to any large expanse of water (cf. Vergil *Aen*. 1.242–46, where *pelagus* refers to the rushing waters of the river Timavus). Second, and what seems more difficult to assess in this introductory scene, this *pelagus* is the memorial of the battle at Actium and the *carina* of Iulus' descendant. But this claim also looks back to the elegist's prior words on Actium, especially the final couplet of 3.11, where the sailor is asked to recall Caesar's achievement at Actium throughout the Ionian Sea as he seeks or leaves port (*Caesaris in toto sis memor Ionio*). The Ambracian Gulf, whose waters tossed Roman bones (*nostra . . . verteret ossa*, 2.15.44) and buried the helpless cries of Antony's men (*fremitu complevit inani*, 2.16.37), was always, at least in the view of the elegist, a memorial of the Roman dead at Actium. What is significant and substantially different in 4.6 is that Propertius refrains from the explicit and painful associations of civil conflict and seeks instead to create a marine setting of apparent calm (*murmura condit* and *non operosa via*) and an occasion of epic glory (*Iuleae . . . carinae*). The sea is still a permanent memorial of the naval battle, but the character of the *Actia monumenta* is strangely left undefined.

The forces of the world converge on this sea of tranquillity, but a powerful and vivid image disrupts the calm. The mass of pine (*moles pinea*) stands on the water. Critics have often noted in this remark a subtle allusion to the vast size of Antony's ships. More probably, the poet refers here to both fleets. The adjective *pinea* emphatically opens its line, and the effect on the reader is much the same as when the brazen fleet (*classis aeratas*, Vergil *Aen*. 8.675) emerges suddenly into the midst of the Vergilian image of the swollen Actian waters. The Propertian stage is also prepared for battle. The subsequent description of the opposing forces reveals, however, how differently Vergil and Propertius wished their readers to view the epic confrontation.

> . . . nec remis aequa favebat avis.
> altera classis erat Teucro damnata Quirino,
>   pilaque feminea turpiter acta manu:
> hinc Augusta ratis plenis Iovis omine velis,
>   signaque iam patriae vincere docta suae.
> tandem aciem geminos Nereus lunarat in arcus,
>   armorum et radiis picta tremebat aqua,
>
> (lines 20–26)

> [. . . not the same fortune favored their oars.
> One fleet had been condemned by Trojan Quirinus,

the javelins were shamefully hurled by a woman's hand.
On this side is Augustus' ship, its sails swelling with Jove's omen,
    standards already experienced in victory for their country.
At last Nereus curved the lines into twin crescents,
    and the water quivered, struck by the glitter of arms,]

The elegist devotes four verses to the description of both forces, one couplet equally bestowed to each side. The sentiment, however, is one-sided. The introductory phrase *nec . . . aequa* in the previous verse has already disclosed the poet's bias. On one side, the *altera classis* (without name or without specific identification) is doomed to destruction by Trojan Quirinus; on the other side, the *Augusta ratis* receives the favorable omen of Jove. Johnson asserted that the elegist's slanted view in his description of the opposing forces "sounds suspiciously like the crassest variety of Augustan propaganda, and Vergil, as we might expect, is subtler in his celebration of this victory than Propertius wants to be."[22] The outcome of battle is already decided, and the battle is an unfair fight. Unlike the treatment of Actium on the centerpiece of the hero's shield in Vergil's *Aeneid*, where the proud name of Augustus initiates the poet's description of the two sides, the Propertian account of the naval battle starts off with the *altera classis*. The enemy lacks any national or cultural identity; the foe is neither Roman nor foreign. The vagueness is suggestive; earlier, in 2.16, Antony's shameful love affair (*turpis amor*) and his deafness (*surdis auribus*) condemned his soldiers to their deaths in the Actian waters (*Actia damnatis aequora militibus*, line 38). In 4.6 *Teucrus Quirinus* condemns the fleet.

The identity of this deity has perplexed scholars. One inferior manuscript (V) and a marginal comment (D_2) offer *tenero* instead of *Teucro*, a reading that might then suggest that Antony is the cause of his soldiers' destruction, as the elegist exclaims in 2.16. Most editors, however, accept the best manuscript reading, though they struggle to explain the epithet attributed to Romulus.[23] Following the earlier recommendations by Passerat and Postgate, Butler and Barber suggested that the name actually refers to Augustus.[24] In his review of their commentary, A.E. Housman smartly rebuked

---

22. Johnson, "Emotions of Patriotism," 161.

23. The explanations seem forced and unconvincing: Camps, *Propertius: Elegies, Book IV*, 107: "because as a son of Ilia he was descendant (in some versions grandson) of Aeneas"; and Richardson, *Propertius, Elegies I–IV*, 449: "because of his descent from Iulus." Fedeli, *Properzio. Elegie, libro IV*, 175, quotes Lachmann without comment: "Antonii classis et Cleopatras arma divo Quirino ab Augusti partibus stanti damnata erant. Sic intellige, non Augustum pro Quirino. Contra Augustus habet postea *plena Iovis omine vela*."

24. Butler and Barber, *Elegies of Propertius*, 356.

the editors for their failure to give a satisfactory explanation for their interpretation and brusquely dismissed their note as that "crazy notion of Passerat's" that should be "packed off to limbo."[25] I hesitate to join in this
editorial lunacy, but an implicit association with Augustus is not as far-
fetched or inexplicable as Housman claimed. Quirinus plays a prominent
role in the elegy, either by his Trojan connection, by his augury of the
Palatine walls, or by the recovered standards of his brother Remus (lines 21,
43, and 80, respectively). This emphasis on the deified founder may reflect
recent events in Rome, Augustus' plans to rebuild the god's temple, which he
formally dedicated before he set off for Gaul in 16 B.C.E. (Dio 54.19.4). The
princeps had once contemplated adopting the title of Romulus. The refurbishment of the god's temple undoubtedly revived the close association between Rome's "first" founder and Augustus.[26]

But the god's epithet of *Teucrus* is odd and perplexing. Though historical
and literary traditions traced the descent of Romulus back to Trojan Aeneas,
the Roman founder was not identified or distinguished (at least not by
Augustan poets) for his connection with Ilium.[27] The choice of epithet may
instead be part of the elegist's efforts, evocative of Vergil's epic, to exalt the
Julian ancestry and its Trojan origins. Earlier, the Augustan ship is identified
by the name of Aeneas' son and founder of the Julian gens (*Iuleae . . .
carinae*, line 17). And in Apollo's speech to Augustus in lines 37–54, the god
reminds the Roman leader of his illustrious Trojan descent by associations
with Iulus (or Ascanius), who founds the city of Alba Longa (*O Longa
mundi servator ab Alba*, line 37) and Hector, the most renowned Trojan
warrior (*Hectoreis cognite maior avis*, line 38). Though Quirinus in line 21
may not directly represent (or substitute for) Augustus as earlier commentators have suggested, the Trojan epithet signifies the reshaping or further
dimension of the god's role in terms of an Augustan political ideology.
Romulus, the deified founder of Rome, is no longer the model that the
aspiring young leader sought to emulate in the formative and still uncertain

---

25. A.E. Housman, Review of *The Elegies of Propertius*, ed. H.E. Butler and E.A. Barber,
CR 48 (1934): 138–39.

26. For a review of the ancient evidence, see K. Scott, "The Identification of Augustus with
Romulus-Quirinus," *TAPA* 56 (1925): 82–105.

27. Bailey, *Propertiana*, 245, cites two passages from Ovid (*pater Iliades*, Fasti 4.23 and
Iliaden humeris ducis arma ferentem, Fasti 5.565) which might seem to refer to the Trojan
origins of Romulus. The examples are neither comprehensive (here one might add *Iliades
fratres*, Fasti 3.62 and *Romulus Iliades Iliadesque Remus*, Am. 3.4.40) nor compelling. The
adjective *Iliades*, though it may be a poetic variant of *Troianus* in other passages, surely in
connection with Romulus and Remus alludes more directly to Ilia, the mother of the twins, than
to an association with Ilium. The name Ilia, of course, evokes the Homeric name of Troy, but
this association must be secondary in the choice of the epithet.

years of the early twenties; more than a decade later, Augustus, the Father and Leader of his country, has now become the model by which contemporaries may look back to and judge Romulus. Before understanding the objectives of the elegist in his brief characterizations of the opposing sides at Actium, it is instructive to recall the earlier treatments of the battle by both Horace and Vergil.

In his prelude to the naval battle in *Epode* 9, Horace revealed his pain and disbelief that the Roman *miles* served a woman and her band of wrinkled eunuchs. The enemy is not named, but the Roman involvement with the Egyptian queen is explicit. Intense feelings of anguish and horror motivate the description of the confrontation in the epode. Although Horace and Propertius both refer to the enemy as a woman (*feminae*, Hor. *Epode* 9.12, and *feminea . . . manu*, Prop. 4.6.22), and though the two poets highlight this unpleasant truth with disapprobation (*turpe*, Hor. *Epode* 9.15, and *turpiter*, Prop. 4.6.22), there is a significant difference in the content, tone, and feeling of the two passages, however similar the language may be in describing Octavian's enemy. For Horace, the declarations that the enemy is a *femina*, that she is supported in her efforts by *spadones*, and that a *conopium* is part of her armament are brought into sharp focus by the fact that the *Romanus miles* has taken up arms and has carried the Roman *militaria signa* in service to the enemy. Civil war is the real cause of the shame—and of the poet's emotional outburst. Propertius, however, is more restrained and reticent in his description. While commentators often point out that the mention of the *pila* in line 22 refers to the "short, heavy javelin with which Roman legionaries were armed and which they hurled at the commencement of action,"[28] the elegist does not make the reality of civil war explicit. Instead, we are forced to admit that Propertius, who earlier in his poems closely linked Actium with the horrors of civil discord, has not allowed us to understand the shame in this context. The note of the elegist's disapprobation, when we compare the description to Horace's treatment of the battle, arises from the fact that a woman hurls the weapons of the enemy, not from the fact that Romans have joined ranks with this female foe and her effeminate crew.

On the shield of Aeneas, Vergil portrayed the enemy of Augustus and the Italians in language that reveals his endeavor to fashion the battle into a confrontation between Rome and the Far East. Foreign wealth and arms support the enemy. He comes from the nations of the Dawn and the Red Sea.

---

28. Richardson, *Propertius, Elegies I–IV*, 449; cf. Camps, *Propertius: Elegies, Book IV*, 107.

He carries with him Egypt, the strength of the Orient, and remote Bactra. Two points are important here. First, while the epic poet does not omit Antony's name and relegates the role of the Egyptian queen to companion (and does not make her the principal or singular enemy), he also painstakingly avoids any overt mention of Roman participation and civil war. Contemporary readers were not unaware of Antony's Roman identity, but Vergil has chosen to identify him conspicuously as an Eastern potentate. This characterization of Antony underscores the peculiarities of the Propertian treatment, where the reality and horror of civil war are not obfuscated but almost expunged. Second, Vergil imagined the foes of Augustus and Agrippa as impressive and formidable opposition. As Johnson has commented, these foes are "capable of putting up a good fight, that is to say, a victory over them is worth something."[29] The elegist, however, has refrained from depicting either the truth of the civil conflict or even the glorification of a foreign campaign. Instead, he ignores historical details and facts. Neither Antony nor Cleopatra is named. The enemy is not the Far East; there is not even a reference to Egypt in the passage. This omission is surely not because of Propertius' adherence to an "official" propaganda that extolled the conquest of foreign lands. All the elegist's reader learns is that the will of the gods has already determined the outcome of battle. The divine assurance of victory (and defeat) is the pointed emphasis of the poet's description. Trojan Quirinus condemns the *altera classis* to defeat, and the favorable omen of Jupiter assures the *Augusta ratis* of the victory in battle. The first of the two verses allotted to the description of each side accentuates this contrast between divine condemnation and approval. The second of the two verses comments on the armament of the opposing forces in a conspicuous structural balance of form and length. The nouns *pilaque* and *signaque*, similar in content and equal in number of syllables, lead their respective verses. Both are coupled with a final *que*. A contrast again defines the antagonists. The *pila* are hurled by the hand of a woman (*feminea . . . manu*); the *signa* are experienced in victory (*vincere docta*). The opposition between Rome and a foreign enemy, an opposition that once served the propaganda aims of Octavian before the naval battle and distinguished the passage in the *Aeneid*, is absent in the Propertian narrative. The struggle, introduced as a confrontation that assembled the forces of the world (*mundi . . . manus*, line 19), is now viewed as a clash between the tested standards of Augustus and the javelins hurled by a woman.

Divine intervention begins the battle. Nereus curves the line of battle into

---

29. Johnson, "The Emotions of Patriotism," 161.

twin bows, and Apollo appears on the scene. The introduction to the god is
carefully handled. Apollo has just left the island of Delos before he stations
himself on the poop of the Augustan ship (lines 27–30). The elegist strains a
bit to assure his reader that this Apollo is an imposing and awesome figure of
war.[30]

cum Phoebus linquens stantem se vindice Delon
    (nam tulit iratos mobilis una Notos)
astitit Augusti puppim super, et nova flamma
    luxit in obliquam ter sinuata facem.
non ille attulerat crinis in colla solutos
    aut testudineae carmen inerme lyrae,
sed quali aspexit Pelopeum Agamemnona vultu,
    egessitque avidis Dorica castra rogis,
aut qualis flexos solvit Pythona per orbis
    serpentem, imbelles quem timuere lyrae.[31]

                                      (lines 27–36)

[when Phoebus left Delos, now standing firm under his protection,
    (for it alone once moved, subject to the angry South winds)
and stood over the stern of Augustus, and a strange flame
    shined, thrice curving into a slanting torch,
he had not come with his hair flowing down on his neck
    or with the unwarlike strain of the tortoise lyre,
but with his face such as when he looked on Pelopean Agamemnon
    and emptied the Dorian camps by greedy funeral pyres,
or such as when he crushed Python and untied the winding coils
    of the serpent whom the peaceful lyres feared.]

Though Apollo the Archer needs neither elaboration nor defense, Propertius seems to place undue stress and special emphasis on the god's change of
roles.[32] Six verses of description (lines 31–36), beginning with a litotes (*non
ille attulerat*), illustrate the transformation of the god from the player of the

---

30. Cf. Johnson's questioning ("The Emotions of Patriotism," 163–64) of the emphasis on
the disparity in the god's roles.

31. *Lyrae* is the manuscript reading. Some editors prefer *deae*. The repetition of *lyrae* might
be not a scribal error or an awkward repetition but a reminder of the Apollo more familiar to
the temple on the Palatine.

32. For a different view on the significance of the Apollo similes ("the elegist's hyperbole too
is tinged with Augustan ideology") see G. Mader, "The Apollo Similes at Propertius 4.6.31–
36," *Hermes* 118 (1990): 325–34.

lyre to the slayer of the Python. The adjectives *inerme* and *imbelles* call direct attention to the contrast between the peaceful and martial qualities of Apollo. That this concern is not simply an expression of fulsome praise or a rhetorical device to exalt the traditional guises and myths of the god can be seen more clearly in the closure of the narrative section, where the elegist again reminds us of the inconcinnity of the god's roles when Apollo exchanges his bow for a lyre.

> bella satis cecini: citharam iam poscit Apollo
>   victor et ad placidos exuit arma choros.

(lines 69–70)

> [I have sung of wars enough: Apollo now demands his lyre
>   in his victory and sheds his arms for peaceful dances.]

The Greek god with the long, flowing locks and tortoise shell lyre is surely more congenial to the concerns of the love elegist, but this aspect of the god is not peculiar to Propertius; the god with the lyre identifies the resident deity of the Palatine temple, the subject of the elegist's undertaken song. From the elder Pliny (*NH* 36.25), we know that the cult statue of the god in the Augustan temple was a famous work by Scopas of Paros in the fourth century B.C.E.; and in *Elegy* 2.31, Propertius describes the statue of Apollo Citharoedus.

> deinde inter matrem deus ipse interque sororem
>   Pythius in longa carmina veste sonat.

(lines 15–16)

> [Then between his mother and his sister the god himself,
>   the Pythian god, clad in a long robe, plays his song.]

This image of the lyre-playing god, not his image as the god of archery carrying his bow and quiver, must have been familiar to any visitor of the temple complex. The elegist's belabored introduction of the god highlights an opposition of roles between peaceful and warlike where the Palatine god of the *carmen inerme* also acts as the death-bringing enemy to the Dorian camps and the savage conqueror of the serpent's coils. The circumspect reader might question whether the elegist's description is convincing or succeeds in making its point. We might expect a scene of fierce battle after such an introduction, but a long speech follows and substitutes for the action.

Apollo's speech to Augustus has provoked discomfort among critics. The god seems to say all the right words, but somehow the overall effect of his words is not quite right. The divine harangue resembles the address of a general to his troops before battle, a familiar piece of rhetorical invention among ancient historians and a feature of Hellenistic verse. Propertius points everything toward Apollo's eighteen-verse speech, which takes up more than a third of the narrative devoted to the elegist's myth of Actium. Apollo begins with lavish praise of Augustus, bringing to the fore his distinguished lineage from both Iulus, the ancestor of the Julian gens, and Hector, the mighty representative of the Trojan race. The noble compliments establish Augustus as the Roman leader and protector of his people. Immediately, the god commands the task at hand: *"vince mari."* The land has already been won, and the burden of his shoulders, his bow and arrows, favors the endeavor. Of course, in the historical battle at Actium, the nineteen legions of Antony surrendered to Octavian almost a week after the defeat at sea. The elegist ignores the factual details; he prefers a myth of battle.

The god's address to Augustus focuses on fear, the fear that holds not only the Roman people but also Augustus.

> mox ait "O Longa mundi servator ab Alba,
>   Auguste, Hectoreis cognite maior avis,
> vince mari: iam terra tua est: tibi militat arcus
>   et favet ex umeris hoc onus omne meis.
> solve metu patriam, quae nunc te vindice freta
>   imposuit prorae publica vota tuae.
> quam nisi defendes, murorum Romulus augur
>   ire Palatinas non bene vidit avis.
> et nimium remis audent prope: turpe Latinos[33]
>   principe te fluctus regia vela pati.
> nec te, quod classis centenis remigat alis,
>   terreat: invito labitur illa mari:
> quodque vehunt prorae Centaurica saxa minantis,
>   tigna cava et pictos experiere metus.
> frangit et attollit vires in milite causa;
>   quae nisi iusta subest, excutit arma pudor.
> tempus adest, committe ratis: ego temporis auctor
>   ducam laurigera Iulia rostra manu."

(lines 37–54)

---

33. I have accepted Markland's suggestion (*Latinos*) for *Latinis* in the manuscript tradition.

[Soon he spoke: "Savior of the world, descended from Alba Longa,
  Augustus, shown greater than Hector and your Trojan ancestors,
conquer on sea: the land is already yours; my bow fights for you,
  and this whole load on my shoulders favors you.
Release your country from fear, who, relying on your protection,
  has placed the vows of the people on your prow.
Unless you defend her, Romulus, the augur of his own walls,
  did not spy the flight of the Palatine birds with auspicious omen.
Look, their oars dare too close; it is shameful that Latin
  seas, under your leadership, endure regal sails.
Don't let it frighten you because their fleet is outfitted with
  hundreds of oars—the ships float on a hostile sea—
or because their prows bear Centaurs threatening to hurl rocks,
  you will find them hollow boards and painted fears.
The cause shatters and supports the soldier's strength;
  unless the cause is just, shame dislodges his arms.
The time is at hand; engage the ships: I, who govern the time,
  will lead the Julian prows with my laureled hand."]

Baker has attempted to explain away this "motif of a burden of fear"—
which he himself recognized—by the fact that Apollo's promise and show of
support will ultimately relieve Rome's fearful anxiety. But there are too
many disconcerting moments in the god's speech to redeem the fear completely by the glorification of the roles of the god and Augustus in battle.
One injunction follows another in such rapid and close succession that the
unavoidable and certainly unwelcome implication is that the man who is the
subject of the elegist's praise received a fair amount of encouragement from
the god before the battle. Apollo bids Augustus to free the *patria* from fear.
It is his responsibility; the people depend on him alone; they have placed
their vows on his ship. If he fails to defend at Actium, the augury of Romulus
on the Palatine will have served no purpose. The remark associates Augustus
with the deified founder of Rome for a second time in the elegy (cf. line 21)
and directs attention to the site of the Palatine, where the Augustan temple
will later be built. This much seems to suit the purposes of the elegist's
aetiological story. Nonetheless, the comparison fails to make its point
smoothly or effectively. The negative condition implies a possibility of failure, part of a pattern that seems to lay unwanted stress on a decidedly
pessimistic outlook to the battle. The epithet of Romulus as *augur murorum*
is striking and double-edged; it hints at the popular and unpleasant story of

the murder of Remus, who jumped over the newly built walls of his brother and was killed in a fit of anger.[34]

Apollo warns Augustus that it is shameful for the waves to endure the sails of the queen (*regia vela*). But this declaration of shame (*turpe*) is somewhat different from the earlier treatment of the woman's involvement in the battle (*turpiter*, line 22). The shame seems not to derive from the fact that the enemy is a woman but from the fact that she is a queen and that the Latins might be forced to submit to her rule. In the same verse, the woman's threat of tyranny (*regia vela*) is placed beside the honorific title and leadership of Augustus (*principe te*). The political associations of the term *princeps* are obvious; the juxtaposition is either awkward or ironic. The motif of fear is reiterated. The god instructs Augustus not to be frightened (*nec te . . . terreat*) by the enemy's fleet. The prows that depict Centaur figures threatening to hurl rocks will prove to be only hollow planks and painted terrors. The god's revelation about the false display of the enemy's superiority may leave one with the impression not only that Augustus was afraid but that his fear was not justified.

The claim that the righteousness of the cause makes or breaks the strength of the soldier follows, with the confident prediction that shame will force the unjust enemy to cast aside his weapons (lines 51–52). The couplet intimates the surrender or the refusal to engage by the enemy in a manner that resembles Horace's description of the Actian campaign (*Epode* 9.17–20). Propertius, however, speaks only in vague generalizations. The boast supports the propaganda of the victorious side or sounds like an empty platitude. The god commands Augustus to commence the naval battle, and the epic-sounding epithet *laurigera* at the close of Apollo's speech anticipates, if not preordains, the victory. The elegist omits the details of fighting, both the surrender of the enemy and the prowess of the victorious side. The battle ends quickly, won by the arrows of Apollo, supported by the spear of Augustus.

> dixerat, et pharetrae pondus consumit in arcus:
>> proxima post arcus Caesaris hasta fuit.
> vincit Roma fide Phoebi: dat femina poenas:
>> sceptra per Ionias fracta vehuntur aquas.

(lines 55–58)

[He had spoken, and he exhausted his quiver's load for his bow;
    next after his bow was the spear of Caesar.

---

34. For the conflicting stories of the murder of Remus, cf. Livy 1.7.1–3.

Rome conquers by the faith of Phoebus: the woman pays the penalty:
her broken scepters are swept along the Ionian waters.]

The woman (*femina*) who challenged Rome is punished with divine retribution; the arrogant symbols of the tyranny (*sceptra*) she threatened are tossed
about in the Ionian Sea.

Even Caesar looks down from his star and approves. The father's immortality is strangely confirmed by the actions of his son.

> at pater Idalio miratur Caesar ab astro:
> "Sum deus; est nostri sanguinis ista fides."
>
> (lines 59–60)

[But Father Caesar marvels as he watches from his Idalian star:
"I am a god; this deed is the proof of our divine ancestry."]

This passage is doubly indebted to Vergil. The star's epithet *Idalius* associates the divinity of Caesar with the goddess Venus and looks back to
Lycidas' admonition toward Daphnis in *Eclogue 9* and the *astrum* of Di-
onaean Caesar (*ecce Dionaei processit Caesaris astrum, Ecl.* 9.47). The
scene more directly alludes to the epic description of the Augustan forces at
Actium on the shield of Aeneas, where the appearance of the paternal star
signals divine approval (*patriumque aperitur vertice sidus, Aen.* 8.681). The
elegist is less subtle in his flattery toward Augustus. Father Julius marvels
from his Idalian star—and speaks. Textual critics have been skeptical of
Caesar's words, and emendations have been rashly suggested.[35] But Caesar's
astonishment and his almost outrageous declaration that his divinity has
been assured (*sum deus*) by the subsequent events at Actium should not be
surprising in the elegist's narrative of a mythic battle where the gods often
and obtrusively intervene on behalf of Augustus.

The description of battle ends abruptly. Nereus had commenced the engagement, and now Triton and the goddesses of the sea applaud the victory
in an exaggerated scene of triumph. The standards of Rome are freed (*libera
signa*) from the rule of the queen.

> prosequitur cantu Triton, omnesque marinae
> plauserunt circa libera signa deae.
>
> (lines 61–62)

---

35. Fedeli (Teubner ed., Stuttgart, 1984) reads *tu deus*; Lachmann suggested *tum deus*;
Baehrens, *tu meus*.

[Triton accompanies with his song, and all the sea goddesses
  applauded around the standards that were freed.]

The flight of Cleopatra (lines 63–66) suddenly turns the reader away
from the fighting at Actium in a manner reminiscent of the passage in the
Aeneid. The differences in the poetic treatments once again are significant.[36]
In the Vergilian treatment of the Actian battle, an impressive and long triumphal procession in Rome quickly replaces the flight of Cleopatra into the
parental embrace of the Nile. In the final scene of the shield, the epic poet
depicts the thronged streets of the city in a roar of joyful applause and
reverent celebration. The victor sits on the shining throne of Phoebus as he
inspects the gifts of the conquered nations. If there is a dimness to the bright
light in Vergil's scene of Augustan triumph, as I argued in chapter 5, it comes
from the poet's pained awareness of the illusions of victory and the sorrowful realities of defeat. The sudden movement from personal loss to public
glory jolts the reader into a greater consciousness of both. In contrast, the
Propertian passage lacks any genuine emotion, rejects any feeling of compas-
sion for the defeated foe, and denies a joyful relief to the victor in triumph.

Cleopatra is not named; she is recognized only by the pronoun *illa*, which
identifies her by gender.

> illa petit Nilum cumba male nixa fugaci,
>   hoc unum, iusso non moritura die.
> di melius! quantus mulier foret una triumphus,
>   ductus erat per quas ante Iugurtha vias!
>
> (lines 63–66)

[She seeks the Nile, weakly relying on her fleeing skiff;
  this one thing she wins, not to die on the ordered day.
May the gods forbid! What a triumph one woman would make,
  through the streets where Jugurtha had once been led!]

The woman flees to the Nile. Her flight is rather pathetic. The royal sails
(*regia vela*, line 46) that once threatened the Latins and the leadership of
Augustus have vanished. The queen's ship is now a skiff (*cumba*), and she
even struggles to escape in this (*male nixa fugaci*).[37] The elegist's fore-

---

36. For an interesting examination of the contrasting portraits of the Egyptian queen in
Horace and Propertius, see V. Cremona, "Due Cleopatre a confronto. Properzio replica a
Orazio," *Aevum* 61 (1987): 123–31.

37. Richardson, *Propertius, Elegies I–IV*, 452, takes *male* with *fugaci* and asserts that her
flight is disgraceful and futile.

shadowing of her approaching death (*moritura*, a favorite Vergilian expression) might seem to recall the epic poet and strike a sympathetic note. But there is no Vergilian pathos here, the pathos of the *regina* who appears amid the carnage of battle *pallentem morte futura*, as she gives sail to the winds and flees to the embrace of the grieving Nile (Vergil *Aen*. 8.707–13). And there is also not the final touch of dignity that Horace lavishes on the defeated enemy at the end of his Cleopatra Ode (*Odes* 1.37). In the lyric poet's composition, the Egyptian queen eludes the chains of the victor at Actium and his haughty triumph (*superbo . . . triumpho*, *Odes* 1.37.31–32). The Propertian scene seems to invite the reader to look back to the earlier scenes of desperate flight by Horace and Vergil, but the elegist rejects the emotional intensity and pathos that characterized these dramatic portraits of the queen's defeat. Throughout the elegist's myth of Actium in 4.6, Cleopatra is always an object of disparagement or ridicule.

Moving from the scene of the queen's pathetic flight to an allusion to her suicide, the elegist declares that the defeated obtains but one thing (*hoc unum*), and it is a dubious accomplishment; she will not die on the ordered day (*iusso . . . die*). As commentators have indicated, the exclamation *di melius* in line 65 takes its meaning from context. The gods knew better; how great a triumph one woman (*mulier . . . . una*) would have been! The outburst should surprise any reader who has been expecting the proud declaration of Augustan triumph. Throughout the narrative of the battle, the Egyptian queen is portrayed as the enemy of the forces of Augustus (*feminea . . . manu*, line 22; *regia vela*, line 46; *femina*, line 57; *sceptra . . . fracta*, line 58; and *illa . . . Nilum*, line 63). This focus on the queen and the elegy's denial of Roman involvement have been viewed as Propertius' adherence to the official version of Actium, the ultimate concession to the Augustan regime. This view distorts the meaning and emphasis of the elegist's words, but it must be admitted, even by those who insist on an espousal of a public ideology, that Propertius conspicuously fails to glorify the victory or exalt the achievement, except for the manifest intervention of the god. The implications of the elegist's outcry in lines 65–66 are unmistakable. The defeat of one woman (the addition of *una*, emphatically placed, further degrades the accomplishment) does not merit a triumph; the *mulier* is no Jugurtha.[38] The victory lacks the honor and renown of a Roman triumph.

The final words of the poet reiterate this message in yet another way. The

---

38. There may be a subtle allusion here to Horace's *Epode* 9.23–24, where Horace compares the victor at Actium to Marius, the *dux* of the Jugurthine war. Horace, however, makes the victorious leader the point of the comparison; Propertius concentrates on the defeated enemy, the *una mulier*, who, as his outcry suggests, would not have been worthy of a triumph, certainly not a triumph in the tradition of past Roman conquerors.

monuments of Actium do not belong to the victor; they derive from the shooting finesse of Apollo.

> Actius hinc traxit Phoebus monumenta, quod eius
> una decem vicit missa sagitta ratis.

(lines 67–68)

> [From this, Phoebus of Actium claims his trophies, because
> one arrow shot from his bow conquered ten ships.]

In this final comment on the battle, the elegist seems once again to acknowledge the epic poet's dramatic scene on the shield of Aeneas, where Apollo draws his bow, puts an end to the fighting, and scatters the motley crew of Eastern foes (*Actius haec cernens arcum intendebat Apollo / desuper, Aen.* 8.704–5).[39] At the end of his narrative, Propertius defines more clearly the *monumenta* of battle. The elegist's narrative began with a vague suggestion of the Ambracian Gulf, the setting of battle, as the *monumenta* of Augustus' fleet (line 17); it concludes with the boastful claim that one arrow from Apollo's bow captured ten ships. Camps explained in frustration that we know of no source for this remarkable feat, and Richardson remarked that the comment was "mysterious."[40] More likely, the number *decem* alludes to the victor's trophy of ten ships, which he dedicated at Actium after the battle.[41] The naval station served as a memorial to the battle and exhibited a representative selection of the enemy's warships. The god has usurped the victor's monuments of battle. Augustus must take comfort that his *hasta* (the symbol of a victory on land) followed close on the god's bow. At the conclusion of the elegist's aetiological narrative, Apollo, not Augustus—the avowed recipient of the elegist's praises—earns the title of *victor*.

> bella satis cecini: citharam iam poscit Apollo
> victor et ad placidos exuit arma choros.

(lines 69–70)

---

39. In an appendix, Cairns, "Propertius and the Battle of Actium (4.6)," 165–67, identifies the passage as the "second piece of Propertian *aemulatio*" where the elegist follows Vergil's scene of the god's decisive intervention in the naval battle. In response to the criticism that Augustus plays a surprisingly insignificant role in the Actian battle, Cairns claims that the Propertian narrative actually directs less attention to the god than does the Vergilian counterpart, since in the former Augustus receives the honor of second place after the bow of Apollo (*proxima post arcus Caesaris hasta fuit*, line 56). But in 4.6, Propertius grants the god the title of *victor* (line 70); he disparages the claim of the victory over a *mulier* (lines 65–66); and perhaps most importantly, he conspicuously ignores the occasion of a triumphal celebration.

40. Camps, *Propertius: Elegies, Book IV*, 112; Richardson, *Propertius, Elegies I–IV*, 453.

41. Strabo *Geo.* 7.7.6. By the time the Greek historian composed his universal geography, however, the ten ships and boathouses had been destroyed by a fire.

[I have sung of wars enough: Apollo now demands his lyre
in his victory and sheds his arms for peaceful dances.]

The elegist has sung of wars enough. The god abruptly demands his lyre
and strips off his armor. The god of the Palatine temple has resumed his
former role as the associate of the Muses and the poets. A festive band
gathers on the soft grass of the grove. It is a peaceful setting of celebration.
Not Calliope but Bacchus now supplies inspiration for the songs of Augustan military glory that follow in succession.

> candida nunc molli subeant convivia luco;
>   blanditiaeque fluant per mea colla rosae,
> vinaque fundantur prelis elisa Falernis,
>   terque lavet nostras spica Cilissa comas.
> ingenium positis irritet Musa poetis:
>   Bacche, soles Phoebo fertilis esse tuo.
> ille paludosos memoret servire Sycambros,
>   Cepheam hic Meroen fuscaque regna canat,
> hic referat sero confessum foedere Parthum:
>   Reddat signa Remi, mox dabit ipse sua:
> sive aliquid pharetris Augustus parcet Eois,
>   differat in pueros ista tropaea suos.

                                                    (lines 71–82)

[Let the brightly clad guests enter the luxurious grove,
   let sweet roses be poured around my neck,
let wine crushed in Falernian presses flow forth,
   and let Cilician saffron drench my hair.
The Muse pricks the talents of the assembled poets:
   Bacchus, you often are of rich service to your Phoebus.
Let one celebrate the submission of the marshy Sugambri;
   let another sing of the dusky realms of Cephean Meroë;
let another tell how the Parthian was overcome by a tardy compact.
   Let him return the standards of Remus; soon he will give his own.
Or if Augustus spares the quivered peoples of the East at all,
   let him put off these trophies for his own sons.]

This party of poets, as Johnson contends, is "neither patriotic and traditional nor of the more modern kinky sort that he and Horace imagine
elsewhere," and the choice of topics "involves scraping the bottom of the

barrel."[42] Baker retorts that these songs of praise are not "Propertius' themes" but "minor themes that he prays the Muse to move other (lesser) poets . . . to take up."[43] Though the defeat of the aggressive German tribe in Gaul and the expedition into lower Egypt may seem "minor" themes, the return of the standards from the Parthians is the most celebrated military accomplishment in the Augustan Age. These songs of the assembled party, of which the elegist presumably takes part, cannot be dismissed so easily; they conclude the poem and are indicative of the elegist's final attitude toward Augustus and his military achievements.

New campaigns are the themes of epic verse by the assembled poets. The mention of the Sugambri starts off the list.[44] The epithet that the elegist has bestowed on the vanquished foe (*paludosos*) is an uncommon word, and this passage marks its first appearance in extant Latin literature. The adjective may be epic-sounding, but the image of a marshy bog hardly evokes a feeling of grandeur or formidable challenge. When Horace foretold the Augustan triumph over the German tribe in his Pindaric ode from his fourth book (*Odes* 4.2.33–36), the Sugambri are described as fierce (*feroces*), and their proclaimed defeat will merit a richly deserved laurel wreath and triumphal procession. For the elegist, however, German marshes and bogs distinguish the enemy, a dubious mark of honor and military glory. In the following verse, the Ethiopian foes, allusively recalled by the father of Andromeda, Cepheus, are famed for their swarthy kingdoms. More suggestive is the elegist's description of the Parthian success. Propertius seems intent on reminding his reader of the shortcomings in the official boast of success that the Senate honored with the vote of a triumph. The enemy has agreed to a compact of peace, but it came late (*sero . . . foedere*). The subsequent verse points out another revealing and unflattering truth. Although the Parthians have finally returned the captured Roman standards, they have not yet yielded their own. The emphatic *sua* ends the verse. These are trophies of war set aside for the next generation, the *pueros* of Augustus, perhaps an allusion to the recent adoption of the infants Gaius and Lucius in 17 B.C.E.

---

42. Johnson, "The Emotions of Patriotism," 170 and 170 n. 17, respectively.

43. Baker, "*Caesaris in nomen* (Propertius IV, vi)," 173.

44. The inclusion of the Sugambri (*paludosos . . . servire Sycambros*, line 77) points to the military defeat of Marcus Lollius in Gaul by this German tribe. The date of the incident is probably late 17 or early 16. Dio (54.20.4–6) places the raid in his narrative of 16, though the historian mentions the incident in a brief summary of military disturbances during an extended period. R. Syme, "Some Notes on the Legions under Augustus," *JRS* 23 (1933): 17 n. 24, cogently argues that the date of 17, also given by Julius Obsequens 71, should be preferred. Most scholars accept the earlier date, but for objections, cf. A.J. Woodman, ed., *Velleius Paterculus: The Tiberian Narrative (2.94–131)* (Cambridge, 1977), 110–11.

The final address to the dead shade of Crassus concludes the laudation of Augustan military achievement on a mournful note.

gaude, Crasse, nigras si quid sapis inter harenas:
  ire per Euphraten ad tua busta licet.

(lines 83–84)

[Rejoice, Crassus, if you have any feeling amid the black sands:
  we may pass through the Euphrates to your tomb.]

The name of the Euphrates should imply the glory of conquest, the expansion of the Roman Empire, and the final defeat of the Parthian enemy. The river's name should provoke joyful celebration and a triumphal procession, and the couplet certainly begins on the appropriate note, *gaude*. The imperative is directed toward Marcus Licinius Crassus, whose failed campaign against the Parthians led to a crushing defeat and his own death at Carrhae in 53 B.C.E. More than thirty-five years later, the return of the captured Roman standards proclaimed that vengeance had been exacted on the enemy. Further conquests in the East should bolster this claim. But the sincerity of the poet's call for Crassus to rejoice is almost immediately cast into doubt by the implications of the subsequent *si* clause. The blackness of the sand (the adjective's position is emphatic) has funereal associations. As Butler and Barber remarked, *nigras* "refers rather to the darkness of the grave than to the colour of the soil."[45] The somber note calls into question whether the success of Augustus concerns the dead at Carrhae. While the *si* clause perhaps reflects the conventional skepticism on the question of life after death—where it often appears in the words of consolation to a grieving friend or relative[46]—the sentiment revokes the mood befitting a celebration of victory. The reward of this military achievement has become, in the words of the poet, a passageway across the Euphrates to the tomb of Crassus (*ad tua busta*).[47]

Connor queried whether Propertius is critical of Crassus and his defeat,[48]

---

45. Butler and Barber, *Elegies of Propertius*, 359.

46. Cf. Cic. *Fam.* 4.5.6: *si qui etiam inferis sensus est, qui illius in te amor fuit pietasque in omnis suos, hoc certe illa te facere non vult*; and Cat. 96.1–2: *si quicquam mutis gratum acceptumque sepulcris / accidere a nostro, Calve, dolore potest*.

47. Crassus, however, never received any formal burial; his head and right hand were cut off from his body, and, as Plutarch (*Crass.* 33) reports, the severed head served as a prop for the character Agave, the mother of the dismembered Pentheus, in a lurid and ghastly production of the Euripidean *Bacchae*.

48. Connor, "Actian Miracle," 9: "but it seems, rather, a cold appreciation of the futility of it all."

and Johnson described the passage's tone as "specially shrill and bellicose and rhetorical."[49] But if there is a note of criticism or shrillness in the elegist's verses, it derives from the fact that the much heralded military triumphs of Augustus, past, present, and future, fail to elicit from Propertius any genuine feelings of applause or approval. In an elegy from his third book that ends with a parting address to the avengers of Crassus, Propertius distanced himself from those who seek the rewards of military campaigns. The final couplet leaves the distinct impression that the elegist's spoken show of enthusiasm for the celebrated Parthian expedition lacks sincerity or interest.

> exitus hic vitae superest mihi: vos, quibus arma
>   grata magis, Crassi signa referte domum!
>
> (3.5.47–48)

> [This end of life awaits me: may you, who instead find
>   pleasure in war, bring home the standards of Crassus!]

The intermittent years and the further conquests of Augustus have not brought the elegist any closer to an acceptance of this way of life.

Elegy 4.6 ends with a final nod toward the ambiguous role of the Propertian *vates*, who will pass the night in drunken revelry. In service to this poet/priest will be his *patera* and his *carmen*.

> sic noctem patera, sic ducam carmine, donec
>   iniciat radios in mea vina dies.
>
> (lines 85–86)

> [Thus I will pass the night with libations and in song, until
>   tomorrow's day casts its rays on my wine.]

The sacerdotal *patera* has become the poet's wine cup. Like Horace at the end of *Epode* 9, Propertius is drunk or at least expects some heavy drinking ahead. But the elegist's intoxication does not arise from the uncertainty and fear about Caesar's affairs (*curam metumque Caesaris rerum*) that troubled Horace as he contemplated a future after Actium. In his previous elegies that handled the theme of Actium, Propertius looked back on the battle with a mixture of pain and bitterness and defiantly refused to ignore the latest

---

49. Johnson, "Emotions of Patriotism," 170.

episode of a nation's shame; he sought instead to revive memories of civil war and to associate the Actian battle with the destruction of Perusian hearths and the tombstones of Philippi. *Elegy* 4.6 surely marks a new direction in the elegist's treatment of Actium—and a farewell. The former intensity and passion have now gone. The elegiac hymn ostensibly celebrates Augustus, his temple, and his victory over Antony and Cleopatra, in an uneasy blend of Alexandrian poetics and Roman politics. But the tension and reality of civil war do not motivate the poem's central narrative. Though Horace and Vergil obfuscated the truth about Actium, the poets revealed their fears and hopes, articulated their joy and sorrows. The battle had dramatic vigor, meaning, and consequence. In *Epode 9*, Horace decried the shame of Roman subservience to a woman and predicted that posterity would deny the truth. On the shield of Aeneas, Vergil represented the struggle in individual terms but also in a public and Roman context, as a mighty clash between two cultures and peoples. The immortal gods took part in this epic conflict, and Apollo Actius played a critical role, but the scene focused on human participation. Augustus and the Egyptian *coniunx*, and even Antony and Agrippa, were leading actors in the Actian drama. The private tragedy of the queen and the embrace of Father Nile were placed beside the public triumph of Augustus and the applause of Rome.

In the Propertian hymn, neither Antony nor foreign foes threaten the ships of Augustus. The Roman *dux* and the Egyptian queen, who once opposed the might of Rome, have no roles in the elegist's epic confrontation at Actium. The enemy is only a woman, an inglorious fact of which Propertius seeks to remind his reader at every occasion (*feminea*, line 22; *femina*, line 57; *illa*, line 63; and *mulier . . . una*, line 65). Although there are allusions to the woman's royal status (lines 46 and 58), Cleopatra is never the *regina* who appears formidable and undeniably majestic in the treatments of the Actian battle in Horace and Vergil. When the elegist turns to describe the events of the naval battle, there is no battle. He chooses instead to place an undue stress, unparalleled in the contemporary literature, on the role of Apollo. The god's prolonged speech of encouragement to Augustus sets the tone. Rome wins by the *fides* of Phoebus, and when all the fighting is over, the god is victor. The *monumenta* of Actium derive from the archery of Apollo. Augustus, although he receives lavish praise throughout the narrative of the battle, never quite emerges as the glorious leader (and Agrippa, the admiral of the Augustan fleet, prominently placed beside Augustus and the Roman senators on the shield of Aeneas, is nowhere to be found). The defeat of one woman fails to merit the honor of a triumph (*di melius!*, line 65).

The Propertian account of the battle of Actium concludes without any sincere or convincing feeling of accomplishment. There is no final resolution that might redeem the occasion of war. Instead, the elegist refuses to acknowledge the rewards that the Actian victory achieved: the cessation of civil conflict; the subjugation of foreign tribes and nations; and, above all, the final establishment of the Augustan Principate.[50] The Vergilian scene of battle has been recast, fashioned anew into a stylized piece of Callimachean finesse and wit, at once fantastic and ultimately unsettling. If the epic poet inspired a national myth of Actium and Roman imperialism, the elegist surely exploits whatever comforts and assurances this myth may have granted. What Augustus in the later years of his political regime may have thought of Actium and the epic myth of the naval battle demands a brief and final consideration.

---

50. Cairns, "Propertius and the Battle of Actium (4.6)," 163, concludes that the Propertian description of Actium "directs the reader towards a moralising view of myth and of past Roman history which had been espoused by the Augustan regime. This was that Rome's recent civil wars had been in part punishment for recent sins mirroring ancient sins which had caused the fall of Rome's predecessor, Troy." But Cairns' reassuring view cannot be found in the elegist's aetiological hymn. Unlike the treatments of Horace and Vergil, and his own previous view of the battle, Propertius ignores the harsh reality of Actium as civil war. The battle is a clash between the experienced prows of Augustus and the javelins of a woman.

Epilogue: Actium *Renascens*

sed eum honorem Germanicus iniit apud urbem Achaiae Nicopolim
. . . igitur paucos dies insumpsit reficiendae classi; simul sinus Actiaca
victoria inclutos et sacratas ab Augusto manubias castraque Antonii
cum recordatione maiorum suorum adiit. namque ei, ut memoravi,
avunculus Augustus, avus Antonius erant, magnaque illic imago tris-
tium laetorumque.

(Tac. Ann. 2.53.1–3)

[But Germanicus assumed his consulship while he was in the city of
Nicopolis in Achaia . . . and so he spent a few days there outfitting his
fleet; as he visited the bay that was renowned for the victory at Actium,
the spoils dedicated by Augustus, and the camps of Antony, he remembered his ancestors; for, as I have mentioned, Augustus was his great
uncle and Antony was his grandfather, and there he imagined a mighty
scene of sorrows and joys.]

The celebration of the Ludi Saeculares in late May and early June of 17
B.C.E. officially heralded the commencement of a new era. Last celebrated in
146, at the end of the Third Punic War, the solemn occasion was a public
ritual that no one living had ever seen before or could ever hope to see
again.[1] The civil war between Julius Caesar and Pompey interrupted whatever intentions there may have been to celebrate the sacred games in the
early 40s, and the anticipated expedition against the Parthian foe by the
victorious Caesar and the political chaos following his assassination must
have dimmed the prospect of joyous festivities and beginnings. The message
of Vergil's fourth *Eclogue*, proclaiming the new order of the ages and the
return of Saturn's rule in the consulship of Asinius Pollio, gave poignant
expression to a fleeting moment of optimism, but the poet's hopes were
quickly shattered. The fragile union and intrigues of the Second Triumvirate,

---

1. See Zosimus 2.5 for a brief description of the traditional ceremonies of the Ludi
Saeculares.

the domestic turmoil in Italy and failed campaigns in the East, and the final struggle between Caesar's heir and Antony for supreme power in Rome thwarted any promise and plans of a celebration. As the oracular speaker of the *Eclogues* predicted, the Roman world still awaited a second Tiphys and second Argo and, yet again, another destruction of Ilium by *magnus Achilles*. More than ten years after his triple triumph ceremony in August of 29, the illustrious descendant of Trojan Aeneas, who had piously restored eighty-two shrines and temples of the gods, decided that the neglected ritual should at last be revived and could be celebrated anew.

The political climate in Rome greatly encouraged the occasion. With his loyal friend, fighting ally, and recent son-in-law, Marcus Agrippa, who now shared with him the consular imperium and tribunician *potestas*, Augustus consolidated his authority and position after a period of unrest and failed conspiracy in 19. The Senate was reorganized and purged, and the social legislation on marriage and adultery was at last successfully enacted. The princeps had been absent from the city for almost three years while he conducted an extensive tour of the eastern provinces. He returned triumphant, with claims of victory over the Parthians and vengeance achieved. The Parthian king, perhaps fearful of a Roman invasion, or more likely dismayed at Roman involvement in Armenian affairs, agreed to a diplomatic arrangement whereby he relinquished the captured standards of Crassus and the surviving soldiers who still lived in foreign lands. Augustus, whether or not he ever seriously contemplated a major assault on Parthia, exclaimed that he compelled the enemy to restore the spoils and standards of three Roman armies and to seek the friendship of the Roman people as suppliants.[2] The euphoria and patriotic feelings arising from the recovery of standards, certainly exaggerated, but nonetheless real, marked an end to the frustrations and disgrace of the past, as Ovid recounted it almost thirty years later.

> isque pudor mansisset adhuc, nisi fortibus armis
> Caesaris Ausoniae protegerentur opes.
> ille notas veteres et longi dedecus aevi
> sustulit.

(Fasti 5.587–90)

[That shame would have still remained, had not the brave arms of Caesar furnished shelter to the Ausonian realm.

---

2. *RG* 29.2; Vell. 2.91.1; Suet. *Aug.* 21.3; Dio 54.8.1–3.

The former stains and long-standing disgrace of a generation
he removed.]

Contemporary coinage offers an indication of the major themes of an
emergent ideology in this still formative period of the Augustan Principate.
With the return of Augustus from the East in 19, the mint in Rome resumed
activities under the official authority of the Senate, but presumably under the
direct influence of the princeps. The coinage of the moneyers, though often
considered "Republican" in style and coin type,[3] nonetheless embraced the
symbols and rhetoric of an Augustan public image extolling martial success
and religious ritual. In a deep reverberation of coin types and legends, issues
blazon the slogans of military conquest, public salvation, and divine vengeance: ARMENIA CAPTA (or ARMENIA RECEPTA), SIGNIS RECEPTIS (or SIGNIS
PARTHICIS RECEPTIS), CIVIBUS ET SIGNIS MILITARIBUS A PARTHIS RECU-
PERATIS, OB CIVIS SERVATOS, FORTUNA REDUX, and MARS ULTOR.[4]

Though the Senate formally voted him a triumph, the princeps declined
the honor.[5] Neither at this time nor at any later occasion did Augustus
endeavor to surpass the glory and boasts of his triple triumph of 29. But we
should not be inclined to regard the decision to spurn the triumph as a sign
of humble modesty or calculated restraint.[6] Augustus proudly accepted public sacrifices and thanksgivings in honor of his accomplishment; he erected
an altar to Fortuna Redux, the deity who represented the protection of
Augustus and the prosperity of the state by granting his safe return from the
East; and finally, the day on which Augustus returned to the city (October
12), perhaps recalling the triumphant return in 29, was commemorated and
duly enrolled in the public *fasti* as a festival to Augustus, named from his

---

3. For an examination of the coin types of the senatorial mint in Rome from 19 to 16, see
C.H.V. Sutherland, "The Senatorial Gold and Silver Coinage of 16 B.C.: Innovation and Inspiration," *NumChron* 3, ser. 6 (1943): 40–49.

4. *RIC*[2] 513, 514, 515–16, 519–20 (ARMENIA CAPTA); 517, 518 (ARMENIA RECEPTA); 41,
58, 60, 80–84, 85–87, 508–10, 521 (SIGNIS RECEPTIS); 522–26 (SIGNIS PARTHICIS RECEPTIS);
131–37 (CIVIBUS ET SIGNIS MILITARIBUS A PARTHIS RECUPERATIS); 29–32, 40, 75–77, 78–79,
323, 325, 327–30 (OB CIVIS SERVATOS); 53–56 (FORTUNA REDUX); 28, 39, 68–74, 103–6, 507
(MARS ULTOR).

5. Dio (54.8.3) records that Augustus rode into the city on horseback and received the
honor of a "triumphal" arch. This would seem to indicate that the princeps earned an *ovatio*
when he declined the triumph, but no other ancient testimony confirms this claim. It is more
likely that the Greek historian assumed that the senatorial honor of an arch and the prominence
attached to the day (October 18) on which he returned to the city presupposed some form of
triumphal ceremony.

6. Zanker, *Power of Images*, 186: "This time Augustus was utterly restrained, in contrast
to his behavior after Actium."

distinguished cognomen, the Augustalia.[7] The deification of the princeps only awaited his mortal demise. An imposing marble arch of three spans flanked the Temple of Divus Julius, perhaps replacing a simpler structure of a single bay that honored the restoration of order in 29.[8] The message of the "Parthian" arch was clear and visible; elaborately carved representations and emblems of the foreign foe, bowmen and slingers, decorated the attics and pillars of the two smaller passageways of the massive arch. Images of winged Victory in relief highlighted the spandrels. An official list of consuls and triumphs (the *Fasti Capitolini*) may also have been inscribed at this time and affixed to the monumental passageway.[9]

The former claims of vengeance against the Parthian foe were finally realized. And as if he had captured the spoils from a vanquished enemy on the battlefield instead of having received the standards of Roman armies previously humiliated in defeat, Augustus wished to fix the standards to the walls of a temple and exhibit the "booty" of a victorious general. The theme of vengeance was reclaimed and confirmed in the image of Mars Ultor, the deity who had previously been invoked in the struggle against Brutus and Cassius. Caesar's son had vowed a temple to the god at the battle at Philippi in 42, but the work for his temple had not been completed; the plans had probably been postponed or abandoned.[10] After Actium, the victor over Antony chose to honor the divinity of his father by the dedication of the Temple of Divus Julius, not by reprisals of vengeance exacted against the Roman citizens who conspired to remove a dictator.[11] The occasion of

---

7. Dio (54.10.4) reveals that Augustus actually returned to the city in the evening and in secret because of the turmoil arising from the contested consular elections of that year. The first celebration of the Augustalia probably belongs to 18.

8. See my earlier discussion in chap. 1: "The 'Actian' Arch."

9. In a series of articles written in response to the publication of Degrassi's *Inscriptiones Italiae*, vol. 13 (Rome, 1947), L.R. Taylor cogently argues that the *Fasti Capitolini* were inscribed on the two lateral openings of the Augustan triple arch erected in commemoration of the Parthian victory. The consular list was inscribed at this time and edited "in the interests of the new order." See Taylor, "The Date of the Capitoline *Fasti*," *CP* 41 (1946): 1–11; "Annals of the Roman Consulship on the Arch of Augustus," *PAPS* 94 (1950): 511–16; "Degrassi's Edition of the Consular and Triumphal *Fasti*," *CP* 45 (1950): 84–95; and "New Indications of Augustan Editing in the Capitoline *Fasti*," *CP* 46 (1951): 73–80.

10. We know that Augustus experienced problems and long delays in acquiring all the property he wished for his Forum (Macr. *Sat.* 2.4.9). And according to Suetonius (*Aug.* 56.2), Augustus never obtained all the land he sought. But this can hardly explain the delay of forty years.

11. Horace seems to have anticipated or inspired the later claims of Augustus. At the end of *Odes* 1.2, the poet exhorts the *iuvenis*, in the guise of Maia's winged son, to turn his intentions of vengeance toward the Parthians, the enemy of the Romans. Cf. A. Oltramare, "Auguste et les Parthes," *REL* 16 (1938): 121–38; L.A. MacKay, "Horace, Augustus, and *Ode*, I, 2," *AJP* 83 (1962): 168–77, esp. 176–77; and R. Seager, "*Neu sinas Medos equitare inultos*: Horace, the Parthians and Augustan Foreign Policy," *Athenaeum* 68, n.s. 58 (1980): 103–18.

RIC²366

RIC²170   *RIC²173a*

RIC²192a   *RIC²196*

Plate 6

RIC²	Giard, BNC	Denom.	Obverse	Reverse
366 [*BMCRE* 95]	362–64	DEN	Head of Augustus (r.) IMP CAESAR AVGVS TR POT IIX	Apollo, holding lyre and *patera*, standing (l.) on platform decorated with naval prows and anchors C ANTISTI VETVS IIIVIR APO-LLINI l. and r. in field ACTIO in exergue
170 [*BMCRE* 459–60]	1394–95	AUR	Head of Augustus (r.) AVGVSTVS DIVI F	Apollo, holding lyre and *plectrum*, standing (l.) IMP X ACT in exergue
173a [*BMCRE* 463]	1392–93	DEN	Head of Augustus (r.) AVGVSTVS DIVI F	Diana, dressed as hunter in short tunic and cloak, dog at her feet, head (r.) IMP X SICIL in exergue
192a [*BMCRE* 481–83]	------	AUR	Head of Augustus (r.), laureate AVGVSTVS DIVI F	Apollo, holding lyre and *plectrum*, standing (r.) IMP XII ACT in exergue
196 [*BMCRE* 489]	------	AUR	Head of Augustus (r.), laureate AVGVSTVS DIVI F	Diana, in long drapery, advancing (r.), taking arrow from quiver, holding bow IMP XII SICIL in exergue

*RIC*² 170, 192a, and 196 reproduced courtesy of The American Numismatic Society, New York.
*RIC*² 366 and 173a reproduced courtesy of the Trustees of the British Museum, London.

the recovered standards offered Augustus a new concept of vengeance, fulfilling his former promise by boasting of his recent success. Impatient, however, to postpone the celebratory event and wait until the temple that he had vowed was completed, Augustus deposited the standards on the Capitoline temporarily, in a Temple of Jupiter or in a hastily erected Temple of Mars Ultor. The depiction of a domed temple on coin issues at this time, identified by the legend MAR ULT and supported by the authority of Dio (54.8.3), might suggest the latter, but the silence of contemporary literary sources and Horace's claim that Augustus restored the standards to "our Jove" (*et signa nostro restituit Iovi*, *Odes* 4.15.6) more plausibly indicate that only one Temple of Mars Ultor was ever erected in Rome.[12] Finally dedicated in 2 B.C.E., the temple was the focal point of the monumental Forum, where an Augustan political ideology was impressively realized in marble.[13] An array of statues adorned the porticoes of the temple complex, Aeneas, Ascanius, and the Julian gens in one hemicycle, and Romulus and the Republican heroes facing opposite in another. Rome's greatest generals and triumphators could be seen in two long, lateral colonnades. A brief *titulus* was inscribed beneath each statue, exhibiting the name, title, and *elogium* of the *laudandus*.

The recasting of the image of Mars Ultor on his return to Rome in 19 reflects the concerted efforts of the princeps to reevaluate Roman history (in particular, his own career in civil war) by linking the past with recent events.

---

12. Since Mommsen (*CIL* I², p. 318), the view has generally been accepted that Augustus erected a temporary shrine to Mars Ultor until the completion of his temple in the Forum. Cf. P. Zanker, *Forum Romanum. Die Neugestaltung durch Augustus* (Tübingen, 1972), 5–6, and, more recently, J.C. Anderson, Jr., *The Historical Topography of the Imperial Fora*, Collection Latomus 182 (Brussels, 1984), 68, who seeks to reconcile the apparently contradictory testimonies of Dio and Horace, suggesting that the standards were actually dedicated to Jupiter Feretrius on the Capitoline but were displayed "in their own small round *sacellum* of Mars Ultor." C.J. Simpson, "The Date of Dedication of the Temple of Mars Ultor," *JRS* 67 (1977): 91–94, has more persuasively argued that Dio (54.8.3) must be in error when he locates the Temple of Mars Ultor on the Capitoline and that the Augustan issues depicting a small, domed temple with the legend MAR ULT commemorated the decree to build a temple, not the dedication. H.R.W. Smith, *Problems Historical and Numismatic in the Reign of Augustus*, University of California Publications in Classical Archaeology 2.4 (Berkeley and Los Angeles, 1951), 194–202, anticipated Simpson's conclusions.

13. For the architecture of the monumental Forum and its political message, see Zanker, *Forum Augustum. Das Bildprogramm* (Tübingen, 1970), and Anderson, *Historical Topography of the Imperial Fora*. On the *elogia* of the Forum, see H.T. Rowell, "The Forum and Funeral *imagines* of Augustus," *MAAR* 17 (1940): 131–43, and "Vergil and the Forum of Augustus," *AJP* 62 (1941): 261–76; M.M. Sage, "The *Elogia* of the Augustan Forum and the *de viris illustribus*," *Historia* 28 (1979): 192–210; P. Frisch, "Zu den Elogien des Augustusforums," *ZPE* 39 (1980): 91–98; L. Bracessi, "Ancora su *Elogia* e *de viris illustribus*," *Historia* 30 (1981): 126–28; and M.M. Sage, "The *Elogia* of the Augustan Forum and the *de viris illustribus*: A Reply," *Historia* 32 (1983): 250–56.

Contemporary coinage from the mints at Spain and Rome also reveal how the memory of Julius was revived and exalted during the celebration of the Ludi Saeculares. An obverse coin type of the moneyer Marcus Sanquinius depicts a herald in a long robe and feathered helmet, standing with a winged *caduceus* and round shield, with a six-pointed star in his hands.[14] The legend, AUGUST(us) DIVI F(ilius) LUDOS SAE(culares fecit), identifies the solemn occasion. The reverse exhibits a youthful head crowned with the laurel, with a comet above. Numismatists identify the male figure as a "rejuvenated" Divus Julius or the Genius Saeculi Novi, perhaps looking back to Iulus, the son of Aeneas and the ancestor of the Julian gens.[15] But the portrait of the cometed head resembles more the finely distinguished features of Augustus on earlier issues, and it is difficult to believe that contemporaries would fail to recognize the remarkable similarity. Issues from the mint in Spain also exhibit the comet of Julius; reverse types prominently depict the comet with eight rays and the tail pointing upward.[16] The legends proclaim DIVUS JULIUS across the field of the coins. The obverse depicts the portrait of Augustus, oak-wreathed, with an encircling title of CAESAR AUGUSTUS. The coinage of Octavian previously recognized the star of Julius;[17] the representation of the comet is new on Augustan coinage.

The impetus for the coin types is probably not the appearance of a comet in the year of the games, a dubious historical event; more likely, the comet is invoked at this time not only as the sign of Caesar's apotheosis but as a harbinger of the new age and the approaching divinity of Augustus.[18] The

---

14. *RIC*[2] 337–42.

15. Mattingly, *BMCRE* I, civ, and Sutherland, *RIC*[2], p. 66. For the suggestion that the youthful head represents the Genius Saeculi Novi, see A.A. Boyce, *Festal and Dated Coins of the Roman Empire: Four Papers*, ANSNNM 153 (New York, 1965), 1–11.

16. *RIC*[2] 37–38, 102. The date is not fixed for these issues, but a period of 19–17 is likely. For the difficulties in dating and attribution of mint for these issues, see Sutherland, *RIC*[2], pp. 25–26.

17. Two issues of Octavian from the period of the Second Triumvirate depict the star of Julius: Crawford, *RRC* 534 (the obverse shows a laureate head of Julius with a star before his forehead), and Crawford, *RRC* 540 (the reverse offers a temple of four columns; within is a statue of Julius wearing a veil and holding a *lituus*; the pediment is ornamented with a star and inscribed DIVO IUL). The dates of both issues are not certain, but the coins probably belong to the period of 38–36.

18. We need not believe the singular report of Julius Obsequens 71 that a comet appeared in this year. The fortuitous reoccurrence would surely not have been ignored by the ancient sources, which duly report the appearance of the comet in 44 B.C.E. Weinstock, *Divus Julius*, 379 n. 3, who readily accepts the claim of the late chronicler of prodigies, seems to suggest that Dio (54.19.7) is confused when he mentions a comet in the following year. This seems unlikely. Dio records a list of portents that occurred in Rome shortly after the departure of Augustus from the city. The flame, which Dio describes as a torch, burning throughout the night and shooting from the southern sky toward the north in the direction where Augustus was traveling,

testimony of the elder Pliny is instructive. Pliny (*NH* 2.94) reports Augustus' feelings toward the comet that appeared during the games he celebrated in honor of his father in July of 44. Publicly, he explained that he dedicated the statue of Caesar in the Forum and crowned it with an emblem of a star, since the people believed that the *sidus* signified the soul of Caesar received among the spirits of the immortal gods. Privately, however, he was especially delighted in the opportune event, because he judged that the comet's "birth" was instead a sign to himself (*sibi illum natum*) and that his "birth" occurred at this sign (*seque in eo nasci*). The image of the comet on these Augustan issues hints at this attitude of the princeps and prefigures the newly defined role of Divus Julius in an Augustan political ideology.[19]

Beside Mars Ultor and the comet of Divus Julius, Apollo Actius emerges on Augustan coinage. The god first appears on a denarius issue by one of the moneyers in the collegium at Rome in 16 B.C.E. (*RIC*² 365 and 366, plate 6). The legend on the obverse IMP(erator) CAESAR AUGUST(us) TR(ibunicia) POT(estate) IIX dates the coin firmly to the annual period beginning on the 27th of June in that year. The reverse type shows the male god in a long robe, standing on a low platform ornamented with what is probably three naval prows flanked by two anchors.[20] In his left hand, the god holds a lyre, and in his right, he makes a sacrifice from a *patera* over an altar. The legend placed above and below the platform offers a dedicatory inscription to Apollo Actius (APOLLINI ACTIO). The name of the moneyer, C(aius) ANTISTI(us) VETUS IIIVIR, who was later consul in 6 B.C.E., encircles the upper exergue of the coin. The depiction of the god is peculiar and unique. Editors of numismatic catalogs have associated the representation with a statue from the

---

was recognized as a foreboding sign of disaster for the city. Public prayers were quickly offered for the safe return of the princeps. The details of the incident do not indicate Dio's confusion or error.

19. For contrasting views on the public image of the divine Julius in the Augustan age, see E.S. Ramage, "Augustus' Treatment of Julius Caesar," *Historia* 34 (1985): 223–45, and P. White, "Julius Caesar in Augustan Rome," *Phoenix* 42 (1988): 334–56.

20. For the suggestion that the three objects depicted on the platform are intended to represent the gilded cases in which the Sibylline books were kept (*foruli*), see H. Cahn, "Zu einem Münzbild des Augustus," *MusHelv* 1 (1944): 203–8. Suetonius (*Aug.* 31.1) records that Augustus deposited the oracular inscriptions at the base of the Temple of Apollo (*sub Palatini Apollinis basi*) but that they were placed in two, not three, gilded coffers (*duobus forulis auratis*). For a convincing refutation of Cahn's claim and an analysis of the coin type, see H. Jucker, "Apollo Palatinus und Apollo Actius auf augusteischen Münzen," *MusHelv* 39 (1982): 82–100. Jucker argues that the figure of the god should not be linked with the Temple of Apollo on the Palatine. His suggestion, however, that the sacrificing god represents a statue of Apollo placed on the memorial that Augustus set up on the site of his camp at Actium is not supported by the archaeological evidence; cf. Murray and Petsas, *Octavian's Campsite Memorial*, 91.

Temple of Apollo on the Palatine.[21] Such an identification has bolstered the claims that the Augustan temple was established and widely recognized as a monument to the victory at Actium. But the god with the *patera* is certainly not the lyre-playing statue of Scopas that stood in the cella of the temple. Others associate the Apollo depicted on the coin of Antistius with a statue of the god that may have stood in the surrounding area of the Palatine temple complex.[22] However attractive these identifications may be, they are speculative at best, are not supported by the ancient sources, and serve as a poor foundation to associate the Apollo of the issues of Antistius with the temple on the Palatine. The distinctive and detailed features of the coin type—the decorated platform, the altar, and the *patera* in the god's hand—may reflect not the efforts of the moneyer (or his engraver) to represent an actual monument in Rome but his attempts to identify the unfamiliar god.[23] The legend of the coin (APOLLINI ACTIO) should seem to bring to mind the cult of Apollo Actius, whose temple stood near the site of the naval battle, refurbished by the Roman victor. The decorated platform of naval spoils recalls the occa-

---

21. Sutherland, *RIC*[2] 365, identifies three *foruli*, not naval prows, on the platform, citing the authority of Cahn, "Zu einem Münzbild des Augustus," and Gagé, *Apollon Romain*, 545. Mattingly, *BMCRE* I, cvi, "The other reverse of the denarius—Apollo of Actium—certainly refers to the temple built by Augustus on the Palatine to the god to whom he attributed his greatest victory." Grueber, *BMCRR* II, 54–55 n. 3: "Type II. commemorates the sacrifices to Apollo of Actium in his temple on the Palatine, which was built by Augustus."

22. Propertius seems to suggest that a statue of Apollo with his silent lyre (*marmoreus tacita carmen hiare lyra*, 2.31.6) stood in the area immediately before the temple, but the text is perhaps corrupt and is the only ancient source to identify this statue. Zanker, "Der Apollontempel auf dem Palatin," 31–32, and *Power of Images*, 85–86, identifies this statue as the "Apollo of Actium," associating it with the depiction of the god on the denarius issue of Antistius Vetus (*RIC*[2] 365–66). The confidence of this assertion is surprising and unfounded, since the description of the statue by the elegist, admittedly brief, fails to correspond to the details of the coin, where Apollo, holding a *patera* in his right hand, stands on a platform with an altar, decorated with naval beaks and anchors.

23. The involvement of the moneyer in the choice of the coin type should not be discounted. The issues of Antistius in 16 exhibit the "Republican" practice of alluding to the moneyer's gens (cf. here Mattingly, *BMCRE* I, cvi, and Sutherland, "Senatorial Gold and Silver Coinage of 16 B.C.," 46. *RIC*[2] 363–64 depicts two veiled priests sacrificing a pig over an altar, in allusion to the ancient treaty between Rome and Gabii, the home of the moneyer's family (the legend reads FOEDUS P R QUM GABINIS). In addition to this issue and the coin type of Apollo Actius (*RIC*[2] 365–66) Antistius minted two issues whose reverses display the symbols of sacrifice. *RIC*[2] 367–68 shows the implements of sacrifice, the *simpulum*, *lituus*, tripod, and *patera*—and *RIC*[2] 369 features a veiled priest holding a *patera* over an altar and an attendant leading a bull (the legend reads PRO VALETUDINE CAESARIS SPQR). This issue may be an allusion to the quinquennial games celebrated in 16. It is tempting to conclude, however, from these four issues, including the figure of Apollo holding the *patera* over the altar, that the moneyer intends a pun on his name (the *antistes* was the priest in charge of a ritual). Later issues by another moneyer of this gens, Antistius Reginus, perhaps minted in 13 B.C.E. (*RIC*[2] 410, 411), revive the earlier coin types of *RIC*[2] 367–68 and 363–64, respectively.

sion of victory and his role in the battle. Whether or not Augustus erected such a monument at Actium, Nicopolis, or perhaps Rome (the silence of the ancient sources is inclined against this view), the recognition of the god fifteen years after the decisive battle is more significant and certain.

Issues from the new imperial mint established at Lugdunum in 15 B.C.E. also feature depictions of Apollo Actius. The coins, dated by the military title of imperator awarded to Augustus, belong to a large series of issues distinguished by a rich variety of coin types.[24] The coins vary in their images of Apollo. Earlier issues depict the god holding the lyre in his left hand and a *plectrum* (not the *patera*) in his right (RIC^2 170, plate 6).[25] Absent are the platform and altar of the issues of Antistius. The legend identifies the god with the title ACT(ius). Later issues adopt a strikingly different pose of the god (RIC^2 192a, plate 6).[26] The figure is in profile, standing erect and facing right. His left hand holds a lyre, but the object in his right hand is difficult to identify; it may be a *patera* or a *plectrum*. The differences might suggest that the engravers at Lugdunum had not seen the cult figure of the god or more likely did not feel compelled to represent the deity except in the familiar guise of Apollo Citharoedus. In contrast, the depiction of the helmeted Mars Ultor, holding the standards, is a fixed type on the issues from the mints at both Spain and Rome. More telling is the fact that all the issues of Apollo Actius are coupled with issues of Diana Siciliensis, the deity who was later associated with the naval victory at Naulochus (RIC^2 173a and 196, plate 6).[27]

The coin types are closely connected by style and legend. The pairing of the twin children of Latona is not surprising, but the association of the two naval victories in civil war seems a later and concurrent development. If we seek an impetus for the exaltation of the gods' roles in battle, we should perhaps begin with the recognition of Mars Ultor, formerly associated with the defeat of the Republican forces at Philippi. The celebration of the Ludi Saeculares and the prominent roles that Apollo and Diana received at this time may also have influenced the coin types. As *magister* of the priestly

24. For discussions of the Augustan issues of the Lugdunum mint, see Sutherland, "The Personality of the Mints under the Julio-Claudian Emperors," *AJP* 68 (1947): 54–55, and Kraft, *Zur Münzprägung des Augustus*, 25–51.

25. RIC^2 170 and 171a–b (with legend IMP X, ACT in exergue); RIC^2 179–80, 190a–b, and 191 (with legend IMP XII, ACT in exergue).

26. RIC^2 192a–b and 193a–b (with legend IMP XII, ACT in exergue).

27. RIC^2 172 and 173a–b (with legend IMP X, SICIL in exergue); RIC^2 194a–b, 195, 196, and 197a–b (with legend IMP XII, SICIL in exergue). A four-aureus multiple (RIC^2 204: legend IMP XV, SICIL in exergue) was found at Pompeii in the late eighteenth century and was stolen from the Museo Nazionale in Naples in 1977. No other specimen is known.

college, the *quindecimviri sacris faciundis* who were in charge of the games, Augustus took a special interest in the preparations. The ceremonies lasted three days and three nights, different in several respects from the earlier occasions, but chiefly in the deities invoked. No longer were prayers offered only to Dis and Proserpina, rulers of the infernal regions, but the Moirae (Fates), Eiliythiae, and Terra Mater received sacrifices during the three night-time ceremonies. The ceremonies during the days, an innovation from the ancient ritual, included sacrifices and prayers to Jupiter Capitolinus on the first day, to Juno Regina on the second, and to Apollo and Diana, the deities enshrined in Apollo's temple on the Palatine, on the third and final day.

Perhaps some in Rome were beginning at this time to make some association between the god of the Palatine temple and Apollo Actius, who had assured the victory. Vergil had already imagined the Augustan triumph in procession before the "snowy threshold of shining Phoebus" (*Aen.* 8.720). And a few years later, Propertius composed his Callimachean hymn linking the origins of the Palatine temple with the divinely sanctioned and divinely won victory at Actium (*Elegy* 4.6). But we should not be so quick to presume official directives or policy for the imaginative scenes of the poets. In his elegy on the dedication of the temple (*Elegy* 2.31), Propertius ignores any memories of the Actian battle in his description of Apollo's new sanctuary. Horace's testimony is also critical. With the death of Vergil, Horace was asked to compose a public hymn to honor the ceremonies of the Ludi Saeculares before the Temple of Apollo Palatinus.[28] The song begins and ends with an address to the twin deities. Apollo is augur and healer, the beloved favorite of the nine Muses, and the archer with the gleaming bow. Diana is queen of the forests, the radiant glory of the heavens, and ruler of the Aventine and Algidus. At the end of the hymn, the poet prays to Phoebus to look favorably on his altars on the Palatine and to continue the prosperity of Rome and Latium for future generations. The Medes already fear the Alban axes on land and sea; even the once arrogant Scythians and Indians seek the clemency and guidance of the victor (lines 53–56). For Horace, the commencement of the new *saeculum* does not invite a reappraisal of the past and civil war; his gaze keeps looking ahead in wonder and greater confidence in the Augustan peace. Apollo Actius and Diana Siciliensis play no role in Horace's prayers.

The attitude of Augustus toward Actium is complex, ambiguous, and difficult to grasp. The grateful Roman and pious victor recognized the god's

---

28. For a sober discussion of the historical and epigraphical evidence on the Augustan celebration of the Ludi Saeculares and an analysis of Horace's poem, see Fraenkel, *Horace*, 364–82.

role at the site of battle and refurbished his neglected temple. He exalted his local games to Olympian status and erected the monument of a victory city. His coinage exhibited the symbols and tokens of victory and broadcast the messages of captured or recovered lands (AEGYPTO CAPTA and ASIA RE-CEPTA). On his return to Rome, he honored the battle with a triumphal procession, voted earlier by a fawning Senate; but the Actian triumph was crafted as just one aspect of a larger and more impressive accomplishment, conquest in the East and the establishment of peace throughout the Roman world. In later years, Roman coinage acknowledges the roles of Apollo and Diana in the victories at Actium and Naulochus, respectively. But even here we should refrain from making bold generalizations or confident assertions. In 2 B.C.E., during the formal dedicatory ceremonies of the newly opened Temple of Mars Ultor and the Augustan Forum, the princeps exhibited a mock naval battle for the citizens of Rome. The occasion is duly recorded in the *Res Gestae* with an astonishing detail of information.[29] Augustus staged the public event in the *nemus Caesarum* near the Tiber and excavated a huge area for the spectacle. Almost three thousand men and more than thirty triremes and smaller ships participated in the dramatic scene of battle. Ovid is a contemporary witness. The *magister amoris* exclaims in grandiose language that the whole world, from the eastern and western shores, gathered in the city for the show (*ingens orbis in Urbe fuit*, AA 1.174); he playfully asks his reader who would not find someone to love in so great a crowd. The occasion might have seemed an excellent opportunity for Augustus to recall his victory won in the Ambracian Gulf and the decisive act in the war against Antony and the Egyptian queen. Augustus instead looked back to a more distant past—and a foreign struggle, the battle at Salamis between the Athenians and Persians. Perhaps the cautious princeps worried that the "victorious" side might not win again. At least the descendants of Cecrops graciously complied with the record of history and the wishes of the Roman master of ceremonies.

The outcome at Actium secured the supreme power and position of Augustus in the Roman world. Of this fact, there can be little doubt or controversy today. From the advantage of our modern prospective, we are inclined to view Actium more as a beginning than as an end. The confrontations at Philippi and Pharsalus are often seen as the signs of the demise of the

---

29. *RG* 23. Julius Caesar (Suet. *Caes.* 39.4) presented the first naumachia in Rome, a combat between Tyrian and Egyptian fleets. The emperor Claudius (Suet. *Claud.* 21.6) recreated the fight between the Sicilians and Rhodians.

Republic, while the battle at Actium betokens the commencement of a new age and political establishment. Subsequent events may defend this opinion, but for the contemporaries of Augustus, who witnessed a long succession of repeated civil wars, the Actian victory was felt as the culmination of a bitter past, no matter what side they had once supported; it could not become the start of a more glorious future until such a future became assured. Attitudes varied on the battle. Horace despaired of the battle and later chose to ignore the victory in his lyrics and public hymn. Vergil fashioned Actium as a final conflict between two mighty cultures and civilizations; the reality and memories of civil strife often obstructed his vision. Propertius bemoaned the occasion of battle in the Ambracian Gulf and exposed the shame and deceit of the victor. More than ten years after his initial *recusatio* to Maecenas to sing of the *bellaque resque* of Augustus, the Roman Callimachus took up the theme of Actium again. The stylized hymn playfully responds to the myth of battle in Vergil's *Aeneid* and the reappraisal of the past in Augustan Rome. But the elegist's belated efforts at imperial panegyric lack sincerity and credulity, making the most critical moment in recent Roman history into an exaggerated account of battle and an exhibition of the effete god's shooting finesse.

Augustus was neither a mad Caligula nor a lyre-playing Nero, a victim of the illusions of his own grandeur or divinity. Prudence and propriety ever directed the life of the man who was inclined to hasten at a sluggish pace. From the ancient commentators on Vergil's *Eclogues* and Horace's *Epistles*, we hear that Augustus had set up in his library adjoining the Temple of Apollo a statue of himself in the guise of the god with all his attributes (*simulacrum factum est cum Apollinis cunctis insignibus* and *Caesar in bibliotheca statuam sibi posverat habitu ac statu Apollinis*).[30] That Servius and pseudo-Acron identify the statue in such terms (not, for example, as a statue of Apollo with the features of Augustus) indicates the perspective of a subsequent generation who looked on the founder of the Principate perhaps in the same way in which Augustus himself once looked on the legendary figures of Romulus or Camillus. I imagine that Augustus would have smiled at the interpretation of the statue. He might explain that he had piously erected an image of the deity whom he revered and worshiped. The resemblance of features was a fortuitous coincidence or the providence of fate and the will of the immortal gods.

As he approached death, Augustus still fretted about his public image. He

---

30. Serv. *Comm. in Verg. Buc.* 4.10 and pseudo-Acron *Comm. in Hor. Epist.* 1.3.17, respectively.

queried if any disturbance befell the city because of his absence and failing health. He called repeatedly for his mirror while attendants combed his thin hair and puffed out his shrunken cheeks. His friends assembled into his private chamber, and the dying princeps asked how well he acted in the comedy of life. Like the lead actor at the end of a play, he sought the final applause and approval of his audience.[31] That judgment, much like the verdict on Actium, must belong to the individual spectator.

---

31. For the final words of Augustus and the scene of his death, see Suet. *Aug.* 99.

Bibliography

Ableitinger-Grünberger/Graz, D. "Die neunte Epode des Horaz." *WS* 81 (1968): 74–91.

———. *Der junge Horaz und die Politik. Studien zur 7. und 16. Epode.* Heidelberg, 1971.

Ahl, F. "The Rider and the Horse: Politics and Power in Roman Poetry from Horace to Statius." *ANRW* II.32.1 (Berlin, 1984), 40–124.

———. *Metaformations: Soundplay and Wordplay in Ovid and Other Classical Poets.* Ithaca, 1985.

Albert, R. *Das Bild des Augustus auf den frühen Reichsprägungen. Studien zur Vergöttlichung des ersten Prinzeps.* Speyer, 1981.

Alexander, W.H. "*Nunc Tempus Erat*: Horace, *Odes* I, 37, 4." *CJ* 39 (1944): 231–33.

Alfonsi, L. "Properzio II, 1, 23–24 e il *Marius* di Cicerone." *SIFC* 19 (1943): 147–53.

———. *L'Elegia di Properzio.* Milan, 1945.

Anderson, J.C., Jr. *The Historical Topography of the Imperial Fora.* Collection Latomus 182. Brussels, 1984.

Anderson, W.S. *The Art of the Aeneid.* Englewood Cliffs, N.J., 1969. Reprinted Bristol and Wauconda, Ill., 1989.

Andreae, B. "Archäologische Funde und Grabungen im Bereich der Soprintendenzen von Rom 1949–1956/57." *JDAI* 72 (1957): cols. 110–358.

Ashmore, S.G., ed. *The Comedies of Terence.* 2d ed. Oxford, 1908.

Auden, W.H. *Homage to Clio.* New York, 1955.

Babcock, C.L. "Erasure of the Antonii Names and the Dating of the Capitoline Fasti." Ph.D. diss., University of California at Berkeley, 1953.

———. "Dio and Plutarch on the *Damnatio* of Antony." *CP* 57 (1962): 30–32.

———. "Horace, *Carm.* 1.32 and the Dedication of the Temple of Apollo Palatinus." *CP* 62 (1967): 189–94.

Babelon, E. *Description historique et chronologique des monnaies de la République romaine vulgairement appelées monnaies consulaires.* 2 vols. Paris, 1885–86. Reprinted Bologna, 1963.

Bailey, D.R. Shackleton. *Propertiana.* Cambridge, 1956.

———. *Profile of Horace.* London, 1982.

Baker, R.J. "Propertius, Cleopatra and Actium." *Antichthon* 10 (1976): 56–62.

———. "*Caesaris in nomen* (Propertius IV, vi)." *RhM* 126 (1983): 153–74.

Baldwin, B. "The Death of Cleopatra VII." *JEA* 50 (1964): 181–82.

Bartels, C. "Die neunte Epode des Horaz als sympotisches Gedicht." *Hermes* 101 (1973): 282–313.

293

Barwick, K. "Horaz Carm. 1, 2 und Vergil." *Philologus* 90 (1935): 257–76.

———. "Zur Interpretation und Chronologie der 4. Ecloge des Vergil und der 16. und 7. Epode des Horaz." *Philologus* 96 (1943–44): 28–67.

Bauer, H. "Das Kapitell des Apollo Palatinus-Tempels." *RömMitt* 76 (1969): 183–204.

Becher, I. *Das Bild der Kleopatra in der griechischen und lateinischen Literatur.* Deutsche Akademie der Wissenschaften zu Berlin 51. Berlin, 1966.

Becker, C. "Der Schild des Aeneas." *WS* 77 (1964): 111–27.

———. "Die späten Elegien des Properz." *Hermes* 99 (1971): 449–80.

Benario, H.W. "The *Carmen de Bello Actiaco* and Early Imperial Epic." *ANRW* II.30.3 (Berlin, 1983), 1656–62.

Benario, J.M. "Dido and Cleopatra." *Vergilius* 16 (1970): 2–6.

Bickel, E. "Politische Sibylleneklogen." *RhM* 97 (1954): 193–228.

Bieber, M. "The Development of Portraiture on Roman Republican Coins." *ANRW* I.4 (Berlin, 1973), 871–98.

Binder, G. *Aeneas und Augustus. Interpretationen zum 8. Buch der Aeneis.* Beiträge zur klassischen Philologie 38. Meisenheim am Glan, 1971.

Bishop, J.H. "Palatine Apollo." *CQ* 49, n.s. 6 (1956): 187–92.

———. "Palatine Apollo: A Reply to Professor Richmond." *CQ* 55, n.s. 11 (1961): 127–28.

———. *The Cost of Power: Studies in the Aeneid of Virgil.* University of New England Monographs 4. Armidale, New South Wales, 1988.

Bonaria, M. "Actionicae." *RE* suppl. 10 (1965): col. 1.

Bowersock, G.W. "Eurycles of Sparta." *JRS* 51 (1961): 112–18.

———. *Augustus and the Greek World.* Oxford, 1965.

———. "A Date in the *Eighth Eclogue*." *HSCP* 75 (1971): 73–80.

Boyce, A.A. *Festal and Dated Coins of the Roman Empire: Four Papers.* ANSNNM 153. New York, 1965.

Braccesi, L. "Orazio e il motivo politico del *Bellum Actiacum*." *PP* 22 (1967): 177–91.

———. "Ancora su *Elogia* e *de viris illustribus*." *Historia* 30 (1981): 126–28.

Breckenridge, J.D. *Likeness: A Conceptual History of Ancient Portraiture.* Evanston, Ill., 1968.

Brendel, O. *Ikonographie des Kaisers Augustus.* Nuremberg, 1931.

Brilliant, R. *Roman Art from the Republic to Constantine.* London, 1974.

Bruhl, A. "Les influences hellénistiques dans le triomphe romain." *MélRome* 46 (1929): 77–95.

Brunt, P.A., and J.M. Moore, eds. and trans. *Res Gestae Divi Augusti: The Achievements of the Divine Augustus.* Oxford, 1967. Reprinted (with corrections) 1970.

Bücheler, F. "*Coniectanea*." In *Index scholarum quae summis auspiciis regis augustissimi Guilelmi Imperatoris Germaniae*, ed. F. Bücheler, 3-26. Bonn, 1878–79. Reprinted in *Kleine Schriften*, 2:311–33. Leipzig and Berlin, 1927.

Buchheit, V. "Mythos und Geschichte in Ovids Metamorphosen I." *Hermes* 94 (1966): 80–108.

Burnett, A.M. "The Authority to Coin in the Late Republic and Early Empire." *NumChron* 17, ser. 7 (1977): 37–63.

———. Review of *Das Bild des Augustus auf den frühen Reichsprägungen*, by R. Albert. *Gnomon* 55 (1983): 563–65.

————, M. Amandry, and P.P. Ripollès, eds. *Roman Provincial Coinage*. Vol. 1, *From the Death of Caesar to the Death of Vitellius (44 BC–AD 69)*. Part 1, introduction and catalogue. Part 2, indexes and plates. London and Paris, 1992.

Butler, H.E., and E.A. Barber, eds. *The Elegies of Propertius*. Oxford, 1933. Reprinted Hildesheim, 1969.

Buttrey, T.V., Jr. *The Triumviral Portrait Gold of the Quattuorviri Monetales of 42 B.C.* ANSNNM 137. New York, 1956.

Cahn, H. "Zu einem Münzbild des Augustus." *MusHelv* 1 (1944): 203–8.

Cairns, F. "Horace, *Odes* 1.2." *Eranos* 69 (1971): 68–88.

————. "Horace *Epode* 9: Some New Interpretations." *ICS* 8.1 (1983): 80–93.

————. "Propertius and the Battle of Actium (4.6)." In *Poetry and Politics in the Age of Augustus*, ed. T. Woodman and D. West, 129–68. Cambridge, 1984.

————. *Virgil's Augustan Epic*. Cambridge, 1989.

Campbell, A.Y. *Horace: A New Interpretation*. London, 1924.

Camps, W.A., ed. *Propertius: Elegies, Books I–IV*. Cambridge, 1961–67.

Carettoni, G. "Excavations and Discoveries in the Forum Romanum and on the Palatine during the Last Fifty Years." *JRS* 50 (1960): 192–203.

————. "I problemi della zona augustea del Palatino alla luce dei recenti scavi." *RendPontAcc* 39, ser. 3 (1966–67): 55–75.

————. *Das Haus des Augustus auf dem Palatin*. Mainz, 1983.

————. "Die 'Campana'-Terrakotten vom Apollo-Palatinus-Tempel." In *Kaiser Augustus und die verlorene Republik*, ed. M. Hofter, 267–72. Mainz, 1988.

Carney, T.F. "Cicero's Picture of Marius." *WS* 73 (1960): 83–122.

Carruba, R.W. "The Structure of Horace's Ninth Epode." *SymbOslo* 41 (1966): 98–107.

Carter, J.M. *The Battle of Actium: The Rise and Triumph of Augustus Caesar*. London, 1970.

————. "A New Fragment of Octavian's Inscription at Nicopolis." *ZPE* 24 (1977): 227–30.

————. Review of *Nicopolis I: Proceedings of the First International Symposium on Nicopolis (23–29 September 1984)*, ed. E. Chrysos. *CR* 40 (1990): 387–89.

Cavarzere, A., ed. *Orazio, il libro degli Epodi*. Venice, 1992.

Cesano, S.L. *Numismatica augustea*. Rome, 1937.

Chittenden, J. "Hermes-Mercury, Dynasts, and Emperors." *NumChron* 5, ser. 6 (1945): 41–57.

Clarke, M.L. *The Noblest Roman: Marcus Brutus and His Reputation*. Ithaca, 1981.

Clausen, W. "On the Date of the *First Eclogue*." *HSCP* 76 (1972): 201–5.

————. *Virgil's Aeneid and the Tradition of Hellenistic Poetry*. Sather Classical Lectures 51. Berkeley and Los Angeles, 1987.

Coarelli, F. *Il Foro Romano*. 2 vols. Rome, 1983–85.

Cohen, H. *Description historique des monnaies frappées sous l'Empire romain communément appelées médailles impériales*. 9 vols. 2d ed. Paris, 1880. Reprinted Graz, 1955–57.

Cohon, R. "Vergil and Pheidias: The Shield of Aeneas and of Athena Parthenos." *Vergilius* 37 (1991): 22–30.

Coleman, R., ed. *Vergil, Eclogues*. Cambridge, 1977.

Commager, S. "Horace, *Carmina* 1.37." *Phoenix* 12 (1958): 47–57.

————. "Horace, *Carmina* I, 2." *AJP* 80 (1959): 37–55.

————. *The Odes of Horace: A Critical Study.* New Haven, 1962.

————. *A Prolegomenon to Propertius.* Lectures in Memory of Louise Taft Semple, University of Cincinnati 3. Norman, Okla., 1974.

Connor, P.J. "The Actian Miracle: Propertius 4.6." *Ramus* 7 (1978): 1–10.

Courtney, E., ed. *The Fragmentary Latin Poets.* Oxford, 1993.

Crawford, M.H. *Roman Republican Coin Hoards.* London, 1969.

————. *Roman Republican Coinage.* 2 vols. Cambridge, 1974. Reprinted (with corrections) Cambridge, 1989.

————. Review of *Zur Münzprägung des Augustus*, by K. Kraft. *JRS* 64 (1974): 246–47.

————. "Roman Imperial Coin Types and the Formation of Public Opinion." In *Studies in Numismatic Method Presented to Philip Grierson*, ed. C.N.L. Brooke et al., 47–64. Cambridge, 1983.

Cremona, V. "Due Cleopatre a confronto. Properzio replica a Orazio." *Aevum* 61 (1987): 123–31.

Crowther, N.B. "The Sebastan Games in Naples (IvOl. 56)." *ZPE* 79 (1989): 100–2.

Curtis, C.D. "Roman Monumental Arches." In *Supplemental Papers of the American School of Classical Studies in Rome,* 2:26–83, New York and London, 1908.

Davis, G. *Polyhymnia: The Rhetoric of Horatian Lyric Discourse.* Berkeley and Los Angeles, 1991.

Degrassi, A. "L'edificio dei Fasti Capitolini." *RendPontAcc* 21 (1945–46): 57–104.

————, ed. *Inscriptiones Italiae.* Vol. 13, *Fasti et Elogia.* Fasc. 1, *Fasti Consulares et Triumphales.* Rome, 1947.

————. "Epigrafia romana." *Doxa* 2 (1949): 47–135.

Deonna, W. "Le trésor des Fins d'Annecy." *RevArch* 11, ser. 5 (1920): 112–206.

Deutsch, M.E. "The Apparatus of Caesar's Triumphs." *PQ* 3 (1924): 257–66.

————. "Pompey's Three Triumphs." *CP* 19 (1924): 277–79.

————. "Caesar's Triumphs." *CW* 19 (1926): 101–6.

DiCesare, M.A. *The Altar and the City: A Reading of Vergil's Aeneid.* New York, 1974.

Doblhofer, E. *Die Augustuspanegyrik des Horaz in formalhistorischer Sicht.* Heidelberg, 1966.

————. "Horaz und Augustus." *ANRW* II.31.3 (Berlin, 1981), 1922–86.

Doukellis, P.N. "Actia Nicopolis: idéologie impériale, structures urbaines et développement régional." *JRA* 3 (1990): 399–406.

Dörrie, H. *P. Ovidius Naso. Der Brief der Sappho an Phaon.* Zetemata 58. Munich, 1975.

Drew, D.L. *The Allegory of the Aeneid.* Oxford, 1927.

Dunston, A.J. "Horace—Odes III.4 and the 'Virtues' of Augustus." *AUMLA* 31 (1969): 9–19.

DuQuesnay, I. M. Le M. "Horace and Maecenas: The Propaganda Value of *Sermones* I." In *Poetry and Politics in the Age of Augustus*, ed. T. Woodman and D. West, 19–58. Cambridge, 1984.

Durante, M. "Triumpe e triumphus. Un capitolo del più antico culto dionisiaco latino." *Maia* 4 (1951): 138–44.

Eck, W. "Senatorial Self-Representation: Developments in the Augustan Period." In *Caesar Augustus: Seven Aspects*, ed. F. Millar and E. Segal, 129–67. Oxford, 1984.

Eden, P.T. "The Salii on the Shield of Aeneas: Aeneid 8, 663–6." *RhM* 116 (1973): 78–83.

———, ed. *A Commentary on Virgil: Aeneid VIII.* Mnemosyne Supplementum 35. Leiden, 1975.

Elmore, J. "Horace and Octavian (*Car.* I. 2)." *CP* 26 (1931): 258–63.

Enk, P.J., ed. *Sexti Propertii elegiarium liber I (Monobiblos).* 2 vols. Leiden, 1946.

———. *Sexti Propertii elegiarium liber secundus.* 2 vols. Leiden, 1962.

Evans, J. DeRose. "The Sicilian Coinage of Sextus Pompeius (Crawford 511)." *ANSMN* 32 (1987): 97–157.

———. *The Art of Persuasion: Political Propaganda from Aeneas to Brutus.* Ann Arbor, Mich., 1992.

Farrell, J. "Asinius Pollio in Vergil *Eclogue* 8." *CP* 86 (1991): 204–11.

Fears, J.R. "The Theology of Victory at Rome: Approaches and Problems." *ANRW* 2.17.2 (Berlin, 1981), 736–826.

Fedeli, P., ed. *Sesto Properzio. Elegie, libro IV.* Bari, 1965.

———. *Sesto Properzio. Il primo libro delle elegie.* Florence, 1980.

———. *Sesto Properzio. Il libro terzo delle elegie.* Bari, 1985.

Feeney, D.C. "History and Revelation in Vergil's Underworld." *PCPS* 32 (1986): 1–24.

———. *The Gods in Epic: Poets and Critics of the Classical Tradition.* Oxford, 1991.

Ferrabino, A. "La battaglia d'Azio." *RivFil* 52 (1924): 433–72.

Ferrarino, P. "La data del *Marius* Ciceroniano." *RhM* 88 (1939): 147–64.

Fischer, T. "Zahlenmystik in der Goldprägung des CAESAR DIVI F. Ein Prinzip augusteischer Ideologie und Propaganda?" *NAC* 13 (1984): 163–70.

Flory, M. "Livia and the History of Public Honorific Statues for Women in Rome." *TAPA* 123 (1993): 287–308.

Fogazza, D., ed. *Domiti Marsi Testimonia et Fragmenta.* Rome, 1981.

Fordyce, C.J., ed. *P. Vergili Maronis Aeneidos Libri VII–VIII.* Oxford, 1977.

Forster, E.M. *Alexandria: A History and a Guide.* 3d ed. New York, 1961.

Fowler, W. Warde. *Aeneas at the Site of Rome: Observations on the Eighth Book of the Aeneid.* 2d ed. Oxford, 1918.

Fraenkel, E. *Horace.* Oxford, 1957.

Franke, P.R. "Apollo Leucadius und Octavianus?" *Chiron* 6 (1976): 159–63.

Fraser, P.M. *Ptolemaic Alexandria.* 3 vols. Oxford, 1972.

Fredricksmeyer, E.A. "Octavian and the Unity of Virgil's First Eclogue." *Hermes* 94 (1966): 208–18.

Frisch, P. "Zu den Elogien des Augustusforums." *ZPE* 39 (1980): 91–98.

———. "Die Klassifikation der παῖδες bei den griechischen Agonen." *ZPE* 75 (1988): 179–85.

Frothingham, A.J., Jr. "A Revised List of Roman Memorial and Triumphal Arches." *AJA* 8, ser. 2 (1904): 1–34.

———. "De la véritable signification des monuments romains qu'on appelle 'Arcs de Triomphe.'" *RevArch* 6, ser. 4 (1905): 216–30.

Gabba, E. "The Perusine War and Triumviral Italy." *HSCP* 75 (1971): 138–60.

Gabelmann, H. "Zur Schlußszene auf dem Schild des Aeneas (Vergil, *Aeneis VIII* 720–728)." *RömMitt* 93 (1986): 281–300.

Gagé, J. *"Actiaca." MélRome* 53 (1936): 37–100.

———. *Apollon Romain. Essai sur le culte d'Apollon et le développement du "ritus Graecus" à Rome des origines à Auguste.* BEFAR 182. Paris, 1955.

———. "Apollon impérial, Garant des *Fata Romana.*" *ANRW* II.17.2 (Berlin, 1981), 561–630.

Galinsky, K. "The Triumph Theme in the Augustan Elegy." *WS* 82 (1969): 75–107.

———. "The Anger of Aeneas." *AJP* 109 (1988): 321–48.

———. "Venus, Polysemy, and the Ara Pacis Augustae." *AJA* 96 (1992): 457–75.

Gardner, P. *A Catalogue of the Greek Coins in the British Museum: Peloponnesus.* Revised and edited by R. Stuart Poole. London, 1975.

Gardthausen, V. *Augustus und seine Zeit.* 2 vols. Leipzig, 1891.

Gatti, G. "La ricostruzione dell'arco di Augusto al Foro Romano." *RendPontAcc* 21 (1945–46): 105–22.

Geer, R.M. "The Greek Games at Naples." *TAPA* 66 (1935): 208–21.

George, E.V. *Aeneid VIII and the Aitia of Callimachus.* Mnemosyne Supplementum 27. Leiden, 1974.

Gesztelyi, T. "Mercury and Augustus: Horace, Odes I 2; Some Contributions to the Problem of Their Identification." *AClass* 9 (1973): 77–81.

Giard, J.-B. *Bibliothèque Nationale. Catalogue des monnaies de l'empire romain.* Vol. 1, *Auguste.* Paris, 1976.

———. "La monnaie coloniale d'Orange: une attribution en question." *RevNum* 26, ser. 6 (1984): 77–84.

Gillis, D. *Eros and Death in the Aeneid.* Rome, 1983.

Goold, G.P., ed. and trans. *Propertius, Elegies.* Loeb Classical Library 18. Cambridge, Mass., 1990.

Gordon, A.E., and J.S. Gordon. Review of *Inscriptiones Italiae.* Vol. 13, *Fasti et Elogia.* Fasc. 1, *Fasti Consulares et Triumphales,* ed. A. Degrassi. *AJA* 55 (1951): 278–81.

Gosling, A. "Octavian, Brutus and Apollo: A Note on Opportunist Propaganda." *AJP* 107 (1986): 586–89.

Gowing, A. *The Triumviral Narratives of Appian and Cassius Dio.* Ann Arbor, Mich., 1992.

Graef, P. "Triumph- und Ehrenbögen." In *Denkmäler des klassischen Altertums,* ed. A. Baumeister, 3:1865–99. Munich and Leipzig, 1888.

Gransden, K.W., ed. *Virgil, Aeneid Book VIII.* Cambridge, 1976.

Grant, M. *From Imperium to Auctoritas: A Historical Study of Aes Coinage in the Roman Empire 49 B.C.–A.D. 14.* Cambridge, 1946.

———. *Roman Anniversary Issues: An Exploratory Study of the Numismatic and Medallic Commemoration of Anniversary Years 49 B.C.–A.D. 375.* Cambridge, 1950.

———. *The Six Main Aes Coinages of Augustus: Controversial Studies.* Edinburgh, 1953.

Greenhalgh, P. *Pompey: The Roman Alexander.* London, 1980.

Griffin, J. "Propertius and Antony." *JRS* 67 (1977): 17–26.

———. "Augustus and the Poets: 'Caesar qui cogere posset.'" In *Caesar Augustus: Seven Aspects*, ed. F. Millar and E. Segal, 189–218. Oxford, 1984.

———. *Latin Poets and Roman Life*. London, 1985.

———. Review of *Virgil's Aeneid: Cosmos and Imperium*, by P. Hardie. *JRS* 78 (1988): 229–33.

Griffith, J.G. "Again the Shield of Aeneas (*Aeneid* VIII. 625–731)." *PVS* 7 (1967–68): 54–65.

Griffiths, J. Gwyn. "The Death of Cleopatra VII." *JEA* 47 (1961): 113–18.

———. "The Death of Cleopatra VII: A Rejoinder and a Postscript." *JEA* 51 (1965): 209–11.

Groag, E. "Beiträge zur Geschichte des zweiten Triumvirats." *Klio* 14 (1915): 43–68.

Gros, P. *Aurea Templa. Recherches sur l'architecture religieuse de Rome à l'époque d'Auguste*. BEFAR 231. Paris, 1976.

Gross, W.H. "Ways and Roundabout Ways in the Propaganda of an Unpopular Ideology." In *The Age of Augustus: Interdisciplinary Conference Held at Brown University, April 30–May 2, 1982*, ed. R. Winkes, 29–50. Archaeologia Transatlantica 5. Louvain-la-Neuve and Providence, 1985.

Grueber, H.A. *Coins of the Roman Republic in the British Museum*. 3 vols. London, 1910. Reprinted 1970.

Gruen, E.S. "Augustus and the Ideology of War and Peace." In *The Age of Augustus: Interdisciplinary Conference Held at Brown University, April 30–May 2, 1982*, ed. R. Winkes, 51–72. Archaeologia Transatlantica 5. Louvain-la-Neuve and Providence, 1985.

———. "The Imperial Policy of Augustus." In *Between Republic and Empire: Interpretations of Augustus and His Principate*, ed. K.A. Raaflaub and M. Toher, 395–416. Berkeley and Los Angeles, 1990.

Habicht, C. "Eine Urkunde des Akarnanischen Bundes." *Hermes* 85 (1957): 86–122.

Hadas, M. *Sextus Pompey*. New York, 1930.

Haight, E.H. "An 'Inspired Message' in the Augustan Poets." *AJP* 39 (1918): 341–66.

Hallett, J.P. "Book IV, Propertius' recusatio to Augustus and Augustan Ideals." Ph.D. diss., Harvard University, 1971.

Hannestad, N. *Roman Art and Imperial Policy*. Aarhus, 1986.

Hanslik, R. "Nachlese zu Vergils Eclogen 1 und 9." *WS* 68 (1955): 5–19.

———. "Horaz und Aktium." In *Serta Philologica Aenipontana*, ed. R. Muth, 335–42. Innsbrucker Beiträge zur Kulturwissenschaft 7–8. Innsbruck, 1962.

Hardie, P. *Virgil's Aeneid: Cosmos and Imperium*. Oxford, 1986.

Harrison, S.J. "Some Views of the *Aeneid* in the Twentieth Century." In *Oxford Readings in Vergil's Aeneid*, ed. S.J. Harrison, 1–20. Oxford and New York, 1990.

Hartmann, L. *De pugna Actiaca a poetis Augusteae aetatis celebrata*. Darmstadt, 1913.

Hausmann, U. "Zur Typologie und Ideologie des Augustusporträts." *ANRW* 2.12.2 (Berlin, 1981), 513–98.

Hekler, A. *Museum der bildenen Künste in Budapest. Die Sammlung antiker Skulpturen*. Budapest, 1929.

Hertzberg, G.A.B., ed. *Sex. Aurelii Propertii elegiarum libri quattuor.* 3 vols. Halle, 1843–45.

Hill, G.F. *Historical Roman Coins from the Earliest Times to the Reign of Augustus.* London, 1909.

Hill, P.V. "The Triumphal and Honorary Arches of Augustus." *NumCirc* 68 (1960): 158–60.

———. "The Temples and Statues of Apollo in Rome." *NumChron* 2, ser. 7 (1962): 125–42.

———. "Coin-Symbolism and Propaganda during the Wars of Vengeance (44–36 B.C.)." *NAC* 4 (1975): 157–90.

———. "From Naulochus to Actium: The Coinages of Octavian and Antony, 36–31 B.C." *NAC* 5 (1976): 121–28.

———. "Buildings and Monuments on Augustan Coins, c. 40 B.C.–A.D. 14." *NAC* 9 (1980): 197–218.

Höepfner, W. "Nikopolis—Zur Stadtgründung des Augustus." In *Nicopolis I: Proceedings of the First International Symposium on Nicopolis (23–29 September 1984),* ed. E. Chrysos, 129–33. Preveza, 1987.

Hofter, M. "Porträt." In *Kaiser Augustus und die verlorene Republik,* ed. M. Hofter, 291–343. Mainz, 1988.

Holland, L.B. "The Triple Arch of Augustus." *AJA* 50 (1946): 52–59.

———. "The Foundations of the Arch of Augustus." *AJA* 57 (1953): 1–4.

Hölscher, T. *Victoria Romana. Archäologische Untersuchungen zur Geschichte und Wesensart der römischen Siegesgöttin von den Anfängen bis zum Ende des 3. Jhs. n. Chr.* Mainz, 1967.

———. "Beobachtungen zu römischen historischen Denkmälern." *AA* 94.2 (1979): 337–48.

———. "Die Bedeutung der Münzen für das Verständnis der politischen Repräsentationskunst der späten römischen Republik." In *Actes du IXᵉ Congrès international de numismatique, Berne, septembre 1979,* ed. T. Hackens and R. Weiller, 2:269–82. Louvain-la-Neuve, 1982.

———. "Actium und Salamis." *JDAI* 99 (1984): 187–214.

———. *Staatsdenkmal und Publikum. vom Untergang der Republik bis zur Festigung des Kaisertums im Rom.* Konstanz, 1984.

———. "Denkmäler der Schlacht von Actium. Propaganda und Resonanz." *Klio* 67 (1985): 81–102.

———. "Historische Reliefs." In *Kaiser Augustus und die verlorene Republik,* ed. M. Hofter, 351–400. Mainz, 1988.

Hornsby, R.A. "Horace on Art and Politics (*Ode* 3.4)." *CJ* 58 (1962): 97–104.

Housman, A.E. Review of *The Elegies of Propertius,* ed. H.E. Butler and E.A. Barber. *CR* 48 (1934): 136–39.

Hubbard, M. "*Propertiana.*" *CQ* 18 (1968): 315–19.

———. *Propertius.* London, 1974.

Huzar, E.G. *Mark Antony: A Biography.* Minneapolis, 1978.

Immisch, O. "Zum antiken Herrscherkult." In *Aus Roms Zeitwende. von Wesen und Wirken des augusteischen Geistes,* ed. O. Immisch et al., 1–36. Leipzig, 1931.

Instinsky, H.U. *Die Siegel des Kaisers Augustus. Ein Kapitel zur Geschichte und Symbolik des antiken Herrschersiegels.* Baden-Baden, 1961.

Jal, P. *"Bellum civile . . . bellum externum* dans la Rome de la fin de la République." *LEC* 30 (1962): 257–67, 384–90.

Johnson, J.R. "Augustan Propaganda: The Battle of Actium, Mark Antony's Will, the Fasti Capitolini Consulares, and Early Imperial Historiography." Ph.D. diss., University of California, Los Angeles, 1976.

Johnson, W.R. "A Quean, a Great Queen? Cleopatra and the Politics of Misrepresentation." *Arion* 6 (1967): 387–402.

———. "The Emotions of Patriotism: Propertius 4.6." *CSCA* 6 (1973): 151–80.

———. *Darkness Visible: A Study of Vergil's Aeneid*. Berkeley and Los Angeles, 1976.

Jones, A.H.M. *The Greek City from Alexander to Justinian*. Oxford, 1940.

———. *The Cities of the Eastern Roman Provinces*. 2d ed. Oxford, 1971.

Jones, J.E. "Cities of Victory—Patterns and Parallels." In *Nicopolis I: Proceedings of the First International Symposium on Nicopolis (23–29 September 1984)*, ed. E. Chrysos, 99–108. Preveza, 1987.

Jucker, H. Review of *Zur Münzprägung des Augustus*, by K. Kraft. *Gnomon* 45 (1973): 428–29.

———. "Apollo Palatinus und Apollo Actius auf augusteischen Münzen." *MusHelv* 39 (1982): 82–100.

Judge, E. *"Res Publica Restituta*: A Modern Illusion?" In *Polis and Imperium: Studies in Honour of Edward Togo Salmon*, ed. J.A.S. Evans, 279–311. Toronto, 1974.

Kahrstedt, U. "Die Territorien von Patrai und Nikopolis in der Kaiserzeit." *Historia* 1 (1950): 549–61.

Karamessini-Oikonomidou, M. Ἡ Νομισματοκοπία τῆς Νικοπόλεως. Βιβλιοθήκη τῆς ἐν Ἀθήναις Ἀρχαιολογικῆς Ἑταιρείας 79. Athens, 1975.

Kähler, H. *The Art of Rome and Her Empire*. Rev. ed. Trans. J.R. Foster. New York, 1965. Originally published as *Rom und seine Welt. Bilder zur Geschichte und Kultur*. Munich, 1960.

Kellum, B. "Sculptural Programs and Propaganda in Augustan Rome: The Temple of Apollo on the Palatine and the Forum of Augustus." Ph.D. diss., Harvard University, 1982.

———. "Sculptural Programs and Propaganda in Augustan Rome: The Temple of Apollo on the Palatine." In *The Age of Augustus: Interdisciplinary Conference Held at Brown University, April 30–May 2, 1982*, ed. R. Winkes, 169–76. Archaeologia Transatlantica 5. Louvain-la-Neuve and Providence, 1985.

———. "The City Adorned: Programmatic Display at the *Aedes Concordiae Augustae*." In *Between Republic and Empire: Interpretations of Augustus and His Principate*, ed. K.A. Raaflaub and M. Toher, 276–307. Berkeley and Los Angeles, 1990.

Kennell, N.M. "ΝΕΡΩΝ ΠΕΡΙΟΔΟΝΙΚΗΣ." *AJP* 109 (1988): 239–51.

Keppie, L. "A Note on the Title *Actiacus*." *CR* 85, n.s. 21 (1971): 329–30.

———. *Colonisation and Veteran Settlement in Italy, 47–14 B.C.* London, 1983.

Keydell, R. "Zwei Stücke griechisch-ägyptischer Poesie." *Hermes* 69 (1934): 420–25.

Kienast, D. "Augustus und Alexander." *Gymnasium* 76 (1969): 430–56.

———. *Augustus. Prinzeps und Monarch*. Darmstadt, 1982.

Kilpatrick, R.S. *The Poetry of Friendship: Horace, Epistles I.* Edmonton, Alberta, 1986.

Kirsten, E. "The Origins of the First Inhabitants of Nicopolis." In *Nicopolis I: Proceedings of the First International Symposium on Nicopolis (23–29 September 1984),* ed. E. Chrysos, 91–98. Preveza, 1987.

Kleiner, F.S. *The Arch of Nero in Rome: A Study of the Roman Honorary Arch before and under Nero.* Rome, 1985.

Koestermann, E. "Die Mission des Germanicus im Orient." *Historia* 7 (1958): 331–75.

Kraay, C. "The Coinage of Nicopolis." Review of Ἡ Νομισματοκοπία τῆς Νικοπόλεως, by M. Karamessini-Oikonomidou. *NumChron* 16, ser. 7 (1976): 235–47.

Kraft, K. "Zum Capricorn auf den Münzen des Augustus." *JNG* 17 (1967): 17–27.

———. *Zur Münzprägung des Augustus.* Wiesbaden, 1969.

Kraggerud, E. *Horaz und Actium. Studien zu den politischen Epoden.* Symbolae Osloenses Supplementum 26. Oslo, 1984.

Krinzinger, F. "Nikopolis in der augusteischen Reichspropaganda." In *Nicopolis I: Proceedings of the First International Symposium on Nicopolis (23–29 September 1984),* ed. E. Chrysos, 109–20. Preveza, 1987.

Kromayer, J. "Die Entwicklung der römischen Flotte vom Seeräuberkriege des Pompeius bis zur Schlacht von Actium." *Philologus* 56 (1897): 426–91.

———. "Kleine Forschungen zur Geschichte des zweiten Triumvirats. VII. Der Feldzug von Actium und der sogenannte Verrath der Cleopatra." *Hermes* 34 (1899): 1–54.

———. "Zur Schlacht von Actium." In *Antike Schlachtfelder. Bausteine zur einer antiken Kriegsgeschichte,* 4.4:662–71. Berlin, 1931.

———. "Actium. Ein Epilog." *Hermes* 68 (1933): 361–83.

Laffranchi, L. "C • A *(Certamen Actiacum)*." *RIN* 54–55, ser. 5 (1952–53): 3–11.

———. *La monetazione di Augusto.* Milan, 1919.

Lambrechts, P. "La politique 'apollinienne' d'Auguste et le culte impérial." *Nouv-Clio* 5 (1953): 65–82.

Lämmer, M. "Die Aktischen Spiele von Nikopolis." *Stadion* 12–13 (1986–87): 27–38.

Langenfeld, H. "Die Politik des Augustus und die griechische Agonistik." In *Monumentum Chiloniense: Studien zur augusteischen Zeit. Kieler Festschrift für Erich Burck zum 70. Geburtstag,* ed. E. Lefèvre, 228–59. Amsterdam, 1975.

La Rocca, E. *Amazzonomachia. Le sculture frontonali del tempio d'Apollo Sosiano.* Rome, 1985.

———. "Le sculture frontonali del tempio di Apollo Sosiano a Roma." In *Archaische und klassische griechische Plastik. Akten des internationalen Kolloquiums vom 22.–25. April 1985 in Athen,* vol. 2, *Klassische griechische Plastik,* ed. H. Kyrieleis, 51–58. Mainz, 1986.

———. "Der Apollo-Sosianus-Tempel." In *Kaiser Augustus und die verlorene Republik,* ed. M. Hofter, 121–36. Mainz, 1988.

———. "Die Giebelskulpturen des Apollo-Sosianus-Tempels in Rom." *Gymnasium* 95 (1988): 129–40.

Laubscher, H.P. "Motive der augusteischen Bildpropaganda." *JDAI* 89 (1974): 242–59.

Lee, A.G. Review of *Horace's Ninth Epode and Its Historical Background*, by E. Wistrand. *Gnomon* 31 (1959): 740–41.

Lefèvre. E. *Das Bild-Programm des Apollo-Tempels auf dem Palatin*. Konstanz, 1989.

Léon-Marcien, Frère. "L'interprétation de la bataille d'Actium par les poètes latins de l'époque augustéenne." *LEC* 24 (1956): 330–48.

Leroux, J. "Les problèmes stratégiques de la bataille d'Actium." *RecPhL* 2 (1968): 29–61.

Lessing, G.E. *Laocoon* (1776). Trans. E. Frothingham. Boston, 1890.

Levi, M.A. "La battaglia d'Azio." *Athenaeum* 20, n.s. 10 (1932): 3–21.

———. "Cleopatra e l'aspide." *PP* 9 (1954): 293–95.

Levick, B. *Tiberius the Politician*. London, 1976.

———. "Propaganda and the Imperial Coinage." *Antichthon* 16 (1982): 104–16.

Lewis, M.W. Hoffman. *The Official Priests of Rome under the Julio-Claudians: A Study of the Nobility from 44 B.C. to 68 A.D.* American Academy in Rome Papers and Monographs 16. Rome, 1955.

Liegle, J. "Die Münzprägung Octavians nach dem Siege von Actium und die augusteische Kunst." *JDAI* 56 (1941): 91–119.

Little, D. "Politics in Augustan Poetry." *ANRW* 2.30.1 (Berlin, 1982), 254–370.

Lloyd, R.B. "On *Aeneid*, III, 270–280." *AJP* 75 (1954): 288–99.

MacKay, L.A. "Horace, *Odes*, III.4: Date and Interpretation." *CR* 46 (1932): 243–45.

———. "Horace, Augustus, and *Ode*, I, 2." *AJP* 83 (1962): 168–77.

MacLeod, C.W. "Horace and His Lyric Models: A Note on *Epode* 9 and *Odes* 1, 37." *Hermes* 110 (1982): 371–75.

Mader, G. "The Apollo Similes at Propertius 4.6.31–36." *Hermes* 118 (1990): 325–34.

Mankin, D. "The Addressee of Virgil's Eighth Eclogue: A Reconsideration." *Hermes* 116 (1988): 63–76.

Mannsperger, D. "Apollon gegen Dionysos." *Gymnasium* 80 (1973): 381–404.

———. "ROM. ET AUG. Die Selbstdarstellung des Kaisertums in der römischen Reichsprägung." *ANRW* II.1 (Berlin, 1974), 919–96.

———. "Annos undeviginti natus. Das Münzsymbol für Octavians Eintritt in die Politik." In *Praestant Interna. Festschrift für Ulrich Hausmann*, ed. B. von Freytag gen. Löringhoff et al., 331–37. Tübingen, 1982.

Massner, A.-K. *Bildnisangleichung. Untersuchungen zur Entstehungs-und Wirkungsgeschichte der Augustusporträts (43 v. Chr.–68 n. Chr.)*. Berlin, 1982.

Mattingly, H., and R.A.G. Carson. *Coins of the Roman Empire in the British Museum*. 6 vols. London, 1923–.

———. "Virgil's Golden Age: Sixth Aeneid and Fourth Eclogue." *CR* 48 (1934): 161–65.

Mayor, J.E.B., ed. *Thirteen Satires of Juvenal*. 2 vols. London and New York, 1888–93.

Megow, W.-R. Review of *Studien zu den Augustus-Porträts*, vol. 1, *Actium-Typus*, by P. Zanker. *Gnomon* 48 (1976): 699–705.

Meier, C. "C. Caesar Divi filius and the Formation of the Alternative in Rome." In

Between Republic and Empire: Interpretations of Augustus and His Principate, ed. K.A. Raaflaub and M. Toher, 54–70. Berkeley and Los Angeles, 1990.

Metcalf, W.E. Review of Ἡ Νομισματοκοπία τῆς Νικοπόλεως, by M. Karamessini-Oikonomidou. *Gnomon* 49 (1977): 632–33.

Meyer, H.D. *Die Aussenpolitik des Augustus und die augusteische Dichtung*. Cologne, 1961.

Michel, D. *Alexander als Vorbild für Pompeius, Caesar und Marcus Antonius. Archäologische Untersuchungen*. Collection Latomus 94. Brussels, 1967.

Miller, P.A. "Horace, Mercury, and Augustus, or the Poetic Ego of *Odes* 1–3." *AJP* 112 (1991): 365–88.

Millon, C., and B. Schouler. "Les jeux olympiques d'Antioche." *Pallas* 34 (1988): 61–76.

Miltner, F. "Das praenestinische Biremenrelief." *JÖAI* 24 (1929): 88–111.

Mingazzini, P. "La datazione del rilievo da Praeneste al Vaticano rappresentante una bireme." *RendPontAcc* 29 (1956–57): 63–68.

Moles, J. "Fate, Apollo, and M. Junius Brutus." *AJP* 104 (1983): 249–56.

Momigliano, A. "*Terra Marique*." *JRS* 32 (1942): 53–64.

Mommsen, Th., ed. *Res Gestae Divi Augusti*. 2d ed. Berlin, 1883.

Morel, W., ed. *Fragmenta poetarum latinorum epicorum et lyricorum praeter Ennium et Lucilium*. 2d ed. Stuttgart, 1963.

Moretti, L. *Iscrizioni agonistiche greche*. Rome, 1953.

Murray, W.M., and P.M. Petsas. *Octavian's Campsite Memorial for the Actian War*. Transactions of the American Philosophical Society 79.4. Philadelphia, 1989.

Mustilli, D. "L'arte Augustea." In *Augustus. Studi in occasione del bimillenario Augusteo*, ed. V. Arangio-Ruiz et al., 307–77. Rome, 1938.

Nash, E. *Pictorial Dictionary of Ancient Rome*. 2 vols. New York, 1962. Reprinted 1981.

Nedergaard, E. "Zur Problematik der Augustusbögen auf dem Forum Romanum." In *Kaiser Augustus und die verlorene Republik*, ed. M. Hofter, 224–39. Mainz, 1988.

Nethercut, W.R. "Propertius 2.15.41–48; Antony at Actium." *RSC* 19 (1971): 299–301.

———. "Propertius 3.11." *TAPA* 102 (1971): 411–43.

———. "The ΣΦΡΑΓΙΣ of the Monobiblos." *AJP* 82 (1971): 464–72.

———. "Recent Scholarship on Propertius." *ANRW* 2.30.3 (Berlin, 1983), 1813–57.

Netzer, E. "Herod the Great's Contribution to Nicopolis in the Light of His Building Activity in Judea." In *Nicopolis I: Proceedings of the First International Symposium on Nicopolis (23–29 September 1984)*, ed. E. Chrysos, 121–28. Preveza, 1987.

Newman, R. "A Dialogue of Power in the Coinage of Antony and Octavian (44–30 B.C.)." *AJN* 2, ser. 2 (1990): 37–63.

Nilsson, M.P. "The Origin of the Triumphal Arch." In *Corolla Archaeologica*, 132–39. Acta Instituti Romani Regni Sueciae 2. Lund and London, 1932.

———. "The Triumphal Arch and Town Planning." *OpusArch* 1 (1935): 120–28.

Nisbet, R.G.M. "Horace's *Epodes* and History." In *Poetry and Politics in the Age of Augustus*, ed. T. Woodman and D. West, 1–18. Cambridge, 1984.

Nisbet, R.G.M., and M. Hubbard. *A Commentary on Horace: Odes, Book 1.* Oxford, 1970.

Noack, F. "Triumph und Triumphbogen." *VBW* 5, ser. 6 (1928): 147–201.

Nodelman, S. "The Portrait of Brutus the Tyrannicide." In *Ancient Portraits in the J. Paul Getty Museum*, 1:41–86. Occasional Papers on Antiquities 4. Malibu, 1987.

Norden, E. *Die Geburt des Kindes. Geschichte einer religiösen Idee.* 2d ed. Leipzig, 1931.

Ogilvie, R.M. *A Commentary on Livy, Books 1–5.* Oxford, 1965.

Oliver, J.H. "Octavian's Inscription at Nicopolis." *AJP* 90 (1969): 178–82.

Oltramare, A. "Auguste et les Parthes." *REL* 16 (1938): 121–38.

Orelli, J.C., ed. *Q. Horatius Flaccus.* Revised by J.G. Baiter and W. Hirschfelder. 2 vols. 4th ed. Berlin, 1886.

Otis, B. *Virgil: A Study in Civilized Poetry.* Oxford, 1963.

Overbeck, J. *Griechische Kunstmythologie.* 4 vols. Leipzig, 1871–89. Reprinted 1969.

Page, D.L., ed. and trans. *Select Papyri.* Vol. 3, *Literary Papyri: Poetry.* Loeb Classical Library 360. Cambridge, Mass., 1941. Reprinted 1970.

Page, T.E., ed. *The Aeneid of Virgil.* 2 vols. London, 1894–1900.

Page, T.E., A. Palmer, and A.S. Wilkins, eds. *Q. Horatii Flacci Opera.* London, 1910. Reprinted 1922.

Paladini, M.L. *A proposito della tradizione poetica sulla battaglia di Azio.* Collection Latomus 35. Brussels, 1958. Reprinted in *Latomus* 17 (1958): 240–69, 462–75.

Paratore, E. *L'elegia III, 11 e gli atteggiamenti politici di Properzio.* Palermo, 1936.

Parry, A. "The Two Voices of Virgil's Aeneid." *Arion* 2.4 (1963) 66–80.

Paschalis, M. "Virgil's Actium-Nicopolis." In *Nicopolis I: Proceedings of the First International Symposium on Nicopolis (23–29 September 1984)*, ed. E. Chrysos, 57–69. Preveza, 1987.

Payne, R. *The Roman Triumph.* London, 1962.

Pearce, D. "Horace and Cleopatra: Thoughts on the Entanglements of Art and History." *Yale Review* 51 (1961): 236–53.

Pelling, C.B.R. "*Puppes sinistrorsum citae.*" *CQ* 80, n.s. 36 (1986): 177–81.

———, ed. *Plutarch: Life of Antony.* Cambridge, 1988.

Perret, J. *Horace.* Trans. B. Humez. New York, 1964. Originally published Paris, 1959.

Picard, G.C. *Les trophées romains. Contributions à l'histoire de la religion et de l'art triumphal de Rome.* BEFAR 187. Paris, 1957.

Piganiol, A. "Fornix Fabianus." *MélRome* 28 (1908): 89–95. Reprinted in *Scripta varia*, vol. 2, ed. R. Bloch et al., 105–10. Collection Latomus 132. Brussels, 1973.

Pillinger, H.P. "Some Callimachean Influences on Propertius, Book 4." *HSCP* 73 (1969): 171–99.

Platner, S.B., and T. Ashby. *A Topographical Dictionary of Ancient Rome.* London, 1929.

Poduska, D. "*Ope Barbarica* or *Bellum Civile?*" *CB* 46 (1970): 33–34, 46.

Pollini, J. "Man or God: Divine Assimilation and Imitation in the Late Republic and Early Principate." In *Between Republic and Empire: Interpretations of Augustus and His Principate*, ed. K.A. Raaflaub and M. Toher, 334–63. Berkeley and Los Angeles, 1990.

Postgate, J.P., ed. *Select Elegies of Propertius*. 2d ed. London, 1884. Reprinted London, 1968.

Poulsen, V. *Les Portraits Romains*. 3 vols. Copenhagen, 1962–74.

Pöschl, V. *The Art of Vergil: Image and Symbol in the Aeneid*. Trans. G. Seligson, Ann Arbor, Mich. 1962. Originally published as *Die Dichtkunst Virgils. Bild und Symbol in der Äneis*. Innsbruck-Vienna, 1950.

———. *Horaz und die Politik*. Heidelberg, 1956.

———. *Horazische Lyrik. Interpretationen*. Heidelberg, 1970. Reprinted 1991.

———. "Virgil und Augustus." *ANRW* II.31.2 (Berlin, 1981), 702–27.

Pound, E. *Personae: The Collected Poems of Ezra Pound*. New York, 1926.

Prayon, F. "Projektierte Bauten auf römischen Münzen." In *Praestant Interna. Festschrift für Ulrich Hausmann*, ed. B. von Freytag gen. Löringhoff et al., 319–30. Tübingen, 1982.

Price, S.R.F. *Rituals and Power: The Roman Imperial Cult in Asia Minor*. Cambridge, 1984.

Prückner, H. "Das Budapest Aktium-Relief." In *Forschungen und Funde. Festschrift für Bernhard Neutsch*, ed. F. Krinzinger et al., 357–66. Innsbruck, 1980.

Purcell, N. "The Nicopolitan Synoecism and Roman Urban Policy." In *Nicopolis I: Proceedings of the First International Symposium on Nicopolis (23–29 September 1984)*, ed. E. Chrysos, 71–90. Preveza, 1987.

Putnam, M.C.J. *The Poetry of the Aeneid: Four Studies in Imaginative Unity and Design*. Cambridge, Mass., 1965. Reprinted Ithaca, 1988.

———. "Propertius 1.22: A Poet's Self-Definition." *QUCC* 23 (1976): 93–123.

Quinn, K. *Virgil's Aeneid: A Critical Description*. London, 1968.

Quint, D. *Epic and Empire: Politics and Generic Form from Virgil to Milton*. Princeton, 1993.

Ramage, E.S. "Augustus' Treatment of Julius Caesar." *Historia* 34 (1985): 223–45.

Reinhold, M. "The Declaration of War against Cleopatra." *CJ* 77 (1981–82): 97–103.

Reisch, E. "Aktia." *RE* 1.1 (1893): cols. 1213–14.

Reitzenstein, R. "Properz-Studien." *Hermes* 31 (1896): 185–220.

Renard, M. "Horace et Cléopâtre." In *Études Horatiennes*, ed. M. Renard, 189–99. Travaux de la faculté de philosophie et lettres de l'université de Bruxelles 7. Brussels, 1937.

Richardson, G.W. "Actium." *JRS* 27 (1937): 153–64.

Richardson, L., jr. *A New Topographical Dictionary of Ancient Rome*. Baltimore, 1992.

———, ed. *Propertius, Elegies I–IV*. The American Philological Association Series of Classical Texts. Norman, Okla., 1977.

Richmond, I.A. "Commemorative Arches and City Gates in the Augustan Age." *JRS* 23 (1933): 149–74.

Richmond, O. "The Augustan Palatium." *JRS* 4 (1914): 193–226.

———. "Palatine Apollo Again." *CQ* 52, n.s. 8 (1958): 180–84.

Richter, G.M.A. *Engraved Gems of the Greeks, Etruscans, and Romans*. Vol. 2,

Engraved Gems of the Romans: A Supplement to the History of Roman Art. London, 1971.

Richter, O. "Die Augustusbauten auf dem Forum Romanum." *JDAI* 4 (1889): 137–62.

Richter, W. "Divus Julius, Octavianus und Kleopatra bei Aktion. Bemerkungen zu Properz 4, 6, 59ff." *WS* 79 (1966): 451–65.

Rieks, R. "Sebasta und Aktia." *Hermes* 98 (1970): 96–116.

Ritter, H.W. "Das Heiligtum des Apollo Palatinus in der augusteischen Münzprägung." In *Actes du IXᵉ Congrès international de numismatique, Berne, septembre 1979,* ed. T. Hackens and R. Weiller, 2:365–70. Louvain-la-Neuve, 1982.

Ritti, T. *Fonti letterarie ed epigrafiche. Hierapolis. Scavi e Ricerche.* Archaeologica 53. Rome, 1985.

Robert, J., and L. Robert. "Bulletin Épigraphique." *REG* 67 (1954): 113–15.

Robert, L. "Études d'épigraphie grecque." *RevPhil* 4, ser. 3 (1930): 25–60.

Rose, H.J. "The Departure of Dionysos." *AArchAnth* 11 (1924): 25–30.

Rowell, H.T. "The Forum and the Funeral *imagines* of Augustus." *MAAR* 17 (1940): 131–43.

———. "Vergil and the Forum of Augustus." *AJP* 62 (1941): 261–76.

Rowland, R.J., Jr. "Foreshadowing in Vergil, *Aeneid,* VIII, 714–28." *Latomus* 27 (1968): 832–42.

Ryberg, I. Scott. "Vergil's Golden Age." *TAPA* 89 (1958): 112–31.

Sadurska, A. "L'art d'Auguste: progrès, regrès, ou transformation?" *Klio* 67 (1985): 70–73.

Sage, M.M. "The *Elogia* of the Augustan Forum and the *de viris illustribus.*" *Historia* 28 (1979): 192–210.

———. "The *Elogia* of the Augustan Forum and the *de viris illustribus*: A Reply." *Historia* 32 (1983): 250–56.

Salmon, E.T. "The Political Views of Horace." *Phoenix* 1.2 (1946–47): 7–14.

Santirocco, M.S. *Unity and Design in Horace's Odes.* Chapel Hill, 1986.

Sarikakis, Th. "Ἄκτια τὰ ἐν Νικοπόιλει." *AE* 15 (1965): 145–62.

———. "Nicopolis d'Épire était-elle une colonie romaine ou une ville grecque?" *Balkan Studies* 11 (1970): 91–96.

Sartre, M. *Bostra. Des origines à l'Islam.* Paris, 1985.

Savage, J.J.H. "The *aurea dicta* of Augustus and the Poets." *TAPA* 99 (1968): 401–17.

Schaefer, E. "Horaz nach Actium." *WJA* 13 (1987): 195–207.

Schenk von Stauffenberg, A. *Die römische Kaisergeschichte bei Malalas. Griechischer Text der Bücher IX–XII und Untersuchungen.* Stuttgart, 1931.

Schlachter, A. *Der Globus. Seine Entstehung und Verwendung in der Antike.* Berlin, 1927.

Schmaltz, B. "Zum Augustus-Bildnis Typus Primaporta." *RömMitt* 93 (1986): 211–43.

Schmitthenner, W. "Octavians militärische Unternehmungen in den Jahren 35–33 v. Chr." *Historia* 7 (1958): 189–236.

Schodt, A. "Apollon sur les monnaies de César Auguste." *RBN* 41 (1885): 5–66.

Schor, B. *Beiträge zur Geschichte des Sextus Pompeius.* Stuttgart, 1978.

Scott, K. "The Identification of Augustus with Romulus-Quirinus." *TAPA* 56 (1925): 82–105.

———. "Mercur-Augustus und Horaz *c.* I 2." *Hermes* 63 (1928): 15–33.

———. "Octavian's Propaganda and Antony's *De Sua Ebrietate.*" *CP* 24 (1929) 133–41.

———. "The Political Propaganda of 44–30 B.C." *MAAR* 11 (1933): 7–49.

Seager, R. *Tiberius.* Berkeley and Los Angeles, 1972.

———. "*Neu sinas Medos equitare inultos*: Horace, the Parthians and Augustan Foreign Policy." *Athenaeum* 68, n.s. 58 (1980): 103–18.

Setaioli, A. "Gli 'Epodi' di Orazio nella critica dal 1937 al 1972." *ANRW* II.31.3 (Berlin, 1981), 1674–1788.

Shipley, F.W. "Chronology of the Building Operations in Rome from the Death of Caesar to the Death of Augustus." *MAAR* 9 (1931): 7–60.

Simon, E. *Die Portlandvase.* Mainz, 1957.

———. "Apollo in Rom." *JDAI* 93 (1978): 202–27.

———. *Augustus. Kunst und Leben in Rom um die Zeitenwende.* Munich, 1986.

Simpson, C.J. "The Date of Dedication of the Temple of Mars Ultor." *JRS* 67 (1977): 91–94.

Smith, H.R.W. *Problems Historical and Numismatic in the Reign of Augustus.* University of California Publications in Classical Archaeology 2.4. Berkeley and Los Angeles, 1951.

Spawforth, A.J.S. "A Severan Statue-Group and an Olympic Festival at Sparta." *ABSA* 81 (1986): 313–32.

Stahl, H.P. *Propertius, "Love" and "War": Individual and State under Augustus.* Berkeley and Los Angeles, 1985.

———. "The Death of Turnus: Augustan Vergil and the Political Rival." In *Between Republic and Empire: Interpretations of Augustus and His Principate*, ed. K.A. Raaflaub and M. Toher, 174–211. Berkeley and Los Angeles, 1990.

Stefanis, I.E. "Ἀθλητῶν ἀπολογία." *Hellenica* 39 (1988): 270–90.

Strazzulla, M.J. *Il principato di Apollo. Mito e propaganda nelle lastre "Campana" dal tempio di Apollo Palatino.* Rome, 1990.

Strong, E. *Scultura Romana.* Florence, 1923.

———. "The Art of the Augustan Age." *CAH* 10 (1934): 545–82.

Sullivan, J.P. *Ezra Pound and Sextus Propertius: A Study in Creative Translation.* Austin, Tex., 1964; London, 1965.

———. *Propertius: A Critical Introduction.* Cambridge, 1976.

Sutherland, C.H.V. "The Senatorial Gold and Silver Coinage of 16 B.C.: Innovation and Inspiration." *NumChron* 3, ser. 6 (1943): 40–49.

———. "The Personality of the Mints under the Julio-Claudian Emperors." *AJP* 68 (1947): 47–63.

———. *Coinage in Roman Imperial Policy 31 B.C.–A.D. 68.* London, 1951. Reprinted New York, 1971.

———. "The Intelligibility of Roman Imperial Coin Types." *JRS* 49 (1959): 46–55.

———. "Octavian's Gold and Silver Coinage from c. 32 to 27 B.C." *NAC* 5 (1976): 129–57.

———. *The Emperor and the Coinage: Julio-Claudian Studies.* London, 1976.

————. *Roman History and Coinage 44 B.C.–A.D. 69: Fifty Points of Relation from Julius Caesar to Vespasian*. Oxford, 1987.

Sweet, F. "Propertius and Political Panegyric." *Arethusa* 5 (1972): 169–75.

Sydenham, E.A. "The Coinages of Augustus." *NumChron* 20, ser. 4 (1920): 17–56.

————. *The Coinage of the Roman Republic*. Revised with indexes by G.C. Haines. Ed. L. Forrer and C.A. Hersh. London, 1952.

Syme, R. "Some Notes on the Legions under Augustus." *JRS* 23 (1933): 14–33.

————. *The Roman Revolution*. Oxford, 1939.

————. "Imperator Caesar: A Study in Nomenclature." *Historia* 7 (1958): 172–88.

————. *Danubian Papers*. Bucharest, 1971.

————. *The Augustan Aristocracy*. Oxford, 1986.

Tarn, W.W. "The Battle of Actium." *JRS* 21 (1931): 173–99.

————. "Antony's Legions." *CQ* 26 (1932): 75–81.

————. "The War of the East against the West." *CAH* 10 (1934): 66–111. Reprinted in *Octavian, Antony and Cleopatra*, by W.W. Tarn and M. Charlesworth, 83–139. Cambridge, 1965.

————. "Actium: A Note." *JRS* 28 (1938): 165–68.

Tarrant, R.J. "The Addressee of Virgil's Eighth Eclogue." *HSCP* 82 (1978): 197–99.

Taylor, L.R. *The Divinity of the Roman Emperor*. Middletown, Conn., 1931.

————. "The Date of the Capitoline *Fasti*." *CP* 41 (1946): 1–11.

————. "Annals of the Roman Consulship on the Arch of Augustus." *PAPS* 94 (1950): 511–16.

————. "Degrassi's Edition of the Consular and Triumphal *Fasti*." *CP* 45 (1950): 84–95.

————. "New Indications of Augustan Editing in the Capitoline *Fasti*." *CP* 46 (1951): 73–80.

Thomas, R.F. "Turning Back the Clock." Review of *Latin Poets and Roman Life*, by J. Griffin. *CP* 83 (1988): 54–69.

————, ed. *Virgil, Georgics*. 2 vols. Cambridge, 1988.

Thompson, M.W. "The Date of Horace's First Epode." *CQ* 64 (1970): 328–34.

Thornton, A.H.F. "Horace's Ode to Calliope (III, 4)." *AUMLA* 23 (1965): 96–102.

Tidman, B. "On the Foundation of the Actian Games." *CQ* 44 (1950): 123–25.

Tränkle, H. "Properz über Vergils Aeneis." *MusHelv* 28 (1971): 60–63.

Trillmich, W. Review of *Studien zu den Augustus-Porträts*, vol. 1, *Der Actium-Typus*, by P. Zanker. *BJ* 174 (1974): 687–93.

————. "Münzpropaganda." In *Kaiser Augustus und die verlorene Republik*, ed. M. Hofter, 474–528. Mainz, 1988.

Versnel, H.S. "Triumphus: An Inquiry into the Origin, Development and Meaning of the Roman Triumph." Ph.D. diss., Leiden, 1970.

Veyne, P. "*Quid dedicatum poscit Apollinem?*" *Latomus* 24 (1965): 932–48.

Viscogliosi, A. "Die Architektur-Dekoration der Cella des Apollo-Sosianus-Tempels." In *Kaiser Augustus und die vorlorene Republik*, ed. M. Hofter, 136–48. Mainz, 1988.

Von Papen, Frère G. "Die Spielen von Hierapolis." *ZN* 26 (1907): 161–82.

Wallace-Hadrill, A. "The Emperor and his Virtues." *Historia* 30 (1981): 298–323.

————. "Image and Authority in the Coinage of Augustus." *JRS* 76 (1986): 66–87.

————. "Rome's Cultural Revolution." Review of *The Power of Images in the Age of Augustus*, by P. Zanker. *JRS* 79 (1989): 157–64.

Wallisch, E. "Die Opfer der römischen Triumphe." Ph.D. diss., Tübingen, 1951.

Wallmann, P. *Triumviri Rei Publicae Constituendae. Untersuchungen zur politischen Propaganda im Zweiten Triumvirat (43–30 v. Chr.)*. Frankfurt, 1989.

Wardman, A. *Religion and Statecraft among the Romans*. Baltimore, 1982.

Watson, L. "*Epode 9*, or the Art of Falsehood." In *Homo Viator: Classical Essays for John Bramble*, ed. M. Whitby et al., 119–29. Bristol and Oak Park, Ill., 1987.

Weinstock, S. *Divus Julius*. Oxford, 1971.

West, D.A. "*Cernere Erat*: The Shield of Aeneas." *PVS* 15 (1975–76): 1–7. Reprinted in *Oxford Readings in Vergil's Aeneid*, ed. S.J. Harrison, 295–304. Oxford, 1990.

White, P. "Julius Caesar in Augustan Rome." *Phoenix* 42 (1988): 334–56.

————. *Promised Verse: Poets in the Society of Augustan Rome*. Cambridge, Mass., 1993.

Wickham, E.C., ed. *Quinti Horatii Flacci Opera Omnia: The Works of Horace*. 2 vols. 3d ed. Oxford, 1896.

Wiesen, D.S. "The Pessimism of the Eighth Aeneid." *Latomus* 32 (1973): 737–65.

Wili, W. *Horaz und die augusteische Kultur*. Basel, 1948.

Wilkes, J.J. *Dalmatia*. London, 1969.

Wilkinson, L.P. "Horace, *Epode* IX." *CR* 47 (1933): 2–6.

————. *Horace and His Lyric Poetry*. 2d ed. Cambridge, 1951.

————. *The Georgics of Virgil: A Critical Survey*. Cambridge, 1969.

Williams, G. "Poetry in the Moral Climate of Augustan Rome." *JRS* 52 (1962): 28–46.

————. *Tradition and Originality in Roman Poetry*. Oxford, 1968.

————. *Technique and Ideas in the Aeneid*. New Haven, 1983.

Williams, R.D., ed. *The Aeneid of Vergil*. 2 vols. London, 1972–73.

Wimmel, W. *Kallimachos in Rom. Die Nachfolge seines apologetischen Dichtens in der Augusteerzeit*. Hermes Einzelschriften 16. Wiesbaden, 1960.

Wistrand, E. *Horace's Ninth Epode and Its Historical Background*. Studia Graeca et Latina Gothoburgensia 8. Göteborg, 1958.

Wlosok, A. *Die Göttin Venus in Vergils Aeneis*. Heidelberg, 1967.

Woodman, A.J., ed. *Velleius Paterculus: The Tiberian narrative (2.94–131)*. Cambridge, 1977.

Wurzel, F. "Der Ausgang der Schlacht von Aktium und die 9. Epode des Horaz." *Hermes* 73 (1938): 361–79.

————. "Der Krieg gegen Antonius und Kleopatra in der Darstellung der augusteischen Dichter." Ph.D. diss., Heidelberg, 1941.

Wyke, M. "Augustan Cleopatras: Female Power and Poetic Authority." In *Roman Poetry and Propaganda in the Age of Augustus*, ed. A. Powell, 98–140. Bristol, 1992.

Zanker, P. *Forum Augustum. Das Bildprogramm*. Tübingen, 1970.

————. *Forum Romanum. Die Neugestaltung durch Augustus*. Tübingen, 1972.

————. *Studien zu den Augustus-Porträts*. Vol. 1, *Der Actium-Typus*. Göttingen, 1973.

————. "Der Apollontempel auf dem Palatin. Ausstattung und politische Sinnbezüge nach der Schlacht von Actium." In *Cittá e Architettura nella Roma Impe-riale. Atti del Seminario del 27 Ottobre 1981 nel 25° Anniversario dell'Accademia di Danimarca*, 21–40. Analecta Romana Instituti Danici Supplementum 10. Copenhagen, 1983.

———. *The Power of Images in the Age of Augustus*. Trans. A. Shapiro. Jerome Lectures Series 16. Ann Arbor, Mich., 1988. Originally published as *Augustus und die Macht der Bilder*. Munich, 1987.

Zecchini, G. *Il Carmen de bello Actiaco. Storiografia e lotta politica in età augustea*. Historia Einzelschriften 51. Stuttgart, 1987.

Zinserling, G. "Die Programmatik der Kunstpolitik des Augustus." *Klio* 67 (1985): 74–80.

General Index

Achilles, 194, 200, 210, 222, 223

Actia. *See* Games

Actium (31 B.C.E.)
 anniversary of battle, 83n.166, 85n.168, 119, 120, 131
 attitude of Augustus, 2–3, 7, 16–17, 84–85, 86–87, 131–36, 213, 245–46, 271, 288–89
 attitude of Caligula, 85n.168
 attitude of posterity, 1–2, 85
 celebrated by Greek poets, 14, 14n.22
 commencement of new era, 1–2, 289–90
 foundation-myth, 3, 7, 46
 monuments, 2–3n.6, 4–6, 7–10, 42n.41, 65–67, 81, 84–85, 131–33, 288–89
 motifs of victory represented on artwork, 13–14, 13–14n.21, 124–87
 motifs of victory represented on coins, 5, 5n.12, 8, 40–41, 47–48, 47–48n.53, 57–67, 62–63, 132, 285–89
 naval battle, 2n.4, 66n.115, 151n.32, 152n.33, 205
 subject of *Carmen de Bello Actiaco*, 14–15, 15n.26
 See also Arches; Games; Horace; Nicopolis; Propertius; Temples; Triumphs; Vergil

Actium-Typus, 53–55, 54nn. 75, 76

Adiatorix, 29

Aemilius Lepidus, M. (Triumvir), 63, 100, 112n.60, 117n.73

Aemilius Lepidus, Paullus (cos. 34 B.C.E.), 116, 116n.71

Aemilius Paullus, L. (cos. 182 B.C.E.), 67

Aemilius Paullus, L. (brother of Triumvir), 116n.71

Aeneas
 ignarus, 244–45, 245n.48
 represented on coins of Octavian, 100
 shield in *Aeneid,* 11–12, 34–35, 82, 134, 209–47 passim, 262–63, 270, 271, 277
 statue in Forum of Augustus, 283
 See also Augustus

Aetolian League, 68

Agrippa, M., 51, 55, 55n.80, 85n.168, 106n.49, 121, 123, 151, 187, 234, 253, 263, 277, 280

Alba Longa, 215n.19, 220, 221, 222, 223

Alcaeus, 138, 139, 160n.44

Alexander of Emesa, 29

Alexander of Macedon, 54, 69, 69n.124, 70–73, 70nn. 126, 127, 102, 132, 243. *See also* Augustus

Alexandria, 1, 19, 72, 93, 102, 119, 132, 159, 179, 196–98, 234
 address of Octavian, 70–71
 anniversary of battle, 119, 131
 battle (30 B.C.E.), 72, 73, 74

Allobroges, 39

Amazonomachy, 116n.73, 238n.43

Amphictyonic League, 68

Amphion, 163

Amymone, 124n.90

Amyntas, king of Galatia, 28n.16, 150, 150n.30

Antipater of Thessalonica, 77n.148

Claudius, emperor, 79, 289n.29
Cleopatra, 1, 2, 7, 16, 19, 22, 33, 45,
    65, 131, 184, 200n.40, 268
    as Danaid, 124–25
    and Dido, 134, 237, 240
    effigy in triumph, 29–30, 131
    in Horace, 10, 147–49, 160n.44,
        201, 201n.41, 262, 270n.36,
        271, 277
    image in Ptolemaic Egypt, 196n.36
    as Medusa, 125, 125n.94
    in Propertius, 11, 189–208 passim,
        262–63, 268–71, 270n.36,
        277
    suicide, 1, 29–30, 29n.17, 30n.30,
        125n.94, 159
    in Vergil, 11, 134, 201, 234–36,
        237, 240, 263, 270, 277
    See also Augustus
Cloelia, on shield of Aeneas, 214, 224,
    224n.30
Columna rostrata, 41, 58, 63, 115
    represented on coin, 50, 57, 58
Commodus, emperor, 79
Concordia, represented on coin, 48–
    49, 48–49n.55
Cornelius Gallus, 105
Cornelius Severus, epic poet, 15n.26
Cornificius, L. (cos. 35 B.C.E.), 58n.86,
    116, 116n.70
Crassus, M. Licinius (cos. 70 B.C.E.),
    243, 275, 275n.47, 276
Creusa, wife of Aeneas, 236
Crinagoras, 14
Curia Julia, 33, 41, 42, 115, repre-
    sented on coin, 50, 61–62,
    62n.105, 132, 162
Curtius, M., 203–4
Cythnia, girlfriend of Propertius, 168,
    169, 170, 183, 207

Dalmatia, Dalmatian, 26, 27, 31
Danaids, 124–25, 124–25nn. 90, 91,
    92
Darius, king of Persia, 243
Decius, P., 203–4
Deiotarus, king of Galatia, 150n.30

Diana
    in Carmen Saeculare, 253, 287–88
    represented on coin, 49, 57, 58, 99,
        287, 287n.27, 289
    Siciliensis, 57–58, 89, 287–88,
        287n.27
    statues, 119, 126
    See also Temples
Dido, 237, 240
Dio Cassius, 1–2, 22, 25, 27, 31, 33,
    36, 39, 40, 41, 50–51, 51n.62,
    52, 59, 67, 70–71, 73, 92, 100,
    101, 110, 121–22, 123, 152,
    181n.22, 274n.44, 281n.5,
    282n.7, 283, 284n.18
Diocletian, emperor, 85
Dionysus (also Bacchus and Lyaeus), 9,
    93, 97, 103, 158, 158n.43, 257,
    273
Diospolis, of Pompey, 70n.125
Dirae, on shield of Aeneas, 238,
    238n.42, 239
Discordia, on shield of Aeneas, 238,
    238n.42, 239
Divus Julius
    altar at Perusia, 94, 176, 176n.15
    image in Augustan Rome, 285,
        285n.19
    in Propertius, 269
    represented on coin, 284–85, 284–
        85nn. 16, 17, 18
    statues, 106n.49
    See also Julius Caesar; Temples
Domitian, emperor, 80
Domitius Ahenobarbus, Cn. (cos. 32
    B.C.E.), 118n.75
Domitius Ahenobarbus, Cn. (cos. 32
    C.E.), 55
Domitius Ahenobarbus, L. (cos. 54
    B.C.E.), 55, 55n.80
Domitius Marsus, 101–2, 101n.38,
    102nn. 39, 40
Dorian mode, 144, 144n.19
Drusus, son of Tiberius, 40n.37

Egypt, Egyptian, 1, 11, 15, 19, 33, 62,
    71, 103, 116–17n.73, 124–25,

Index of Ancient Authors

Acron (*also* pseudo-Acron)
  Commentarius in Horatii Carminum
    Libros
    1.37.30: 30n.18
  Commentarius in Horatii Epis-
    tularum Libros
    1.3.17: 290n.30
  Commentarius in Horatii Epodon
    Librum
    9.25: 154n.38
Ammianus Marcellinus (Am. Marc.)
  21.16.15: 37n.32
Anthologia Palatina (Anth. Pal.)
  6.236: 14n.24
  6.251: 14n.24
  7.692: 77n.148
  9.553: 14n.24
Appian
  Bella Civilia (BC)
    2.26: 116n.71
    2.28: 198n.39
    2.101: 20n.3, 23, 23n.5
    2.106: 122n.83
    3.16: 92n.14
    3.19: 92n.14
    4.134: 98n.26
    5.32–49: 176n.15
    5.73: 118n.75
    5.129: 59
    5.130–32: 41n.40, 58, 62n.107,
      63nn. 109, 110, 106n.49
  Bella Illyrica (Illyr.)
    16–28: 25n.10
    28: 26n.12
  Bellum Mithridaticum (Mithr.)
    105: 69n.125
    115: 69n.125

Asconius
  In orationem in toga candida (tog.
    cand.)
    80–81: 124n.87, 257n.19
Augustine
  de Civitate Dei (Civ. Dei)
    4.29: 49n.56
Augustus
  Res Gestae (RG)
    1: 225n.33
    2: 93
    3: 185n.25
    4: 25n.8, 27–28, 84
    9: 84, 121
    10: 84
    13: 16, 84
    19: 26, 110, 257n.19
    23: 289n.29
    24: 84, 106n.49, 110, 126n.96
    25: 16, 134, 146, 164, 176n.14
    27: 16
    29: 280n.2
    34: 16, 221n.27

Carmen de Bello Actiaco:
  14, 15, 15n.26
Catullus (Cat.)
  96.1–2: 275n.46
Cicero
  Arati Phaenomena (Arat.)
    129: 236
  Epistulae ad Atticum (Att.)
    4.16.3: 106n.50
    4.16.14: 116n.71
  in Catilinam (Cat.)
    3.24: 173n.9
    4.21: 173n.9

Index of Coins and Inscriptions

Coins

(coins illustrated in plates are in italics)

Inscriptions

DATE DUE

DEC 1 0 2003			

GAYLORD

PRINTED IN U.S.A.